UNIVERSAL PREDATOR

UNIVERSAL PREDATOR

A Lone Woman's Fight To Expose
Serge Benhayon and His Universal Medicine Cult
— The Inside Story

ESTHER ROCKETT

Copyright © 2024 Esther Rockett

All rights reserved. No part of this publication may be reproduced, distributed, stored in or introduced into a retrieval system or aggregator, or transmitted in any form or by any means, including photocopying, recording, or other electronic or mechanical methods, without the prior written permission of the copyright owner.

ISBN: 978-0-646-89623-6

Cover design by Christa Moffit @christabelladesigns
Cover photographs: AAP Image, AAP Image/Joel Carrett

A catalogue record for this book is available from the National Library of Australia

Foreword

In 2015, Serge Benhayon commenced a defamation action against me over a blog and tweets I authored that were keenly descriptive of his character and conduct. By then, I'd been investigating him and his Esoteric healing enterprise, Universal Medicine, for three years, blogging my findings and making complaints to disinterested regulators.

Over ten years earlier, in just a handful of encounters, Benhayon showed me what he was. It wasn't until 2012, however, that I learned he'd amassed substantial wealth and a fervid international following, and that he, his supporters, and his vulturous business, posed a far greater threat to the community than I could have foreseen. Universal Medicine had evaded scrutiny for twelve years. Its victims were too frightened to speak out or make complaints. Cancer patients, sexual abuse survivors, and children, were among Unimed's prey. As someone with dirt on Benhayon, it was not a situation that I could walk away from.

This is the story of the 2018 trial of Benhayon versus Rockett in the Supreme Court of New South Wales, the fight to have my defence heard, and the circumstances that flagged Serge Benhayon as the universal predator.

Dialogue exchanges from the trial of Benhayon versus Rockett, while reproduced as faithfully to the court transcripts as possible, have been edited for brevity. Where transcripts were not available, I've recounted as accurately as I could from notes and memory. Transcripts of recorded materials have been similarly edited.

Some names have been changed to protect privacy or for legal reasons. Those are indicated with an asterisk*.

Esther Rockett, 2024

In memory of Laurie, Maurie, Madeline, and Mary.

Contents

Part I – Forums _____ 9

Part II – For the Love of Serge _____ 97

Part III – Ash _____ 199

Part IV – The Scales _____ 277

Epilogue _____ 374

Afterword _____ 384

List of characters _____ 388

    Acknowledgements _____ 393

    Endnotes _____ 393

Part I

Forums

i Squall

My new umbrella had a snakeskin print; a choice Serge would have disapproved of. The self-anointed emissary from the sixth dimension, the luminous embodiment of transcendental purity rails against our animal tendencies. But a snake's belly cannot get closer to the earth, and I liked to remind him that we all have a touch of reptile in us; we're all slithering through the dirt. Provoke any of us enough and we'll bite.

It was a short walk from chambers to the Law Courts Building at Queens Square. On the fifth of October 2018, the twenty-second day of the defamation trial of Serge Isaac Benhayon versus Esther Mary Rockett at the Supreme Court of New South Wales, the stirring sky was mottled grey. All the evidence had been heard, counsel had closed their arguments, and Her Honour was to commence her summing up.

A sprinkle of rain and a fitful breeze greeted us at the corner of Martin Place. Mr Tom Molomby SC had manila folders and notebooks tucked under one arm, and carried a sleek dark umbrella with an oak handle and tip. Junior counsel, Ms Louise Goodchild, strode two steps ahead, the luxurious pleats of her black robe swaying, the curled tails of her wig bouncing, and even Tom, a good head taller, had to liven his step to match her pace. She had her smartphone, her pencil case, and her favourite parasol with the musical motif; merry bars of black crotchets and quavers dancing across white sateen.

Louise and I raised our umbrellas as cold raindrops spattered our faces near Queens Square, where a press photographer trained his lens on us from the courthouse steps. The traffic broke, we started across the street, and the breeze quickened as it often did near the entry. A wind that might rate as slightly spirited in any other part of Sydney could build there into a howling southerly that would swirl from Hyde Park through the sandstone plaza, recoil at the steeple of St James Church, and swoop down Phillip Street, knotting and whirling into a mini tornado.

Suddenly, a fierce blast had me using both hands to push my umbrella into its face as it whipped Louise's wildly about before ripping whole bars of crotchets from its frame. I was thumbing for my collapse clip when my canopy flung upward and yanked backward, turning my snakeskin inside out. Yet Tom's umbrella was still folded, and he advanced across wind, squinting into the squall. Skipping in his wake, I thrust mine against the gale to turn it back on itself. 'I think it's bloody broken,' I muttered, clumsily pulling it down. Moments later, the photographer snapped me with damp hair flying skyward; Medusa in the CBD.

Molomby forded Phillip Street like a battleship, judicious nose in line with his umbrella tip, compass needle steady —chest out, robes flapping, horsehair wig bristled, but undisturbed. His voice trailed back as if from faraway… 'Don't give up,' he said.

ii Extraordinary ordinary

> What you need to believe in is what you can see... If you see me as your friend, I'll be your friend. As you see me as your father, I'll be your father... If you see me as your saviour, I'll be your saviour. If you see me as your God, I'll be your God.
>
> Jim Jones[1]

The sergebenhayon.com website was packed with glowing testimonials authored by nearly fifty of Benhayon's devoted 'students'. Its tabbed pages were arranged by theme: Serge Benhayon the author, Serge Benhayon the philosopher, Serge Benhayon the practitioner, the teacher, the family man, the friend. Some acolytes were so effusive in their admiration of the man and his multimillion-dollar enterprise, Universal Medicine, and so incensed by his treatment by the media, that they'd contributed two testimonials. Beneath each article was an invitation to leave a reply, followed by hundreds of unanimous responses; admirers often leaving numerous comments.

> Beautifully said Michelle. And it's an absolute yes from me as to the amazingness of Serge Benhayon and Universal Medicine. So in the face of the lies that are being told about them let's not hold back how we feel as everyone else in the world deserves to hear the truth and to have the choice to experience the healing that is possible...

Each carried its author's full name and a beaming photo avatar, and each was immaculately spelled.

> I agree Ingrid, well said, everyone deserves to hear the truth and to experience deep healing. I too, as have many many others, have had huge transformation in my health and life from the inspiration, deep love and truth lived and presented by Serge Benhayon.

That a businessman based in suburban Goonellabah, on the outskirts of Lismore, New South Wales, could inspire a whole website with so many positive raves is remarkable, but between 2012 and 2018, the Universal Medicine corporation and its associated spiritual community launched over fifty websites lauding its proprietor. Ten were blog sites, each featuring hundreds of devotional articles and tens of thousands of assenting comments from the 'student body'. The sites had titles like *The Truth About Serge Benhayon*, *Words on Serge Benhayon*, and *Medicine and Serge Benhayon*, and with so much repetition, students had to strain to find new superlatives.

> I feel so blessed to know Serge. As mentioned before he really is an extraordinary ordinary man.

Not a word of criticism was found on those thousands of webpages. Serge Benhayon was flawless.

The plaintiff's evidence in chief, where he entered the witness box and was questioned by his own lawyer, was his chance to portray himself as the innocent victim of defamation, and to persuade the court that his reputation and feelings had been so grievously harmed by my publications that I should pay him hundreds of thousands of dollars in damages. Benhayon claimed sixty-two defamatory imputations were conveyed by a blog article I'd authored and a series of tweets, and his lawyer, Kieran Smark SC, read out some excerpts, beginning with the opening paragraph of my blog post, 'Universal Medicine's sexual abuse apologism hits a crescendo'.

> Complementary health conglomerate and religion, Universal Medicine, has launched what could be its greatest fiasco with an hysteria ridden public promotion of the molestation they call 'healing'. UM's Esoteric hysterics mob, led by propaganda drill sergeant, Alison Greig, label our concerns about the organisation's predatory behaviours and our questions about the welfare of the most vulnerable members as 'sexualizing' and 'dangerous to children'. The UM *Facts* battalion then justifies inappropriate touching with anatomical confusion, New Age quackery and testimonials from Serge Benhayon's young female houseguests... It's a perfect demonstration of the mix of dishonesty, delusion, stupidity, abuse apologism, bullying and exploitation that screams 'cult'.

Smark, well-known in the defamation circuit, was a slightly built chap around fifty with a slack face that was too doleful for someone so well paid.

'It can fairly be said that presently Ms Rockett is not a fan of Mr Benhayon,' the barrister observed.

Before the judge, Serge looked more like an accountant than a cult leader. In grey tweed trousers, a blue business shirt and a navy sweater, he was short in stature and slim, and his wiry, grey-flecked hair was combed neatly. His posture, however, was the only straight thing about him. He recounted how he'd migrated from Uruguay in 1970, at age six, his family settling in Maroubra, a beachside suburb of Sydney. He'd been devoutly religious from an early age, he said, and if his statements were true, his religious upbringing was as eclectic as his latter-day New Age bent. Circumcised by a Jewish Mohel, he was baptised Catholic, worshipped at the Church of England, became a student of Messianic Judaism in his late teens, and learned about the Koran from his father. 'I've never not believed in God,' he said.

He added that his first nine years were deeply joyful and insightful, and that it was 'a very beautiful experience to be in one's body.' But his bliss was disrupted by the schoolyard attacks that plague migrant children. 'At the age of nine I made a decision to depart from that state of being...The pressures were basically to survive bullying, to survive being called a "wog".' Born with the name Sergio, perhaps the taunts led him to change it to Serge, and he said the hardships pushed him to excel at sport, which led to his career coaching tennis.

About fifty observers filled the court's public gallery, the majority stalwart UM students, rugged up in heavy coats and scarves despite the mild September weather. Seated behind his legal team, his wife and adult children wore woollen mittens. Smark needed testimony about hurt to his client's feelings, and asked of his first exposure to my crescendo post: 'How did you feel when you read it?'

Moist eyed Benhayon replied through trembling lips. 'The raping of my integrity, the raping of my... the attempt to demolish my reputation and the intrusion into my marital status...'

The barrister interrupted. 'But I'm asking how you felt about it. How did you feel about it?'

'Well, you feel raped.'

iii Intent

'Then you say this at line six,' said Smark. '"My claim that Benhayon is a sexual predator is not false"?'

It was early in my cross-examination, and Smark was quoting the crescendo blog. 'You were saying Mr Benhayon was a sexual predator, weren't you?'

'Yes.'

'You've said, "I've seen him in action"?'

'Yes.'

'You were referring to your experience with him in his consultation room, weren't you?'

'Yes, and at the workshop I went to as well.'

Benhayon skimped on a lot, but not on his leading barrister. Tom said it more than once during our preparations: 'Kieran is one of the smartest lawyers I know.' In the three years since Serge had filed his claim, Smark represented international cricketer Chris Gayle, and actor Geoffrey Rush, in successful defamation claims against Australian news outlets over 'Me Too' allegations.

Yet, despite the calibre of Benhayon's legal arsenal, and much of the public gallery praying to the Ascended Masters that I would slip up, the witness box was an unexpectedly serene place. The stops and starts, the paper shuffling, the legal arguments and procedural pauses make for a stilted process. Our preparations had been so hectic, it was a dramatic drop in pace.

Benhayon's Senior Counsel was too obviously tethered to *terra firma* to be a cult devotee. 'At line sixteen on page four, you say, "Even if that were true, how does it make it okay for Serge to touch people's private parts"?' Balding under his coarse wig, Smark was not flamboyant, and his weary expression suggested he'd heard every possible iteration of every possible argument. If he had a blind side, it was well hidden. 'Then at page six you style him as an "unqualified ex-bankrupt self-styled messiah pressing at erogenous zones for extended periods"?'

'Yes.'

If he'd ever had cheek muscles, they'd atrophied from lack of use. We never saw his teeth, he didn't jeer or scoff or raise his voice. Eyes steady and alert, his delivery was even, and he never looked or sounded pleased with himself, or anyone else. 'Then at page nine, at lines twenty to twenty-one, you refer to "treatment room perverts," do you see that?'

'Yes.'

'And you were clearly, in the context, referring to Mr Benhayon, weren't you?'

'And others.'

'You were calling Mr Benhayon and others, if you will, a "treatment room pervert"?

'Yes.'

'A "sleazebag guru"?'

'Yes.'

Smark's agile arguments during pre-trial hearings told me that he would not be a predictable foe. I could only hope that telling the truth would be enough to defend my publications. Sometimes his questions seemed clumsy, but I suspected it was a strategy. 'Now, do you really say that you didn't intend, when you wrote this blog, having written all of it, including the matters I took you to specifically, you really didn't intend to convey to ordinary readers who read the whole thing that Mr Benhayon had intentionally indecently touched you during a consultation in his treatment room?'

I took a breath. 'Could you ask that again?'

'Sure. Do you really say that you did not intend to communicate the meaning, the message, the allegation that Mr Benhayon had intentionally indecently touched you, his client, during a consultation in his treatment room?'

'I did not intend it.'

iv Translators

My colleague described Serge as a healer. That was the first red flag: strike one. I cringed, but my study-buddy, who lived in the Byron Bay region, insisted that Serge's methods were 'interesting' and worth experiencing. We'd always been interested in exploring diverse healing approaches in case they might help our patients or improve our understanding of the therapeutic process.

At my first meeting with Serge in his waiting room, he smiled broadly and extended his hand but stepped so close to me that I reflexively stepped back. He continued to chat cheerily as if nothing had happened. That was strike two. I'd practised acupuncture for ten years by then, and been a patient for longer, seeking alternative medicine when doctors were not able to help my chronically ratty digestive and immune systems. I knew a lot about personal boundaries and I knew what kind of reptiles were out there.

Aside from the space-invasion, Benhayon looked harmless. It was 2004, he was forty, still coaching tennis occasionally, and lively; his olive complexion relatively dewy, his green eyes bright. Media photos eight years later showed him haggard and emaciated, with pale, thin lips and yellow teeth, vampirish rings around his cloudy eyes. More recently, Universal Medicine's photographers light him so that his complexion looks fairer, and he's not been seen in short sleeves for over a decade. Whether at UM's

Vietnam retreats or in steamy Northern New South Wales summers, he's in his uniform of dark suit trousers and an untucked business shirt, buttoned at the cuffs.

In 2004, Serge operated from rooms beneath his white and mission brown brick veneer home on Pineapple Road, Goonellabah, where his front yard was adorned with a white concrete birdbath. A weather-beaten statue of Roman wench waded in its slimy shallows, surrounded by an imprisoning moat of glinting white pebbles. Strike three. A Benhayon acolyte bought the renovated house for about a million dollars ten years later and that birdbath, or a replica, is still there.

I was holidaying near Byron Bay, two hours' drive from my Brisbane home. Run down and grumpy, I told Serge that I'd just graduated my Arts degree, which I'd worked on while building my practice, and it was my first holiday in years. In 2000, I'd returned to Australia from four years post graduate training in clinics in Japan, where I'd worked for a shifty expat practitioner for a year before upgrading to the clinic of his reputable senior teacher, a renowned author of textbooks on Traditional Chinese Medicine. Over several years, I translated a couple of his books, top sellers in the field in Japan, but despite their prospects for publication in English, the cantankerous Sensei was fickle and uncooperative, the work thankless and unpaid, and with the expat white-anting me behind my back, I quit.

I laughed along when Serge responded with a tale about my past-life as a samurai warrior sent into exile by feudal overlords. Generating reincarnation clichés remains one of his sidelines. Smark asked if Benhayon had talked about kidney energy and energy flows, but if he had, I hadn't taken notice. There are major distinctions between the sophisticated metaphors of the Chinese Medical classics and New Age fantasies about magical 'energy'. My interest wasn't piqued by what Serge said, but what he did; his hands-on practice.

I lay on his treatment table and he placed his hands on my back and shoulders and told me to empty my mind. Keen to discover what my friend found so fascinating, I made an effort to do so. As minutes passed, my breathing deepened, and unusual sensations arose throughout my body. I wasn't concerned at first. Subtle sensations commonly arise during acupuncture, but these soon escalated into strong involuntary movements, unlike anything I'd experienced. I didn't fight them, which I blame on reading a little too much Carl Jung, and concentrated on keeping my mind empty. Jung had explored his own psyche via extended bouts of lucid dreaming where he resolved not to resist whatever emerged from his unconscious. It was a risky experiment, and he descended into psychosis at times, but I saw no harm in complying with Benhayon's instructions for those short sessions.

He kept his hands in place, and as I worked to suppress my thoughts, the bodily tingles intensified into twitches. As minutes passed, they graduated into tremors, and soon those were so pronounced that I was shaking all over and writhing on the couch, heaving gulps of air, legs jolting. If Benhayon said anything while I was in that state, I don't remember, and I lost sense of time, but he must have had his eye on the clock, because he eventually talked me through slowing my breathing until the reactions ceased.

I did feel lighter afterward; but that's to be expected from a large intake of oxygen — probably more exercise than I'd done in a while. The second session, a week later, was the same; casual chat, laying on of hands, and a physical catharsis, followed by Benhayon riffing about chakras and past lives. I hadn't entirely deactivated my critical faculties, though, and his decor earned him another strike. A painting of a female nude hung on the waiting room's purple walls, the creation of one of his assistants, Désirée Delaloye, rendered in lurid acrylic swirls of crimson, violet, orange and gold, and a male voice bellowed a New Age melody from the sound system, a wordless 'ahh ah ahhh ah ahh ah a ahhhhhh...' to a dirge-like synthesiser track. Women breezed in and out, and a meek young receptionist appeared from a cupboard or somewhere to take payment — Benhayon still gets other people to handle the lucre, lest it sully his pristine hands.

As I left one of my first sessions, Serge exercised one of his truly supernatural skills. He was chatting chirpily when I noticed indigo covered books on a shelf; *Ponder on This* by Alice A. Bailey. I don't recall why I asked about them, but he said, 'I keep a few copies here. Some people find it interesting. I don't push anyone to buy it…'

As much as I love a crack at Serge's tightfistedness, I could give him a good run in the thrift race. I never buy a book without inspecting the contents, yet I bought the Bailey book when I'd always thought Theosophy was nonsense. From weird to worse, I asked if the CDs on the shelf, *Silk in the Clouds*[2], was the music that was playing. The cover art was similar hued to Désirée's tacky painting, and Benhayon said the performer was a local friend of his, Chris James. Next thing, I bought the CD too, which I've never played.

After a cleansing swim in the surf at Broken Head, I sat on the sand to read a few short chapters of *Ponder on This*. Organised by themes: 'The New Group of World Servers', 'Triangles of Light', 'The New World Religion', 'The Reappearance of the Christ', 'The Master Djwal Khul', and the like, the book reacquainted me with Helena Blavatsky's Ascended Masters of The Hierarchy, light-filled beings 'who have triumphed over matter' and reside in Shamballa, an 'etheric plane' located somewhere above the Gobi Desert. Bailey postulated that Ascended Master Maitreya, a mystic caricature lifted from Mahayana Buddhism, was the same character as the Christian Christ and lined up for a second coming, and Blavatsky and Bailey asserted that all their 'Ageless Wisdom' writings, a hodge-podge of mistranslated Eastern spirituality and self-serving bourgeois projections, were dictated to them by an imaginary 'Tibetan' hermit, Djwal Khul. Schisms formed in the Theosophical movement as rivals claimed they were also channelling the invisible sage.

What a waste of twenty-five bucks. Serge didn't know that I'd majored in studies in religion, focusing on Eastern traditions, New Religious Movements, and cults. I didn't choose the field because I was shopping for a faith — growing up Catholic cured me of religion by my teens — I'd always been interested in the ways people find meaning, as well as the influences of belief on behaviour.

That was not the only oddness as I left Goonellabah's Shamballa, either. Benhayon mentioned that he too was a translator, and said, with a smile, 'I'm translating the Yoga Sutras.'

'Oh,' I said, surprised, 'you speak Sanskrit?'

Benhayon's eyeballs pinned and his smirk dropped. I waited, and he gave an ambiguous, coughed out laugh. 'Ugh-herghh.'

You wouldn't know Sanskrit if it bit you on the arse, I thought, and left. Still, I went back.

v The Patanjali channel

After the first session, Benhayon phoned to invite me to a yoga 'study group'. I'd always warned patients about health practitioners who contact them out of hours or ply them with stuff they haven't asked for. I told him I wasn't interested, but he persisted, telling me it was just a few friends getting together to translate Patanjali's sutra. Again, I went against my better judgement, and before sunset the following evening, found myself driving an unsealed road overlooking Byron Bay, where breaks in the roadside brush revealed a sheer unguarded drop from a precipice.

I went telling myself that perhaps someone in his group was a genuine scholar with something interesting to say about the challenges of translating, but 'a few of us getting together' turned out to be Serge packing a function room beneath the Bay FM radio towers and charging a ten dollar entry fee, which he hadn't mentioned. On the lawn outside, two women worked at a table stacked with copies of *Ponder on This*, taking cash flat out as customers grabbed for books that had been in print for over thirty years. Serge hovered, chatting merrily, watching the money change hands.

'Hi Heather, glad you could make it,' he said when he saw me.

'Esther,' I replied, as his attention flitted to someone else.

Odd looking white postcards with indigo splotches were also on offer, and I learned that they were 'healing symbols'. Serge produced them in partnership with Désirée Delaloye, but he claimed credit for the designs — crude, block coloured shapes. One looked like a sort of geometric duck crossed with a cassowary, another a cubist Michelin man, and others like splats found at the bottom of bird cages. Someone said the cards were for clearing bad energy, and they sold for seven dollars fifty each, while some laminated sheets of A4 paper went for eighty dollars apiece.

I kept tallying the demerits as more punters rolled in, most of whom were older women. Serge appeared with another carton of Bailey books, and the meeting was delayed when his volunteers discovered there weren't enough seats. While we waited, someone brought a chair outside for a young woman to receive an impromptu healing session. Maura*, a stout matron in her fifties, steadied her stance behind the seated waif, and placed one hand on the younger woman's forehead and the other on the nape of her neck. Eyes half-closed, Maura began to emit a series of startling belches: not your dainty Perrier burps, but loud, sonorous croaks that seemed to emanate from the bedrock of her base chakra. Elongated, multi-tonal, and arguably more melodic than Chris James' *Silk in the Clouds*, I thought it odd that her performance didn't draw a larger audience. From those gathered, I learned that each belch was a release of noxious energy drawn up through Maura's powerful hands. The louder the burps, the worse the patient's energetic state, and Maura would remove one hand occasionally and give it a few shakes, a succinct burp accompanying each flick of the wrist, before embarking on a new round of gaseous volleys, all with the stony countenance of a veteran of many violent seances. It reminded me that Serge had quietly burped during my sessions, unburdening some of my inner evils, I suppose, but I'd just thought he was disagreeing with his lunch.

At least a hundred eager yogis crammed into that meeting room that humid night, wedged flesh to sticky flesh. Beside me was acupuncturist, Neil Ringe, who I'd met when he visited Sensei's clinic in Japan five years earlier. In his early fifties, he had a busy practice near Mullumbimby, and he told me that he'd been friends with Serge for years. The longtime Zen Buddhist said that the yoga sutras weren't his thing either.

The evening's show was not a translation at all but Serge posing before his audience and pretending to channel. He'd close his eyes, take a dramatic pause, and then burble some fake platitude, making out that it was the 'true text' conveyed exclusively to him from the etheric sphere. He had no text with him, couldn't identify which part of the sutra he was transmitting, and nothing I heard bore any conceptual relationship with the original, yet, no one seemed to care. Benhayon's first book, two years later, audaciously titled, *The Way It Is*, claimed that 'The Tibetan' Djwal Khul was Patanjali in a former life, and that his Raja Yoga was practised in Atlantis.[3]

The meeting room had a view across Byron Bay, glowing under a pearlescent full moon, and as the night dragged on, Cape Byron's lighthouse flashed warnings. Serge spent more time on tangential banter with Chris James and other male accomplices than on the 'text', and his barest witticisms drew peals of over-appreciative laughter. It was one of those hot, still, subtropical nights where the humidity and the etheric magnetism of the lunar apogee brings everything that creeps and crawls out of its respective crack and cranny. The place was riddled with cockroaches, scurrying over sandalled toes and ankles, up walls and across the ceiling, yet Serge's sweating students did not stir or complain. Irritation swelling, I contemplated climbing over twelve clammy devotees for a clear run to the door.

Meandering onto the topic of meditation, Benhayon called on Neil to describe his experience of the optimal state. My counterpart blustered that the peak of his practice was 'what I can only describe as pure love.' It was difficult not to scowl. Zen is a predominantly male sect of self-focus that never bothered with the concept of compassion and revels in the violent use of the 'wake-up stick'. Aloof Neil struck me as an ideal proponent, and I couldn't fathom why he'd spin a cultural fiction characterising inhuman levels of detachment as 'love', or would play straight man to Serge's farce.

The full moon beamed and the cockroaches scuttled. It occurred to me that Benhayon was trying to start a cult, but so were a lot of oddballs and most don't succeed. His seemed too obvious a scam. Two tedious hours in, I had a growing urge to shove past the converts, find a copy of the weekend paper, roll it up, and start whacking the cockroaches into oblivion. Perhaps the others held back out of a belief that they were some of their past lives. At that point, a robust specimen interrupted its trek across the ceiling to drop twitching and scratching onto my lap. I flicked it to the floor with an open hand, and it began scuttling afresh. Raising my knee, I stamped my foot down. Under my sole, I felt a satisfying squelch.

vi The reading

You bastard.

It was February 2005, my third and final session. I was alone in a treatment room with Serge, and I was annoyed with him and annoyed with myself for being there. Despite his Patanjali pretensions, I remained curious about his ability to put me into a trance and whether his technique was reproducible. I expected the session to proceed as the previous two had, and I'd settled myself on the table when he came straight out and said: 'Today I think we should do an ovarian reading.'

My reaction was instant. Without hesitation, and with firmness, I said 'no'. I didn't know what an ovarian reading was, and I didn't want to know. I told him, 'I don't need that.'

He hadn't questioned me previously about my private life or medical history, so I assumed he knew the limits of his competence. But he didn't accept my rebuff. 'It's not invasive,' he said.

I repeated irritably. 'I don't need it.'

'I think it would be good for you,' he answered in his soft, squeaky voice, adding an unimpeachable little smile.

That's when I came to doubt my common sense. 'What is it?' I asked.

He explained that I'd remain fully clothed, and he'd lay his hands on my lower abdomen, and 'feel into' some information from my ovaries.

'What kind of information?'

'Everyone is different, it depends…'

Again I insisted I didn't want it.

'I wouldn't do it if I didn't think it would be good for you…'

'Is it a psychic reading?' I asked.

He gave the same incongruous chuckle as when I caught him out on his Sanskrit proficiency. But instead of taking that as a cue for a spectacular exit, I began to think that I was overreacting, that I was missing something. Surely a pipsqueak like him wouldn't try something inappropriate on an assertively unimpressed woman. To reassure me, he said that I didn't have to say anything during the reading. 'I'll pass on the information from your ovaries and you can decide whether or not it resonates.'

With some impatience, I gave in. 'Oh, all right.'

With that he placed his finger tips on my lower abdomen about a centimetre superior to the upper boundary of my pubic area. For some long uneasy moments he was silent, eyes closed, hands in place. Eventually he said, 'when you were five years old, a man in your life let you down.'

You bastard.

He continued with more conjectures, pausing between each. 'When you were seven years old, a man in your life wasn't who he seemed… When you were eleven years old, a man in your life wasn't there for you…' He worked his way up random ages and more suggestions about 'a man in your life', reaching the teens, where he alleged, 'a man in your life tortured you'.

We women hear a lot of shitty lines. The rogue expat practitioner in Tokyo used that kind of psychic fakery, waiting until his clients were relaxed before saying, with feigned care, 'who hurt you?' or 'a man has caused you pain…' It ignited a heated confrontation between us over his behaviour with women, which he repaid by bad-mouthing me for years. After I quit his clinic, his male staff confirmed that the married man was a serial tryster with patients and visiting therapists.

It doesn't take a psychic to guess that a man in anyone's life has let them down. Or a woman for that matter. 'Yeah Serge, my Dad let me down every time we passed the corner shop and he didn't buy me a Paddle Pop.' Shonks have used cold reading to extract information from their victims for centuries. Co-operative targets confirm or correct their guesswork, and it's likely that some of Benhayon's clients did surrender information about their male-inflicted vulnerabilities; anything from Paddle Pop deprivations to histories of serious abuse — while his mitts were placed over their reproductive regions.

He said I didn't have to comment, so I lay still as a plank, fuming. He lost patience and opened his eyes. 'Err…am I right?' he said.

'No,' I croaked. 'Not really.'

Compared with the dark colonial era courts across the square, with their wooden floors and creaking joinery that echoes every clunk and clomp, the forty year old Law Courts are muted, with fluorescent lighting, pale woodwork, and white walls. The youngster's carpeting and upholstered chairs absorb extraneous sounds. On a dais to my right, overlooking the witness box, was Her Honour Justice Julia Lonergan and her Tipstaff. On the same level as me, a step above the bar table and public gallery, was the judge's Associate and the court reporter. To my left, an elderly court officer dozed in a chair.

Tom stood at a lectern facing Her Honour. Unlike Smark, he did not hunch, but held a regal posture, chin up. 'Just to clarify there,' he said, 'Mr Benhayon was identifying certain sorts of incidents at particular ages. Had anything at those ages or around them happened to you like that?'

'It was all very vague, so I couldn't tie it to anything in my experience,' I answered.

On Benhayon's side, Smark and his junior, Nicholas Olson, in matching wigs and robes, tapped notes on identical tablets. Behind them sat the plaintiff and his solicitor, Paula Fletcher, a UM community member and one of a clutch of lawyers in Benhayon's thrall, her haughty eyes fixed on me while he stared into middle distance, into space.

'What happened after that?' said Tom.

'I was relieved at turning over and not having to look at him.'

Several women journalists were among the observers. To date, I was the only woman willing to go on the record about the real reptile Benhayon, and while it was uncomfortable to give that evidence, the court had heard much weirder testimony before mine: Serge's own.

vii The professional

Tom was surprised that my readers were suspicious of Smark, but UM seemed to have tentacles everywhere, so it was natural to question whether he had links to the group. After all, Charles Wilson, a Brisbane barrister and Benhayon acolyte, was Smark's original junior in the proceeding, practising outside his usual area of commercial litigation.

Tom worked at a desktop piled with papers and notebooks, drafting documents by hand as his dilapidated notebook computer balanced on a teetering stack. I spent weeks seated opposite on his worn blue sofa, flanked by bundles and binders, computer on my knee. On a bureau stood a brightly enamelled toy Ferris wheel, and the lawyer wound it up for me once to play its carnival music. Otherwise, he played classical CDs as we worked, tapping his toes, and he'd lift his eyes above the mountain of papers at times to say something like, 'Can you hear that?… There, the organ coming in… It's a subtle undertone… Saint Saëns is one of the most underrated composers don't you think?'

He had a point, but I had my own question. 'Do you think Smark's concerned he might get a bad name acting for clients like Serge?'

Tom replied that most lawyers wouldn't have a practice if they were choosey about who they represented. He respected Smark, and guessed he had good reason to work for Benhayon. 'Kieran has an inordinate number of children,' he said, adding that he'd lost count. 'He's probably sending them to private schools… That gets expensive. A client like Benhayon doesn't come along often — obsessed, vindictive, and with the money to push a big claim like his all the way.'

viii Bruised

'You can't have complete freedom of speech or there would be no right to reputation,' Justice Lonergan remarked to the court. 'You can't have a complete right to reputation or there would be no freedom of speech, so the law has to strike balances.'

The defamatory imputations Benhayon claimed to find in my blog and tweets ranged from allegations of sexual misconduct to charlatanism, dishonesty, exploitation, and bullying, and that he was the leader of a socially harmful cult. I pleaded that the majority could be proven true, truth being an absolute defence, and also that most imputations could be defended as expressions of honest opinion. Relying on a further defence of qualified privilege, I pleaded that my publications were reasonable under the circumstances, even if the court found the other defences did not apply.

To defeat the truth defence, Smark had to convince the court that the evidence I brought did not prove the allegations. To defeat the opinion defence, he had to make out that my allegations were not expressions of opinion, but false statements posed as facts, or were not rationally based on facts or proper material, or that I did not honestly hold those opinions. To beat the reasonableness defence, he had to convince the court that I had not acted reasonably in publishing, or that I published out of malice. The law distinguishes malice as an improper intention, such as a deliberate intent to inflict damage on the plaintiff, or knowingly or carelessly making allegations that are false.

'When you published each of the matters complained of, you did so as part of an overall campaign to harm Mr Benhayon,' said Smark. 'What do you say to that?'

I surmised from the question that he was wrapping up the cross-examination, and imagined he was as weary of me as I was of him. 'No.'

'I suggest to you that in publishing each of the matters complained of, you turned a blind eye to the risks of the harm that you would cause Mr Benhayon. What do you say to that?'

'That makes no sense,' I answered. 'I was considering the harm being done by this organisation to countless people.'

'Finally, I suggest that in publishing each of the matters complained of, you intentionally used strong and inflammatory language designed to maximise the harm caused to Mr Benhayon. Do you agree with that?'

'No.'

In the lead up to trial, I envisaged that Smark could only try to entrap me into making false admissions, or try to distort the evidence to confuse the issues. When I was released from the witness box, I was less enamoured of his professionalism than my lawyers were, although they were more experienced with what passes on the legal battlefield as fair. Witnesses are not permitted to consult their lawyers while they are under cross-examination, and we regrouped in the empty foyer before Benhayon's entourage trooped out. Tom wasn't brimming with compliments over my performance. He'd maintained that it was unlikely that I'd be able to defend my publications one hundred percent. 'Well I did say, Esther, that no one gets through a cross-examination without taking some hits,' he said. 'And shall we say that Kieran dealt you a few bruises?'

ix Commuters

> If her allegations were true and her concerns as great as she expresses… why would she follow the alleged incident with her attendance at a course run by the very man who she considered was a sexual predator? It makes no sense.
>
> Universal Medicine Facts website, 2014

There's nothing advanced about Sacred Esoteric Healing Advanced Level One. The entry level course to the Universal Medicine workshop cycle is open to anyone who pays, and I paid. After the ovarian reading, the compulsion to get out of that purple dungeon and never go near Benhayon again was overruled by a burning need to find out the extent of his exploits. You never forget being preyed upon, just as you never escape the suspicion that the culprit is preying on others. I considered going to the police, but imagined recounting a New Age ovarian reading to some surly rural cop and doubted I'd be taken seriously. Consumer safeguards were non-existent. Any shyster could call themselves a therapist.

I was never scared of Serge. Patients can be disturbingly compliant, so I feared for those who believed him. Many would not have understood that he was not qualified to inquire about their reproductive organs or their private lives, or to put them into trances, or touch them the way he did.

Of the sixty or so who attended the workshop at the Lennox Head Sports Stadium in April 2005, a handful were men. At least eight women attended as Benhayon's assistants, including Maura the belcher, Désirée, and a Brisbane naturopath, Jenny Ellis. The other helpers, previous Level One graduates, didn't have much to do that weekend except swan around trying to look important. None, aside from Ellis, had formal health qualifications, and at the top of a distinct pecking order, Maura, Désirée and Jenny received most of the proprietor's coveted attention.

On the first morning, I overheard Ellis tell another woman that Serge had called her to a meeting the coming Monday night, adding that she'd have to drive straight from work to arrive on time, and 'yes, he still wants us at Wednesday's.' It was a two hour commute each way and she would do it twice in the three nights from Monday, at his whim, having spent the weekend helping at the workshop. It reminded me of a Queensland based yoga group run by Vijay Yogendra. I'd attended its yoga classes in Brisbane around 1994 and the elderly guru was one of the iciest characters I've ever met. He had genuine knowledge of yoga philosophy, at least, but the regular attendees were unnervingly humourless and deferential to him. Yogendra extolled humility, detachment, selfless service, and being mindfully present in the moment, and he excoriated the use of foul language. I was never going to fit in.

In 1999, at sixty-nine, Yogendra dumped his wife of thirty-five years, took up with a woman thirty-four years younger and absconded from his community near Warwick, Queensland, taking money that was raised to fund its school and other initiatives. When I got back from Japan in 2000, the group tried to recruit me to fill a vacancy left by a practitioner who'd bolted with him. I asked a doctor I knew about it. He'd been part of Yogendra's inner circle, and he looked me in the eye and told me it was a cult.

Many years earlier, the old con had commandeered a non-profit foundation set up by followers, and he recruited medicos, psychologists, teachers, and business managers to toil away in health centres and other enterprises attached to it. Vijay did not practise the humility and selfless service he expected from acolytes, whom he systematically ripped off while cruising around in a Range Rover, investing in real estate, and exerting himself in extramarital yoga.

After he fled Warwick, Yogendra set up a 'wellbeing' practice in North Queensland. He died of cancer in 2005, at seventy-five, having promised clients that he could cure them of the same disease. But that wasn't the end of the strife. Days after his death, his healthy and wealthy forty-one year old wife, Kate, took her own life. In a note to her cousin, she told her not to be sad, that she was not depressed, and that her choice was intentional and willing. She left nothing for her family in her will, and they were barred from the funeral, while the couple's terrier received thirty thousand dollars per annum for its care. Kate wrote of her extreme final act that there is no death; that she was just passing on to another stage in life.

In my view, Vijay was culpable. I saw the hold he had on his supplicants. His foundation still limps along in Warwick, his followers believing he died of a spider bite, and they glossed over his wife's suicide with fairytales about the couple reuniting in the afterlife.[4] Yogendra, of course, could gain nothing from manipulating Kate into believing her life was not worth living without him, except for the malign gratification that he had the power to dispense with her existence.

Yogendra's professionals spent unhealthy amounts of time commuting to his allied health sweatshops and out of hours meetings. Rackets of that type purposely keep devotees busy, exhausted, and isolated from those who might challenge their devotion to the leader and their dubiously urgent cause. Neither Jenny Ellis nor the recipient of her message hesitated at Benhayon's command.

Jenny and Désirée were of similar age, mid to late thirties, a little older than me. Unusually soft-spoken and demure, they looked to be in decent health and put noticeable effort into their grooming. Cult red flags were flapping as I watched Svengali Serge go to work, approaching each in turn, cheerily rattling off ideas and instructions, as if they were paid staff. The two nodded meekly, obviously smitten, but neither looked comfortable or content, and they had the same look of defencelessness in their watery eyes; submissive and on edge; infatuation imbued with fear.

He's screwing these women, I thought — if only figuratively.

x Entities

Benhayon set the chairs for the morning's lecture with their backs to the windows; no doubt conscious that the view of the cloudless blue sky and the rocky, bush-covered Lennox Head looming over a glittering ocean was a stinging reminder that we weren't just wasting money on his madness, but wasting perfect weather. From his opening talk, it became clear that Sacred Esoteric Healing had nothing to do with health or wellbeing. Benhayon was agitated, dropping his Patanjali wisecracking and pacing as he talked, and his talk was rapid-fire. He veered erratically through topics, from claiming Christ was an avatar of Ascended Master, Lord Khuthumi, to deriding competing belief systems. Catholicism was evil; Buddhism was a 'belief in nothing'; teachings about chakras were all 'bastardised'; Helena Blavatsky had sold out to glamour and illusion; and tarot readers, psychics and mediums were all false angels and spiritual deceivers, mired in the Dark Rule of the Astral plane. Occasionally, he'd assert something that sounded genuinely insightful, but before it was possible to properly consider, he'd descend into gibberish: the story of Noah's Ark is an inaccurate tale of the sinking of Atlantis; inhabitants of the distant star Arcturus built Egypt's ancient pyramids eighteen thousand years before the pharaohs, and regularly revisit to create crop circles. I didn't have the confidence or the speed to take him on, and courageous audience members who challenged him were bludgeoned with aggressive *non sequitur* responses.

The hands-on training was worse. We set up portable treatment tables, formed pairs and took turns to play practitioner and patient. Our host closed the blackout curtains and turned out all the lights so that only a thin shard of daylight crept into the room where he left the door ajar. He handed out workshop manuals, but no one could see them well enough to read Serge's dotty prose, or properly inspect the black and white photographs of Benhayon demonstrating his hands on healing techniques on a girl who looked to be in her early teens. If I'd not cast the thing aside, repulsed, I would have found the images of his hands on the young girl's backside and chest purporting to clear 'stagnant sadness'.

No out of bounds touching occurred that weekend that I was aware of, but in the darkness, Benhayon revealed more of his true self. Instructing all participants in the breathing technique, he told them to empty their minds, insisting that the healing would not work unless all parties focused on doing so. The technique for inducing altered states was indeed reproducible, and dedicated to my experiment, I followed the directions faithfully to experience roughly the same physical reactions with each new partner and new technique. I'd writhe with tremors, hyperventilate, and at some points found myself speaking in tongues. Others reacted similarly, some thrashing about more strongly, wailing and crying, while some responded minimally or not at all. A woman paired with me for one session lay dead still, eyes wide open, staring at the ceiling, lips pursed, perhaps having realised she'd made a terrible mistake.

Once participants had entered the trance, Benhayon began a macabre rave, telling the group that our reactions were evil energies escaping our bodies, and that malevolent spirits — 'entities' — were being released. Violent traumas occurring over many lifetimes had created openings in our auras that allowed them in, he said, and he strode around practically shouting this stuff to the flailing patients as the volume of panting and wailing swelled to a peak. He'd then talk them down, returning to a focus on breathing.

The partners would change places, and the process, with Benhayon's narrative, would begin again. We'd change partners for the next technique, and repeat it, each episode building over twenty minutes or so to a hellish commotion in the dark, and as the day wore on, his rhetoric became more medieval, more violent and more perverse. 'You've been tortured! You've been raped!' he shouted. We'd been branded, beaten, flogged, and disembowelled with swords in our martyred past lives. Some of us had been angels tortured for heresy, had our limbs and wings hacked off, were burned at the stake, or drowned. As his tirades intensified, the catharses escalated, men and women erupting in sobs and full throated screams. At one point, Benhayon dragged a plastic garbage bin to the head of a table where an unfortunate was heaving and appeared to vomit.

xi Tongues

'Yes, no, get off the stand,' was Louise Goodchild's advice for answering questions under cross-examination. It was the day before Smark was to start on me, and like a boxer before a big bout, I was getting some final slaps around the chops before my trainers shoved me into the ring. 'It's not a soapbox,' she said. 'Don't get up there and try to argue your case, that's what we're here for. Don't be defensive; give short, yes, no answers; don't give him anything…'

None of my team could guess how long Smark would question me or where he'd go with it. Because I didn't want to invite accusations that I was seeking coaching, I barely glanced at our side of the bar table, keeping my gaze on saggy faced Smark, or allowing it to wander into the public gallery, often to Benhayon, who spent a lot of time staring at the back of his lawyer's knees. Tom agreed with Louise that it was best to keep my answers short. Any clarifications could be made under Tom's re-examination.

Smark referred to the transcript of my evidence in chief: 'You said you can recall "moving around on the table almost involuntarily… Quite a strong physical reaction, kind of trembling, hyperventilating and moving around on the table". Was that the complete list of what you say were your physical reactions to the sessions from Mr Benhayon in late 2004?'

'To the best of my recollection, yes.'

'Nothing else, no other behaviour?'

'Not that I can recall.'

'Are you sure?'

'Not that I can recall.'

'What about speaking in tongues?'

'I don't recall that happening in the treatment room, but I remember that happening at that workshop I went to.'

Passed a copy of one of my blogs, Smark asked me to read a paragraph he'd selected, which mentioned me speaking in tongues during one of the visits to Pineapple Road. 'I'd asked you about the experiences that you said you'd had on the table when you saw Mr Benhayon in late 2004. What about speaking in tongues in those sessions?'

'I don't remember that now. This blog was written six years ago, so it could just be a difference in memory.'

'It's right, isn't it, that some years ago, that is to say, in 2012 you blogged that during these sessions you had experienced speaking in tongues?'

'Well, if it's in there I blogged it.'

'You were saying that a man who, on your experience, in these sessions in late 2004 simply by gently laying his hands on you and instructing you to empty your mind and breathe deeply, had led you to speak in tongues. Is that the claim that you blogged in 2012?'

'That's what I blogged in 2012.'

'Isn't that an extraordinary claim?'

I halted, unsure how to answer a question about 'claiming' something as opposed to describing what happened. Smark pressed. 'Don't you regard that as a surprising claim?'

'A surprising…?'

'That a man could simply by laying his hands gently on you, asking you to empty your mind and breathe deeply could lead you, on the treatment table, without any drugs or other influencing mechanism, cause you to speak in tongues?'

'I found it a surprising experience.'

xii The Monads

Benhayon pointed his finger at me. 'And you, Hannah,' he said: 'Monad.' This time I didn't correct my name. Finger extended, he moved to the next person. 'Monad.' We were between practice sessions and he was delivering readings to each workshop participant, tagging them as either a Monad or an Angel. No other options were available. Monad was a term Blavatsky and Bailey had borrowed from a Pythagorean concept of divine singularity or oneness, but Benhayon's version anthropomorphised it into a troupe of occult beings superior to Angels. Serge said that we'd all lost our connection to God, but Angels had become Monads' underlings in 'restoring Brotherhood on Earth'. Scandalised at being tarred an Angel, a woman called after him, 'But why? Why?!' Benhayon ignored her.

That sideshow was a forerunner to his 'School of Initiation', where, for a fee, he rated each followers' proximity to God. Predictably, he ranked himself at the top of the scale, first as a fifth degree initiate, a step up from the Dalai Lama, a clear two to five dimensions above his students, and the closest thing to God on this globe, but in 2015 he mocked his admirers further by catapulting himself to the sixth dimension — a level of transcendence so celestial that the initiate usually dumps their physical body to waft around the Etheric Plane like some sort of gas. Benhayon was so underfed by then that it was plausible, but he claimed to be the first sixth degree Master in history to remain incarnate, selflessly staying on Earth to shower us with his gifts.

He delivered the initiation readings in front of the whole congregation, awarding the highest to his most abrasive acolytes, giving the most servile the lowest, and shifting the most neurotic up and down the scale arbitrarily. Former students said it created havoc; tears, wails, and demands to know why so and so got a better score, and he'd invariably follow with a scolding lecture on the evils of jealousy and comparison.

The exorcisms recommenced apace, and I lost sight of Benhayon's harem of assistants in the dark, apart from formidable Maura, who moved among the tables, drawing forth evils with her fulsome belches. With all the shrieking, moaning and burping, I was unable to make out whether anyone else was speaking in tongues, but by late afternoon I understood Jenny and Désirée's stupefied gazes. They'd been hit with the Serge-stick one way or another. The other assistants were less subdued, but perhaps they were less 'advanced', so to speak, and the ringleader had to intervene when a bossy young woman's policing of her colleagues' Esoteric language descended into verbal scrapping.

At the workshop dinner on the Saturday evening, I learned that most other participants were Northern Rivers locals. No one talked about the day's sensations, opting for small-talk about travel, childcare, and car trouble. Aside from the bickering assistants, they were decent and unpretentious people; a few humanities students, a couple of musicians, office admins, retail workers, and mothers or grandmothers you might meet on tuckshop duty. It was a relief to be back on planet earth.

xiii 2,300 lives

Access to the Ageless Wisdom is available to everybody at any time, during any, and every reincarnation, and we've had at least two thousand three hundred lives each…

Serge Benhayon[5]

Sunday morning I stopped at a beachside bakery at Lennox Head to scrounge for breakfast. Across the way, the Pacific Ocean heaved and fizzed, glaring white under the climbing sun. I recognised a mother and daughter from the workshop at an outside table, the younger woman weeping helplessly, tears streaming down her cheeks. The mother put a roll and a cup of something hot in front of her, but the daughter did not touch them. When practice resumed that morning, she deteriorated, and sobbed uncontrollably all day as her mother and Maura fussed around her. I wanted to tell the women to cut their losses, get out of there, and seek professional help before they copped more damage, but I maintained my cover, and felt like a traitor.

As Sunday wore on, I grew bored. Benhayon rehearsed the occult schlock at every session, and the cathartic reactions didn't peter out, as I thought they might with repetition. He insisted we've all had countless past lives, implying that the supply of demons, pernicious energies and bad *karma* was inexhaustible; a standard New Age ploy to generate repeat business. Customers have to keep returning to have it all cleared. But the catharses delivered no insights or existential relief, I didn't trip into higher dimensions or receive relays from Djwal Khul. Speaking in tongues was novel at first, but ultimately empty. Serge would probably argue that I was too unevolved to realise I'd been impulsing the blank-brained Wisdom of Lord Khuthumi, or somesuch, but squirming and hyperventilating all weekend just left me spent.

Under cross-examination Benhayon said that getting money out of me was not among his motivations for suing. He was only concerned about damage to his reputation. Molomby returned: 'I suggest to you that actually the reason you brought this case right at the start, knowing that you had far greater resources than her, and predicting that she wouldn't be able to fund a defence, was to close her down, to stop her publishing the things she was publishing about you?'

'Absolutely not,' said Serge.

'It's never been any part of your objective to stop her publishing the sorts of things she's been publishing?'

'I understood she would never stop.'

xiv Natalie

Physiotherapist Kate Greenaway, a practitioner at Benhayon's rooms at Pineapple Road showed up on Sunday, and I was horrified to hear her advising workshop attendees on how to set up their Esoteric healing practices, and how to use Serge's techniques on children. The complementary medicine market was already overflowing with well-meaning incompetents taking people's money, but Esoteric hobbyists exorcising children ratcheted the hazard to a new high.

Benhayon's second eldest child, fifteen year old Natalie, also joined the practice sessions. I'd heard grown women talk about her as if she had superpowers, but with dark brown hair and big green eyes, she seemed like any ordinary fifteen year old, except that she was small and could have passed for twelve. Sitting beside her for the workshop closing ceremony, I asked if she planned to practise healing after she graduated high school, and she said she hadn't decided yet.

That afternoon, when Benhayon switched the lights back on, some recruits wandered around grinning senselessly, while others seemed startled, mouths open, lips quivering, out of breath. The woman who'd cried all day was red-eyed and snivelling, but Benhayon was pumped. When he reprised some of the claptrap from his opening lecture, his converts responded with wide-eyes and tipsy smiles; no sign of the puzzled frowns of the previous day.

In closing, he had us sit in a circle and join hands to feel our 'connectedness' while he 'impulsed' us with the energy of the Ascended Masters. I took the trembling hand of a university student, who was majoring in religious studies, and as Serge recited an occult prayer, the boy's body began to shake so strongly I had to ask if he was okay to drive. He seemed on the verge of either hysterical laughter or tears.

Whatever became of him, a number of participants I met that weekend, including Jenny Ellis and Désirée, are still in the group, and I didn't escape mentally unaffected. On the long drive home, my mind was rushing, despite my exhaustion. Beset by a tumult of contradictory thoughts, I was conscious of how deplorable the whole thing was, but as torpidly drunk as some of the new believers. Pangs of disgust mixed with strange feelings of fascination. Irrational doubts badgered me, telling me Serge wasn't that bad, he's harmless, just a bit quirky, and maybe he's right and there is some universal, unifying, homogenising, emulsifying spiritual lineage that connects Christ and Buddhist and Yogic and Ancient Egyptian traditions via Galileo and Helena Blavatsky, followed sharply by sensible bursts of fury. 'Atlantis? Arcturans? Angels burned at the stake??'

It's also possible that I'd misread the reactions of others, who, beneath the elation, might have been similarly confused and fighting just as hard to resist disorientation, fatigue and implanted suggestions. Another chilling thought was that the majority had been in the treatment room with Benhayon, and he'd probably manipulated them into personal disclosures. Nothing was stopping him from exploiting histories of domestic violence; drug, alcohol, and porn habits; mental breakdowns; gynaecological disorders; relationship conflicts; or sexual abuse. No participants were warned he'd render them suggestible and pull every trauma trigger he could that weekend, in full knowledge of their vulnerabilities.

Mind muddled, physically wrung out and numb, it took days to recover. I struggled to focus at a study date with a couple of acupuncturist friends the following day. One exploded when I told them about the previous weekend. 'Who is this fuckwit? This Serge? What the fuck were you doing going to that?' Slumped in his office, slack jawed and weak, his salvo of profanity came as a merciful shot of clarity. That hangover was like nothing I'd experienced. I'd never had to fight so hard for control of my own mind.

Over seven years later, within hours of writing about the event on an online anti-cult forum, I received messages of gratitude. 'Thank you for posting about what happens in those workshops,' said one. 'Now I understand why my wife comes back from those things spaced out like she's on drugs.'

xv Hypnotic

When Smark began dissecting the press kit I worked on late in 2012, two years before I'd published the crescendo blog, it made me wonder how many documents he was going to dredge up from the mass of material I'd authored since.

'And then in the third paragraph you say: "Followers known as students of Universal Medicine are seen to undergo personality changes consistent with states of psychological dissociation, anxiety and paranoia as they become increasingly involved with the group." Do you see that?'

'Yes'

'Now, this was one of those matters to which your statement, "We can provide evidence for everything stated herein" applied, as you would understand readers to take it, wouldn't it?'

'Yes.'

'When you say "they are seen," what you're putting that forward as, I suggest, in this press kit was a statement of fact of general application, do you agree with that?'

'Yes.'

'Did you hold any degree in psychiatry or psychology at the time?'

'No.'

'What enabled you to say that students of Universal Medicine, as a general statement of fact, underwent personality changes consistent with states of psychological disassociation, anxiety and paranoia? How were you able to say that?'

'I'd spoken by then to, I don't know, at least forty people about their family members and friends who were involved in Universal Medicine.'

'My question to you is do you accept you did not have qualifications that enabled you to identify the conditions there stated?'

'I don't have those qualifications, no.'

Smark moved to another part of the press kit, waving the document disdainfully as if it was permeated with criminal DNA. 'This section, I suggest fairly plainly, is saying that Universal Medicine is a cult and Mr Benhayon is the leader of the cult?'

'Yes.'

'In the section beginning "Serge Benhayon employs deceptive behaviours", you were stating that Serge Benhayon employed thought reform or mind control techniques in recruiting followers and securing their dependency, weren't you?'

'According to my analysis, yes.'

'You were stating it as a fact?'

'According to my analysis and I've given the reasoning within this document.'

'You state as a matter of fact that Benhayon uses hypnotic techniques, don't you?'

'The press understand that this is coming from a member of the public and that this can only be my analysis.'

'This was something that you said you could provide evidence for everything stated in this, wasn't it?'

'Yes.'

'You said, "Hypnotic techniques were employed to induce psychological dissociation in recruits and increase their suggestibility."'

'Yes.' A term I'd used in the document, 'covert hypnosis without informed consent', came from the book, *Dangerous Persuaders*, by psychologist, Louise Samways.

'You stated that as a matter of fact, didn't you?'

'Yes. According to the people I'd spoken to who had seen this occur. And myself, I'd been to a workshop, I'd seen this happening.'

'You were saying weren't you, that Mr Benhayon was hypnotising people?'

'Yes.'

xvi The Da Vinci Mode

On my forty-fifth birthday, late August 2012, *The Sydney Morning Herald* ran a feature, 'The Da Vinci Mode', about a suspected cult in Northern New South Wales. Its leader claimed to be the reincarnation of the original Renaissance man, and the majority of his estimated two thousand followers were women. His name was Serge.

Living two hours' drive away in Brisbane I'd heard little about Benhayon for seven years. After the workshop, I'd phoned Neil, hoping to persuade him to talk some sense into his friend. 'Reading ovaries?' I said. 'He shouldn't be going near anything gynaecological.'

Neil conceded that Benhayon could be 'pushy'. He also agreed that the occult stuff was extreme. He'd seen Benhayon teach students to remove energetic swords from each other — imaginary blades inflicted by past-life demons — and was taken aback at how many could be pulled from a person, and their length. One workshop-goer kept pulling from one of the women until he was out of the conference room door, but Neil's response to me was, 'Don't overlook all the good things for the bad.'

In the intervening years, I'd searched the internet and found the universalmedicine.com.au website, which was loaded with Esoteric waffle. Around 2008, Benhayon began marketing Esoteric Breast Massage® with the dubious caveat that it was practised exclusively 'by women, for women'. Still, I found no criticism.

According to The Da Vinci Mode, however, fifteen thousand customers had 'flocked' to Benhayon's events in Australia and Europe since 2002, and locals complained that he was telling seriously ill people that they were infested with evil spirits. His ego had also soared to new dimensions. Leonardo also claimed to have been Alice Bailey, Pythagoras and ancient Egyptian statesman, Imhotep, in past lives, while his stepdaughter, Simone, was Winston Churchill. Followers were spending large sums on UM services, expressing animosity toward non-believers, and relationships were breaking under the strain.

Alarmingly, Benhayon's solicitors, Cameron Bell and Paula Fletcher, held a book-burning at their acreage with texts on competing spiritualities and health modalities thrown onto the pyre. Doctors, psychologists and dentists were also plugging Benhayon's 'Esoteric Medicine'. Bangalow opthalmologist, Dr Anne Malatt, told journalist David Leser that Serge is all about 'energetic integrity', and UM physiotherapist, Kate Greenaway, put in her reverential two cents. The photo of ghoulish Benhayon, however, contradicted their praises of Esoteric wellbeing.

The article also echoed some unsettling scenarios. Serge had dumped his first wife, Deborah, the mother of their four children, and married Miranda Smith, seventeen years his junior. Serge and Miranda met when she was thirteen and he was thirty, and he'd sold her parents his 'elite' coaching programme. In 1995, at fourteen, she moved into the Benhayon family home, beginning with one night per week, but it soon became full-time, and mother, Trish, told Leser she was against it. The arrangement created irreparable rifts between Miranda's parents, and Trish had seen her daughter just once in twelve years.

Leser described a tense interview at the UM clinic headquarters in Goonellabah, with Miranda and ex-wife Deborah present. Serge denied telling Trish that he could coach her daughter to Wimbledon, and Miranda backed his version, dutifully slandering her mother. The report said that in the days after she spoke with the journalist, Trish twice found her car smashed with eggs[6].

I emailed David Leser, and sent a letter to the editor. The report was missing a critical element. Benhayon had pressured me into a sleazy ovarian reading. Surrounded by women as he was, I couldn't have been the only one he tried it on. Someone needed to dig deeper.

xvii Richardson

Benhayon filed his defamation claim in November 2015, months (that felt like an eternity) before I learned the name Tom Molomby. Living nearly eight hundred kilometres from Sydney, near Byron Bay, with limited finances, no experience of legal trouble, and no connections, I had to navigate the ruthless legal marketplace of Australia's largest city on my own, and soon learned that persuading my initial lawyers that my publishing was justified could be as challenging and demoralising as trying to persuade the court.

I wanted to plead truth to all imputations, but my nuggety solicitor, Smith*, mulishly dismissed what I considered to be clear evidence. For example, I wanted to plead that the imputation that Serge Benhayon had intentionally indecently touched me was true, but Smith didn't think my account of the ovarian reading would hold up. Images I put forward to prove the imputation that Benhayon intentionally indecently touched his clients met resistance, and my proposal to get a medical expert to verify the anatomical locations copping Serge's hands was rebuffed: 'A lot of people practice alternative healing,' Smith said. 'All sorts of touching is widely accepted. The plaintiff will argue he's genuinely seeking to heal them, and that he gets consent.'

We didn't disagree on everything, however. Benhayon had limited his claim about the crescendo blog to sexual imputations, so Smith proposed a defence of contextual truth. That is, we would plead that there were additional defamatory meanings within the blog and those could be proven true. The defence would assert that because it's true that Benhayon engages in an array of crooked behaviours I'd mentioned, his reputation could not be further harmed by imputations of sleaze. But Smith grumbled that a lack of official findings made it difficult, if not impossible, to substantiate claims of wrongdoing. We then debated whether a person who says that 'The

Horse, Elephant, Eagle, and Cat will evolve to a Dog, Dolphin, or Whale' is delusional.[7]

'Plenty of people believe odd things. It doesn't make them delusional,' said Smith.

'I thought believing demonstrably untrue things does precisely that.'

'Yes, but then you have people believing in a virgin birth…'

The solicitor was thorough and methodical and a good firewall against Benhayon's legal team, but he was not backward in charging and refused to work unless his bills were paid instantly. Briefing my lawyers and the drafting of a lengthy defence was grievously time consuming and became staggeringly expensive; the cost compounded by time spent in obstinate arguments. Over the weeks leading up to filing that first defence, I burned through twenty thousand dollars in crowdfunding and my bank balance of over fifty thousand dollars plummeted. Each sober and terrifying transfer of funds — my savings and other people's money vanishing at the click of a mouse — felt like stepping off a cliff.

The defence still needed a lot of work when barrister Matthew Richardson joined my team. When we first met at his chambers, I couldn't tell whether he was unimpressed with the whole mess and unhappy to see us, or whether he behaved that way by default — or both. He showed us to a conference table in his brightly lit war-room, its white venetian blinds closed tight, its benches and tables arrayed with industrial strength office equipment, and its shelved walls precision loaded with binders. We had an hour, my solicitors showed up late, and Richardson didn't hide his irritation. He'd read through the particulars I'd provided to back my defence of truth and was underwhelmed.

From his manner I guessed he was in his early forties, but he could have passed for older with his rectangular glasses and pale, somewhat inflamed complexion. He read out some imputations in a severe tone. "'Serge Benhayon is a sexual predator? Serge Benhayon had intentionally indecently touched a number of his clients in his treatment room?'" Lip curled, he eyeballed me over the statement of claim.

I glared back. 'He is... and he did.'

'You're in serious trouble,' Richardson said. He practically sputtered it.

xviii Forum

> So my advice to guys is - if you meet a girl and she invites you back to her place.... and in the lounge room or bedroom there is a GIANT painting of the Mona Lisa - RUNNNNN!
>
> Frodo Baggins

David Leser replied to my email, and the Herald published my letter, name withheld, but there was no follow up. I considered letting go of the Benhayon problem altogether to audition a casual boyfriend, or write a novel, or learn another language, but the malignant growth of Universal Medicine and its endorsement by health professionals kept bugging me. A new web-search led me to the Cult Education Forum, a United States based website run by expert Rick Ross. In January 2012, a forlorn husband in the US calling himself Herbert Kane had started a thread dedicated to Universal Medicine on the website's discussion forum.

> My wife has become involved. All very scary as she is falling more and more in to their control and her thought patterns/beliefs are changing beyond recognition... Any advice you can give me about how to extract my wife would be much appreciated![8]

It took a couple of months to warm up, but by September the discussion had over two dozen pseudonymous contributors sharing information and concerns about partners, friends and relatives. It extended to one hundred webpages and had been viewed tens of thousands of times.

For twelve years, until David Leser and other journalists took an interest, Serge had been running his healing sham without media scrutiny. In a 2012 TV interview, Benhayon said that his business turned over two million dollars per year. He was also claiming that he received exclusive transmissions of Ageless Wisdom from the Ascended Masters, and the forum confirmed a pattern of odd behaviour among UM followers. They didn't just avoid drinking booze, they wouldn't allow it in the house, and they believed that a growing list of healthy foods, including grains, dairy products, certain vegetables, legumes, fruits and meats were full of bad 'pranic' energy. Literature and music were also pranic, unless produced by Benhayon and approved sycophants, and UM patrons had given up interest in sport and reduced their exercise to 'gentle' Serge sanctified movements. Most were in bed before nine each evening — when Serge said the evil entities became active — and up each morning at three.

Disciples also dismissed all competing belief systems and complementary health practices. They refused to be touched by non-UM practitioners, and that extended to relationships. Esoteric Breast Massage clients shunned physical intimacy with their partners, while slavish attendance at the group's activities left loved ones, including children, abandoned. UM students commonly repeated the entire cycle of Benhayon's commercial workshops, lectures and retreats, annually, and filled their homes with Da Vinci prints, posting them on their computer and phone screens as well. Benhayon's teaching that tattoos retain the bad energy of the tattoo artist's drug or alcohol use also saw Dr Anne Malatt do a cracking trade in laser tattoo removals from her Bangalow opthalmology rooms.

Enduring households controlled by Benhayon's commandments, the forum contributors were united in frustration, and none had confident words of advice on how to extract loved ones. All agreed that attacking the topic head-on was fruitless, and they recommended treading carefully, but none had gotten anywhere with reason and gentle persuasion either. Unimed's promoters, meanwhile, swarmed onto news outlets' websites and social media pages to criticise their reports. They swamped newsrooms with complaints of bias, characterising the content of every report as 'lies'. In reaction to the initial media coverage, UM's student body established four blog sites in July 2012, churning out scores of articles to repeatedly declare that anyone with a beef about the group was a disgruntled male 'looking for someone to blame for their problems', and that journalists were all missing the truth. Benhayon was always keen to tap the commerce in 'truth' that's proved lucrative for all sorts of phoneys, like Alex Jones and Donald Trump.

The Cult Education forum thread was long and disorganised, and the format was cumbersome. I found no mention of ovarian readings, exorcisms, or Astral flavoured burps, and it had scant detail of what UM's services entailed; albeit more than could be gleaned from the glut of words on the organisation's websites. When I posted my account of my UM experience, I received private messages from forum contributors, warily holding to their pseudonyms, not wanting to risk being tagged as a sexist or a conspirator, making their domestic hell worse.

'The woman in tears who was at that workshop with her mother could have been my wife,' wrote one husband. 'Her mother's in it too.' His description didn't match the women I'd met, but he explained that his wife was a victim of childhood sexual abuse and had been an emotional mess since encountering UM. According to official statistics, one in three women have experienced sexual abuse, and by those odds, there are hundreds of sexual abuse survivors among Benhayon's student body. Like most of the spouses who contacted me, his marriage was doomed.

Lance was the first to contact me using his own name. A business owner and resident of Bangalow, he was a big chatty guy in his late forties. He'd come to suspect UM was a cult as his wife Anna became less communicative, more secretive, and increasingly absent from home-life. He feared the impact on their preschool aged daughter. Anna had thrown out all non-UM books in the house, had attempted to dispose of the couple's music collection, and would only play the wind-filled Chris James, or tinny 'Glorious Music' — a din produced by Benhayon's offspring, whom Serge marketed as an Esoteric version of the Osmond Family. The marriage fell apart in April 2012 when Anna returned from UM's five day retreat in Vietnam to book straight into an Esoteric healing workshop she'd already done, and another five day retreat at Lennox Head, over near consecutive weeks.

It was then that a pop-up notification on a shared computer alerted Lance to an email exchange between his wife and Benhayon.

Hi Serge,

Lance has been in denial about moving out, I spoke to him this morning about it and he is devastated, and loads of sadness and calling in a lot of forces trying to get to me.

I am staying steady and know what I am doing is right... I want to make this transition about love, he is in a lot of emotion and drama at present, been interesting to see how what he calls loving me so quickly turns to being nasty towards me. Not sure why I am writing to you, perhaps for reassurance.

Thanks Serge,

with love Anna

Hi Anna,

If you re-tell your story in other words, what you are saying is that -- you come home feeling great and ready to be more of who you are, to be more love and allow more love not only in you and for you but equally so for Lance ...... and in that, he channels more than ever before ...... and conveniently lying ...

question to you

why would he want to steal your thunder so to speak?

why sabotage you in your glory?

why would you allow the real you and your love to be sabotaged?

its time Mr. Lance became more honest and much less scared of love and the truth.

with love,

Serge

Lance began visiting affected locals. Within a few weeks he found that over forty committed partnerships had broken down, each with a similar pattern. The common denominator was Serge.

xix Millikan

Benhayon predicted a New Era would begin in 2012; a change in the universe's energy that would expose pranic pretenders and bring the power of his Esoteric Sons of God to the world's fore. While his first press coverage certainly marked a renaissance for his reputation, it also kicked off a series of firsts for me. I'd always kept to myself, and never wanted a social media account or blog. I'd never made complaints to regulators, read law, or had any reason to front media cameras. I didn't jump at the invitation to go on national television, either. No one wants their fifteen minutes of fame focused on a suburban swindler's interest in their ovaries, but Nick Farrow, a producer for the national current affairs programme, *Sunday Night on Seven*, practically pleaded. Plenty of people were willing to gripe to him about Universal Medicine, until asked to go on the record. He couldn't get a report to air without complainants willing to speak out, and we'd miss a precious opportunity to expose Benhayon.

I knew what high demand groups do to people who blow the whistle. Scientology has an established 'Fair Game' policy, and has sought to justify stalking, physical harassment and defamation in the USA under first amendment protections of free speech[9]. But I also knew that extremist groups rely on secrecy and intimidation to thrive, and in the absence of meaningful government regulation, media exposure is the most powerful weapon against them. I saw speaking out on television as one way to stay ahead of any retaliation; that I'd be safer in the public eye. I'd used a pseudonym online, but suspected Benhayon would put resources into identifying me.

The interviewer was cult expert, Reverend Doctor David Millikan. Tall, gregarious and dressed in a black leather blazer and blue jeans, he had a cropped beard and impish blue eyes. A former director of religious broadcasting at the Australian Broadcasting Corporation (ABC), the preacher was as comfortable before the camera as he is in the pulpit.

Dramatically elongating his vowels, he pronounced Benhayon's first name as an expression of disgust, 'Serrrje.'

'You understand that some people might say that you're criticising this group's religious beliefs?' he asked for the cameras. 'Don't you think people are entitled to their beliefs?'

'Of course. They're entitled to believe whatever they like... that Serge flew in on a flying saucer if they want.'

'I think they do believe that!' laughed David.

'But the beliefs are not the problem,' I continued. 'The problem is the harm.'

Off camera, David was pleased to hear that I was starting a Wikileaks inspired blog publishing factual, primary source material the group attempted to conceal from the public, plus critical analysis of its health claims and cult characteristics. He asked what I'd be naming my website, but before I could answer, he shouted, 'GET SERGE!' and gleefully punctuated, 'dot com!'

Universal Medicine Accountability was a comedown after that, but blogging was never meant to be an end in itself. I saw the online exposé as a way to inform the public until action was taken on a series of complaints I made to regulatory authorities about Benhayon and the couple of dozen health professionals endorsing the enterprise and its toxic products and services.

Registered health practitioners who worked at the Goonellabah headquarters, Kate Greenaway and psychologists, Caroline Raphael and Brendan Mooney, advertised their Esoteric healing services with their professional ones, and Raphael and Greenaway were practising a frightening rip-off of acupuncture called 'Esoteric Chakra-puncture'. UK National Health Service surgeon Eunice Minford was running a website named *Medicine and Serge Benhayon*, and was pushing Esoteric Breast Massage, the insane Esoteric eating restrictions and other quackery, citing her medical credentials.

> Esoterically and energetically the fundamental truth is that it is living in separation to our true nature or essence of love that results in illness and

disease and indeed suffering of any kind…What is also clear is that most of us do not actually live very self-loving or self-caring lives… For example, being self-loving includes being aware of how all foods impact the body and choosing not to eat those that are detrimental like gluten, dairy, excess sugar, caffeine and alcohol. This is only looking at a small aspect of the 'what' we eat without looking at how we eat (eg rushing it down in a hurry) or why we are eating (eg for comfort, reward, numbing etc).[10]

While Minford was happy to push her puffery to the fore of UM's advertising, she was fastidious in her nondisclosure of the extent of the group's dietary restrictions. Universal Medicine's publicity provided no information either; just a lot of blogs reproducing the same mystical malarkey. All its student blogs were written to a template, that before they met Serge, his adorers were lost, unhappy, unhealthy and not living their truth, and now they were basking in 'self-loving choices', radiant with the best health they'd ever experienced. Locals and loved ones of cultists, however, reported the contrary. Those trudging Serge's Way of the Livingness were identifiable for their greyish green complexions, their tortoise-like gait, their 'thousand mile stare', as Lance put it, and many were alarmingly underweight.

My earliest investigation looked for the source of UM's disordered eating, and I found that Benhayon had circulated 'Esoteric Food Charts', in which he'd chaotically categorised 'foods' on a scale of 'evil' (coffee, marijuana, ayahuasca), 'pranic' (dairy products, grains, root vegetables, mango, and other fruits and vegetables and protein sources) and 'fiery' (a short list, including green apples, spinach, and red onion). He said that pranic foods 'hinder the flow of the light of the soul in the body', whereas the fiery help 'to re-create a body of love & light'. The charts had not been made public until I analysed them on my blog. Benhayon also preached that human beings use food to 'numb themselves', and that the more lovingly a person lives, the less they require food[11].

As a result, households, including kids, were subjected to such delights as sea vegetable bouillabaisse; broccoli and hazelnut soup; bright green pea and basil soup; and meat-free, grain-free, dairy-free, seaweed lasagna, with fibrous green matter in the place of pasta. Served regularly as part of a limited and flatulence producing menu, each dish was a recipe for irreconcilable differences, and the regime also produced a dietary neurosis so extreme that one chap said he'd seen a mother sprint to her child to bat a bread-crust out of a little hand as if it were a live grenade. Dr Minford and her fellow bloggers, moreover, never cited any scientific basis for cutting out entire food groups. Like all UM's austerities, they were wholly based on 'Serge says so.'

Eric Dobbs*, on the Cult Education forum, reported that his wife had been on the diet for eighteen months, transforming so radically from 'a rosey-cheeked, healthy woman' to emaciated and anaemic that her family and friends organised an intervention.

> Fortunately she went for a real MEDICAL check up, the doctor firmly suggested she return to her former sensible diet which she did, thank God. Moral to the story: Don't go to a JUNIOR TENNIS COACH for anything but tennis!!

David Millikan had some suggestions regarding UM's devotee health professionals. 'Name them,' he said conspiratorially. 'Put their names on your website; their professions, where they operate.' My 'Naming Names: Unimed cult cartel' directory came into being that way, with doctors at the top of the list, followed by allied health professionals, and then amateur practitioners with no formal credentials, including Benhayon and his offspring. Only Serge's eldest son Michael had a recognised certificate; in acupuncture. I included non-practitioners that promoted UM too, including the book burners at Universal Law Solicitors, and the proprietors of Bed and Breakfast property, The Lighthouse, in Somerset, England, which served as UM's European hub.

Before we parted, I told David Millikan about Yogendra's posthumous murder of his young wife. Nick was nodding as I drew parallels between Yogendra and Benhayon's behaviour, and the similar make up of their groups. 'How dangerous is Serge?' I asked.

xx Missy

When Richardson said I was in trouble, I half expected him to add the word, 'Missy'. 'These allegations are extremely serious,' he said brusquely, and restated Smith's view that the evidence I'd put forward of Benhayon's sexual impropriety was unlikely to cut it in court. 'If you plead the defence of truth to some of these sexual imputations, the plaintiff might apply to have that defence struck out!'

The words stung and the blood must have drained from my face. Softening slightly, he said, 'I'm sure you're a good person and this Benhayon is not a good person, but that won't win your case. You could lose everything.'

For a few minutes I floundered as he persisted, relentlessly bleak about my defence. To be fair, hardened lawyers know the law and the courts a hundred times better than I ever would, and that got me at first. But lawyers also make an ample living from their powers of persuasion. I was properly intimidated, yet something instinctive sparked. Benhayon had gotten the better of me when I gave in to self-doubt; led me to think that I was overreacting and that his motives were harmless. My lawyers were trying to persuade me of something similar, that the court would side with Serge.

My obstinacy reflex kicked in first. 'I'm going to fight all the way,' I said, and explained my strategy, inexpert as it was. I had no hope of raising enough money to pay lawyers to represent me up to and through the trial. I didn't tell him that I also considered it immoral to try; that Benhayon's vanity defamation claim did not deserve the disposal of that much cash. I'd had no luck finding pro bono assistance, so I planned to represent myself when the funds ran out — imminently. In the meantime, I wanted our money spent on filing the best possible defence.

Richardson's sceptical gaze sharpened my resolve. I knew what I'd discovered about UM. I knew about quacks and cults, and I knew how I'd planned and checked my publications. It wasn't perfect, but I'd read the

Defamation Act and legal articles about it before I blogged a word. I also knew the extent of press and public interest in Universal Medicine, and I knew myself well enough. Sun Tzu said, 'know thine enemy', but he also said self-knowledge is more important than knowing one's foe.

'I'm not losing to these people,' I told him.

Richardson's tone remained severe. 'I don't think you understand the consequences.'

'There's no losing to Benhayon,' I said. Nothing could convince me that the public would find the plaintiff's behaviour acceptable. 'As long as I get the evidence in front of the court,' I added, 'it'll be a moral victory.'

Richardson explained that even if I won, the way that costs are awarded meant that I'd never recover my money.

'That's not fair,' I muttered. 'It's Benhayon that's up to no good, I'm just the messenger…'

'Do you think you're the first person to complain that court outcomes are unjust?' was the barrister's sharp retort. Smith and the other body with him advisedly kept their mouths shut. 'Do you think being in the right is going to help your case!?'

At the peak of his caustic questions, I broke into a wry smile. He tailed off with a grudging smirk. Although he thought little of my chances, his fierceness suggested he was on my side. 'This Benhayon, he's full of shit, isn't he?'

At last he was speaking my language. 'All of it's bullshit,' I said.

Richardson squinted at me. 'It's bullshit. He's a bullshitter.' His pen was poised over his legal pad. 'Do you have any of his bullshit documented?'

'There's mountains of it,' I said, and wondered why my solicitor hadn't briefed him to that effect.

'That's how we come at him.' The lawyer spoke gravely. 'We gather his shit and throw it back at him.'

I sighed with exasperation. 'That's what I've been saying…' I said aloud, but there was no time to pontificate about the difficulties of getting it across to Smith.

'I need you to put together particulars of the worst of his bullshit, the weirdest, the nastiest…anything a judge will hate,' said Richardson.

'He says schizophrenia is caused by evil spirits…'

'You have that in writing?'

'And there's recordings… He says disabled people were abusers and tyrants in their past lives…'

The lawyer paused as if deciding whether to believe me. 'Good,' he conceded. A glimmer of hope lit in his face. He explained that the strategy might not win the case but it was a powerful way to hit back. 'Bullshit like that is good. What else have you got?'

xxi Esoteric Breast Massage

Archive.org became a valuable tool in my investigation, storing captures of UM's online materials, including copies of its Esoteric Breast Massage website dating back to 2008. UM pulled the whole website down in 2012 when journalists began asking questions. 'What effect, if any, did discovering this material have on your general attitude to Universal Medicine?' Tom asked for the court.

I answered that the organisation was making unjustifiable health claims to deceive the public, and had behaved dishonestly in erasing them when media scrutiny commenced. Published in cerise font on a pink background, with a cluster of Désirée's puce flowers, the site was filled with grotesque claims about women's health, including Benhayon's fictions that lack of self-nurturing was 'the energetic cause of breast cancer', and that the breasts were repositories of disease-causing energy.

> It is not surprising to see the amazing results, but most importantly, the deeply revealing discoveries that women are making about themselves through the release of what is insidiously held in their nurturing centres — their breasts.

UM never republished its most outlandish claims.

> Every time your breasts get affected, that is, sore or lumpy, it can contribute to a lung condition, and a digestive issue. And if the breasts are affected, so too are the ovaries, which emanate the 'light of Femaleness', and hence, they too are suppressed and contracted from their natural way of impulsing…they then affect the breasts.

> This sacred esoteric technique assists to heal many issues such as painful periods, polycystic ovaries, endometriosis, bloating/water retention, and pre-menstrual and menopausal symptoms.

The breast massagers charged seventy dollars per session, and another page recommended women undergo a series of 'EBMs' to 'clear the imposed ills that come from ourselves and from those who impose on us.'

> We recommend at least 10 to 12 to start with…You can attend weekly, fortnightly, monthly etc. In some acute and extreme cases, you may need to have one a day.

Men were the culprits imposing ills on women, according to Serge, but he also blamed babies. UM mothers had been observed to abruptly wean their infants, and the website suggested why.

> If there is no nurturing energy in the breasts the baby suckling will receive the milk, but will not get the nurturing energy. All is energy, and if the breasts are not clear when the baby is feeding, the baby will also receive the ill-energy that is in the breasts.[12]

xxii Heath

Heath must have been nervous entering the witness box. UM still cast men who spoke out about the group as abusive, but Smark opted not to cross-examine him. A placid cat-lover in his thirties who liked books and vinyl records, his concern for his ex-girlfriend Ellen was unchallengeable. They'd became a couple in 2011 and she seemed easy going until she began following UM's diet, refusing to eat anything she hadn't prepared herself, 'because someone else's energy may have impacted that food.' Heath told the court that he tried the diet himself for several months but found it made him fatigued and weak.

He was one of the respondents to a questionnaire I sent out early in my research. My survey of students' daily habits and engagement in UM's activities helped me confirm the group's cult characteristics and Benhayon's methods for keeping followers under his control. Loved ones on three continents replied with striking uniformity about the dietary restrictions, that followers refused to listen to music unless it was produced by UM, read Benhayon's books repeatedly, and listened to his recorded lectures, which were released once a month, daily. A former student confirmed she'd read Benhayon's books cover to cover three times each and listened to his audio recordings for at least an hour per day.

Heath testified that adherents feared they'd be possessed by spirits if they didn't keep to sleeping hours prescribed by Serge. 'We were in bed by eight-thirty every night — nine o'clock at the latest. Anything beyond that and you were open to entity activity.'

Ellen also used the Healing Symbol postcards, and Lance reported that Anna put one under herself when she lay in bed listening to Benhayon's lectures through earbuds. Heath saw Ellen place receipts from her grocery shopping on a symbol to clear the *prana* from the items she'd bought. 'Some of them were displayed on the walls,' he told the court. 'Most of the electronic appliances in the house had one either under it or taped to it. A water purifying jug would have one underneath to clear energy from water.'

Ellen was also preoccupied by Esoteric rituals. 'If, say, you were making a cup of tea, it had to be stirred anticlockwise. And if I forgot occasionally, she was really strict about it, it had to be the other way.' But as much as Heath struggled with her habits, he avoided criticising them, and said he never thought she should have to choose between him and her beliefs. He wasn't asked in court how the relationship ended, but privately confided that the differences in lifestyle and thinking caused profound difficulties. The concept of moderation doesn't exist in UM, and he told the court about a conversation the couple had about liquor, and how there's no safe way to imbibe even the tiniest amount of booze. 'I've never been much of a drinker,' he said, 'but I said something to her like, "If someone else enjoys a drink and I don't, that's not really any of my business." But she was adamant that it's incredibly damaging to everyone if someone occasionally drank alcohol.' He confirmed that the idea came from Universal Medicine. 'She explained what she believed and about being open to being entered by entities if you drink.' My defence tendered quotes from Benhayon's books where he claimed that using drugs or alcohol creates openings in one's aura through which spirits can enter to 'have their way with you'.

After a pause, Heath added: 'The thing that she said that took me aback though was, "Saying I only drink a little bit is as bad as saying I only watch a little bit of child porn."'

xxiii A blessing

> Reporter: It's the controversial healthcare movement which had its origins on a toilet thirteen years ago.
>
> Serge Benhayon: I just gave myself time to sit and feel that moment, and I could feel something really really beautiful.
>
> Today Tonight programme, Seven Network Australia, 2012

To report Benhayon to authorities, I needed proof of his threat to public health. That meant examining his enormous output of toilet inspired works, dumped on me by informants. I began with recordings from his Study of Esoteric Medicine lecture series, but with his infernal digressions, it took hours to transcribe a few excerpts from the first two hour lecture. It didn't help that I type like I roller-skate. I type the way Alison Greig runs UM's public relations. Serge, with two fingers, probably types faster and more accurately than me. Between hitting play, pausing, blundering, cursing, forgetting the maestro's wording, rewinding too far, fast forwarding too far, rewinding again, effing, blinding, and repeating the process, the air in my flat turned blue with Yogendra's reviled foul language. Fortunately I lived alone.

The guru commenced many of his presentations with a session of guided Gentle Breath Meditation, indistinguishable from hypnosis. From his recordings, I recognised that his subscribers were reproducing his phrases verbatim in their online writings. His soft, monotonous voice and repetitive language probably heightened his listeners' suggestibility.

Not far into the first lecture, I transcribed an excerpt we'd play in court six years later:

> We don't stand here and go 'how did this lump happen?' Or 'why am I infertile, why can't I fall pregnant?'
>
> Because you haven't been a woman for thirty years. You've been using mental energy to please your dad, you've been using male energy.[13]

He repeated his teaching that breast cancer results from women failing to nurture themselves, and claimed it could

> all be cured — not a good word — healed, if we just taught that a woman needs to be fragile and honour that, to be nurturing, to not pick up heavy things...'

He added that merely teaching mothers and daughters his bespoke style of self-nurturing could eliminate breast cancer from their family tree.

In the second hour, Benhayon described the genesis of his sewer-bound philosophy.

> When I first started 10 years ago, I was a tennis coach who got shown by the loveliest, sweetest, most amazing voice that could speak to me things; that never asked me what to do, but asked me to put them to the test. And when I was sitting in the toilet, you know, that came, and 'the heavens shine on those whose hearts bleed with love and compassion bestowed upon you is my kingdom'.

He said the toilet voices told him that everything he needed to know was within his body, and all the knowledge in the universe could be accessed, not by his mind, but by feeling into his innermost heart — an ability he referred to as clairsentience.

> The impulses to start the healing, to start Universal Medicine, to start the workshops, the modalities and everything, comes from my body, my impulses, my energy… All I have to do is tune into someone and whatever they need, the impulse is there. I don't have to question, it's just there. And that's how I do the readings you know I'm a little bit famous for… illness and disease and so forth. And I do readings all over the world.

In an interview celebrating his New Era he'd explained that he knows more than any scientist. 'In my inner-heart I know everything about the universe and how it works…I can answer any question about any mystery in the world, any mystery in the universe…[14]'.

Now, in the first of his Esoteric Medicine lectures, he said that his knowledge was available to all 'equally', that it was simple to intuit, but added that no one apart from him had ever done it. Even the students who'd slavishly adhered to his teachings for ten years were failing to choose the right energy, he said.

He announced that he was before an audience of over two hundred, with half a dozen medical doctors present, including lung specialist Dr Sam Kim, and close to the end, he said something about the medico that made me sit up and grasp for my keyboard, my phone and the roots of my hair all at once.

> So imagine walking down the corridors doing my rounds, Sam, and the other specialists that are here; and you walk with gentleness as Sam does. He walks into this room to see his patients. They get a blessing the moment he walks in. The corridor gets a blessing and Sam has, if I'm allowed to say so, assisted people to die…

A staffer at a national agency advised me to send the recording to the office of Federal Attorney General, Nicola Roxon, and local police. Still a tech novice, I fiddled and fumbled through Googled instructions until I produced a clip and transcribed the excerpt to send with it.

Sam has, if I'm allowed to say so, assisted people to die faster than or sooner than holding on. Because he brings them a blessing, they go 'I get it, see you later Sam, say hello to my folks'; boom, pass-over, right?... you bring someone harmony, and it's time to go, they say 'see you later, I'm outta here,' because they feel the loveliness of who they are, the loveliness of what they will go into, the moment they leave their body. That's grace.

xxiv The list

'Would you accept that UM has become a major focus in your life?' said po-faced Smark.

'Unfortunately, yes.'

'I'm going to show you a document which sets out various of your blogs over the period of late 2012 through 2014. I'm going to ask you, if you're minded to, to look at it overnight.'

I wasn't minded to. The tabulated list ranged to several pages. I could see what it was. In courtroom theatre the observers glance between the clever lawyer and the plucky witness to see who blinks. I waited, looking appropriately bored, as he niggled about the document. 'It's just a schedule that's been drawn up for this court case. I won't distribute it yet because I'm not going to tender it at this point...' He told me I ought to check it for inaccuracies, and that his client would permit me to consult my lawyers about it and its subject matter et cetera et cetera; all in a condescending tone that inferred that he was talking about some red hot item of incrimination and that I should be grateful for his client's largesse.

'Yes, I understand,' I said flatly. I didn't return to it until he did the next day. I knew I'd published about two hundred and fifty articles about Universal Medicine over the two years to November 2014. I'd published scores more since. I knew where he was going with it.

xxv The purple books

I resisted as long as I could, but it wasn't possible to identify the teachings that were leading UM students to flush their health and relationships down Benhayon's talking toilet from his convoluted audio recordings alone. I had no choice but to read his self-published tomes.

Within two years of selling me Alice Bailey's *Ponder on This*, Serge worked out that he could make more money from churning out his own fiction. More again if he monopolised his customers' reading habits. So he told them that all works of literature except his were 'bastardised'. Even Bailey's were 'past energy' and out of whack with his New Era, but his claim to have occupied her body in a past life gave him uninhibited licence to her intellectual property. He co-opted all her concepts, down to designing near indistinguishable indigo book covers — although Serge's bindings were a tinge more purple, to match his prose. He also picked up the Theosophists' gift for pseudo-telepathy, not just quoting Master Djwal Khul, but channelling his predecessors' entire pantheon of divinities. Citing 'The Hierarchy' as co-authors, he rendered the cacophony of their Ageless Wisdom in a different font for each voice. Several fonts competed in each paragraph at times, but when it came to copyright, his etheric collaborators asserted none.

Benhayon's idiosyncratic use of language, or what I dubbed SergeSpeak, was his only true originality. He had remarkably loose spelling and punctuation for such a rigid personality, and his promiscuous use of hyphens created peculiar Esotericisms like 'beauty-full', 'truth-full' and 'love-able'. Sadly, he and his spectral colleagues wrote the way he talked, and the term he used for his delivery — 'spherical wisdom' — was apt for his endlessly looping statements that never reached any logical point.

SergeSpeak also radically uncoupled words from their dictionary definitions, and when passed through the reality tester (the soft matter located between one's ears), they usually emerged with the opposite meaning. Esoteric love more closely resembled hate. Esoteric healing was shorthand for a suite of abuses, and 'self-loving choices' translated to self-harm and damage to all associated.

My spherical reading confirmed that Benhayon had nothing positive to say about human wellbeing, and no constructive advice for promoting health or enjoying life. The Sanskrit concept of *prana*, traditionally meaning breath and the life-energy cultivated in Eastern health practices, was Serge-spoken into an intrusive 'lower life-force' that 'pulls away from God'.[15] Fire, on the other hand, was 'Soul-full'; the good to prana's evil, and designated the few dreary things Benhayon approved of. His healing practices, moreover, sought to 'clear' pranic life-energy, as in eliminate it. Seeking to relieve pain and sickness was unacceptably pandering to clients' desire for wellness, he said, and ran counter to his objectives.

> The use of Esoteric Healing is not for one to live to a 'ripe old age', and nor is it about survival or getting better or curing diseases etc. It is an ongoing process of becoming more love until you are back to the full you = Soul. And hence the process of releasing all that which is not...that which we have chosen to lovelessly let in. This may take several if not many, many lifetimes...[16]

His moralistic misanthropy was also self-serving. Where he taught that pranic music enters the body and is 'ten times more damaging than food poisoning', and that listeners can be physically infected by the energy of a musicians' 'undealt-with emotions' or their drug and alcohol habits, he was cursing all of it, except for the stuff he or his underachieving offspring could make money from.[17] Benhayon can't play or sing a note, yet he wangled co-writing and production credits on collaborations with the Esoteric minstrels, presumably earning a cut of the sales. Quality was never an energetic consideration, and when Michael's first wife, Emmalee, fell out of favour as the Glorious Music vocalist, Miranda was put out front with results that made us wish she'd stuck with tennis.

Sport too was deemed evil, pranic and 'divisive', and Benhayon, no doubt embittered by his failed sporting career, said that it 'ingrains animal behaviour in human beings'[18]. He was even more damning about sex, preaching that most people only partake so that others will like them, or 'for relief' — surely a projection of his own sordid propensities. Pleasure and intimacy were worth nothing on Planet Serge, unless he controlled them, and limiting followers' endorphin production was a way to keep them subdued and pliable, just as nutritional restrictions weakened them physically and cognitively.

In disparaging everything healthy, Benhayon was damning anything that might challenge disciples' attention and loyalty to him. His teaching that emotions are pranic and 'the cause of all disease', was calculated to corrode their relationships. Sympathy and empathy were condemned as 'poisonous to our physical body'[19]; 'love has not one ounce of emotion in it', and he extended that to parenting advice. 'If you love your children with and from emotional love,' he said, 'you are just passing down to another generation a form of love that has not ever worked.'[20]

Having unseated them emotionally, Serge also indoctrinated his followers to distrust their own minds. All intellectual and critical functioning was controlled by spirits, he said, and if a friend or relative questioned a student's allegiance to UM, it was not their loved one speaking, but an evil Astral entity that had taken control of them, sent to sabotage the Hierarchy's work on earth.

Benhayon psychologically hijacked his subscribers to the point where they believed his doctrines absolutely. The damage has been unquantifiable. Eric Dobbs reported that his wife returned from interstate pilgrimages so 'completely and utterly emotionally blank' that his eleven year old son became anxious and clingy and started wetting his bed for the first time since he was two. Another reader shared her concerns that a young mother in the group was suffering from postnatal depression and hadn't bonded with her infant. She asked her friend if she ever worried about her baby the way she had about her own children, and the acolyte unnervingly replied, 'if something ever happened to him I would know it was his soul wanting to return to the soul plane.'

The purple books also revealed Benhayon's world-rejecting ideology that romanticised disease and death.

> If we wake up with a cancerous tumour, or diabetes, or with arthritis or even just exhaustion, with a sneeze, a cough, a runny nose — then there has been a way that we have been living that has caused it. Because everything is energy, the way you have been living energetically has allowed your body to operate with an ill energy that then manifests the ills you physically, physiologically, emotionally and psychologically will have.
>
> Death is always a healing — and not part of the failure.[21]

xxvi The Pineapple Post

Jim Jones is said to have learned from another cult leader to 'find an enemy'; a focus for galvanising followers.[22] But cults also need an enemy to wear their psychological projections — the loathsome traits they refuse to acknowledge within themselves. Serge relied on supernatural foes at first, lazily borrowing the Four Lords of Form from Alice Bailey, who'd described them in passing as opponents of the Lords of Light. He installed them in the Dark Lodge, the dimmest recess of the Astral Plane, to assume 'the Dark Rule', commanding the legions of invasive spooks behind all the corruption in the universe. They debuted as the Four Horsemen of the Apocalypse[23], and Serge said they lurked outside UM meetings, peering menacingly through the Lennox Head Community Centre windows. None of his believers seemed troubled that no one else could see them.

But in Reverend David Millikan the flock finally had an enemy they could all see and name. The Seven team needed footage of Benhayon, none was publicly available, and the distinguished reincarnate refused an on-camera interview. David had formed a relationship with him over some months, attending some of his Friday night presentations at Lennox Head, and on the fatal evening, the producers planted some undercover camerawomen in the audience to start filming when cued. The main camera crew waited outside in a van.

'I fucked up,' David told me, mournfully. 'I really did.'

Serge asked him if he was alone, and in his zeal to get the footage, he lied. Benhayon invited him onstage to address his flock, and when David faced them, he gave the cue and told the congregation that they were all in a cult. 'Serge just about COLLAPSED!' said the Reverend with his pulpit rattling flourish. 'He went into a PANIC and began shrieking like a frightened chiiiild.' But as the main camera operator was about to burst in through the double doors, an unusually quick-witted acolyte wedged an umbrella though the handles, barring entry, and although the photographers in the audience continued to film, David decided to pull them out when the jostling began.

UM's management called the police, and Benhayon was so shaken that he stayed up all night botching together a counterfeit news item in a fruity olde worlde typeface that he emailed to followers at four the next morning, indirectly finding my inbox. Filled with characteristically spherical grammar and spelling, it decried the media ambush, and I blogged it as a breaking despatch from 'The Pineapple Post'; adding advice to Serge to wait until Desirée is awake in future before he chooses a font.

UM's student body then unleashed in blogs with titles like: 'David Millikan: Man of God For Sale'; 'David Millikan: Media Bullying at Universal Medicine Event'; 'Millikan at Lennox — Memories of South American military oppression'; 'The Betrayal'; 'Night of the Inquisition' and so on.

I didn't see a problem with telling a harmless porky to expose a bloke running a multimillion-dollar health scam, but the report was shelved. The event was held at a Ballina Shire Council property. 'It was in the public interest,' I said.

'Yeah I know,' said David. 'But Nick wouldn't use it — not based on a fib.'

Benhayon's management probably sent legal threats to the network as well. However it transpired, the press backing I'd hoped would insure me against retaliation and help me get more public support was gone. I'd have blogged anyway, but failing to factor the caprices of the media cycle was one of the miscalculations I made.

xxvii Danger markers

> Have you been part of a brainwashing cult that Unimed's teachings have pulled you out of?
>
> ...our temporal world to-date, life as we conventionally know it, is predominantly under the impulse of the Astral Plane. It is one big cult by the very meaning the temporal has of that word.
>
> Serge Benhayon[24]

UM had all the signs of a dangerous group.[25] It had a patriarchal authority structure with quasi-kin relationships (the group's mainly female following referred to themselves as a Brotherhood of Sons of God). It was secretive, intolerant of dissent and criticism, sought to suppress negative information about the group, and adherents believed Serge's assertions of divinity, that he was 'The One', as in the second coming of Christ. He'd predicted an energetic apocalypse of sorts in his 2012 New Era, and although Unimed hadn't established a physical compound, students were clustering in the Goonellabah region and around The Lighthouse at Tytherington, near Frome, in Somerset, England. It had the makings of an online compound as well, using webcasting, digital conferencing and private online forums to reinforce its indoctrination and carry out internal surveillance.

I was also alert to any indication that followers could be persuaded to die for Benhayon or his ideology, as Yogendra's second wife had. Or to kill. Worst cases ended in the mass deaths of David Koresh's Branch Davidians in Texas, or the mass murder at the People's Temple in Guyana, where parishioners who refused Jim Jones' command to drink cyanide laced cordial were forced to, or shot. The most dangerous groups accumulate armaments, and although I had no reason to think that UM were interested in guns, it was the potential to weaponise medicine that had me scrambling to notify authorities on Benhayon's announcement that a devotee doctor was 'blessing' his patients with death.

Before Aum Shinrikyo's attacks on the Tokyo subway, Shoko Asahara practised a corrupted Tibetan Buddhist ritual, *poa*; a meditation performed by clergy to expedite the spiritual transcendence of the dying or deceased. He ordained a 'priesthood', which included medical doctors, with authority to cleanse karma, and over time, Aum's *poa* became 'killing to heal', a religious justification for murdering those the guru deemed impure. The cult operated a private hospital in Tokyo where its doctors murdered more than twenty patients, and Asahara eventually envisioned healing the world by bringing on an apocalypse, *Destroying the World to Save It*, as psychiatrist Robert Jay Lifton named his book. Lifton noted that medicos are often exalted by their mystique 'as gatekeepers between this world and the next', and that the cultic environment can make them a little too amenable to that feeling of omnipotence.[26]

Eunice Minford also glorified disease and death, parroting Benhayon's preachings alongside her surgical credentials, including in her blog 'Assisted Suicide - is it really the end?'

> Knowing that lovelessness and the emotions are the energetic root cause of illness and disease, then it is also possible for healing opportunities to occur right up until the patient's death and death itself is also healing — healing our separation from God, from Love...
>
> Whilst [assisted suicide] may appear to end the suffering in this lifetime, the unhealed emotional conditions that led to the cancer or terminal condition will be carried through to the next incarnation and re-lived again and again until true healing occurs.[27]

Minford was advertising her services in Sacred Esoteric Healing and other hocus pocus from her medical rooms in Antrim, Northern Ireland.

Other UM bloggers wrote about death as something to celebrate rather than mourn. In a blog about her mother's funeral, UK Esoteric Breast Massager, Jane Keep, complained that she'd 'always found funerals overwhelmingly sad and intense occasions' where she 'felt very uncomfortable and unsettled'. She bolstered herself on the day 'with a loving walk in the countryside, a hearty breakfast, a long hot bath' and picked out a pretty dress. Having resolved to keep her interactions light-hearted and 'playful' she reported that 'it was a joyful day for me.' God knows how it was for everyone else.

But the discovery that Universal Medicine held a memorial service for a community member, Rita, at a 2010 Esoteric Developers' Group (EDG) meeting, had me clutching at my scalp again. Rita was alive and present. Benhayon was master of ceremonies, and student notes taken at the event reported that the sixty-seven year old, who was suffering a relapse of cancer, had come into her light and was 'serving at a very high level'. 'Serge says it's time to go,' said the notes. The time had come to 'dump' her prana into her body to prepare for an 'esoteric passing over'. She died later that year.

Benhayon sermonised that Rita would be spared the loveless recycling of a non-Esoteric death. No hauling her pranic baggage onto the Astral Plane to await a new human carcass like the rest of us plebs. She would be rewarded with an expedited return to 'greater service' in a 'clearer' incarnation, and Serge projected a slide showing her future parents, Michael and Emmalee Benhayon. According to the notes, 'Serge said he will be Rita's Grand-Dad and not to forget the hyphen.'

More notes taken at EDG meetings reported that UM were holding retreats for seriously and terminally ill patients in Australia and England, and Benhayon had bought a cold storage warehouse on five acres at Converys Lane, Wollongbar, between Lismore and Ballina, to convert into Universal Medicine's new centre. He planned, with Dr Kim, to establish an Esoteric aged care facility there.

'I guess that's one way to look after your nearest and dearest,' said Inspector Matt Kehoe of Lismore police when I shared the info. That quip aside, the inspector took it seriously, including the recording of Benhayon talking up Sam Kim's hospital rounds. He was aware of Benhayon from a previous investigation, but didn't elaborate. Because the recording didn't identify recipients of Dr Kim's blessings, Kehoe referred me to the New South Wales Health Care Complaints Commission (HCCC), saying the regulator could refer it back to police if it found evidence of a criminal offence. A Lismore detective also took a short statement about the ovarian reading, but the police doubted it could secure a conviction for indecent assault.

In answer to my question, 'how dangerous is Serge?' David Millikan answered that the most hazardous groups are those that are secretive; that form compounds in secluded locations. 'They're usually the ones you don't hear about,' he said. 'The ones that go under the radar, evade scrutiny…'

Investigative journalists ordinarily gather material for some time before publishing their findings, but I resolved to blog most of the information revealing UM's dangers as I found it. To me, any delay in making facts public increased UM's risk to the community, especially with the group expanding so aggressively. SergeCorp's propaganda machine cranked up a gear as I continued to publish, pumping out sycophantic hyperbole at higher volume, with no acknowledgement of the issues I raised. Universal Law, however, without notifying me, made defamation complaints to Google that got my first blog shut down. The Google Blogger platform provided no course for redress, so I republished my site on the US based Wordpress, and into 2013, raced to expose as much as I could, constantly expecting to be sued.

I never set out to publish hundreds of articles about UM, or to spend years neck-deep in Benhayon's muck. I'd failed to anticipate how little support I would get. But now I was stuck with the dilemma that the more I investigated, the more I found, and the more I found, the worse it got.

xxviii Louise Hay

Benhayon was also an avid plagiarist of magical thinking mogul, Louise L. Hay. The popularity of the author of *You Can Heal Your Life*, which has sold fifty million copies worldwide, hinged on her unverified claim to have cured herself of cervical cancer without medical treatment. 'The way to control your life is to control your choice of words and thoughts,' was her core belief, and she matched a catalogue of diseases to a list of causative thoughtcrimes.[28] Anger, for example, gives rise to cellulite and cancer; longing for love causes physical aches; and too much 'self-pity' causes cystic fibrosis. Years before Benhayon claimed that breast cancer is caused by lack of self-nurturing, especially among mothers, Hay had written that the disease was caused by 'refusal to nourish the self. Putting everyone else first. Overmothering.'[29]

All pastel rainbows and airbrushed cheerfulness, she peddled a thought modification cure of daily affirmations. 'I release the pattern in me that created this. I am at peace. I am worthwhile,' was typical, and its reverse tells us what she thought of the sick and the suffering. They're at fault for their misfortune, they're chaotic, flawed, inferior. Hay told an interviewer that she did not expect other people to be able to cure their own cancers — but not because her approach did not work. 'I just don't think other people would necessarily give it one hundred percent, the way I did,' she said.[30]

Serge was one of thousands of uncredentialed imitators who devised similar lists of thought and emotional sins behind disease. Heart disease happens in people who don't know how to love properly, he said. Brain tumours are the residues of 'un-expressed truths', and those with mental or physical disability were villains in their past lives.[31]

Hay also had no qualifications to speak of, and her remedy was not based on research or clinical experience either. She claimed her knowledge was channelled to her, beating Benhayon to that furphy as well. Yet her belief system remains pervasive, especially in the increasingly extremist 'wellness' movement that casts health and financial success as pinnacles of modern virtue, and where disease and disability exist as punishment for failing to be irrationally upbeat and intuitively attuned to dubious 'truths'. Health professionals have had to pick up the pieces for decades, counselling patients who believe they can will themselves free of serious illness without medical interventions, and treating their depression when the feel-good mantras inevitably fail.

Hay, like Serge, blamed her quackery's inefficacy on customers' past-life sins. She admitted to her interviewer that she thought Holocaust victims had it coming for misbehaviour in previous lives, but she knew better than to share that view with her fans. 'I don't go around making people feel bad,' she said, and added, nonchalantly, that it was only her opinion.[32] Indeed.

But pinning all misfortune on personal failings overlooks crucial causative factors that are not within any individual's control. Nobody chooses to be marginalised or disabled, or to have their water supply poisoned by a multinational corporation, or to go hungry because of a climate change related drought, or a war, or the inequitable distribution of wealth. Critical faculties, legitimate expertise, and the grief and anger that instigate movements toward justice, however, are offensive to magical thinkers. Hay wrote that 'rebellion against authority' causes accidents; implying that it's worse to complain than to be crushed.[33]

At trial, I had to prove the imputation that 'Serge Benhayon dishonestly promotes fraudulent ideas of karma for self-gain', and I pointed out that according to the traditional doctrine of karma and reincarnation, a person's actions have consequences. While harmful actions may invite blowback in future, it's also believed that helping others improves karmic outcomes. The traditional teaching therefore had the potential to benefit society, but New Age proponents are ruthlessly self-interested. The belief that individuals have complete control over their circumstances allows mercenaries like Hay and Benhayon to imagine themselves superior and to abandon the less fortunate to their plights.

While Hay was carefully vague about the details, Benhayon was assertively fundamentalist, portraying karma as purely punitive. He referred to it as 'great medicine' at one talk, adding that if a child is sexually abused, it's because they were an abuser in a past life.[34] His appropriation of karma was fraudulent because he completely omitted benevolence as a mitigating factor. He even preached that 'the highest good on earth is the highest form of evil,' extending his condemnation to all forms of altruism.[35] That jaundiced outlook guaranteed conflict between UM acolytes and those putting up with them.

Psychiatrists in the US have defined a 'four Ds' model for the process of cult conversion: debilitation, deception, dependency and dread.[36] People are deceived into joining cults, often while in a state of physical or emotional debilitation; they take on beliefs that inculcate dependency on the leader and group, and they're threatened with adverse consequences when they try to break free. In UM, the four Ds weren't just implemented to expand Benhayon's cult of personality — they were his business model.

He therefore had no use for Hay's positive affirmations because he did go around making people feel bad. Limiting the options for avoiding hell in this or future lifetimes made his students dependent on him to guide them through a universe of consequences he fabricated. The only way to dodge karmic payback on his Way of the Livingness was not to do good, but to do as he says, and eternally commit to his Unimed consumption cycle. The only relief Serge offered was in death — a death on his terms, under threat that incomplete compliance to his Way would lead to lifetimes of torment.

xxix Esoteric Womens Health

The Livingness death package was just one branch of Benhayon's business. He also targeted the lucrative women's health market, and in 2012 chose his second eldest child, Natalie, to head promotional front, Esoteric Women's Health Pty Ltd, despite her lack of relevant tertiary education. He'd been grooming her for a role in his business since he had her join him onstage as a schoolgirl. At eighteen, she dropped out of studies in architectural drafting to massage ovaries at his Goonellabah clinic, and at twenty, in 2011, Serge appointed her to the board of several of his companies, including his newly registered charity, the College of Universal Medicine. His youngest offspring, Michael and Curtis, also worked for UM as practitioners, trainers and presenters, but their male energy apparently precluded them from executive roles.

According to the Esoteric Womens Health website, Natalie's business was 'inspired by, made possible by' and 'based on the work of Serge Benhayon and Universal Medicine', and UM's Women in Livingness were conspicuous for dressing in line with his ideal of 'lovely and gentle' ladies and 'true beauty'. Frocked like Jehovah's Witnesses on church days, in skirts, heels, and meticulous makeup, they devoutly accessorised with his healing symbol pendant — a small gold rendering of one of his bird-crap splats that he retailed for three hundred dollars. Silky neck scarves were another must-have, believed to protect from vampire entity attacks.

UM's women unquestioningly accepted Natalie's pretence at expertise, and no one could accuse her of taking a scientific approach. She gave a long talk at a 2012 event about painting her nails, and student notes recorded a contribution from her father, who seemed to shadow his star-earner wherever she went:

> Serge then came on stage and said that the energy of a tampon in our body is like having sex with the dirtiest guy you know all the way through your period.

That launched the occult misogyny and recruitment roadshow that Unimed shopped around Australia and Europe.

During UM's early growth spurts, followers were commonly recruited by individual Esoteric practitioners or through singing workshops run by Benhayon's favoured wind instrument, Chris James. Esoteric Women's

Health became UM's main recruitment gateway for Serge's New Era of commercial aspirations, exploiting a critical gap in conventional healthcare that leaves women floundering in prolonged suffering and uncertainty. The front ran wellbeing events, with Lismore GP Dr Jane Barker, UM-affiliated nurses, and an array of Esoteric practitioners offering self-loving promotional plugs for Esoteric Breast and Ovary Massages. In time, the presenters were joined by Goonellabah GP Dr Elizabeth McGregor, rheumatologist Dr Maxine Szramka, and Melbourne psychologist Cynthia Hickman.

Wellbeing for Women love bombers swarmed on fresh bodies, feigning sympathy for their problems and using small group discussions to extract personal disclosures. Escapees told me that from the moment they surrendered their contact details, Serge's snoopers would not leave them alone. None had set out to join a religion — UM was advertised as a health service.

Some observers wrongly assumed that Esoteric Breast Massage gained recruits via titillation, so to speak; that the massages 'by women, for women' gave them sexual pleasure. However, customers I spoke with were pressured into it, and found it deeply unpleasant. One said she felt sick when she discovered that her masseuse was a lesbian, as around half the EBM practitioners were. She didn't want to complain because she didn't want to be perceived as homophobic, but in my view, the practitioners had no business passing it off as therapy at all.

The testimonials on UM's website indicated that even the most contented EBM consumers were uncomfortable with it, describing it as 'incredibly confronting', and they expressed distress at being told of their loveless 'self-abuse' before meeting the patriarch of their dreams. A twenty-two year old client was stunned to learn of the 'junk' she'd been carrying around in her breasts despite feeling perfectly fine. Others revealed more serious implications.

> The EBM sessions have given me insight into feeling and clearing the patterns that I have lived, which led to the breast cancer. (age 37) AUS[37]

The client seemed unaware of the lack of scientific foundation for that belief, and that breast massage is medically contraindicated for breast cancer.

Esoteric Women's Health is where debilitation, deception, dependency, and dread met Benhayon's commercial death drive. Lured by fraudulent health claims, the Women in Livingness were sold an unending course of bogus remedies for a perpetuity of phantom ailments, and led to believe they were in for terrible diseases if they didn't keep up their subscription.

xxx The HCCC

The New South Wales HCCC responded to my notifications about UM's hazardous health practices and its medical promoters by losing some in their system, refusing to return phone calls, or with obtuse excuses for refusing to investigate. The ovarian reading had occurred too early, they said, before regulations for unregistered practitioners had been introduced, and I'd left my complaint too late, they added, citing a limitation period that came into effect post 2008.

The authority had powers to ban unregistered practitioners from operating health services if they were found to be in breach of its legislated Code of Conduct and to pose a risk to public health, but I soon found that their misconduct thresholds were fatuously high. The regulator fobbed off Benhayon's dietary nonsense, claims about serious illness, exorcisms, Esoteric Chakra-puncture, and breast rubs. It did nothing about him training hundreds of amateurs in all of the above, and telling a cancer patient to drop dead.

The HCCC also had powers to discipline registered health professionals who misled patients or the public, but when I complained about the doctors and psychologists promoting UM's health disinformation, the

Commission's bureaucrats replied that they were entitled to their opinions. It was painful to learn that Australian health authorities only take action after a patient has been exploited, assaulted, or killed by a registered practitioner, and only when the injured or deceased has the wherewithal to lodge a complaint and endure the official process.

At least my research put me in touch with Emeritus Professor John Dwyer, a founder of public health advocacy group, Friends of Science in Medicine. The Professor of Immunology, formerly of Yale University, and former head of the Faculty of Medicine at the University of New South Wales, knew of Universal Medicine and had given media statements about its 'dangerous nonsense'. His warning to me that health watchdogs in Australia were 'pathetic' was exemplified in the Commission's response to my complaint about Esoteric Breast Massage enabler, Dr Barker, stating that her conduct would not 'attract the criticism of her peers to the extent that further action is warranted.'

Professor Dwyer emailed his disagreement:

> My dear Esther Rockett what are you doing up and writing at 10 at night when you should be getting your beauty sleep? Seriously this is a serious matter for when doctors endorse what 99.9% of their peers would ridicule they should be censured if not deregistered. To have Dr in front of your name with that title endorsed by a national registration board is supposed to give the public some confidence that competency can be expected.

He urged me to 'stay angry, and keep up the letters.'

The HCCC did not investigate Benhayon's public statement that Dr Sam Kim had assisted patients to die, either. It would only do so if I provided the names and addresses of the patients whose deaths he'd hurried along. Not wanting to take chances, I notified the Australian Medical Association, and the chief of staff at the private hospital Dr Kim worked at, forwarding the audio. If I was running a hospital, I would want to know if a quackery cult leader was broadcasting that a specialist on staff was consecrating its patients with assisted death.

xxxi Darkly Venus

> One does not become enlightened by imagining figures of light, but by making the darkness conscious.
>
> Carl Jung[38]

Esther Rockett has been my name since birth. We made that clear at trial in case it came across as one of those made-up monikers, like Deirdre Discoball or somesuch. At the outset of my blogging though, I'd used the pseudonym Darkly Venus; partly because I'm a brunette, and as I told the court, I wanted Universal Medicine to know that I was a woman and that I was not pretending to be full of love and light like they were.

Darkly Venus chose an avatar image of a dark-haired woman on all fours against a pitch black ground. Flashlit by twin lightning bolts and electric-blue Japanese characters for 'fury', she's flanked by two snarling hyaenas.[39] My initial blogging, which leaned toward sober academic analysis, didn't fit that picture, but as media backing fell away, UM's critics proved too fearful to speak out, and I realised how gravely I'd underestimated authorities' capacity for inaction, it became clear that I'd need more oomph to sustain the scrutiny.

The problem was, I had no resources, just reckless tenacity and my underdeveloped skills in researching and writing. Against such a wealthy and deranged Goliath, authorly restraint felt not only impotent but inappropriate, and playing at impartiality was a mistake. That behemoth of fakery did not deserve to be dignified. It needed to be forcefully debunked and deprecated as the trash it was.

The group's righteous charades reminded me of Jung's writings on the psychological shadow. He said that people are not as virtuous as they imagine themselves to be, and he'd hoped that the atrocities of the world wars would awaken humanity to our capacity for evil. The most dangerous are those who refuse to acknowledge their inglorious potentials, as exemplified by the Nazis' bogus 'master-race' ideology, and Jung said that the more we disown our base characteristics, the more likely they'll devolve into full-blown corruption. Consciousness of one's shadow requires sustained moral effort, he said.[40]

Criticising UM's hypocrisy from an affectation of intellectual superiority never sat right. The only genuine counter to phoniness is authenticity, and I made the decision that Darkly Venus had to confront everything the group sought to repress, and *be* everything that UM was not. In its simplest form that was a one-woman blitz on their mindless reverence.

Where UM deified Benhayon with unquestioning solemnity, I mocked him. David Millikan said he was self-conscious about his height, so I dubbed him the Munchkin Messiah. Sergio directed followers to revert from their diminutive or assumed names to their birth names, so I used his. He preached that cats are controlled by the Lords of Form, so I posted cat memes. Everything UM's commander condemned, I celebrated. Counter to Benhayon's teaching that classical music is the most noxious of poison, I installed a YouTube music player with a playlist of fine performances. Where he condemned art, except for the energetically pure works he'd produced during his stint as Leonardo, I illustrated my blogs with shadowy, mostly contemporary artworks: V. R. Morrison's disembodied portraits of glamorous women; Heidi Yardley's nightmarish female figures; Louise Hearman's lone children aglow in ominous semi-twilight; and Juan Ford's photorealist compositions that lay bare the clash of nature and artifice.

Where SergeProp's output was hackneyed and repetitive, bogged down by editorial committees, I switched topics frequently, cycling my exposure of greed, quackery, sleaze, cultishness, and their death drive, so they never knew which angle the cannon balls would come from. Where UM's blogs were militantly moderated, with critical comments and questions, no matter how civil, held and deleted before they could be published, I opened my blog to all. Where Unimed attempted to suppress information, I installed a contact form inviting readers to provide it. Where the truth-bloggers clung to consensus, I encouraged a free-for-all. Venting, dissenting and profanity were not only unrestricted on my site, but encouraged, although the person who indulged most was probably me.

Venus also tactically sought online confrontation. Alerted one morning to Eunice Minford and company protesting in the unmoderated comments area on a Frome news website, I waded in and questioned how many of them had been plied with Benhayon's ovarian readings and other repugnant rot. My questions met with a slew of accusations, but no answers. Eventually they leaned on the publisher to remove the article, shutting the discussion down.

Later that day, I reproduced the news item on my blog and invited 'the Brides of Serge' to comment with the same gusto they had on the Frome site. My little blog earned a thousand page-views that afternoon; the ladies indulging the only emotional excitement they were energetically allowed — devout indignation — yet none had the courage to comment. The encounter confirmed that they were deliberately avoiding my complaints, but Darkly Venus did not accept denial. What they saw was their shadow hissing back at them. On one of my anti-propaganda posts, I embedded a music clip of the Morrissey song, 'The more you ignore me, the closer I get'.

xxxii Splitting

When I found out that Esoteric Women's Health were organising an International Women's Day recruitment event, I blogged Benhayon's blather about how breast cancer could be cured 'if women were lovely and precious and didn't pick up heavy things' and his mansplanation for female infertility:

> You've been using mental energy to please your dad, you've been using male energy. You've been involved in sport which women should never be because they're competitive. It means their right ovary gets more powerful than the left ovary, and then they come to here, they're ready to have a

child, but the ovaries are totally out of whack, vaginal walls are as thick as, and they're not a woman energetically, even though they have breasts, the vagina, uterus and so forth. And so they can't work it out. 'Why can't I have a baby like other women?'[41]

Notwithstanding the amateur gynaecologist's ignorance of reproductive anatomy and physiology, I didn't want to contemplate the investigations he'd undertaken to gain expert knowledge of vaginal walls. My readers and I were also appalled by the gynaecological exhibitionism on the *Women in Livingness* blogsite — women writing at fulsome length, under their full names, about their sexual histories, their menstrual experiences, and their breast and gyne disorders — in praise of Benhayon's business.

I disagreed when a male reader complained that Serge exalted women at men's expense. The grifter guru was an equal opportunity hater, insulting everyone with his stereotypes. Women in Serge's universe were only useful when submissive. He was fixated on female victimhood, sexual violence, and breast and gynaecological disease, which he often linked. Motherhood, to him, was martyrdom, and the female body was nothing more than a site of exploitation, abuse, and disease, which he described in disturbingly lurid detail.

He never spoke of women taking pleasure or strength from their physical and sexual gifts. Rather, sex was 'energetic rape', and the hint of a desirous look from a man could inflict women with carcinogenic male energy. On the rare occasions that cultists were willing, partners were subjected to Benhayon's stipulations for 'gentle' and emotionless love-making: women on top for intercourse, vigour forbidden, and oral sex was out. 'Imagine trying to make love to your partner with pervy Serge right there in the room,' I wrote on my blog, ' — BLURGH!!!'

An Esoteric relationship casualty replied, recounting healing symbols under the bed and printed on pillowcases, and '*Mona Lisa* looking down on us watching… It's enough to put anyone off sex, oops sorry, I meant Esoteric Love.'

A traumatised Eric Dobbs, whose marriage hadn't survived, added, 'you forgot to mention the presence not only of Serge the Perve but that old crooner Chris James, bellowing away in the corner of the boudoir serenading us with those rancid songs.'

Benhayon viciously resented women who did not fit his ideal, attributing them with 'male' traits where 'male-energy' was SergeSpeak for any quality that threatened his dominance. Aside from compelling customers to spend on healing services to clear it, the aim of demonising male energy was to denigrate challengers and competitors, and to keep followers subdued, and it was not limited to women. Sergio the passion killer recommended circumcision to curtail men's animalistic urges, as in reduce their sex drive. Despite the lack of any scientific basis for that contention, some UM parents sought it out for their young sons.

When Natalie added a menstrual cycle app to her product range, to capitalise on her father's teaching that the menstrual period is a way for women to clear 'all that she has unnecessarily taken on[42]', UM's students predictably flooded the internet with promotions. What I wasn't prepared for was Lee Green's testimonial on the *Women in Livingness* blog, 'Men, Periods and the Our Cycles Period App'. Lee Green is a bloke. The app had helped connect him with his cycle, he wrote.

> On awakening that morning, knowing deeply that this was the first day of my period, I felt everything. The holding back, the pushing, the drive, the burdens I had stacked up...
>
> I had time in my morning to run a bath and soak me, to really honour this event, this celebration of a man returning to tenderness.[43]

Lee's UM devoted wife and daughter went along with his manstruation, with no interventions, and on the same website, a woman wrote of UM's male members that 'it is a true relief to be around non-creepy men — I prefer to call them real men.'[44]

More of Benhayon's perverse fixations came to light. Before Millikan's attempt to get Serge on camera, journalist Joshua Robertson secured a rare interview in which he focused on questions about Benhayon's commercial activities. Contrary to assertions of financial success before starting Universal Medicine, Josh had discovered that Djwal Khul's latest conduit was bankrupted in the mid-nineties and discharged just months before the cistern Sirens told him to start a cult. But as if to divert from the money questions, Serge embarked on a weird rave, alleging in grisly detail that teenage boys in Goonellabah were injuring adolescent girls with violent sexual assaults.

Some months later, I received another batch of student notes, including some taken by Esoteric Breast Massage practitioner Elizabeth Dolan at an EDG meeting in December 2011.

> Serge spoke about something that 10, 11, 12 year old girls are doing in Goonellabah and no doubt the rest of the world. It is called 'splitting'- meaning that these young girls are having sex with older boys and the sex has to be rough and hard enough that it causes the girl to bleed (not from breaking the hymen but from the roughness of the act). The name of the game is that the boys have to make the girls bleed while the girls have to be able to prevent themselves from bleeding.

Two other notetakers at the same meeting concurred.

xxxiii Laurie

Mid 2012, a couple of months before The Da Vinci Mode article was published, my younger brother Laurie became acutely ill with a life-threatening disease. He spent a few weeks in a Brisbane hospital and struggled in the months afterward. The illness kicked the life out of him. By Christmas 2012, he seemed to be getting better, but I didn't trouble my family with the inexplicable news that I'd publicly taken on a cult. They'd been through enough that year. The few friends I told disapproved. Their question was always, 'do you have to?' The answer was always yes.

Early February 2013, I was working four days a week in my acupuncture practice and spending all available time bashing UM. It took up too much of my focus, and before I left on a holiday to Tasmania, Laurie told me his recovery had stalled. We planned to explore new treatment options on my return. The day after I landed in Hobart, he died.

A few weeks later, a reader alerted me to intrusive questions in UM's online event booking form. A search of the labyrinthine website unearthed a 'consent' form for its one day workshops. Obviously drafted by lawyers, the form required customers to answer comprehensive questions about their medical history under a guise of giving consent to undergo hands-on healing and meditation practices at a five hour event. It also featured a dubious disclaimer releasing the Benhayons from liability for adverse reactions. Workshop participants were required to disclose any history of psychiatric illness, Hepatitis B or C, their HIV status, any other significant illness, and all the medications they were using. A space on the form requested details of any 'major life events'.

Australia has laws around the collection and storage of personal information by health services, but privacy authorities would not act on the firm's harvesting of sensitive information unless a UM client made a complaint that it had been collected or stored unlawfully or misused. All I could do was blog the form and warn of the predatory uses of personal data. UM could potentially exploit it to focus their sales efforts, and for targeted trauma triggering, shaming and blackmail — the manipulations that keep people beholden to high-demand groups. Scientology, for example, keeps records of disclosures made in its faux psychotherapy auditing sessions. It's one of the reasons I don't share my personal life on social media. I refuse to surrender the scarce remnants of privacy we have left, so I won't do Laurie's memory the indignity of poring over his illness in a book about my battle with a crappy cult, except to say that he died at forty-two, much loved, and all who knew him were gutted by his loss.

In Brisbane, Rocketts and friends assured me there were more than enough of them sorting his funeral arrangements and that I shouldn't return from Tasmania early. My old friend Riz was therefore sentenced to a holiday with a heaving wreck, not knowing whether to try to cheer me up, prop me up, or knock me out. His first response was to head to the bottle shop, and when I told him I didn't need a drink, he replied, 'I do.'

The next day we kept to our schedule and drove to Port Arthur, the nineteenth century Tasmanian penal settlement and site of the 1996 mass shooting. It was a cool, overcast day on the breezy peninsula, haunted by pain and death. Riz and I wandered the sandstone ruins of the barracks and cell blocks, those cold chambers of torture. Strolling the bare slopes of the park, where a gunman had unleashed on families, I dawdled down the hill while Riz took selfies. Shouting to me cheerily, he snapped my response — a feigned smile and a two fingered gesture of endearment known in Australian vernacular as 'the forks'.

Some weeks later I introduced my pseudonymous self to my blog readership, publishing Riz's photo under the title 'Brimful of PRANA! — A special and 'joy-full' message for the Universal Medicine Cult from very scary Darkly Venus.' I couldn't complain about UM's presence in my life because I took them on, knowing the risks. It was now a matter of confronting the monster and managing it.

But as Riz and I drove through gentle plains, wind rippling the dry grasses, as we wound through the burnt out forests around Dunalley, puffed our way up the bush track to the Wineglass Bay lookout, and trekked around Dove Lake under the sharp-peaked spectre of Cradle Mountain with Riz complaining about all the walking, death was like a sludge that dragged through my veins. The only breaks in the leaden helplessness were pangs of exasperation at taking a saucepan-headed run at the flailing blades of UM. My miscalculation of the obstacles left me exposed to legal action, stalking, and harassment, and I felt stupid and hollow. I didn't do enough to help my ailing brother; had allowed myself to be distracted from his needs. Now the madness I'd chosen to do battle with, the constant expectation of attack, was holding me back from the outpouring of grief he was worthy of. It was stopping me from screaming at the top of my lungs until all that was left of Port Arthur's sandstone cracked and crumbled to dust.

xxxiv Deeper Femaleness

> I've been a seer, and I still am. A true seer attempts to be wrong. Not right. Fact. And that's the difference when you see an Astral influence psychic. They're proving that they're right all the time, and their proof is the accuracy of their predictions… I'd like to be wrong… So what I do is I put out predictions that allow everyone to make a choice for them to not come true. And that's the secret of a true seer.
>
> Serge Benhayon, 2011[45]

A true seer turns out to be right. Fact. I was right when I suspected that I was nothing special to Serge and that the guy made a habit of preying on clients. The more I discovered, the more I understood UM's refusal to acknowledge my existence, and their efforts to shut my publishing down. It doesn't take a seer to recognise a coverup.

Prompted by my posts critiquing UM's women's health quackery, Heath sent me his copy of the Sacred Esoteric Healing Advanced Level Two manual. He'd endured levels one and two with Ellen in 2011, but, like me, hadn't examined the manuals at the time. Within hours I'd posted some of its photographs on my website and forwarded them to the HCCC with a complaint. They showed Benhayon demonstrating a healing technique called 'Deeper Femaleness'. The adjacent text claimed it was 'great for cases of rape recovery'. Serge had his hands on a clothed woman who lay face up on a treatment table in the Pineapple Road treatment room: the fingers of his left hand pressed to her breastbone; the fingers of his right pressed to her mons pubis — her external genitals.

Esther Rockett

xxxv The idiot test

> Certainty is hugely seductive, and certainty is offered by all successful leaders: it is an important part of their charisma... As every politician realises, the image is more compelling than the reality.
>
> Anthony Storr

At his peak, Goonellabah's most celebrated philosopher attracted audiences of up to six hundred to the two dozen or so workshops he ran annually. Pilgrims paid from one hundred to three hundred dollars per day to attend. But if fifteen thousand customers had filed through his Esoteric checkout by 2012, his rate of retaining them was lousy. The majority rejected his nonsense and never returned. Although it's unlikely that he had two thousand followers in 2012, as claimed in media reports, Serge was extremely effective at maintaining his stranglehold on those who hung around. According to a 2015 UM document, the community numbered seven hundred and fifty regular clients, and of the several hundred who identified themselves on the group's social media; most had been attending events for years.

Outsiders wonder how anyone could fall for such obvious bunk, but UM's manipulations are highly devious and multilayered. Benhayon, like most heads of high demand groups, had honed his manipulative skills for decades. Many ask whether such leaders study the same playbook, seeing their methods are so similar, but the pattern results from their common personality traits. Charismatic con-artists are invariably self-absorbed, ambitious, and convinced they are superior. Voraciously needy, their foremost priority is getting what they want, and they learn, often from a young age, how to get others to do as they say.

They also learn that their unshakeable confidence, their conviction that they have all the answers, attracts people who want to believe. Psychiatrist Anthony Storr observed that the 'charisma of certainty is a snare that entraps the child who is latent in us all' and he said we should avoid any individual claiming special knowledge who preaches that theirs is only way forward, and who claims to be surrounded by enemies and paints the world as divided into 'us and them'.[46] Such characters, while they may appeal to our unconscious yearning for a guide and protector, are too high on their own hubris to be troubled by any kind of moral conscience and are indifferent to the impacts of their demands on others. They justify their exploitative habits as doing their victims a favour — even 'healing' them.

Benhayon became remarkably deft at pinpointing the weaknesses of those useful to him and tailoring his manipulations accordingly. He often found his openings through flattery. A former follower told me that Serge took a dramatic, seemingly reverential step back on their first encounter. 'You!' he said to his mark for all around to hear. '*You!* You've got it!' He gestured toward the workshop podium, 'I'm not needed here. I can step down and let you take this — *you* have it!' The fiery etheric plane would freeze over before Benhayon would give up his spot on the stage, of course, but his target believed for a time that perhaps he was some sort of special vessel, although nothing of the sort had occurred to him before.

Observers are especially mystified by UM's attraction to allegedly brainy acolytes; the academics, lawyers and health professionals. 'What on earth do they see in this little worm?' said producer Nick Farrow about the affluent, well dressed people he saw rolling up to the Church of Serge. But the lures aren't necessarily sophisticated. A senior doctor in a medical lobby group found himself the focus of strange and sudden attentions from a collection of women who'd infiltrated the organisation without identifying themselves as Benhayon believers. 'I was flattered at first,' he said, 'and I must say it had an odd effect on me.' Safe at home with his wife, however, he told her of their fawning and asked if he'd become attractive all of a sudden.

'No,' she said.

'I understand now what it's like to be groomed!' he exclaimed.

Another doctor told of a colleague 'cavorting' with the same pack of Esoteric flirts.

While UM's saucy wowsers were encouraged to populate dating websites (their profiles conspicuous for their self-descriptions of 'playful', and for listing their religion as 'other'), their success at boosting UM's male ranks was mixed. Within the UM community, Benhayon played at matchmaking to keep recruits interested, nudging unlikely couples together with tales that they'd known each other in past lives. Some of the male devotees were cycled through multiple couplings that way.

Other followers found their devotion significantly enhanced by the guru promoting their businesses, seeing students spent enthusiastically on anything he endorsed. In essence, Benhayon and company resorted to any means to draw in assets and keep them: followers' intellectual or spiritual curiosity, physical vulnerability, emotional insecurity, lust, loneliness, and greed, were all tapped to his advantage.

Serge especially ran rings around recruits whose emotional intelligence was wanting. In a 2014 promotional video, *Healing Chronic Pain*, Brendan Mooney, a devotee psychologist who worked at the Goonellabah headquarters, claimed that Benhayon was responsible for healing his shoulder pain. Concerningly scrawny, yellow-complexioned and glassy eyed, soft-spoken Mooney recounted a copybook performance of quack manipulation in which his idol told him that anger was the cause of his pain and that it was 'congregating' in his arm.

> That was the first time anybody had ever mentioned that I had anger... I didn't disagree but I was defensive. I said to Serge, not my family, not my friends, not my partner have ever mentioned I have any anger.

Mooney explained that he was severely overworked from studying psychology full-time while practicing and teaching piano and violin for hours each day. His brother, Andrew Mooney, a UM-affiliated physiotherapist, could have told him it was a repetitive strain injury, and eighteen minutes into his spiel, Brendan revealed that it took more than two years after Serge's diagnosis to be rid of it. He didn't associate the relief with giving his arm a rest, either. Goonellabah's guru must have felt fiendishly satisfied every time a health professional publicly compromised themselves on his account.

'The idiot test' is a simple theory on cult recruitment I learned from 'Anticult', an anonymous contributor to the Cult Education Forum. The con-artist conducts the test by saying outlandish things in their initial sales pitch; tales about Atlantis or extra-terrestrials, for example. Critical thinkers quickly reject it and walk or sprint away, while those who stick around are identified as easy marks — idiots. Benhayon seemed to run the test daily, almost as a kind of sport. The dunny epiphany was pivotal, emblematic of the quality of output his followers were willing to sublimate.

In fairness, there's a difference between being an idiot and being made an idiot, and the blarney was just one of Benhayon's ploys. His promise of 'wondrous spiritual prizes' as David Millikan put it, and the subtleties of his trance inductions and methods for encouraging physical and social bonding helped seal the devotion. His supercharged motor-mouth, a peerless capacity to talk competitors and victims under the table, pulverising all sense and resistance, was another crucial manipulative resource. Disciples' investment of time, money. and labour, plus the coercive threats of blackmail, shunning, and supernatural consequences, then made it difficult for them to exit.

The idiot test is an efficient method for weeding out dissenters before they create trouble. Why waste energy arguing with common sense critics when there are customers who'll become aware of Deeper Femaleness, or hear that a horse will evolve into a whale, or that the US presidential election was stolen, and still spend and donate generously without question? Gullible or accepting people with money are the motherlode for Benhayon's ilk. That's the ruthless rationality of the idiot test: those who believe anything will buy anything.

xxxvi The chariot

Making idiots complainants seemed to be a HCCC policy. The Commission's officers would not investigate Deeper Femaleness, responding that 'there does not appear to be any sexual misconduct evident or likely to be proven.' Working my way through its switchboard to the assessments manager, I asked how on earth the photographs were not evidence of sexual misconduct. 'We consider that it would be difficult to prove a client did not consent,' he said with confidence.

'Consent?' I couldn't help raising my voice. 'People don't attend a health service looking for sex!'

The Commission would not budge, which meant I'd have to toil harder at writing letters and continuing the online exposure, but I was going to work red-eyed and struggling to focus on my patients. Doing the work that smug, taxpayer-funded paper pushers were supposed to do — protecting the public — was costing me, in every way.

The anger I felt was searing, hair-tearing. The memory of the woman at the workshop who couldn't stop crying gnawed at me, and as I drove home from work in peak hour, after dark, the tears came and I could not stop them. There was nowhere to pull over on the crowded main road, and I was aware that beneath the frustration and rage was seething, inconsolable grief.

Lance had been supportive and we talked often on the phone. He was the only other person actively making inquiries and putting in complaints, but he had a business to run and a child to take care of. He'd lost a brother too just a few years before, the same age Laurie was when he died. 'I know exactly how you feel,' he told me. 'To this day when I think about his death it feels like being kicked in the guts.'

That was the most reassuring thing anyone said to me. Laurie wasn't the only loved one I'd lost too young, in terrible circumstances. Some losses drop an axe through your life, breaking it into pieces of before and after.

You're a different person in the dark after, seeing life with less of the adornments you'd imagined before.

I pulled into a basement carpark, but stayed in the car, unable to move. Tears streamed uselessly down my face as I clutched the steering wheel. I knew it was not sustainable to crumble and weep every time things didn't go my way. Professor Dwyer had warned me about the regulators; I needed to accept it. I'd made a commitment based on an estimation, albeit a poor one, that I had the skills and tenacity to tackle Benhayon's expanding industry of abuse, and that it had to be done before the cult got bigger, wealthier and more powerful. I figured that organisations like Scientology could not have expanded or prospered as much in the internet age, with its unprecedented means of exposure. Laurie never knew of my campaign, but he appreciated guts.

Parked there I thought of Arjuna, the ambivalent warrior in the *Bhagavad Gita*. Sitting in his chariot on a battlefield before fighting begins, faced with having to kill or surrender and allow his loved ones to be killed, he's paralysed with despair. But his chariot driver, who is Lord Krishna in disguise, tells him to get up and fight like hell with no thought of winning or losing. The outcome is beyond Arjuna's control. All that he can control is the quality of his effort toward the most just result. To fight is to suffer, but for me, walking away and allowing UM unfettered access to the vulnerable was also to suffer. I couldn't stomach the guilt and regret.

I could investigate, raise the alarm, take the fight to the political level. I had to accept it would be thankless and exhausting, and I needed to focus on what was achievable, on managing my resources better, including the passions that fuelled me. Wiping away the tears, I turned the key to my chariot, resolving not to ride an emotional rollercoaster. Against shiftless bureaucrats and irrational aggressors the only options are to go hard or go home. I chose to go hard.

xxxvii Stopping

Smark asked if I had any thoughts about the document he'd given me to study, 'and the extent to which it corresponds to blogs that you posted up to the eleventh of November 2014?'

'Yes, no, get off the stand' was sound advice, but sometimes I needed to wrest control of my evidence. 'I can paraphrase, if you like,' I said. 'These are the blogs that I posted between the twenty-fifth of September 2012 and the eleventh of November 2014 and there are two hundred and fifty-three of them.'

The barrister nodded. 'Is it right that the great bulk of them are about Mr Benhayon or Universal Medicine?'

'They're all about Universal Medicine.'

'Many of them are about Mr Benhayon?'

'As leader of Universal Medicine, yes.'

Smark turned to Justice Lonergan. 'I tender that document.' He said it as if it was my ticket to the gallows. He then sneered out a lengthy list of complaints I'd made to regulators that were not acted upon. 'Would you accept that the list of complaints between October 2012 and October 2014, just before the first matter complained of, is extensive?'

'It's as extensive as Universal Medicine and Serge Benhayon's misconduct,' I answered.

'It's right to say then that, in your perception, by the time you came to publish the first matter complained of, the response to the complaints that you made had not been one that attracted action from the regulatory bodies to which you were writing?'

'Yes, it was unsatisfactory.'

'Did it occur to you that that should give you pause before you continued to make your allegations publicly?'

'No.'

'The fact that your allegations had been made and in some cases you were told investigated and that there had not been what you regarded as a satisfactory response, are you saying that didn't give you pause to think, "Oh, maybe I should not keep making these allegations"?'

'No.'

'It didn't make you stop? It didn't make you stop to think about that?'

'I think about everything I do, and stopping the exposure of this misconduct was never a possibility where there was an issue with patients — victims — being too frightened to come forward, and where there's clear evidence of inappropriate behaviour, and certainly molestation.'

Smark kept prodding. 'It's right to say, isn't it, that by the time you published the first matter complained of you had made a range of complaints about a range of issues to a range of government bodies about Mr Benhayon?'

'Yes.'

Perhaps he was going through the motions of cross-examination. I knew what was coming. 'Would you accept that by the time you came to publish the first matter complained of, you had formed something of an obsession about Mr Benhayon?'

There it was, the lukewarm flare of the forensic gaslight. The only thing that moved on my face was my lips. 'Not at all.'

Part II

For the Love of Serge

xxxviii Flames

'They are freaking!' said Matthew Richardson under his breath.

It was May 2016, six months into proceedings, more than two years before the trial and Richardson's first and last court argument for my defence. My money was gone, I was borrowing from family and friends, and Tom and his umbrella had not yet appeared in my life. Before filing my defence, I'd made a strategic offer to settle the case. Smith advised me that if I made a reasonable offer and the plaintiff's rejected it, that could help me retrieve more of my legal costs if I won. I therefore offered to take down the crescendo blog and make no claim for costs if Benhayon withdrew his claim, and mentioned that a trial would involve an enormous public airing of his conduct. As expected, he refused.

We didn't expect the Esoteric counter-proposal, however, which Team UM had the cheek to call an 'offer of compromise'. It sought vastly more in settlement than what Benhayon could get from going to trial and demanded 'complete vindication', including that I sign an apology stating that from 2012 onward I'd published unfounded allegations about him and that

> I unequivocally accept that I falsely accused Mr Benhayon of matters which I acknowledge that I published without evidence, without justification, and without belief in the truth of them... deliberately intending to hurt and embarrass Mr Benhayon and harm his personal and business reputation, in a way which I knew, would, and did, cause him harm...

Falsely incriminating myself wasn't what I'd call a compromise.

It was standing room only in Court 12C and I'd elbowed through a forest of suits to find Richardson. Every Friday, Justice Lucy McCallum worked through the defamation list, a weekly cattle-call of media lawyers, where she sorted case management before the tweed thinned out for a succession of interlocutory arguments over the rest of the day. Bucketing Benhayon with his own excrement proved to be an excellent plan, and the toilet bowl prophet promptly applied to strike out my contextual truth defence. We weren't having it, and Matthew was raring. Hugging a pile of binders, eyes darting around the courtroom, he murmured, 'they know we can hurt him with this.'

The barrister had five arguments that day and mine was the last. I spied Benhayon on Queens Square at the end of the lunch recess, ambling to court with Miranda tagging behind. She wore a russet jacket the same colour as the wall behind the stage at the Wollongbar hall; a menstrual hue which made an unsettling backdrop for Benhayon's video sermons. The couple are the same height, but she was thirty-five, attractive, and anxious looking, and he was fifty-two, unappealing, and cocky. Catching his eye, I gave him a wide smile and a wave, and mistaking me for a fan, he waved back, as friendly as the day I first met him, but his mouth and hand dropped when he realised it was me.

The couple were accompanied by loyal Alison Greig, a former lecturer in trade practices law who became UM's spokesperson from 2014, fronting its deteriorating image. In her late fifties, she wore prim cardigans, beflowered frocks, and a killjoy expression, and she was in the throes of an Esoteric romance with barrister Charles Wilson, who appeared at the hearing to assist Smark. Six foot nine and implausibly thin, Wilson seemed constructed from ether and straw, with a demeanour to match. Even his voice was a husk. The couple seemed as made for each other as they were made to serve Serge, and as I sat near the barrister in the front row, I got the impression that I could have stripped naked and cartwheeled around the courtroom singing show tunes, and UM's legal ramrod would have barely blinked his glassy eyes.

Serge, Miranda and Alison skulked to the back corner, before Alison crept forward to convey some last minute Ageless Wisdom to her beau. Despite her online stridency, she was a tremulous figure, clutching a notebook and a blunt HB pencil, and although I lavished her with my winning smile, she wouldn't look at me. Whatever vital message she whispered to Wilson barely roused him from his coma and he didn't pass it on to Smark. Serge probably sent her to test whether I would be rattled by one so fiery, or how she'd fare near the snapping jaws of the pranic beast.

To get rid of my contextual truth defence, Smark needed to argue that our imputations, including allegations that Benhayon was dishonest, delusional, and exploitative, were not conveyed by my crescendo blog. Beginning with a negative review of my writing style; 'this flaming language she uses', he argued that a number of the imputations referred to 'the Brides of Serge', the organisation as a whole, and not its innocent leader. He likened it to pinning allegations about employees of a corporation on its CEO.

Having observed his cordially restrained arguments all day, where no one spoke out of turn, Matthew surprised me by abruptly heckling Smark's submission: 'She called him a cult leader, it's completely different.'

Smark then argued that I could not have conveyed a meaning that Benhayon was making false claims about healing when complementary therapies like naturopathy and chiropractic are well accepted in the community these days, to which Matthew sputtered, 'it's not complementary, it's bogus!'

Justice McCallum listened intently, with solemnity, barely blinking when Matthew interjected, but Smark was amid a submission that the meanings of dishonest and delusional are not conveyed when she interrupted: 'I'm reading a line on page two of annexure A, where the defendant writes, "Mine began when I was subjected to a sleazy ovarian reading from Benhayon in 2005."' She levelled her cool gaze at Smark. 'If I was an ordinary reasonable reader and I came upon that line, I might think, "What is an ovarian reading? What does it entail?" I might ask "Is it an internal examination?"'

Smark didn't speak. She continued. 'An ordinary reader will have read the preceding paragraphs referring to Mr Benhayon as a leader of Universal Medicine, with the words "molestation they call 'healing'", "New Age quackery", "idiotic Esoteric diet", and at line forty, "disturbing exorcistic practices". Then on page four the defendant refers to "Serge's unqualified hands".'

Justice McCallum had presided in many high profile defamation and criminal cases. She ran marathons in her free time. She had read my blog closely. 'An ordinary reasonable reader,' she went on, 'who came upon "sleazy ovarian reading" might gain the impression that it was a procedure of ill intent, or at least of misguided intent. The reader might therefore assume that such a procedure could only be performed by a person who is mad or bad.'

Bam! Bazooka fire from the Supreme Court bench. I didn't turn. I didn't move, but I could practically feel Benhayon take the hit. Oof! A friend had quietly entered the courtroom and sat in the same row as Serge, and told me later that he and his lady bodyguards looked shaken.

Smark moved on to argue that the imputation that Serge Benhayon is exploitative was not conveyed in the blog either. 'Nothing in this article attributes exploitative behaviour to him. To other parties perhaps, but not to him.'

Again Justice McCallum referred to the blog. 'There are references throughout this article to Mr Benhayon engaging in what is described as "inappropriate touching",' she began. 'Then, here at page ten, is a heading that says, "Exploitation of the vulnerable".' Her delivery was bone dry.

The Crescendo blog was a critique of Alison Greig's public denials of Unimed's inappropriate touching. In that section, I'd written about UM publishing testimonials from teenage girls who'd stayed in the Benhayon home. Justice McCallum read my words aloud: 'One of many young girls to file through that home in the last twenty or more years. Only three of them…'

Her Honour halted. She frowned. She began the sentence again, inflecting it as a question. "Only three of them have ended up marrying a Benhayon so far??"

xxxix Houseguests

After Miranda went to stay at Serge's and ended up married to him, Paula Fletcher's daughter, Emmalee, moved in at around fifteen and went on to marry Michael. Following her to the Esoteric altar was Isabella Benhayon, who married Serge's youngest son. Curtis Benhayon's expertise includes 'Esoteric men's massage' and Esoteric Uterus Massage 'for women only' — techniques likely 'impulsed' to him by his handsy old man.[47] My public questioning of what those practices entailed went unanswered.

Over time, I learned more names of girls who'd stayed in the Benhayon household. Student notes named nine year old, Haley*, from Perth, and Lance remembered a European girl who was staying with the Benhayons around 2010, doing 'work experience'. Lance's housemate, Matt Sutherland, remembered seeing her at the UM clinic looking miserable. Work experience was SergeSpeak for cleaning the place, unpaid.

When Matt heard that girls were sent to stay in the Benhayon household without their parents, his former partner Sarah Baldwin dodged the question. The ten year old daughter of Sarah's new boyfriend turned out to be one of them. Heath also told me about a girl of about thirteen who was lingering around Benhayon at the workshop he attended in 2011, wanting to give him hugs, but she seemed to be there without a parent. When Serge needed a model for the treatment demonstration, he overlooked several hundred adults to call her by name, and she happily went to the stage and lay down on the table. Lance noticed another girl in her mid-teens hanging around the guru at Dr Sam Kim's wedding. Defectors told me that cultists believed a hug from Serge would clear them of entities and prana. They lined up for them, with their kids.

Heath had also witnessed Serge preach, in front of children, that if a man feels paedophilic lust toward his niece, it's not his fault because entities from the Astral Plane are making him feel that way. Heath had seen a member of UM's hierarchy standing behind a seated young woman, stroking her face with the backs of his fingers, and assumed she was the chap's wife, until he realised she was a teenage girl.

Joelle* was one of the tennis pupils Serge roped in to his live-in coaching programme. In 1998, aged fifteen, she'd shared a room for a couple of months with an unfriendly seventeen year old Miranda, and found the atmosphere in the household weird and tense. Serge told the girls they were not to shut the bathroom door when they showered.

Each time I learned the name of an unaccompanied girl who'd stayed with the Benhayons, I reported it to the NSW Child Protection Helpline. The authorities would only act on a complaint from a child or their parent or legal guardian, but I thought it best to put the names on record. The Helpline's social workers always asked the same question: Why were parents sending girls there when Benhayon's own children were adults and there were no other children there of similar age? Without identifying children publicly, I posed the question on my blogs. In 2014, Alison Greig published something of a reply.

> ...it is no secret that teenage girls from interstate and abroad stay at the Benhayon home from time to time, often to do work experience at the

Universal Medicine Clinic or to attend courses. The fact is Serge has always shared his financial success with others.

Some girls were younger than teens, but it was an admission nonetheless.

Smark, during cross-examination, swiped at me for creating a meme image from a UM photo of Serge and Miranda strolling hand in hand among Goonellabah greenery, staring lovingly at each other. I'd inserted a speech bubble with the caption: 'Remember when you were thirteen and I was thirty?'

Smark's glare was merciless. 'Was that, do you accept, a particularly nasty thing to put into your blog?'

'No. It was a commentary on facts.'

'Can I suggest to you that by the time you were putting that photo in you had an abiding dislike of Mr Benhayon?'

'I had an abiding dislike of Mr Benhayon long before that.'

The barrister was angling for an admission of malice. 'At all relevant times which the matters complained of in this case were published you accept you had an abiding dislike of Mr Benhayon?'

'I do, yes.'

'It was your desire to bring him down?'

'It was my desire to bring him to account for his misconduct.'

Justice McCallum's brow remained raised at the revelation that juvenile houseguests had gone on to become Benhayon brides. 'Whether any allegations related to these young women can be proven is a matter for the trial,' she said, 'but the imputation that Mr Benhayon is exploitative appears to be quite clearly conveyed.'

I couldn't scribble notes quickly enough. Matthew, at the bar table, had his head down, preparing for his turn. Inside I was cheering. 'Flaming language,' I thought, as Smark pushed on. The argument was not over but I allowed myself a private chuckle. It wasn't my fault if his client's behaviour was flammable — incendiary even.

xl Susceptible

Where Smark was circuitous, Richardson didn't muck about. 'The defendant clearly identifies the plaintiff as the leader of this group and his conduct as the basis of her criticisms. I submit that the imputations are plainly and powerfully made out, because all of them are susceptible to proof.'

Justice McCallum listened carefully. Matthew directed her to a group of subparagraphs in my defence's particulars of truth, quotes from Benhayon's writings about gynaecological disorders that I would use to support the allegation he'd made false claims about healing.

> (vi) "Women have achieved equality, in some measure, by 'out-male-ing' the man. Therefore, they too, are in the excessiveness of male energy. This why there are so many cases of ovarian cancer, fibroids, cysts, endometriosis, breast cancer, etc…Become racy or driven and you have asked the male energy to dominate your body. Looking like a woman but being run by a male energy is not the whole and true you…will women stop and listen to this teaching or will breast and ovarian cancer…need to get so bad that they are forced to pay attention to it?"[48]

The judge slowly lifted her eyes and fixed them on my lawyer. Her features might have been carved from stone. Matthew's speech was impassioned; 'Your Honour will see that those are just four subparagraphs in sixteen pages of material particulars. The imputations are made out because my client fully intended them to be. They are clear and strong allegations due to their abundance of substance.'

He was still shaking his head and muttering as we walked the empty corridor to the lift. 'You're not going to tell a Supreme Court Justice — a woman judge — that the work she does will cause gynaecological disease!' He shuddered. 'This stuff, touching those woman all over their torsos…' He practically hissed. 'It's despicable.'

As we parted in Queens Square, Richardson turned and squinted. 'Do you think he'll go through with this?'

xli Pranic Princess

Google kept caving to requests from Paula Fletcher of Universal Law to remove links to my blog from its search index. I figured that the only way around it was to set up a second blogsite, *Universal Medicine Exposed*. My blog stats indicated that hundreds of readers were visiting the Accountability blog daily, but they were shy about leaving comments, so I decided to embody an interlocutor for Venus, who seemed too tame on her own. Pranic Princess, a lusty, somewhat gluttonous, sport-loving amateur performance artist presided over the new site. Focused on countering UM propaganda and broadcasting gossip, she lavished her writings with glorious profanity and poked fun at the puny patriarch. Her 'Cult Bashing' YouTube playlist rebuffed the strains of Miranda and Chris James with Abbe May's Mammalian Locomotion, Wolf Alice, MS MR, and others, favouring women artists who embodied the qualities Benhayon deplored.

Some readers found her too confrontational at first, but Princess and Venus articulated what many felt, and their recreational mockery kept my growing readership returning to my sites, if for nothing more than an antidote to UM followers' deranged piety. My dual personas infuriated Serge's mostly female Sons of God, who, for years after my identity was out in the open, remained outraged by my use of internet pseudonyms.

Princess was never short of ammunition. A couple of readers had reported seeing healing symbols protruding above UMers' waistbands when they bent down — postcards stuffed down their panties. That inspired Princess to road-test the cards with the occupants of the Accountability bunker, beginning with one labelled, 'Removalist 1: Heavy Duty Energy

Cleanser': Benhayon's remedy for the imposition of other people's anger, and to 'assist during periods of low self-esteem and general heaviness.'

> The Lords of Form reckon they suffer low self-esteem because people make fun of their capes and how wimpy they look when they get off their horses. This caused Venus to feel imposed upon, because she's tired of them gloating about how cult members are scared of them, particularly when they are seen coming out of the bottle shop with more than one bottle of pinot gris. Then they reckoned her anger and frustration was imposing on their feelings. We all, however, agreed they are in a period of general heaviness, especially after that last pastry bender.
>
> Anyway, we sat on the symbol, laid on it, burnt candles, prayed to it, meditated on it, and all that. We really wanted the thing to work, but in the end we still got cranky at the mention of Serge and UM, the Lords of Form still had paunches and continued to fight over the remote control, Venus got the snarks and started ironing right in front of the telly obscuring the LOF's line of sight and causing an uproar, the dairy products were still fat, the toast still had gluten in it and I was still strident, provocatively dressed, rude and Pranic.
>
> I think we can safely say they didn't work.
>
> Later we took our clothes off and played scrabble, and that sorted everything.

xlii Esoteric Practitioners

Given that his products and services were, at best, utterly worthless, Benhayon couldn't possibly grow his enterprise by operating honestly. His real genius lay in establishing a sprawling and profitable apparatus of deceit. The health and other professionals who endorsed it were instrumental to his manipulative reach, while the involvement of lawyers maximised the difficulty of bringing him to account.

Before Paula Fletcher and associates worked at getting my blogs taken down, an enormous pseudolegal effort had gone into passing off Esoteric healing as legitimate health practice. In 2009, Benhayon registered a business named the Esoteric Practitioners Association (EPA) Pty Ltd, and branded it the 'accrediting body' for UM therapies. Lawyer, Serryn O'Regan, joined Natalie on its board of directors, and that of several other Benhayon companies, including the College of Universal Medicine charity and Esoteric Women's Health. The forty-something mother of an adolescent son, divorced from her pranic ex-partner, O'Regan also practised Esoteric Breast Massage and Chakra-puncture from her home in Viewbank, Melbourne.

Like other New Age business operators, Benhayon had worked out that training practitioners in bogus therapies was exponentially more lucrative than working on one patient at a time at seventy-bucks an hour, and the more elaborate the training, the more they could profit. UM management devised a scheme offering practitioner accreditation to customers who completed five levels of Sacred Esoteric Healing workshops, plus optional training in Esoteric Breast Massage, Esoteric Connective Tissue Therapy, Chakra-puncture, and the like. Practitioners and students paid membership fees to belong to the EPA, subject to an 'energetic assessment', but because no UM business is a registered training organisation, the accreditation was as genuine as the extra-terrestrials behind crop circles. What the firm called a 'professional' qualification was not officially recognised, but practitioners misleadingly advertised their sham accreditation to the public.

As a proprietary limited company, with one Glorious shareholder, the EPA wasn't an association at all, but a private business set up to hoodwink consumers. Health professionals, including Sam Kim, Eunice Minford, Kate Greenaway, Caroline Raphael and Sydney rheumatologist Dr Maxine Szramka, served on its practitioner advisory committees, while paying members were roped into authoring and producing training materials. The few Esoteric Practitioners who earned income from Serge's sham therapies usually fell back on more legitimate modalities for their living, while the majority of graduates rarely earned enough to cover their outlay. Benhayon answered complaints by accusing students of being in the wrong energy — his standard out-clause.

Meanwhile, the cult's lawyers devised a practitioner Code of Conduct, which combined a series of Esoteric prohibitions with some standard legalese. Whenever SergeCorp had to answer to authorities or institutions that questioned the group's practices and claims, its apologists produced the manuals and codes. Never mind that the founder and his enablers didn't abide by them, UM students and others fell for the fakery, including misleading ethics statements like the following from the Esoteric Healing manuals:

> CAUTION! — particularly to male practitioners treating women.
>
> As the breasts (nurturing centre) are so close to the heart, at no time must inappropriate contact be made with the breast during Heart Chakra treatment.
>
> ABSOLUTELY NEVER!

But flipping a few pages in the level two manual found photographs of Benhayon with his hand on the model's breast. In another, his hand is pressed to the crease between the younger model's buttocks. Back at the ethics page, it says:

> It is imperative that in healing we must allow the placement of hands where we are in truth guided...
>
> Explain if necessary the importance and why it may be necessary to hold such a hand position.

The text accompanying the Deeper Femaleness technique was a similar mix of counterfeit propriety and blatant scamming:

> Applied with extreme caution and with absolute trust and permission from the client...
>
> Great for cases of rape recovery in woman (after proper treatment), impotence in men, low sex drive and stagnant kidney energy. Over-use of sex drive in men and women.

The manual had been in use for years and Benhayon had gotten away with it. It appeared that he could say or do anything as long as he paid lip-service to integrity. We might expect that from a cheap charlatan, but the role of the health professionals and lawyers, unduly influencing those who didn't know better, was impossible to get past.

xliii Pehm

I requested a Commissioner's review of the HCCC's decision on Deeper Femaleness. In my complaint, I'd made the point that the New South Wales Attorney General's Department defined sexual and indecent assault as a situation in which 'a person is forced, coerced or tricked into sexual acts against their will or without their consent'. No client could genuinely give consent if they'd been deceived that it was legitimate therapy. Registered practitioners would not be permitted to carry out such a technique. However, the HCCC's propensity for inertia could not be overestimated.

Commissioner Kieran Pehm cited the bogus disclaimers in the Level Two manual and said that I hadn't provided sufficient evidence that Benhayon had engaged in sexual misconduct. The Commissioner identified that the 'therapist' in the photo was 'placing a hand over the genital area of a fully clothed patient'. He accepted that 'there may be circumstances in which it would be inappropriate for an unregistered practitioner to be touching genitalia, regardless of consent', and he acknowledged that there was no genuine clinical basis for the technique, but said he wasn't satisfied it was a risk to public health or safety. He added that there could be 'sufficient scope for a practitioner to argue that treatment was provided in a therapeutic setting and that in the course of obtaining consent it had been explained to the patient that the clinical evidence for the procedure was limited'.

The Commissioner of a consumer complaints authority was the last person I expected to use the word 'limited' where he should have used 'non-existent', or to believe Benhayon's sham about caution and permission, or insinuate that it's not molestation if the victim is clothed. He signed off stating that the 'decision should not be viewed as an endorsement or any other support for Mr Benhayon or Universal Medicine', but a health authority refusing to investigate false and misleading healing claims and brazen practices of inappropriate touching could not be a better endorsement for a quackery scam.

Again I complained to parliamentary representatives, and later to a New South Wales parliamentary inquiry and the Australian Health Ministers Advisory Council, that within current legal definitions

> it's acceptable for an unqualified, self-appointed healer to touch genitals if the patient is fully clothed, and as long as the practitioner does a good enough job of deceiving the patient into thinking they are entitled to do so. Under that logic, any sex offender could call themselves a sexual abuse counsellor and molest clients with impunity as long as they told them it was therapy... the same sex offender could run 'healing' workshops and teach the technique to others...

I raised a HCCC case in which a tribunal found, years after a complaint was lodged, that a massage therapist had indecently assaulted a client. It was not referred to police. The penalty was a two year ban from operating a health service in New South Wales, with nothing to prevent the offender doing it again in another state, or signing up for Serge's workshops to practice on UM's women. I recommended that genital touching in healthcare settings be criminalised unless it's performed by a qualified worker for legitimate, officially approved health or hygiene reasons, and I called for a uniform national law to address such abuse. But nothing has changed to this day. There is no legislation in Australia that addresses sexual predation in treatment rooms.

xliv Charity

Benhayon hit the jackpot when he got his fangs into some of Britain's upper-crust money. Chartered accountant and old Etonian, Simon Williams, landed in Benhayon's treatment room in 2002, when he was thirty. His wife, Janet Williams, would go on to organise Benhayon's annual workshops in the UK from 2004, starting at Mells Barn near Frome, a fourteenth century village hall and likely site of a few witch trials. Janet's 'What If Treatise' was published on UM's website in 2005, where she referred to Serge as a 'divine messenger' and asked:

> What if ... there really is a legion of disembodied spirits instructed by the Lords of Form to prevent us from stepping fully into our light?... For many, astral beings are as real as physical forms and a part of daily life management... Until we claim ourselves, they will always have access to our physical vehicle and will use our energy (kidney chi) to fuel their existence.[49]

Around 2008, Serge's eldest child, stepdaughter Simone Benhayon, moved to the UK to teach swimming. Simon and Janet joined her on the board of Universal Medicine UK Ltd, before the couple purchased The Lighthouse, a seventeenth century estate at Tytherington, for nearly two million pounds. All cobblestones and clipped hedges, its thirty-five acres of gentle pastures came with a lake to jump into, and the couple converted the building into Bed and Breakfast accommodation that would double as Universal Medicine's European hub.

Simon Williams was part of the effort to have Benhayon's Way of the Livingness recognised as a religion by the Charities Commission of England and Wales. The Commission rejected the application, however, on the grounds that the movement did not meet the definition of a religion; the charity did not demonstrate a public benefit; and the dissolution clause in its founding document had the potential to allow the trust's assets to be applied for non-charitable purposes.[50]

EDG student notes from 2011 and 2012, yielded useful intelligence about breakthroughs in Benhayon's charity campaigns nevertheless.

> In both the UK and Australia we now have charity status. This means that people can donate money. In the UK there has been 2.5 million pounds raised and this money belongs to the student body and the student body has built a conference centre where all the courses can be held as well as retreats and also free retreats for those who are ill.
>
> The charity commission in the UK would not give UM charity status. Fortunately for us Chris James, one of the esoteric students had an existing charity called "the sound foundation" which he is allowing UM to use, as he does not need it.[51]

Unimed took over Chris James's latent charity without disclosure to the Commission. The Williams donated a parcel of land subdivided from The Lighthouse property and within months SergeCorp's European division had poured the charity money into construction of the Sound Training Centre, a two-million-pound conference premises that included treatment rooms, dorm accommodation, and a commercial swimming pool facility. The single largest donor was another chartered accountant, wealthy Somerset local and Esoteric convert, Michael Nicholson, who threw in over a million pounds of posh tax-deductible dosh.

Simone Benhayon wedded Nicholson's son David in 2011, but like many Esoteric marriages, its temporal existence was short and fiery, and a spirited argument saw Nicholson the younger plead guilty before a local magistrate of keying Simone's Alfa Romeo. Nicholson the older became a charity trustee, nevertheless, together with Simone and a couple of Esoteric Breast Massagers, and with wife Tricia, great granddaughter of tobacco baron Alfred Dunhill, they opened their own swish B & B, Upper Vobster Farm, within a short drive of The Lighthouse.

Shortly after the Sound Foundation charity opened the Sound Training Centre in April 2012, Benhayon restarted his annual programme of UK workshops and retreats in the new digs.[52] It's difficult to say how much Benhayon turned over in the three months he spent in the UK each year, but it had to be, at minimum, half a million pounds. Between the dozen or so scheduled workshops, the Benhayon family were fully booked providing individual and group healing sessions in the facility's treatment rooms, as well as classes in their Esoteric dancercise routine, True Movement, with a sideline selling UM merchandise. The Williams' and Nicholsons' accommodation businesses thrived through UM's event season, but the conference centre remained virtually unused the rest of the year.

None of that resembled charitable activity to me, so I lodged a complaint with England's Charities Commission, which commenced an investigation. In time, the charity's publicly available accounts would reveal that Serge paid a ludicrously small rate of hire; four to five thousand pounds to take over the premises May through June and for the month of November, yearly. To put that in perspective, the sum did not cover the building's energy bill for the same period, which averaged around seven thousand pounds per quarter. Meanwhile, Simone took the lease on the heated pool facility, paying a measly ten thousand pounds per year to operate her swim school. Serge and Simone's rent would barely cover half the centre's annual energy bill, while the rest of its running costs were paid by the charity's Esoteric donors. Simone would also write off up to ninety-five thousand pounds per annum of 'swimming activities' as a 'donation in kind' to the Trust, presumably avoiding tax on those sums. In effect, Serge and Simone's commercial overheads were generously subsidised by Her Majesty's taxpayers.

EDG notes also discussed UM's Australian charity, The College of Universal Medicine, which was set up for the purpose of 'advancing education' — SergeSpeak for promoting his anti-intellectual claptrap. He who preached that emotions are the cause of all disease busted his precepts when he learned of his luck:

> We are now also a legal charity… and any money that is donated is tax deductable. Serge read out a letter that he wrote to the tax department. He held nothing back in this letter yet it was passed. In the middle of reading out the letter Serge broke down in tears. He could not stop crying so Natalie had to finish the letter. He was crying because the Hierarchy were in the room and it was so amazing to feel them. It was a very profound moment.

Inspired by the glimpse of official exertion in the UK, I gathered what I knew about the College and made a complaint to the newly established Australian Not-for-Profit and Charities Commission (ACNC) that the College was operating to benefit individuals rather than the public. It was a similar setup to the UK sham, except that Serge was named as the College's founder. He appointed himself chairman in perpetuity, but resigned from his Ageless directorship less than twelve months later when journalist Josh Robertson began asking questions. Serryn O'Regan took over, and barrister Charles Wilson joined a board that included Natalie Benhayon, Alison Greig and multipurpose Désirée.

Lance, with his business background, helped me put the picture together. Benhayon had bought the cold storage warehouse in Wollongbar, near Goonellabah, for two point three million dollars. He told the student body he'd purchased it on their behalf and had plans to convert it into a conference centre, with a clinic, accommodation for workshop pilgrims, and Dr Kim's hospice. The charity established a school building fund to accept tax deductible donations for the renovations, with plans to lease the Hall of Ageless Wisdom from Serge. By karmic coincidence, the warehouse was a former nut processing facility.

Benhayon even admitted to Josh Robertson that he'd set up the charity as a repository for his self-published works, portraying his provision of teachings as a noble public service. Josh was not distracted by Serge's self-promotions, however, and questioned him about the clauses within the charity's constitution that allowed its directors to charge the College for their products and services; empowering Benhayon and associates to financially exploit a charity that by law is required to benefit the public. He could use it as a promotional front for his profit making business; to raise public money to improve his private property; to lower the commercial overheads of running UM events; and to remunerate himself and the other directors.

Followers were fed some exuberant Esotericisms to inspire them to throw money too. A 2012 letter penned by one of Benhayon's overworked proofreaders, Gabriel Conrad, urged students to donate to 'our very own building'. She'd just returned from the first retreat held at the spanking new centre in the UK where two hundred and thirty seven participants had paid one thousand pounds apiece to attend. Many of those who'd helped pay for the construction of the Sound Training Centre would pay to attend workshops scheduled in the following weeks and years, forking cash again and again into their guru's bottomless pockets.

Sparing His Holiness the vulgarity of grovelling to his Australian customers directly, Conrad referred to Serge as a '5$_{th}$ degree Initiate... a member of the Hierarchy' and 'the voice from heaven for our times'. In the short term, he needed half a million dollars to ready the Wollongbar space for events, she said. His Hierarchical projects required the full backing of the student body to have proper energetic effect and he also wanted them to come up with two and a half million dollars to buy the building from him. Conrad said that the Dark Forces of the Astral Plane would halt the works if students did not 'make the call', and at an EDG meeting, Serge said he would sell the property if they failed to come up with the loot. The energy of donation would reward donors' kidney energy, he added, but insisted that donations were made anonymously.

Some weeks after the ACNC accepted my complaint, something unprecedented happened: an officer of a regulatory body picked up a telephone and called me. Klaus* was a senior investigator and he said that the info I'd provided also made a case for 'harm to beneficiaries' — another breach of charity law. UM's bonkers facade concealed a coldly rational commercial structure sustained by a systematic spiritual and healing fraud, and where the HCCC's officers seemed indifferent to the threat posed by UM, Klaus got it. He even requested more information.

Noticing his email address had the suffix ato.gov.au, I asked if he worked for the Australian Tax Office. He said he'd been an investigator there before his transfer to the ACNC, and although they are separate statutory bodies, he had the authority to refer issues to the tax regulator.

When, over five years later, Smark read out the list of complaints that authorities took no action on, those I made to charity regulators were not among them. Tom would bring those to the court's attention. 'This is very helpful to my enquiries,' said Klaus, when I complied with his request, but he surprised me with his next remark. 'Please take care of your health'.

xlv Therapy

Klaus too was a seer. I'd said nothing about my circumstances, but I was unwell. For months, I put off seeing a doctor because I'd dismissed my worsening symptoms as caused by grief, overwork, and my career's dwindling rewards. I'd never been a commercially minded practitioner, and worked to resolve my patients' complaints with the minimum number of treatments. I did not make promises I couldn't deliver, and didn't charge enough. In a marketplace oversupplied with incompetents peddling deceptive healing claims, and with running costs climbing, my practice was facing extinction, and I no longer had the passion to save it.

Overwhelmed at times by sadness and frustration, I'd isolated more since Laurie died. A neglected friend pestered me to see her psychologist for grief counselling, and in seeking therapy, I also had to ask myself why I'd taken on a dangerous cult. Why did I not value my wellbeing more?

By mid 2013, the illness was seriously debilitating and a botched surgery led to an internal infection. I visited the psychologist a couple of times before the worst of it, to receive an uninsightful diagnosis of survivor guilt. Her idea of therapy was to tell me that I'd failed my dead brother by not finding him better medical help.

I then made the mistake of going along with her suggestion of a guided meditation, wrongly assuming that as a registered psychologist, she knew what she was doing. She had me close my eyes, slow my breathing and focus on the physical sensations in various parts of my body, but after a few minutes, I felt so ill I almost tipped face-first onto her carpet. She asked how

I felt and was surprised when I told her I thought I was about to collapse. 'I told you how ill I was,' I muttered, head in hands. I looked it. Klaus had figured it out from my voice. 'What were you trying to do?'

'It was to help you get in touch with your pain,' she said.

She didn't do lasting damage, but it was definitely painful paying one hundred and fifty dollars an hour for a blind stab at therapy that made me worse; to professional listener who hadn't heard a word I'd said. I'd even complained to her about Serge unethically using meditation to covertly hypnotise people. 'My pain?' I replied. 'My pain is staring me in the face.'

xlvi The update

I cut my working hours, but Unimed's commodified craziness charged on relentlessly. I notified Klaus when the College of UM charity launched its Fiery Building Fund with a website that stated that it was raising cash for the 'new Universal Medicine Centre': evidence that UM's management, who weren't yet aware they were under investigation, didn't distinguish the charity from Benhayon's profit-making business. The site displayed a photograph of Benhayon guiding donors on a tour of his unrenovated nuthouse, with at least three cancer patients among the group, as well as GP Dr Jane Barker, psychologist Caroline Raphael, and Paula Fletcher, whose specialty included wills and bequests. By then, the charity had raised nearly six hundred thousand dollars to spruce up Serge's building.

Encouragingly, a UK news service reported a success. The Charities Commission hit the Sound Foundation Charitable Trust with a mandatory compliance order to address issues of public benefit and trustee conflicts of interest, invoking a delectable image of Winston Churchill Benhayon and colleagues scurrying around Tytherington like lemmings.[53] With the news, I authored a series of blogs laying out UM's charity scams.

Unfortunately, though, information about the Australian investigation evaporated. The last I heard from Klaus was that the ACNC wasn't granting him the resources he needed, but he confirmed that he had an appointment with the tax office to discuss issues he'd identified. A couple of months later, a newspaper reported that several investigators had quit the Commission and were complaining that the regulator was dysfunctional and they'd been prevented from properly investigating serious malfeasance.

Meanwhile Paula Fletcher and her sourpuss Brothers got busy with baseless copyright and trademark infringement complaints to Wordpress, which I staved off with DIY legal counter-notices. My Facebook page was also taken down, and Zuckerberg provided no mechanism for getting it back. Mystic Dentist, Dr Rachel Hall, an anti-fluoride campaigner and Benhayon champion, also made a police complaint accusing me of stalking after I emailed her asking her if she was aware of Deeper Femaleness and Benhayon's other predatory techniques. A police officer phoned to say that I could be charged if I emailed her more than twice. 'Don't send her any more,' he said.

UM's psychologists, Brendan Mooney, Caroline Raphael and Marianna Masiorski, also launched an offensive, complaining to the Australian Health Practitioner Regulation Agency (AHPRA) of harassment and defamation, and arguing that I should be deregistered from my profession. It didn't get anywhere, but I had to waste time submitting a written response. Naturally, I blogged all intimidation attempts. It wasn't me that was stalking UM's professionals, but their own misplaced consciences, and the facts.

In October 2013, the internal infection and the unremedied original ailment escalated until I was so ill I had to cancel my patients. I was on antibiotics, but they didn't seem to be helping. It was a weekday morning when I woke with a high fever, strong nausea, diarrhoea and vertigo, and having made it to the bathroom, I ended up on the floor, losing consciousness. Alone at home, locked in my concrete box unit, with the neighbours all at work, I knew the signs of septic shock, and that I needed an ambulance. My vision darkening, I crawled to my charging phone only to find its screen black. Apple Incorporated had chosen the moment of my near death to commence an operating system update, which, with my lousy internet connection, could take hours. I didn't think I could make it to my front door, or down the steps to the street without collapsing into unconsciousness. I didn't want to die by Apple update, alone in my flat, and I began to weep. No one but Lance knew I was ill.

xlvii Sutherland

Matt Sutherland had been a second-rate cultist. Having inhabited Benhayon's universe for a few years, he'd broken up with fiancé Sarah Baldwin, the mother of their two young sons, around the time Lance and Anna separated. Matt moved in with Lance and their lively kids spent a few days per week with their fathers. At our first meeting, as Matt cooked dinner and the kids played chase, he told me Sarah's siblings and parents were all UM frequent flyers and the Baldwins had sunk substantial cash into 'the work'.

'All they ever talk about is UM,' he said. 'They go on and on about how amazing it is, and they keep telling each other how amazing they are.'

As tall as Lance, Matt performed stand-up comedy in his spare time, sometimes as a guru character named Sergio Benbullshit who said he'd been Jesus Christ in a former life. His wife Miranda had been his donkey.

'So did the cult break up your relationship as well?' I asked.

'No,' he said. 'The breakup with Sarah was a relief.'

Money was tight and the couple argued a lot. Between parenting and work as a chef, the cult was his only social life. He tried healing sessions with a variety of Esoteric practitioners, but not to any cathartic effect — mostly he fell asleep. He tried sessions with Serge, but the character love-bloggers dubbed the 'healer's healer' responded to his problems offhandedly, obviously bored — as he did with anyone who was no use to him. Still, Matt persevered, attending events at Sarah's urging, although he said that sometimes it was nice to just get out of the house, sit at the back of the hall and take a nap.

The couple tried counselling sessions with Sarah's choice of therapist, newlywed Miranda Benhayon, who was about thirty. Serge probably wanted his latest wife earning like the rest of the clan, but her business card listed no credentials; just the words 'Soul-full Solutions - for Spiritual and Emotional Blockages' in Désirée's Esoteric Breast Massage font. It wasn't quite the therapeutic arsenal she'd need to tackle Matt and Sarah's dramas, and Matt described her blinking and stammering through sessions of their bickering. Her Esoteric counselling career was short lived.

Depressed, Matt booked a session with psychologist Caroline Raphael, whose consulting room was adjacent to Serge's. But when he gave an account of his difficulties, she said, 'you're angry with God.'

Matt replied, 'I don't know if God exists.'

'He's in the next room,' said Raphael.

He was such an unconvincing cultist that it took me a year to learn that he'd attended two levels of Esoteric Healing workshops. He never read my blogs, so wasn't abreast of the scandals. I happened to whinge to him about the HCCC inaction on Benhayon's inappropriate touching, and that led him to complain about the stress of avoiding contact with women's breasts or genitals when practicing the techniques. The majority of Benhayon's students are not trained in anatomy, and when Serge instructed them to reach for their partner's pubic bone, their hands could end up anywhere. A shrill little zealot's hand landed on his penis. 'I had to ask her to take it off!' Matt said.

And then there were the snakes. Benhayon convinced followers that their pelvic regions were infested with the writhing phantoms of bad sex energy. Our hapless friend was lying face down during a practice session, when, without warning, he felt his male practice partner poking his fingers lightly around his anus. When Matt asked what the heck he was doing, the guy said that he was pulling an energetic snake out of his backside and inquired whether he'd been looking at porn.

Matt knew of the Deeper Femaleness technique — not by its name, but by what it entailed, and when Benhayon taught it at the workshop in 2007, he went looking for Sarah. Hundreds attended those workshops, and Benhayon had graduated from the conference room at Lennox Head to the indoor stadium. Matt didn't want to be paired with anyone other than his girlfriend if it involved putting his hand on a woman's genitals.

He didn't see any children learning the practices but affirmed that some were present, and Serge didn't hold back from talking about masturbation, paedophilia and supernatural rape in front of them. 'There were kids at all the events,' Matt said. Heath and Lance said the same.

The HCCC's Commissioner Pehm had stated that the authority could only investigate if there was a complaint from a person who had not consented to the inappropriate touching. Matt could confirm that he'd been touched inappropriately without his consent and that Benhayon was the instructor. The risks to children were also clear. Surely the Commission would have to act.

xlviii Life force

> There is no such thing as death. No-one ever dies. We are all immortal. The carnal body however, is not eternal and one day it will completely cease. The Dark Force is the light that serves to preserve this day from coming.
>
> Serge Benhayon[54]

By the time my phone came to life, I was properly conscious and the vertigo had subsided. My doctor later ruled out septic shock, but understood my terror at the storm of symptoms. It was not a death I'd imagined for myself, at forty-seven, alone, not found for days, my family having to deal with the loss of two of us in one year. Dead, to me, meant extinct; no angel wings, or rides on clouds, no rapturous ascent into the ether to await karmic repurposing. I get why people want to believe something Glorious awaits. It's hell to grapple with the loss of everything one was or could be. But cults like Benhayon's can sublimate that anxiety into a dangerous romance with a fantasy afterlife — a death wish.

I'd found a better specialist who said the botched initial procedure should never have been undertaken. My only option now was major surgery but I was too ill to risk it, and needed medical treatment to get well enough to undergo it. Still, I kept hammering the cult. The question of the harm I was doing to myself was often on my mind, but bashing UM was the only thing that vitalised me. My one-woman slog had dramatically curtailed UM's growth, I was expanding my skills and knowledge into stimulating areas, and the group was an easy and worthy target for my own projected shadow — a well of aggression I'd never properly tapped. Their behaviour was so detestable that I could lay into them without guilt, making the fight gruelling and annoying and fabulous all at once. But it had gone on too long, and aside from terrible health, I was in a career that was getting me down, in a city I didn't care for, not seeing my loved ones enough, and going backwards financially.

Up to the day of my surgery, a fortnight before Christmas, I was working on my seventy page submission to the New South Wales Parliamentary Inquiry into the Health Care Complaints Commission's handling of false and misleading health information and practices. In it I concluded that the HCCC was a giant taxpayer-funded filing cabinet, a place where complaints of public health risks go to die, and that Australia's practitioner regulation authorities could be abolished and no one would notice a difference in patient outcomes. I emailed it minutes before my lift to the hospital. Having fasted since the day before, I was light headed and running a fever by the time I was admitted. A nurse took my vitals and showed me to a lounge, but after a few minutes I waved her over.

'Is there a chance I could lie down?'

xlix Certification

Matt Sutherland's complaint to the Health Care Complaints Commission saw Caroline Raphael undergo an interview and counselling before a professional standards panel of the Psychology Council of New South Wales. The authority notified him that he'd identified 'issues of concern...which may constitute a departure from acceptable standards of practice', but did not elaborate. His complaint about Benhayon, however, hit the usual wall of bureaucratic absurdity, although this time the authority sought a response from the guru. Serge denied everything.

> ...the Commission found that the practice of massage used by UM is overseen by a Code of Conduct. This Code appears to stress the importance of placing one's hand in the appropriate position... and states that no touching deemed inappropriate will be accepted by those delivering the course. There appears to be no evidentiary basis to suggest that Mr Benhayon himself teaches students to massage the breast or genital area...

Yet I'd provided the photographs showing Benhayon doing just that, in a manual he'd authored and published. Matt had notified the Commission that he taught the techniques to him.

> ...and if a student should ignore the warning in the Code, that may be considered to be outside of Mr Benhayon's control...

In reviewing that decision, Commissioner Pehm restated that the authority would need evidence that individual patients considered that consent was obtained improperly. But that was the substance of Matt's complaint. The HCCC officers would believe anything but a complainant.

In response to Matt's allegation that children were present during Benhayon's graphic sex talks and exorcisms, they said that 'there is no indication he would act in an inappropriate manner whilst in the company of minors.' Again, no indication other than statements from first-hand witnesses. The Commission also disclosed that UM's proprietor had a current Working With Children certificate, setting off alarm bells all over again. Only those who work with children without parents or guardians present, or provide homestays to kids, require the certification in New South Wales. It's only denied to those who've been convicted of sex crimes and major crimes of violence. As I complained fruitlessly to state MPs, the certificate gives parents and guardians a false sense of security. It does not protect children from unapprehended predators or other dubious characters. Benhayon held one, but the question for us was, why?

1 Christmas 2013

Christmas has no meaning for people who believe the Second Coming of Christ hatched in 1964 and flogs ovary readings and magic postcards from semirural Goonellabah. In 2013, Esoteric greetings came as pseudolegal threats from Désirée Delaloye, psychologist Marianna Masiorski, and Serge's media managers, a pair of thirty-something ultra-Benhayonites, the unctuous Rebecca Baldwin, and humourless psychology graduate, Sarah Broome. Broome's was the warmest, sent at five-thirty on Christmas morning. All claimed my publishing was illegal under some law or other, no one was sure what, and demanded I remove their names from my blogs.

At the same time, a Serge-struck mother and daughter made festive enquiries with relatives of theirs, bemused childhood neighbours of mine, about whether I had a history of mental illness. The mother, a former patient of my acupuncture practice, phoned me a few weeks later to book an appointment, which I refused. She was not off the phone a minute, however, before her daughter called to say the two of them wanted the booking, not for acupuncture, but to talk about my blogging. 'We've seen your blog, and… well, we're worried you're not yourself.'

'What fucking bullshit,' I said to her and the inevitable eavesdroppers on the line. 'We've met twice. Or was it once? You don't know me.' The mother went on to complain to AHPRA that I'd refused to treat her, that I was persecuting a religious community, using swear words and pseudonyms on the internet, and that the agency should order me to take down my blogs.

Intel from the cult warned of more payback to come. I'd noticed that the Esoteric Practitioners Association was advertising discounted professional indemnity insurance to members, so I sent the insurer some material from Benhayon's workshop manuals and suggested that the EPA might have failed in its duty of disclosure. No policy indemnifies past life regressions, molestation, and exorcisms, after all. The members' insurance was cancelled and the leak suggested that the Sons of God were displeased.

Registered psychologist, Marianna Masiorski, who openly advertised that she was a practitioner of Benhayon's 'Esoteric Psychology', renewed her complaint to AHPRA demanding my deregistration. She was probably miffed that I'd reported her to the authority for her blogs on the *Medicine and Serge Benhayon* website, where she'd spouted Esoteric nonsense about mental health pathologies and described her extremely scientific test of Benhayon's 'sexual energy'.

> Now don't get me wrong, I didn't go to one of his courses wearing a short skirt and a low neckline, I just tested a hypothesis, "He's a man and all men I have met have had a sexual desire that can be tapped into". Well, when I felt for this within Serge I felt NO sexual drive, but a very definite strength that was not imposing in any way... It was clear that I was not going to get Serge's attention with any form of sexuality. It was a new level of inner integrity for me that I had not met before...

> He passed every test that I could think of, as a woman and as a psychologist and there was nothing but love.

Masiorski's complaint about me cited studies on cyberbullying and trolling, and diagnosed me *in absentia* with The Dark Triad of psychopathy, narcissism, and Machiavellian sociopathy, with psychosis and sadism thrown in. Signed by the whole roster of UM-invested health professionals, they evidently thought of me as a high achiever.

Again, I could have done without the work of writing responses. My recovery was long and incomplete, and I was unwell for some time. The surgery that was expected to be a one hour procedure had taken more than three, and I'd been in enough danger to rattle the surgical team. 'You had me on my toes!' the doctor said, beating his fingertips to his chest. He'd saved my life, but the revelation felt strangely academic, as if the person on the operating table had been someone else.

Knowing the group would exploit any weakness, I made none of my misadventures public. I had to appear invulnerable. They never gave up. Tipped off by SergiLeaks that the cohort listed on my Naming Names page had complained to the Australian Consumer and Competition Commission about me, a Freedom of Information request revealed they'd swamped the regulator with one hundred and fifty complaints, comprising five thousand pages of materials. I had no information about the substance of their complaints until the trial, where I could divulge that UM's promoters accused me of publishing false reviews of UM businesses, but all were dismissed on initial assessment — a spectacular accomplishment from a community with three commercial lawyers among its hallowed hierarchy.

After going through the motions, the AHPRA complaints went away too. The phone call from the Eso-snoopers at least gave me an opportunity to quiz a cultist on exorcisms, initiations and the like. The daughter confirmed that if a person drinks liquor, entities can leave the imbiber's body and sexually assault nearby children, Serge says so, and she said she knew people it had happened to. She admitted taking her young kids to UM events.

li Messages to Miranda

A few weeks after the Da Vinci Mode article was published, Lance introduced me to Miranda's mother, Trish, during a chance-meeting on Bangalow's gentrified main street. In her early fifties, she was petite and soft-spoken, with curly honey-coloured hair, and a local friend of hers had only just described her to me as frail. After speaking with journalist, David Leser, Trish had left work on two occasions to find her car smeared with eggs. UM also spread vicious and defamatory rumours about her at their Friday evening Church of Serge services. The gutter campaign worked. Trish never spoke with the media again.

On the day we met, she confirmed that she never allowed Miranda to move in with the Benhayons in 1995. Their family lived only half an hour away and she preferred to drive the teen to training. Miranda behaved secretively as soon as she entered Benhayon's orbit, but Trish made it clear that she'd never witnessed any intimate behaviour between her daughter and her ex-tennis coach.

In 2014, a year and a half after I'd met her, another of Trish's friends told me that the mother was still desperate to reunite with her daughter, but that Miranda was shunning her out of disapproval of the people Trish was associating with — implying Lance and me. It prompted me to post a message to Miranda on my blog. Aside from that one encounter, I'd emailed Trish once to check that she was okay after she'd posted a comment on my site.

> I am Miranda's Mum, can you tell her I love her? Can you say THERE IS NEVER ONE SINGLE DAY THAT I NEVER ever ever stop thinking about her xoxoxoxoxo

I told Trish that we were available if she ever needed our support, but otherwise we left her alone. 'So Miranda, you may have your own reasons for not wanting to contact your mother — that's your affair, but don't use us as an excuse. It's not fair to punish your mother for an association that doesn't exist.'

My message also encouraged Miranda to get out of the cult: caring people would be there for her if she did. She was an elusive figure then — less photographed than the Four Lords of Form, and her name and image did not appear in UM's floods of propaganda until mid 2014. But observers said that she attended all Benhayon's events and was rarely out of her husband's sight. She too was idolised, and a contact who attended a workshop in 2013 told of great excitement when Miranda performed vocals to Michael Benhayon's labours — the audience roused to their feet to sway arm and arm with tears rolling down their faces. 'I could have cried too,' said my friend, 'as I thought about how much Serge earned during that hour.' She'd clocked him slouched down the back, hands in his pockets.

Not long after I published the message to Miranda, Glorious Music (which would rebrand as 'GM Records') released new material and provided audio samples on its website. When I heard the stuff, I understood the weeping. They also published the first photos of Miranda I'd seen, enabling me to identify her and find more by scouring Facebook. She was thirty-three then, with longish light brown hair and green eyes; beauty to Benhayon's beast.

It occurred to me that Trish might not have laid eyes on her daughter in years, so I emailed them to her, and she thanked me for the 'gorgeous' photos:

> I adore them xxx, and I am glad you sent that [message to Miranda.] I know why she turned her back on me, it was because the first time I saw Serge, I disliked him, and he knew it.

She said that she couldn't have her name anywhere near ours 'just in case Miranda wants to come looking for her Mum, she won't have in her head I was to blame for bringing her husband down,' and she wrote of her fear when Miranda was a child that someone would take her away. 'The awful day I met Serge, the feeling went, and after a while I realised I'd met the man that would steal my daughter.'

lii UM FACTS

I'd never heard of Alison Greig until I received messages leaked from UM's private online forum. Behind the love-blog façade, Serge's Brides used a vast password-protected echo chamber to organise their hostilities. Alison put her name to many of its bulletins, including those confirming plans to out me as a cyberbully and troll, and she coached the group on dealing with my stuff.

> When you read the blogs be aware that they are configured energetically and are intended to place seeds of doubt in your body... be present as you read it and remember that reaction to the material only feeds it.
>
> Personally I sit on a healing symbol and also have one under my computer!

It was May 2014, and in preparation for the onslaught, I converted my Darkly Venus tag to my real name throughout my websites and launched estherrockett.com to exert some control over my name and message. For want of better branding, I called myself a healthcare activist.

UM's anti-detractor website, 'The FACTS About Universal Medicine', went live a few days later, sub-headed, 'Addressing the lies and distortions of Cyber-bullies, Cyber-stalkers and Internet trolls.' Its initial half dozen articles named and character assassinated Lance, me and a few others, and over the next four years, the FACTS campaign sprawled to over one hundred and twenty defamatory articles about us on a dozen cult websites, where they identified our professions, business names and locations in their subheadings, ensuring that anyone looking for us online would find UM's smears.

According to its organisers, the site was published

> to address over 2 years of cyber-bullying and trolling by a small gang... planned and executed with hate and indecency as its vigour... They kept their public identity anonymous but are now exposed.

Its authors, Alison, Désirée, Charles Wilson, Sarah Broome, and Rebecca and Jonathan Baldwin, called themselves the UM FACTS Team, and asserted that UM is not a cult, and that the website was a student initiative, 'not the product of any design on the part of Serge Benhayon.' Lance, however, found its domain was registered to the crackpot in chief, using his name, Universal Medicine business address and phone number.

Its articles lifted passages verbatim from the Masiorski complaint to AHPRA, citing the same academic studies and diagnosing Lance and me with an identical dark pentad of Machiavellian psychopathy, psychosis, sadism, and other antisocial pathologies, and Alison used the group's favourite Einstein misquote to attack my livelihood.

> If everything is energy as Albert Einstein proclaimed it begs the question; what energy is Esther Rockett bringing to her healing table?..
>
> The fact is that Serge Benhayon never performed an 'ovarian reading' on Esther Rockett and regardless of Esther Rockett's description and accompanying innuendo of sexual impropriety, the event she described never occurred.

It was a confident statement for someone who wasn't there.

Greig was listed as author of most of the blogs, although the style and content were the same regardless of whose name was on them. All were torturously overwritten, up to eight thousand words each, and incongruously illustrated with photos taken by Deborah Benhayon's latest husband, photographer, Clayton Lloyd, of scrubbed and coiffed Esoterics alongside the worst photos of Lance that Anna could dredge up. Riz's shot of me at Port Arthur now flipped the forks at them from within their own fortress.

The titles of the posts about Lance are too false and defamatory to repeat, but Greig accused him of 'indecent obsessions' because he'd expressed concern about girls staying at Serge's house. Anna put her name and Cheshire cat mugshot to a series of blogs 'to present the truth' and 'expose the motivation and dysfunction behind my ex-husband's vicious and corrupt attack on Universal Medicine, its founder Serge Benhayon and anyone associated.' Some articles attracted over a thousand assenting replies, with UM's defenders condemning Lance as an 'abuser'. Benhayon donor and former CEO of Sydney's Star City Casino, Neil Gamble, wrote: 'Let's hope the real men in the village of Bangalow where this monster resides show Lance what happens to bully boys.'

A local court, however, had dismissed two applications for apprehended violence orders that Anna had taken out against her ex. Despite her accusations, she'd continued to drop their daughter at the alleged ogre's place on her way to UM meetings, often stopping for a chat, and the magistrate advised her at each hearing that a disagreement about lifestyle choices was no basis for a restraining order.

I could get why people irrational enough to hitch their wagons to a sixth dimensional scammer would be angry with me for spit-roasting their sacred bull, but their vendetta against Lance was inexplicable. He was a fraction as active and public as me. Perhaps UMers' identification with their guru was so strong that they adopted his alpha-male pretensions and his hostility toward the better adjusted blokes who challenged his monopoly of the group's women. They publicly paraded Anna like a kind of trophy.

Alison also wrote that Lance was behind my accountability 'crusade' and had manipulated me into becoming his mouthpiece. Benhayon's sexism was contagious apparently. Independent agency didn't accord with UM's fantasy of women as helpless damsels, incapable of standing up to their idol, let alone yanking him down from his jerry-built pedestal.

Lance indulged Anna with more tolerance than I thought she deserved, telling me that despite her hurtful behaviour — the website destroyed one of his businesses and profoundly damaged his reputation — she was a good mother. He ultimately decided against taking her to court because he didn't want to upset the relationship between her and their daughter. 'I can't do that to them,' he said. A couple of years later, though, the couple's nine year old, previously shielded from the anti-Lance campaign, was learning how to use Google at school. Searching her Dad's name brought up a torrent of UM's grotesque libel, illustrated with glossy shots of her grinning mother. Lance had hoped to have a few more years to prepare. 'How was I supposed to explain that?' he said of the girl's confusion and distress.

Those of us named and flamed expected blowback to a degree, but we were not prepared for its scale or insanity. The Esoteric rank and file took all criticism of Benhayon and UM as a personal assault. UK child safety worker, Ariana Ray, whose name I'd never heard before, wrote:

> What an awesome exposure of what has been an attempted tyranny by this woman over so many. The foul mouthed lies she has spread about myself and anyone associated with Universal Medicine is finally exposed.

Eunice Minford, Dr Sam Kim, Kate Greenaway, and other health professionals joined in, as well as Mystic Dentist Rachel Hall, who described my blogging as 'criminal'. The mob would parody themselves too. One comment simply read 'Liar, Liar!!' with the commenter later adding: 'How powerful would [Esther Rockett] be if she started to work for humanity.'

UM FACTS wrecked our sleep for a while and gave me an attack of gastric reflux that I feared would develop into a stomach ulcer. Lance was distraught. We floundered in those first weeks, paying a couple of thousand dollars for a defamation lawyer to tell us that litigation carried a high risk and the outlay to sue would be hundreds of thousands of dollars we didn't have.

The Sons of God fanatically shared the defamations on social media and as the months and years passed, with many of them posting about me daily, it seemed that I occupied their thoughts more than Serge did. Their obsessive attention to my every word led me to blog that 'the real leader of Universal Medicine is me.' The circulation of our names also turned out to be such a boon for our cause, I almost regretted not coming out sooner. Long-suffering loved ones of cultists were alerted to a public ally, gifting me with new readers and new information, and bringing them the reassurance that they were not alone in their misgivings.

Eventually, my reflux and sleeplessness eased. The cult's smear-specialists were so limited in what they could invent that they had to recycle the same falsehoods. Anyone with functioning wits could see what loons they were. That's not to say UM's efforts didn't do us damage, but I announced to readers that I would not waste time answering the deluge of lies, it was exposure as usual. Unlike the FACTS Team, I was constantly uncovering new and damaging material, and I posted documents, links and references, inviting readers to fact-check for themselves. I persisted with questions. Why didn't the Benhayons put their names to the attack posts? Where does the money go? And I cautioned readers not to be distracted by the sideshow. The malnourished millionaire had gone to ground, refusing to speak with the press, but he vigorously persisted with raking his dishonest livingness. 'Keep your eye on the puppet-master,' I said.

While nothing on the FACTS site was credible, it was their most honest advertising to date. I wrote in my crescendo blog, 'Alison and a couple of hundred self-loving investors have done a magnificent job of validating our concerns about the dangers of Serge and his venomous Bride army.' Dispensing with the hug-fest and Désirée's love-hearts, they were, at last, broadcasting what they really were, unleashing their long-repressed angst, lunging into the public arena as a rabid chattering online Hydra, baring its thousands of fangs.

liii Dark past

Unimed's attacks inspired Lance to hire a private investigator to look into Benhayon's background, especially around his bankruptcy in 1995. He discovered that Serge absconded from Sydney to Northern New South Wales in 1991, with his young family, owing over six hundred thousand dollars to creditors; large debts even by today's standards. Over half was owed on the lease of a tennis centre in Sydney's northern suburbs. As an ambitious young tennis coach at the Northbridge Tennis Club in the late 1980s, Serge talked three investors into installing him as tenant and coach at the Evergeen Tennis Centre at Brookvale, but it appears that he paid less than a quarter of the one hundred and fifty thousand dollars per annum in rent over the three years the business limped on. According to court documents, he blamed 'extremely inclement weather',[55] and he and

Deborah had taken out the bank loan to keep the business operating. The tennis centre's owners gave up pursuing the debt in 1991 because they were led to believe the Benhayons had fled to South America, but Serge and Deborah owed a further one hundred and fifty thousand dollars to the Commonwealth bank.

In 1994, the bank tracked them down to Alstonville, ten kilometres from Goonellabah, where Serge was working as a tennis coach. On his tax returns for each of the financial years ending in 1993 and 1994, Benhayon declared less than fifteen thousand dollars income, including Social Security benefits. Three of his children were under six years old, with the youngest, Curtis, born in 1992. In his official statement of affairs, Serge declared that he earned less than one hundred and thirty dollars per week in 1994 and 1995.

The Benhayons were tenants at a property called 'Waratah' that had a tennis court. Thirteen year old Miranda Smith became a pupil in 1994 and Serge persuaded her father to pay tens of thousands of dollars to upgrade the court for his coaching business, without telling him that the property was owned by someone else. A big talker even then, he boasted that he could coach Miranda to professional ranking, and Benhayon told other locals that he could get their kids winning major tournaments.

Coaches and players who worked with him during his bankruptcy period said he had hundreds of pupils: so many that he paid young players to assist him for up to thirty hours each week. Some parents paid one hundred and fifty dollars per week, in cash, for the coaching, but by the late nineties he'd not delivered on his promises, and many of his pupils had quit or defected. His berating style was described as 'cop-like', and a parent reported that he pushed Miranda to practise through severe blisters. Trish was thoroughly alienated by then and Miranda quit competition around 1999.

Benhayon's pattern of despotic behaviour was therefore on display long before the toilet bowl called to him, as was his pattern of exaggerating his abilities to persuade others to fund commercial premises for his profit. In his 1995 letters to the bank and an affidavit to the New South Wales court, Benhayon showed the form that he'd also resort to in future. Claiming surprise at the bankruptcy notice, he accused bank officers of corruption and criminality. Without disclosing to the bank or the court that he owed hundreds of thousands of dollars to additional creditors, he claimed that he was the victim: 'These actions only typifies (sic) the CBA's attitude and bullying tactics that have led to our current financial position.' Years later, between his tirades accusing me and others of dishonesty, criminality, and bullying, he would lecture his students at length on 'Responsibility', spelt with a capital R.

He also had a history of fruity money-making schemes. His amazing 'Athletes Powder', which was supposed to help tennis players grip their racquets, was, in fact, clay dug up from his rented Waratah backyard. One local described it as 'Serge's magic dirt'. It didn't take off.

Of most interest to Lance, though, was the Benhayons' miraculous rebound from bankruptcy. Serge and Deborah were discharged mid 1998, but went on to purchase land at nearby Macleans Ridges and build a four bedroom house for a total of two hundred and thirty-nine thousand dollars within two years. Less than eighteen months later, Serge bought the Pineapple Road house as well for one hundred and ninety thousand dollars.

Lance and the investigator spoke with enough locals to get evidence that Benhayon was turning over a healthy income during the bankruptcy, when all the couple's assets and income were supposedly managed by the bankruptcy trustee. Benhayon also told also David Leser that he spent up to sixty thousand dollars per year 'helping families that couldn't afford tennis.' If he was broke until 1995, and then bankrupt until 1999, when the lavatory fairies told him tennis was a sin, it's unlikely such largesse would have met the approval of the trustee.

In June 2014, Lance fired off a complaint to the Australian Financial Security Authority about possible breaches of bankruptcy law. At the same time I reported seventy pages worth of deceptive and misleading claims in UM's commercial publicity to the Office of Fair Trading. Frustrated by silence from the Australian charity regulator, we also applied to the state licensing regulator to have the charitable fundraising permit of the College of Universal Medicine revoked. The Fiery Building Fund website was erased in 2014, but the charity was still running sessions of Serge's 'Ageless Wisdom Teachings' between his profit-making events on 'Unimed Saturdays'.

This time when we emailed the complaint and copied in the relevant government Ministers and MPs, one of them forwarded it to investigative journalist, Jane Hansen, whose special interest was dangerous quackery. Within hours she was on the phone to Lance and me and put together a feature report on Universal Medicine for *The Sunday Telegraph*. Matt Sutherland went on the record to complain that 'Serge Benhayon controlled every aspect of our lives', and the paper published my account of the ovarian reading.

The first major press attention in almost two years gave UM a new enemy, and Alison Greig set upon her with a series of gutter-based articles, including 'Jane Hansen Journalist and the internet troll', and a six thousand word diatribe, 'Jane Hansen: A seasoned journalist with a murky past', that exploited the death of Jane's infant child.

> But would this life-changing moment signify fundamental change in how she works? Would it mean that she would take action to arrest harm if it would get in the way of a good story? Possibly not…

liv Judith

Benhayon bragged at one of his 2011 Esoteric Medicine performances that he knew the causes of all cancers.

> You need thirty years of science to tell you what I can get in one minute. Fact. So why are you spending all that brainpower and resource and lovelessness in your body and thirty years of trials, when I can tell you right now with not another cent spent wasting money of charity, I can tell you right now how women get breast cancer?..

He acted out a treatment room exchange between himself and a client:

'I bet you I can describe — as I can — your lifestyle. And I can bet you that that lifestyle will be accurate, and that accuracy will tell you why you have cancer.' At that moment that person has cancer, they will listen. But if they don't have cancer, they have the arrogance. You see? If you're not brought to your knees, you're not willing to listen...

'If you did what I told you eight years ago, you wouldn't have cancer,' I say...

Sarah McIntyre, a PhD student in neuroscience, made contact soon after I burst out of the detractor closet. Her mother, Judith McIntyre, was 'going to retreats, buying the silly symbols and writing blog posts for the group' and she wanted to communicate with others skeptical of UM, without posting online. Sarah worried that directly criticising UM would make it harder to maintain a good relationship with her mother, but I had to tell her that forming any kind of network was impossible given the group's success in deterring aggrieved parties from identifying themselves, even privately, to each other.

Judith's blogs revealed another textbook case of cult conversion. By 2011, her forty year marriage had ended in a rancorous divorce, and she was living hundreds of kilometres from family and friends on a high maintenance rural property near Byron Bay. She blogged that she'd been a longtime follower of a self-styled New Age goddess, who alternated between exploiting her financial generosity and snubbing her devotional acts. 'I had little confidence in dealing with financial or legal matters or in standing up for myself,' Judith wrote. 'I was lonely, struggling, "homeless", exhausted, and increasingly disillusioned with my spiritual path. Then, in retrospect, unsurprisingly, I got cancer.'[56]

Just three months after Benhayon touted his instant oncology expertise, he manoeuvred a speaking engagement at the Byron Bay Writers Festival, attended by newly diagnosed and terrified Judith.[57] She was taken in by his speech about breast cancer. 'His comments about being true to ourselves as a way to be healthy made sense to me. I knew I had many times looked after others even when exhausted.'[58]

He'd just released his self-published book, *Esoteric Teachings and Revelations*, in which he devoted a chapter to what Tom would call cancer voodoo, and after his presentation, Judith moved to the front of the marquee.

> He turned toward me and as he looked at me, inspired by his message to say and express the truth, I simply told him that I had breast cancer. He said to me that what I needed was deep self-nurturing. I didn't know what that meant at that time, but I knew I wanted to know.
>
> With only a momentary conversation I felt that he had met me. He met me where I was, broken open, detached from the world, where no family member, friend or professional, however caring or supportive, had been able to come.[59]

Benhayon worked quickly. In those days, he'd boast that his healing sessions were fully booked a year in advance, but when he heard the cancer was not in remission, he suddenly had a cancellation and fit her in straight away. She'd visit him weekly for 'counselling and esoteric acupuncture' until the end of her life, and Benhayon, famous for his thrift, and for wringing every cent and every bit of profitable labour out of his minions, was suddenly the paragon of generosity.

> Universal Medicine provided me with a beautiful and nurturing space in which to stay within a short distance of the hospital so that I was able to drive myself to the [chemotherapy and radiation] treatment even though I was still tired and became more so. This accommodation and much of my sessions with Serge have actually been free of charge.[60]

The accommodation was the Benhayon owned Unimed House — a bed and breakfast across the street from the Blue Hills Avenue clinic, which he'd told reporters was partly set up to accommodate terminally ill clients.

Judith was readily persuaded that the disease had resulted from her personal failings.

> I talked to him about death and how I had been living my life for others rather than for myself. I could see how I had squandered my life energy and made myself vulnerable to cancer in spite of my 'healthy' lifestyle…[61]

> The diagnosis changed everything. I felt cracked open. All the spiritual wisdom I had been acquiring seemed useless. I was deeply humbled... Although I am very intelligent, what bothered me most was that I could die knowing nothing, that I had wasted my precious time.[62]

Her cancer was real, but its connection to her attitudes and relationships was not — no matter how much it appealed to her to believe it. Where an authentic healer would have encouraged her to come to terms with her life's path and choices, Benhayon pounced on her anxieties, convincing her of a fictitious causative process so that he could sell her a bogus remedy — his brand of Livingness death.

'It's not the disease that's the enemy,' Benhayon preached. 'The disease is a cleansing, the disease is the blessing.' He added that cancer is a disease of those who 'live in misery'.

> And you don't understand you're living in misery because you have an arrogance that allows you to function...
>
> The real illness is not the cancer. That's a clearing. That's actually a blessing. That's something that's getting rid of the energy that you've been choosing. But what chose the energy? The arrogance. The lovelessness. So the real healing that I do is help them remove the arrogance...[63]

Benhayon's believers might have been less inclined to buy his victim blaming if it wasn't endorsed by the flock's health professionals. Eunice Minford was a big fan of cancer and its opportunities to wallow in Esoteric martyrdom and self-reproach. Restating the healing powers of death, she said that oncology patients had told her that the disease was 'the best thing that ever happened to me,' and she described it as 'an amazing opportunity to clear all of those poisonous thoughts, beliefs, emotions, resentments, grudges, hurts and more.'[64]

As editor of the *Medicine and Serge Benhayon* blogsite, Minford published an article by a cancer patient in her late twenties titled, 'Congratulations! You have cancer!'

> I understood that cancer was my body's way of clearing harmful energies I had taken on. By that I mean, that I had for years been living in a way that

was not very loving, indeed it had been quite abusive and those choices... had been energetically harming for my body... Even if I were to die, I would know that my body would have cleared the harmful energies I had taken on.[65]

Dr Anne Malatt reinforced the dogma. Diagnosed with lymphoma, the opthalmologist authored 'Getting away with it', on the same site. 'When I was younger, I used to drink like a fish, smoke like a chimney and root like a rabbit,' she wrote. 'I did not get away with it, any of it.' The gist was that her cancer resulted from failing to meet Esoteric standards of behaviour. 'Is it possible that the way I have lived has led to this?' she asked.[66]

Lifestyle factors are known to contribute to disease, but UM, with no scientific evidence, cast innocuous and sometimes healthy behaviours as carcinogenic. The group's cancer bloggers spouted Benhayon's gospel that the disease put 'a big stop' to their waywardness.[67] Instead of decent therapy, they got Serged.

Judith died in June 2014 leaving Sarah feeling conflicted. It gave her some comfort that her mother was not discouraged from conventional medical treatment, and that UM provided a support network and helped Judith overcome her fear of death. 'But that doesn't mean I don't think their ideas are crazy and potentially dangerous,' she said. And Sarah had another reason to feel uneasy.

> Mum left quite a lot of money to Serge Benhayon personally, and my brother and I are probably going to contest the will... I think that if she had been well she would have eventually seen through their bullshit...
>
> Serryn O'Regan is the executor of the will, so Unimed students were very much involved in its production...

I didn't ask for details of the estate, but offered to provide any information that might help the siblings' legal bid. When their case went to trial, I learned that Sarah was financially supporting her partner who has a disability. Her brother, a building maintenance worker, was on a smaller income again, and had two children to support. They couldn't fund the litigation and relied on 'no-win no-fee' lawyers. Six months before she died,

Judith's estate was valued at over two million dollars. She left the bulk of it to multimillionaire Serge.

lv Retreat

Perhaps UM's FACTS site was intended to deter me from exposing the corporation's expansion drive; a proliferation of new front organisations, websites, and recruitment events from mid 2014. Suddenly, carefully styled images of the Benhayons, including colour coordinated family portraits, were posted in every corner of the internet, including new photos of Serge, attempting to make him look clean-cut.

UM's unpaid workforce was key to Benhayon's commercial success, growing from the snooty troupe of workshop assistants to legions of helpers cleaning and maintaining his properties and Esoteric practitioners who introduced friends and clients to his workshop mouse wheel. From 2012, UM's publicity warriors, including Search Engine Optimisation professionals, were marshalled to hit back at news media and to keep the firm's propaganda ranking at the top of Google searches. The love-blogs and the sprawling Unimed Living website would become gargantuan Benhayon promoting content mills, powered and funded by hundreds of volunteers.

The firm's 'Expression Program' was part of the effort: a monitored quota of Unimed sites to visit, comments to contribute, and links to share on social media. Supervisor Simone Benhayon stipulated a minimum of five blog comments per day and accused under-performers of holding back humanity's 'evolution'. Where other enterprises use social media bots to promote their agendas, UM used automated human beings.

Its proselytisers also infiltrated any sector of the Astral plane that might advantage the organisation. Some ran for local government seats in

Australia and the UK, with Samantha Chater-England winning a council seat in Norfolk. Others attempted to lift their profiles by authoring articles for mainstream publications, and submissions to government inquiries, or by joining community and professional groups. Universal Medicine's Chief Financial Officer, Deborah Benhayon, was one of a number who sought executive positions on local chambers of commerce, including in Byron Bay, Ballina, Lismore, and Frome. Deborah became a board member of the Lismore Chamber of Commerce and Industry, and its chairperson from 2015, and for four years running, Universal Medicine won the Chamber's 'People's Choice' Business Award, decided by an online 'popular vote', wide-open for exploitation by organised mobs. Deborah's uninspiring immediate family also took out awards in various categories.

It was all about lifting the Benhayons' profiles and diverting cash their way. UM's customers weren't just pressured into repeat consumption, they were hassled into reducing the Benhayons' business overheads, persuaded their monetary gifts and unpaid labour expressed their love of God. Business connections with the wider community, meanwhile, helped the corporation look legitimate, and Benhayon's Brides could also be found wherever there was money to be made from the vulnerable, inserting themselves into government schemes providing services to disadvantaged groups like First Nations and disabled people, to milk their funding. The College of Universal Medicine and the Sound Foundation Community Care ran courses training carers and sent visitors into Aged Care facilities, pursuing the lonely and infirm.

I tried to alert the media, but Serge's minders had sent legal threats to everyone who reported on them, and some journalists had to answer complaints UM made to the Press Council. All I could do to alert the public was send out notifications, blog and tweet.

Esoteric Women's Health joined the offensive, and Natalie appeared as cover girl of *Women in Livingness* magazine, where she was credited as a 'business woman' and its editor in chief. Still looking young for her age, she wore a lot of makeup and a big hairstyle, and dressed the way a woman in her early twenties dresses when most of her friends are middle-aged or older; lamb dressed as mutton dressed as lamb, in loud prints, mucky colours and pushing the elastane to its limits. Her vanity magazine was another project from the Eso-sweatshop, filled with glossy photos of the group's women caught in the act of self-loving, staring into mirrors and cradling mugs of herbal tea, and eighteen of its twenty-five articles focused on breasts, including one titled, 'Breasts - how do we really feel about them?'

Around the time of Judith McIntyre's death, Esoteric Womens Health escalated its targeting of breast and gynaecological cancer patients. Mindful of the laws restricting claims about cancer treatments or cures, the front offered 'self-care' presentations to support groups instead. A Northern Rivers group member who'd had a double mastectomy, tipped me off about its 'Breast Cancer Care Retreat' to be held at Lismore City Hall, offering 'gentle, nurturing hands on healing by accredited female practitioners'. She was horrified at UM's intrusion, but wary of raising objections, so as tactfully as I could, I sent a notification to the group's convenors and the national management of the non-profit that oversaw it, including images, and asked that they consider whether dealings with UM were in the best interests of members.

The retreat flyer's blurb about helping women 'get to know their bodies as the accurate marker of truth they are' came directly from Benhayon's teachings, without disclosure of his nihilistic extremes.

> If we have disease, then there has to be an energy that caused that disease. So, what has occurred? What have I done? What have I been involved in, what emotions do I allow, how do I walk, sit speak and interact with everybody from an energetic point of view that allows some form of energy to enter that is not good for me to come into my body and create what we call a cancerous cell or a cancerous tumour?[68]

I included that quote and others in my notification, which circulated to some support group members. The national managers backed me, stressing that the groups should provide a safe and supportive environment for all, but the convenors ignored us. Some were offended at my intervention and one member wrote in an email to the convenors that we all have a free will and if we are not comfortable with something we should just say 'no thanks', and gracefully back away, everyone should try to be open to other ideas... I had never had a massage, meditated or tried yoga before either, but with your careful planning and thoughtfulness I can now say I have tried those three experiences and what I think of them is now my business.

The response led me to question whether there was a flaw in the way I was communicating the risks of UM's infiltrations. I didn't know how to make them clearer without insulting recipients' intelligence. It was not a matter of trying a harmless wellbeing practice. The women were targets of an organised deception, a predatory multimillion-dollar scam in which venal fanatics were hawking notions that cancer patients deserve their disease, and 'death is a healing' — because one damaged bloke said they didn't walk, sit, speak, and interact right.

lvi Sirius

August 2014, Jane Hansen reported on a HCCC complaint about an unidentified doctor who worked at the Universal Medicine clinic in Goonellabah. A fifty-five year old patient from Ballina, Rosie*, had been under his care for two years and claimed she was misdiagnosed, wrongly prescribed chemotherapy drugs and told she needed a lung transplant. The specialist charged her thirty-five thousand dollars and also referred her for Esoteric treatments, including Chakra-puncture for 'chemo-washing', a bogus Serge-contrived detox. The doctor wrote in medical progress notes that the number one option for Rosie's treatment was to 'Fly [her] to Sirius (star 6.32 light years away)'.[69]

Rosie contacted me to ask if I knew the significance of Sirius in UM beliefs. The medico was Dr Sam Kim, and he'd signed the notes with a hand-drawn smiley face. According to space-cadet Sergio, the star is 'our next plane of life', a destination for the ascended soul after death.[70]

When Rosie gave the records of the previous drug regime to her new pulmonary specialist, he lifted his eyes from the papers and stared at her for a long time without saying anything. He went on to treat her successfully for bronchiectasis, a benign condition that did not warrant chemotherapy, and certainly not a prolonged course, nor a lung transplant. All she'd needed was some standard anti-inflammatory medication.

It was not mentioned in the report, but Dr Kim had discouraged her from seeing her GP, and took over her general care, prescribing medications unrelated to her lung condition. He also failed to refer her to an appropriate specialist for a painful orthopaedic condition that needed surgery, sending her to Neil Ringe for useless Chakra-puncture, and to his wife Jasna for an Esoteric massage. Rosie refused his referral to Serge. She'd had enough.

Jane's article quoted Professor Dwyer, who was due to appear before the parliamentary inquiry into the effectiveness of the Health Care Complaints Commission. The professor's input ensured that UM was mentioned in the Committee's report as one of the organisations advertising misleading health information or providing potentially unsafe procedures. The Committee acknowledged that Unimed's treatments lacked any sound basis, and that none of the courses and qualifications offered to practitioners were legitimately accredited.[71]

Professor Dwyer brought up my complaints at the hearing, and the HCCC's response that the doctors were just expressing their opinions when endorsing UM:

> despite the fact that the code of practice for doctors makes it perfectly clear that you can only refer someone in good conscience if you know the clinical competence of the people you are referring to and that that clinical competence would be accepted by the vast majority of your peers…To me, it is a classic example of the fact that the HCCC is crippled by a lack of capacity to act. You would have thought that a prohibition order would have gone out immediately saying, 'Cease and desist. You cannot continue

to do this to the public. If you continue to do that we will prosecute you'. But no.

The Chairman asked if the HCCC legislation should be amended to rectify it. 'Absolutely,' the Professor replied.[72]

lvii Girl to Woman

Next, Universal Medicine went after kids. The lead organiser of the initiatives was UM FACTS Team member and recruitment dogsbody, Sarah Broome. She and web-designer, Rebecca Baldwin, were Serge's go-to propaganda managers, founding, with Sarah's journalist husband, Hamish Broome, UM's disinformation front, Real Media Real Change, to combat negative press.

Sarah ran two cyber-bullying conferences in Lismore for UM, attended by school teachers and pupils. The College of Universal Medicine 'Combatting Cyber-bullying' forum took place a month after the UM FACTS website was launched, with Natalie Benhayon, UM psychologists, Marianna Masiorski and Caroline Raphael, and the firm's most libellous FACTS bod, Alison Greig, as keynote speakers. Simone Benhayon, with helpers including Serge-worshipping film director, Otto Bathurst, also launched an anti-cyber-bullying front 'All Rise Say No' to run presentations in UK schools.

Sarah Broome and Michael Benhayon then launched 'Teachers are Gold', a front pitching Wellness Days and self-care workshops to educators, and Curtis Benhayon, promoted his 'True Movement' programme to schools. UM's occult zumba was based on his father's demonising of non-Esoteric dance and exercise, and designed to release 'pockets of prana' from the body[73], but its publicity didn't disclose its origins, and its website featured a photograph of a group of school children in uniform at Tytherington's

Sound Training Centre who'd attended Simone Benhayon's swim classes, but had nothing to do with the cult's lurching aerobics.

All I could do was blog warnings and send notifications to school principals and the New South Wales Education Department. The group's threat to kids remained a primary motivator long after I'd grown thoroughly sick of the whole stoush. Benhayon's juvenile sleepovers were a serious concern and I'd been hearing reports of UM children crying from hunger and requiring therapy for anxiety about spirits coming to get them at night.

Devotee parents, meanwhile, engaged in ugly Family Court clashes with their exes. In England, a father, Graham*, concerned about his underweight and unusually tired little daughter, Lara*, sought court orders to protect her from UM. His relationship with the mother, Fran* had broken up amicably, and he doesn't know when she joined the group, but she became increasingly uncommunicative, making it difficult for the father to maintain regular contact with their toddler. He realised something was really wrong when Fran asked him to pick Lara up from an Esoteric healing clinic while she attended an appointment, and he arrived to find his child in distress, sitting on the floor bawling as her mother and the practitioner stood nearby staring vacantly at her. Neither woman made an attempt to comfort her. When Graham went on to raise concerns about UM's influence, Fran contacted social services to allege that he was sexually abusing the girl. A five month investigation found no evidence for the accusation.

Graham and his mother Leonie contacted me for help in gathering materials to demonstrate the group's risk. My sites provided the only useful information on UM that they could find, and enabled them to understand the cause of Lara's stress. She'd wanted to know what colour apples go into apple juice, for example; and Graham discovered that red apples are pranic. She told him that if he were to have an accident, it would be his choice — a belief that came directly from Benhayon. One day, Lara tearfully told her father he would die from a heart attack because he was not love. 'You're not love, Daddy,' she said. 'Serge is love.'

September 2014, the bankruptcy regulator notified Lance that it would not act on his complaint because an investigation of events of over sixteen years earlier was not a good use of its resources. The Office of Fair Trading didn't act on my complaint of misleading advertising, either, because it only had powers to act on complaints from consumers who'd paid for the services in question. The charity fundraising licensing office also let us know that they didn't have the authority to address issues we'd raised, prompting College of UM director, Charles Wilson, to put out public statements labelling Lance and me vexatious complainants, and falsely claiming that no authorities had taken action on any of our complaints.

In fact, the licensing officer told us he'd communicated with the Charities Commission, and although he was given limited information, I'd had a significant win. The ACNC had examined the College's proposal to lease the Wollongbar Hall of Ageless Wisdom from its owner and identified a potential for Benhayon to unlawfully profit from the charity. Consequently, the authority imposed lease conditions to safeguard the charity's public assets, the tax-deductible funds it collected. SergeCorp abandoned the lease proposal, and sure enough, Benhayon quit running events with the College. From then on, its courses dwindled to short 'wellbeing and self-care' presentations and the 'The Lineage of the Ageless Wisdom' course taught by Professor Bill Foley. We'd have preferred that the charity was deregistered, but I'd managed to halt the majority of its intended operations. The ACNC's policy left me open to defamation, however, because they would not publish official confirmation.

By then, illness and time away from work had hastened the demise of my acupuncture practice. I wasn't losing money, but I wasn't making it either, and I decided it was the right time to get out of Brisbane and move to Byron Shire, near the ocean, where I'd long wanted to live. I hoped to spend more time in nature with the whales and dolphins, and improve my health, but UM's aggression never slept. Days before I moved, Rosie told me about the launch of another event run by Esoteric Women's Health and Real Media Real Change. The Girl to Woman Festival was scheduled for January 2015 at the Lennox Head Community Centre and its publicity promised a programme of presentations aimed at kids: workshops and panels on 'self-confidence, body image, relationships, sexual health, healthy use of social media, cyber-bullying, eating disorders and self harm'; areas in which UM's presenters were peerless exemplars, for all the wrong reasons. Natalie Benhayon was mistress of ceremonies and a 'True Beauty tent' was slated, offering 'personal beauty sessions for under 18s'.

So it continued, with me chasing down one advance after another, the cult's callow enablers — not-for-profit welfare organisations, local media outlets, school officials and the like — moving sluggishly, if at all, against the threat. To be fair, some proactive community leaders copped legal threats or other forms of harassment, cultists phoning, emailing and otherwise bailing them up and whingeing about criminal trolls, but it should not have been so difficult to expel a commercial quackery corporation from community welfare services and public institutions.

I had to push for months to get Esoteric Women's Health thrown out of Lismore Women's Health and the Queen Victoria Women's Centre in Melbourne, for example. I was never permitted to see UM's responses to my notifications, but was told that EWH sent their codes of conduct and training manuals, an 'analysis' of the workshop manual photos (probably provided by one of the medical sycophants), and statutory declarations from clients as to the amazingness of its invasive services. Although the letters were probably signed by lawyer Serryn O'Regan, the Deeper Femaleness images alone should have ended all associations. I only succeeded after escalating letters to the organisations' boards, imploring members to examine the photos, the maniacally excessive FACTS site attacks, and the misogynistic tenets that 'inspired' the firm.

It would have been smart to quit Chinese Medicine and find another way to earn a living, but I staggered into Byron Bay in September 2014 and half-heartedly started a new practice. Within days, UM FACTS had updated all their publicity to read, 'Esther Rockett, acupuncturist Byron Bay'.

The following month, I got a call from the Lismore Police detective who'd taken my statement about the ovarian reading two years earlier. He invited me to the station to give a more detailed one. Police prosecutors were considering charging Serge with indecent assault.

lviii Crescendo

Matthew Richardson won our argument outright and Justice McCallum dismissed Benhayon's application to strike out my contextual truth defence. She stated in her ruling that my blog, 'Universal Medicine's sexual abuse apologism hits a crescendo':

> makes serious accusations against Mr Benhayon and Universal Medicine, backed by cogent (if at times extravagantly expressed) argument…
>
> It is plainly intended to be understood [as] part of a vigorous, determined campaign.

She described part of the dispute:

> A later passage in the blog, headed "Esoteric Anatomy", includes photographs from a Universal Medicine "workshop manual" which Ms Rockett says she has blogged previously. The context suggests that her posting of those photographs prompted an exchange with proponents of Universal Medicine as to what they depict. In the blog, Ms Rockett records (and then responds to) comments seeking to discredit her claims…

Those tilts at discrediting me were a three blog series Alison Greig authored on UM FACTS in October and November 2014. The firm chose to publicly acknowledge the workshop manual images, for the first time, via a barrage of distortions, and Alison began with an article, 'Esther Rockett Byron Bay Acupuncturist engineering fear: from brainwashing to false child abuse claims — Part 1 — Sexual abuse', and part two, 'Lies about sexual abuse and incest'.

If you look at the pictures relied upon you might imagine Esther Rockett is playing pin the tail on the donkey with her awareness of anatomy. The hands depicted are nowhere near a woman's vulva or anus and are not in contact with the breasts.

This is all fabrication. There has never been and is no touching of genitals. Ms Rockett's reference to touching the client's genitals in the photograph is anatomically false and is evidently not the case on any consideration of the image shown.

In my crescendo blog, I described Greig's series as a 'gift to our exposure' and used screenshots of UM FACTS' falsehoods to highlight the Esoterics' hypocrisy in their outraged blogging about the Catholic Church's cover-up of sexual abuse. The same Brotherhood that whined for years about how terrible it was when the Church's victims were not believed, publicly savaged those who poked their pranic pate above the parapet to complain about UM, including Rosie, while claiming the group had 'no victims'.

'Rolf Harris had no victims either. Until two years ago,' I replied.

My screenshots showed comments on Greig's article by Dr Maxine Szramka, German physiotherapist Kerstin Salzer and Brisbane acupuncturist Rebecca Poole alleging that my acupuncture practice involved needling the parts of the anatomy that were copping Serge's hands. Salzer wrote: 'A practitioner who doesn't know where the vulva, the anus or the breasts are is certainly not reliable concerning the healing practice that she claims to offer to do.'

The screenshot captured my reply 'awaiting approval' before the Esoteric goon squad made it disappear.

Hi Rebecca Poole, Dr Maxine Szramka and the rest of you lot…

…if Serge doesn't have his hand on that woman's vulva or that young girl's anus, um, where is it?

We've all been trained in anatomy… tell us precisely where his hand is.

Next, I don't know where you trained, Rebecca, but in nearly twenty years of practice I've never needled anyone's anus, and nor have I needled anyone's vulva.

Like most acupuncturists I had worked on muscle strains in the groin and hip.

> Either way that puts me working decently lateral to where Serge's unqualified hands are in those photos above. AND in all cases I was working on local injury or pain — I wasn't an unqualified, ex bankrupt, self-styled messiah pressing at erogenous zones for extended periods and calling it a 'healing' for sexual abuse or *sadness*.

To Rebecca Poole's claim that Serge's Deeper Femaleness 'is far less invasive than the equivalent acupuncture technique,' I replied, 'There is no "equivalent" acupuncture technique, Rebecca.'

Greig's publication of high resolution originals of a selection of manual photos was of great assistance, though, in clarifying the inappropriateness. She did not post all the images I'd taken issue with, or the accompanying text and its claims regarding 'rape recovery' and gynaecological disorders, so I posted some she'd omitted. Justice McCallum described them in detail in her ruling:

> In one, a man is shown placing his hands above and below a (clothed) female's breast with the following explanation:
>
> *8 to 10 years*
>
> *This is the period of a new world when the child explores its new perceptions. Look for hard or sensitive reactions. Feel the emotional experience.*
>
> A second photograph (apparently of the same male and female) shows the man's hands closing in on the breast; one is directly on it and one is directly above it. The explanation:
>
> *13 to 18 years*
>
> *In this period the teenager will live according to what was successful in their 8 to 12 year bracket. This may be obscure and vary far from who they really are. First developments of angst are experienced.*

The woman in the photos was in her thirties, but others featured a much younger woman, who looked about thirteen.

> *Two further photographs appear under the heading "transmuting sadness", depicting a male pressing his right hand firmly against the lower bottom of a female lying face-down on a table (clothed). The photograph carries the following explanation:*

The sacrum is the storehouse of sadness from the heart. The practitioner applies this hand technique to help release the sadness back up into the heart...[74]

When I initially blogged copies in 2013, I'd misidentified the younger model as Natalie. Lance and Matt thought it was her, and the cult castigated me for the mistake, so I included an apology, but added,

> if it isn't Natalie, who is it? How old was that young girl when the photo was taken? And whatever her age, why is it necessary to press a hand to someone's anus to *transmute sadness*? How does that work, Dr Szramka? Eunice Minford? Why is it necessary for Serge Benhayon and his legion of unqualified 'healers' to touch erogenous zones at all?

Alison's blog also placed a testimonial from a seventeen year old girl, including her name and photo, between two headings; 'Lies about sexual abuse and incest' and 'Creating a Moral Panic'. It read, 'Staying with the Benhayons was an amazing opportunity for me to see and feel what a true family is...' A footnote stated that it was published with the girl and her parents' consent, leading me to remark that the parents were major investors in the Benhayon scam. They'd dragged their whole family into it.

UK child protection worker, Ariana Ray, was also quoted:

> 'To professionally consider the online behaviour indices and sexualising language used by Esther Rockett and Lance ... would place them in a high risk category in relation to children.'

Yellow-eyed psychologist, Brendan Mooney, was among those who waded into the comments:

> Yes the fury and jealousy by Lance and Esther is obvious, and they might as well pack up shop and go home as Love has come to town!

Part three of Greig's series, '...More lies of paedophilia and grooming,' featured further photographs and testimonials from UM's teens, prompting an update to my blog.

> The testimonial of the 17 year old mentioned above has been expanded to admit she has lived at Serge's house, which begs the question, how many young girls have lived under the roof of this sleazebag guru?

The youngster had added to her statement:

To have 'Serge Benhayon accused of a grooming process for sexual abuse' does not make sense. As a young woman that has stayed with Serge and his family, and experienced living with them I can say with authority that this statement is completely false.

'Because seventeen year old girls are now authorities on predatory grooming in Ariana Ray's unprofessional opinion', was my response.

No UM FACTS post was complete without Anna taking a swipe at Lance:

> A bit further down the page a woman about to undertake family court proceedings publicly trashes her husband. Again.
>
> That's 'Ageless Wisdom' in action.
>
> For the love of Serge.

The whole farce left us with no doubts about the organisation's integrity.

> Does anyone who hasn't subscribed to Benhayon's occult philosophy, death and bequest drive, now feel comfortable with the cult's targeting of the women's health market, cancer patients and schools? It also casts a grim light on UM's upcoming Girl to Woman Project Festival, again where the cult is using girls as young as eight to publicise their predatory grooming.
>
> Followers describe Unimed as the One True Religion, and while the Catholic church presided over a history of appalling abuse, denial and denigration of victims, the church never mounted a campaign encouraging adherents to publicly slur and defame complainants whilst refusing to engage in public discussion.
>
> Only cults do that.
>
> The Universal Medicine cult takes that vile behaviour several steps further with bizarre excuses for inexcusable behaviour and by marketing that mess as 'Medicine', 'Truth' and 'Love'.

Benhayon filed his defamation claim in November 2015, a full year after I'd published the crescendo post. Richardson and I walked out of court in May 2016 confident. His victory allowed me to bring damaging evidence to prove the contextual imputations that Serge was a dishonest, exploitative charlatan. Alison Greig, Charles Wilson, Serge and Miranda would not look at me as they slunk out of court, but Matthew was upbeat, still voicing disgust at Benhayon's utterances.

'Do you think he'll go through with this?' he asked before we parted.

'Yes,' I answered firmly.

It wasn't that I was certain — it's impossible to second-guess a maniac. Supporters were laying bets that Serge would balk. Lance had his money on him folding on the first day of the trial. I'd answered with the attitude I needed to take on a cashed-up blowhard and his deluded backers. I had to be prepared to go all the way. 'I'm fighting to win,' I added.

The barrister gave a cheerless laugh, and with a squint and shake of his head, he said, 'Why did you have to mention Rolf Harris?' He hurried away.

lix 3(a)

'You can defame someone all right. You can say quite awful things about someone if you've got a defence.' Tom was giving his opening address after seven days of Benhayon and his witnesses' evidence. 'I and Ms Goodchild are saying, for various reasons, Ms Rockett has not defamed Mr Benhayon in a way that results in any liability. We say she's got a defence.'

The court transcripts reveal my stumbles, stammers and half-formed sentences, but Tom's words read like fine prose. Smark too spoke precisely, but Tom was more fluent and succinct. He'd been a television journalist before practising law, and went on to found and host the ABC Radio programme, 'The Law Report', where one of his aims was to make complex legal principles easier for laypeople to understand.[75]

Benhayon had pleaded that sixty-two defamatory imputations were carried by my blog and tweets. Under Australian law, the defamatory meanings within a publication are defined by the plaintiff, and those meanings might not be what was stated or intended. Tom explained that the court's first task after all the evidence was heard and the lawyers had made their arguments was 'to decide if that's right, that is, if an ordinary reader would understand each of these publications as saying those things,' and that the court would hear some dispute about whether imputations were conveyed. 'You would understand it would be quite unfair if a plaintiff could get an article and say, "that's saying this about me" but the plaintiff has given it a bit of a tweak up to something a little bit more serious than what was actually said. It would be unfair to hold the defendant responsible for something more or worse.'

The first defamatory imputation in Benhayon's statement of claim was '3(a) Serge Benhayon had intentionally indecently touched his client Esther Rockett during a consultation in his treatment room.' That's not what I wrote in the crescendo blog, but I had to defend it. Smark's job was to convince the court that the meaning was carried, that I'd intended to convey that meaning, and that I'd set out to falsely accuse Benhayon of indecently assaulting me. I'd mentioned being preyed upon and that he'd given me a 'sleazy ovarian reading', but had not characterised it as touching. I doubted the court would find it was carried, but my lawyers were more concerned. If Smark succeeded and was able to twist it his client's way, we presumed my case would be lost.

'Do you really say that you did not intend to communicate the meaning, the message, the allegation that Mr Benhayon had intentionally indecently touched you, his client, during a consultation in his treatment room?' asked Smark.

'I did not intend it.'

'Do you accept, looking now at the first matter complained of, that was a meaning which was reasonably open to people to derive from it, including by reference to those passages I've taken you to?'

'No.'

'I suggest to you that your position in relation to that is unreasonable, what do you say to that?'

'I'd say you haven't read the blog properly.'

'I suggest to you that you must have at least foreseen, when you wrote these matters, that there was a real chance that people reading it, ordinary people who read the whole thing, would understand it in the way that I am putting to you, that is, in substantially the meaning contained in imputation 3(a), what do you say to that?'

'No.'

'You say there's no chance of that?'

'I reject it, that would be a misreading.'

'Do you accept that you used colourful language in this blog?'

'Certainly.'

'Do you accept that you made a range of allegations against Mr Benhayon?'

'Yes.'

'I'm suggesting to you that you accept that the colourful language that you used and the strength and number of the allegations you included in relation to Mr Benhayon in this blog was part of the context in which ordinary people reading the blog would have understood what it was you were saying had happened between you and Mr Benhayon in his treatment room, do you agree with that?'

'But you haven't...' I stopped, remembering Louise's advice. The blog was about UM's denial of the inappropriate touching in the workshop manual images — and the organisation's fitness to run activities for kids and the debilitated. The blog article was already in evidence and we'd read through it for the court. There was no need to elaborate. 'No, I don't agree with that.'

lx The big adventure

> A lot of cancer people go, 'but I know a lot of people that deserve it more than I do.' Fact. They say that in private session. 'But I know so and so, and you know, I've been good, and I got cancer.'
>
> Sorry madam, you've been good, or sir, but you've also been extremely loveless.
>
> And this is the blessing.
>
> Serge Benhayon[76]

Benhayon's money trail was as meandering and obscure as the dark digs of the Four Lords of Form, and all I had to trace it was publicly available real estate records. That's where I recognised a surname among the previous owners of one of Benhayon's titles. Early 2011, Serge acquired a half-share of a residential property in Goonellabah, formerly owned by deceased cancer patient, Rita. The transaction seemed to explain why he singled her out for beatification at her pre-mortem memorial in 2010 and offered her reincarnation as Michael and Emmalee's child; her assets in exchange for an Esoteric rebirth into the Benhayon hierarchy.

The maestro shopped his cancer doctrines more boldly after Rita died. Judith McIntyre became his client around the time he took possession of Rita's half of her home, and we may never know how many followers have bequeathed him major assets. I've sighted a will prepared by Paula Fletcher of Universal Law in which a devotee leaves her entire estate to Serge and Natalie, and many relatives of cultists suspect their loved one has done the same. Student notes reported that Benhayon was moving to establish a trust to receive such gifts as early as 2008. His commerce in deceit was therefore never limited to quackery claims and selling shonky practitioner accreditations. It incorporated a comprehensive structure of undue influence — a horde of love-bombers and useful professionals helping him harvest bequests.

Judith's exploitation didn't end with her life either. In reply to Sarah and Seth McIntyre's legal challenge, Team Benhayon tendered a video testimonial, which UM's publicity team filmed on her deathbed as evidence that she was of sound mind when she made her final will. In it, Judith sits up, wasted and breathless, full of praise for her favoured beneficiary. 'I've learned a great deal about how disease is actually a form of healing… And this time because of the understanding I had that I had created the disease — all my self-neglect, my choices — and I had time to work with the teachings of Universal Medicine, to really — I just changed everything in my life, everything…

'Not too long later, this is April, I got the third diagnosis. It had spread to organs, and I've got very little time,' said sixty-six year old Judith. 'The truth is I feel excited.' She gave a girlish laugh. 'I've gone from terror to lovely acceptance. To, okay, now's the big adventure.'[77]

lxi Nemeses

'Why call me now?' I thought before I gave my statement to the detective. During the interview, he must have told me three times to pass his contact details to anyone who came to me with allegations about Benhayon, even if they didn't want to formalise a complaint. I knew I wasn't the only one, but I also knew the detective wouldn't tell me if he'd become aware of other incidents.

Whatever was happening, UM were determined to keep pressure on me. The FACTS posse had already published a dozen or so articles vilifying me, but in November 2014, soon after I published the crescendo blog, they launched a website dedicated to trashing my livelihood. Désirée Delaloye purchased the domain acupuncturebyronbay.com, and its home page read:

> Byron Bay Locals Be Warned — Esther Rockett Is A Cyber-Bully Who Also Practises Acupuncture
>
> Esther Rockett has engaged in religious discrimination that at its root is no different to a witch hunt of past times and is unacceptable in our fair and accepting Byron community...
>
> We are exposing Esther Rockett who is bringing her particular brand of divisiveness, lies and hatred to the Byron Shire.

Its ten pages lambasted me, my practice, and my professional skills — as if UM wanted to end my career more than I did. 'Our' Byron community was curious, seeing only a handful of its thirty-six signatories lived there. The majority, including Désirée, Alison, and Rebecca Baldwin, lived sixty kilometres away in Goonellabah, and the site made no disclosure of their common connection to UM.

But if their goal was to deter me from publishing about the Girl to Woman Festival, it didn't work. I blogged the organisers' links to the Esoteric Breast Massage cult and its instigator, but it didn't come to much. Local media was impervious to my complaints. 'We've been told it's a child welfare initiative,' said a radio station manager I phoned, who refused to say whether she'd read the notification I'd sent. She added that the station would treat UM like any other 'Christian group', and stopped listening after that.

Determined to enjoy the area, I got outdoors more. Matt Sutherland lived a few kilometres away and became my regular walking and whingeing partner. Lance lived half an hour away and was a reliable coffee date. I joined local friends for Chinese Medicine study sessions, but underneath everything I was dejected. I tried to bust out of the rut by keeping Pranic Princess active in my blogs. UM's hypersensitivity to pseudonyms and alter egos remained good for some entertainment.

> It's been a hectic few weeks in the bunker. Princess has been organising her inaugural French pastry and erotic film festival for months now, and just days out she realised she'd forgotten to make the films.
>
> They took longer than expected, partly because it was more fun than we thought it would be, and partly due to lack of talent.

Anyway, knowing Princess we'll probably have to make the pastries too.

But it wasn't enough to lift my mood. The more UM attacked us, the more they proved me right. The cult could no longer hide what it was. But what was I? I wanted to be healthier, but had shackled myself to a group that was everything I despised, and a fight that was immeasurably more strenuous than it should have been. That began a discussion with my new psychotherapist, Hayes. I could psychoanalyse the cult readily enough, but wasn't so sharp about my own drives. He recommended I back off and move on. 'You've done enough.'

'But they're preying on more people, getting more aggressive…'

'There are hundreds of these groups in Australia,' he said. 'You won't beat them. If it's not UM, it'll be some other crowd.'

'I have dirt on this one though.'

'Where is it getting you?'

We were sitting in a pagoda in Hayes' serpentine garden, a pond bubbling nearby. He suggested that I make my wellbeing a priority; make more 'self-loving choices' I suppose, and brought up my protracted history of working for nothing. The more I worked, the less I earned. He didn't laugh when I quipped that I was the most underpaid workaholic I knew.

'The problem with being their nemesis,' I said, 'is that they're so focused on the enemy it distracts them from examining their own faults. But am I doing the same thing?' The question was often on my mind. 'What am I projecting?'

lxii Upside down

Serge said that the toilet chorus told him to 'think with your heart, feel with your heart', and that the phantoms returned ten days later to ask what he'd learned. He answered that his heart was telling him the opposite to his head, that 'the world's upside down. Everything is back to front. We've been robbed, we've been stolen. Everything is wrong. Everything we've been told is not right. We've been lied to.'

UM's love-bloggers didn't twig that he was spelling out the subversions that he was inflicting on them. They kept churning out their upside down oeuvre, including the testimonial, 'My first Esoteric Breast Massage: Unveiling the Hidden Harm of Pornography', on the *Women in Livingness* site.

Despite their lack of qualifications, EBM practitioners took detailed gynaecological and reproductive histories from clients,[78] and the blogger's first session commenced with a discussion of her polycystic ovaries.

> [Practitioner, Mary-Louise Myers] tenderly moved the towel, which was covering my chest, to one side to expose my right breast. I was still feeling wonderfully relaxed. As she delicately placed massage cream around my breast, I felt at ease. I was doing well. I felt wholly supported and respected. The love in the room was palpable.
>
> The massage was slow and gentle and moved in lovely big anti clockwise circles around my breast. This continued for a few moments and then I started to feel something change. I felt a little uneasy. My body contracted and, like a clam, it swiftly shut.

Mary-Louise halted the procedure but continued her probing, asking the client if she'd ever been sexually abused. 'No Way!' the blogger responded. 'My idea of "sexual abuse" is being interfered with against one's will. I couldn't recall this ever happening to me.'

With further verbal massage she disclosed that she'd come across her father's 'porn stash' as an adolescent, and was speedily convinced that it 'marked a long journey into self-abuse'. She confessed that as an adult she

> went to parties, drank, and flirted. I told men I liked porn, and this got their attention: they thought it was really sexy, and I loved it...
>
> Little did I realise, I was deeply caught in an undercurrent of loveless-ness that I had come to accept as normal.
>
> ...but my session today has made me question the nature of sexual abuse. I now realise that it isn't just abuse in the literal sense, but can be something

that occurs energetically between a father and daughter or between partners, or in the way I treat my SELF.

The blog's publishers were the crowd that broadcast apologia for Benhayon's Deeper Femaleness and accused me of making false allegations of sexual abuse.

The author hoped

> to bring awareness to women that sexual abuse doesn't just mean being touched in an unsavory or aggressive way against your will. I never realised that what I was doing and whom I was sleeping with, was harming me. I CHOSE to do it. I ENJOYED it.[79]

That was the story fed to her when she resisted having her breasts rubbed by a mercenary busybody — that discovering porn that had been hidden from her was 'sexual abuse', as was consensual sex, as an adult, that she'd enjoyed. For aeons, societies and religions have been shaming women's sexual pleasure, but pathologising it was a brave new extreme. Unimed's sales-Brides made her believe, with zero scientific basis, that sex causes gynaecological disease, and charged her for phoney healing services that in themselves were molestation.

lxiii Fishing

I couldn't convince Matthew Richardson to plead truth to imputation, 3(a), that Benhayon had intentionally indecently touched me, but Tom saw it my way and amended the pleading, adding it to the dozens of allegations I needed to prove. It would be my word against Serge's and I'd spend five days in the witness box: four under Tom's questioning, and another under cross-examination.

'When you went to see Mr Benhayon in 2005,' said Smark, 'you had a conversation with him about feeling low in energy or down or tired or something like that?'

'It's possible. I was, yeah, still tired from the last year, that's why I took a holiday again in February .'

'It's fair to say you don't have a very clear recollection of this session?'

'Not anymore.'

The public gallery, three long rows of taupe upholstered chairs squashed together, was about a metre from the bar table, with no barrier between spectators and barristers. The Benhayons took up a bloc behind the plaintiff; his four children, Deborah with Clayton Lloyd, and Miranda with her minders, the Johnstons, a wealthy elderly couple. Like a grim pair of bookends, Josephine Johnston and Miranda sat with knees crossed, chins up, and lips puckered into what my father used to call a cat's arse.

From day one, Serryn O'Regan squatted in the seat behind mine, while one of Benhayon's wealthy donors, Nicola Lessing, took the seat behind Tom. Otherwise, only a small propaganda crew of Alison Greig, Rebecca Baldwin, and Sarah Broome's journalist husband Hamish, attended Tom's examination of the plaintiff's witnesses. Sitting apart initially, perhaps to avoid looking cultish, they kept their laptops open, scraping for material to diminish me and deify Serge.

'He said he would do a technique where he would put his hands on your belly or abdomen?'

I'd already given my account of the ovarian reading under Tom's questioning. 'Yes.'

'He put his fingertips on your belly or abdomen as he'd said he was going to do?'

'Yes.'

'You were fully clothed all through the session?'

'Yes.'

When Smark commenced my cross-examination, a stack of UM's faithfull, including the Mystic Dentist and psychologist Caroline Raphael, paraded into court and piled over to the defence side of the room. They surrounded O'Regan, as close to the witness box as they could cram themselves, having waited years for Serge's blue-chip lawyer to finally tear down the troll.

'I suggest to you he didn't say to you he was going to do an ovarian reading.'

'He definitely said he was going to do an ovarian reading. I remember that very distinctly. I don't remember the parts of the session very well apart from the ovarian reading, but that part — I remember it quite well.'

My box seat had a good view of the Sons of God, conspicuously grey-faced, overdressed and testy, Natalie squeezed among them, healing symbols presumably stuffed into handbags and down underpants.

'He asked you whether you'd felt in any way intruded on, whether it was by abuse or something sexual?'

'I don't remember him saying that.'

'He said your body was definitely registering compromise or words to that effect?'

'He may have. I don't remember that.'

'He didn't ask you what had happened about particular ages or at particular ages in your past?'

'He definitely asked that.'

Every question was a potential trap. 'Mr Benhayon during this session told you that you didn't have to comment during the technique where you were lying on your back and he was touching your belly or abdomen, didn't he?'

'He said that. He said I didn't have to comment.'

'You knew you could comment if you wanted to or not comment if you didn't want to?'

'Yes.'

'If we take what you say he said in your evidence-in-chief, he didn't physically do anything that he didn't say he was going to do?'

'Yes.'

'On your version, what happened was he asked you some questions which you didn't agree with him asking you, that's a fair characterisation with what occurred, isn't it?'

'He made statements.'

'I didn't mean to exclude that. Let's go back. On your version he made some statements and then on your version asked you whether you agreed with them or whether he was right, words to that effect?'

'He said, "Am I right?"'

'You understand I'm suggesting to you that that didn't happen and you say it did happen?'

'It did happen.'

'Taking your version, if I can respectfully put it that way, what he was doing as a matter of activity, was he was asking you a question, "Am I right?" That was the activity he was engaging in. He was asking for your comment upon his statements?'

'Yes.'

'We know from what you've said before that you knew you were free to give an answer or not? You were free to comment or not upon his statements, that's right, isn't it?'

'I took it that way.'

'This is something that various places you've called a "fishing exercise", isn't it?'

'Yes.'

'On your version what you took exception to in this session was that, in a context where you'd come to Mr Benhayon for treatment, he was asking you questions which you thought he shouldn't be asking. I'm trying to put this neutrally but tell me if you agree with that?'

'He was making inferences about my relationships with men related to my ovarian function.'

'He was asking you questions about that; seeking your comment on that?'

'It appeared to be that way. After he'd put these statements to me and said, "Am I right?" it appeared that they were, in fact, questions.'

'He was seeking your response, a response you could give or not give?'

'It appears that way, yes.'

'Do you accept that engaging in — and here I'm using a term that you've used — a fishing expedition or a fishing exercise is very far short from intentional indecent touching?'

'The questions themselves are not indecent touching.'

'Take the statements and the questions. That fishing exercise of statements and questions is very far short from an intentional indecent touching, isn't it?'

I answered sharply. 'He had his hands where he said my ovaries were.'

Smark's glare was unmoving. He was terse. 'Can you answer my question or are you not able to answer my question?'

My brow creased into a hard frown. Tom rose to object.

No sooner had he spoken than I heard another voice, from above, to my right, one I'd rarely heard through my evidence. 'Mr Smark,' came the unwavering voice of Justice Lonergan, 'she answered the question.'

lxiv The shadow

Many are fascinated by cults, but few, if any, know how to deal with them. They are our collective shadow — our most primitive, deluded, and antisocial behaviours condensed into mobs — and I declared war on one. The reasons to do it were obvious to me, but why weren't the reasons not to? Why martyr myself to a public fight with a giant adversary?

Hayes and I devised an exercise to explore the question. In psychoanalysis, the characters and scenarios within dreams can be symbolic of interactions between aspects of one's psyche or history. If you dream of a fight with the school bully, for example, it may symbolise a struggle with the petty, domineering parts of your own personality. But Hayes suggested I apply similar analysis to the interactions in my waking life. 'What are you drawing to yourself to see about yourself?' he said.

Identifying my points of conflict with Serge and his nasty Brides was easy — I was against everything they represented. It was more critical to scrutinise what we had in common. I identified martyrdom, nitpicking, and I had wowserish moments, but Pranic Princess was a sincere revolt against that. More of her might have come through in my offline life if her appetites weren't so incompatible with my allergies. Still, the martyr and the prude seemed mere supporting characters to a broader and more insidious maladjustment. 'I'm not like Serge,' I said. 'Or am I?'

Hayes waited, a quizzical lift at the corner of his mouth.

'Do I have a cult leader in me?'

'What does that mean to you?'

'Demanding, power-hungry, an egomaniac… Is that what I'm like? Ego driven? Domineering? Needing people to do what I want?' Scoffing at Benhayon's galaxy-sized ego and control-freakishness was practically recreational, but who did I think I was in taking on a large, wealthy, lawyer-riddled conglomerate? Wasn't that grandiose self-deception?

Hayes smirked. He knew cults. He'd been in one. I didn't ask, but given his age, his loose style of dressing and his bare feet, it plausibly involved a bearded guru, chanting, and nudity.

'Or an inner sycophant?' I wondered. 'Am I looking for some sort of approval?'

I couldn't decide which was more loathsome, but I had to question. 'Is it both?'

Hayes was smiling, enjoying himself. His little terrier, who sometimes joined me on the couch, padded into the garden to dig for bones. A creeping nausea grabbed at my guts — the cult within.

'Ugh,' I groaned.

lxv True Sexy

> Sexuality in cults is almost always monitored or controlled in some way. Pairing off with another means you may care more for that person than for the leader or group mission. So cult leaders develop ways to ensure that allegiance goes to the top, not sideways in pair bonding.
>
> Margaret Singer[80]
>
> Sex = energetic rape.
>
> Serge Benhayon[81]

'This is the problem with cults,' said Matthew Richardson, reverting to doomsaying. 'When put under pressure, they double down.'

After Justice McCallum allowed my contextual truth defence, Benhayon effectively tripled his defamation claim, alleging seventeen tweets I'd published had also damaged his reputation. I could no longer afford the barrister's services, though, and Smith's tenure was also precarious as my funds bottomed out. Richardson thought it spelled the end and suggested that I stop publishing altogether, which was exactly what the cult wanted. 'Some of these imputations are very defamatory!' he said.

'They're true!' I replied.

One of the new imputations, that the plaintiff engaged in bizarre sexual manipulation to make money for his business, was based on my 2015 'Sex and Serge Benhayon' blog, inspired by Natalie Benhayon's improbable 'True Sexy' campaign. The Esoteric version of 'sex sells' had her prancing around UM events in tight red dresses, table-top dancing under a spotlight, thrusting her hips, elbows up, messing her hair; strip club dancing without the strip. Given UM's condemnation of all normal intimacy, down to Serge referring to sex as 'energetic rape', it was difficult for UM's sufferers to stomach.

But it wasn't the Benhayons' first sexy charade. In 2011, Lance agreed to accompany Anna to a UM Couples Workshop in the hope it would help their ailing marriage. It had the opposite effect. He was one of few among hundreds in attendance who did not laugh as Serge lewdly described how women could seduce their partners and give their men 'an erection like they've never had before'. Some devotees had brought their kids.

I'd also written about Benhayon's karma-con, where he claimed sexual abuse left a disease-causing energetic 'seed' in the victim's body that could not be cleared without UM's special services. At trial, I referred to a passage in his level two training manual:

> In these cases, trauma and chronic conditions are occurring as a direct result of the wounded chakra...
>
> A great example of this is a woman or a man experiencing rape and not having it cleared energetically for many lifetimes. This can be 100s sometimes 1000s of years old. But if not cleared it will still be in the chakra.

I'd given evidence that the plaintiff's healing for rape entailed touching clients' genitals for minutes at a time — a more compromising therapeutic scenario and more damaging indoctrination for survivors is difficult to imagine — and like all his toxic output, he was making money from it.

True Sexy was a cynical fundraising campaign to kickstart Natalie's 'international TV career'. Her *Natalie with Love* talk show was slated for a subscription digital channel, 'Lovelife TV', and publicity claims that the programme would be 'seen by millions', that donations were 'investments', and that those over five thousand dollars were tax-deductible, were arguably as bent as her father's sex talks. UM's management aimed to raise one hundred and twenty thousand dollars to create it, and her old man pitched for her on Facebook: 'what she brings is what we all are; spunky, powerful, sexy, committed, dedicated and a work ethic worth embracing.'

The fundraiser video opens with three elderly women fighting over a mic to gush about the 'gorgeous' and 'super super sexy' Esoteric starlet. The eldest, Sydney psychotherapist, Jean Gamble, says, 'She's made me a sex bomb, and I was too scared to be that before.'

The next shots feature Natalie on the Lennox Head stadium stage, anti-entity scarf at her throat, wearing a t-shirt with **'YOU'RE JUST JEALOUS'** printed across the bust. 'I should be on TV,' she says. Scenes follow of her applying makeup and bounding around in tight outfits before the mic wrestlers admire the six mirrors in her bathroom, asking: 'Why wouldn't you want to see her from every angle?'[82]

The True Sexy gimmick was peak SergeSpeak in that no one had heard of the twenty-five year old having lovers. She'd firmly declared herself 'single by choice' on *Unimed Living*, and set out to 'redefine sexy' in the most Esoteric way possible, as an 'emanation from the eyes'. Only UM could reimagine sex as thoroughly disembodied, experienced strictly from the neck up. Another of her videos unironically posed the question: 'Is there a difference between being sexy and sexual objectification?' Natalie was pretty much the poster-girl for getting them arse about.

The Women in Livingness reacted to my criticism of their sexual commodification by accusing me of slut-shaming, which was ripe from a bunch of pseudo-religious money-grubbers who'd made an industry of it. I responded that I have nothing but respect for sex workers — they are vastly underpaid in my opinion; besides being honest about what they're selling. Princess also struggled with the further reaches of the campaign.

> Hold on to your urinary valves everyone. UM has released another earth shattering documentary prophesying the end of the world as we know it. The end of meaning. The unhappy ending to end all ends.

The video proclaimed that 'Being sexy...it's not about sex'. Although sexless sexiness was just another clip of Natalie's talking head, seemingly designed to bore the viewer into celibacy, its logic was consistent with the other guff UM promulgated to get away with molestation. Eunice Minford asserted that Esoteric Breast Massage has 'not a whiff of anything sexual about it', and SergeCorp convinced customers that having their intimate body parts palpated was not sexual, even when simultaneously questioned about their sexual experiences.

In prosecuting the plaintiff's case, Smark laboured a falsehood that only a blatant physical assault on an unclothed person can be considered sexual predation; as if groping, indecent exposure, and non-consensual pornography don't exist. He was also representing a self-styled preacher who bluntly taught the opposite, as revealed by the EBM customer who'd been persuaded, while having her breasts rubbed under a pretence of therapy, that sexual abuse can occur, not 'in the literal sense' but 'energetically'.

True Sexy went on to infect UM events for a while. A video promo of the 2015 Lennox Head retreat has Natalie in her 'just jealous' t-shirt strutting through the stadium to Michael's musical toils, pouting and pushing her hands through her hair. The performance triggers an Esoteric dirty dancing contagion; a clutch of women in high heels, lacy underwear peeping out from tight, skimpy dresses, dancing suggestively with each other. Choreographed by Natalie, they stare into each other's emanating eyes, elbows up, messing hair, shimmying before an all-ages audience.

In court, Tom made a point that any of these behaviours, when viewed in the singular, might just appear a bit odd, but when taken as a whole, UM's upside down mosaic was disturbing: a commercial religion peddling confused sexual messages and disordered personal boundaries; female Brothers manipulated to reject non-cult partners directing homoerotic enticements to fellow devotees. Like Esoteric Breast Massage, the performances struck me as staged for Serge's enjoyment, and I suspected that he got as much carnal satisfaction from knowing he'd driven UM's women to separate from his competitors as he did from watching them bump and grind for the cameras in front of the group's real men, and kids. The same women were committed to recruiting more women and girls to display themselves in the same way — fuelling his empire of sleaze.

My readers and I were dismayed as money poured into *Natalie with Love TV*. Within a few days, the fundraiser had attracted over three hundred donations and raised one hundred and twenty-six thousand dollars.

lxvi Resistance

'I'm not despotic,' I said. 'I don't make demands of people…' A drama-hungry friend once complained that I was the lowest maintenance person they knew. 'Or do I?'

Hayes laughed heartily and loud. 'What about the demands you make of yourself?'

Clang. The insatiable tyrant was me. The simpering, stoical dupe was also me; a sycophant working unrewarded for a relentless taskmaster. Hayes tracked them to early authority figures, voices impressed on a young mind, a loop of demands and reprimands that would replay until I worked out how to shred the tape. Grappling with it was not easy, and in argumentative monthly sessions I kept up the resistance, not convinced that externalising an unconscious battle with my inner cult was entirely unhealthy. 'Some of it's exciting.' I protested. 'Stimulating.'

'Avoidance,' Hayes retorted. Any benefits from the fight could have been achieved in healthier ways, he said.

When I mumbled that 'I shouldn't complain. There are people who have it a lot tougher than me…' he stopped doodling in his notepad and whacked his pen down.

'There it is,' he cried. 'Bang on cue. Martyr o'clock!' He wouldn't cop me exploiting other people's adversity to justify my own.

It didn't stop me from trying. 'If no one made sacrifices there would never be any justice.'

'You're telling me you want a healthier life… I want the same for you — imagine if you put the same energy into building something better for yourself.'

lxvii New horizons

'New Horizons, New Frontiers' was the optimistic title of my farewell blog. I'd exceeded what an individual could afford to do against UM, and had been offered a career change. My announcement departed from my policy of never making personal disclosures public, but I wanted readers to start doing their bit. Tired of them whingeing but leaving all the action to me, I blogged instructions on how to make notifications, and assured them that 'no one will ever tell me that I did the wrong thing in standing up for the vulnerable. No one will ever shame any of you for standing up for your families — your kids.'

But I was aware the announcement could bring out the worst in UM. 'Acquired situational sociopathy' was the term Lifton used for the malign transformation of ordinarily harmless people in extremist regimes. I knew that you don't simply walk away from a sociopath. They bear grudges, sometimes for life, so I was aware of the paradox in my assertion of freedom.

A Unimed defector told me that throughout the period that she'd been indoctrinated to hate me, she sensed that she would confide in me someday. UM's diehards needed their projection whipping-girl: someone to function as their displaced conscience and to embody their repressed yearnings for emancipation. They needed me as much as they were dependent on their shonky shaman and would struggle to let me go. So when I published the New Frontiers blog, it was with another of Lifton's terms in mind; one that described the radical final acts of apocalyptic cults like Aum Shinrikyo — 'forcing the end'.

lxviii Girl to Woman

The detective from the local station called ahead. I was at home, it was late September 2015, and the head of a cybersecurity firm had offered me a job, an exit route from my dead career. I'd closed shop, sold my treatment tables and was awaiting my contract. The police were not in a hurry. Four months earlier, between her regular social media posts calling me a liar, a cyberbully, and a troll, Dr Rachel Hall reported me again, probably for replying to her defamatory tweets, and sent police to Lance's house — fifty kilometres from where I lived. UM's entertainment starved faithful must have been disappointed to learn that the pranic tenants of the Dark Lodge don't all bunk together. I phoned the station to let them know where I was if they wanted to speak with me.

    A couple of grumpy looking detectives strolled listlessly from their car, but as I watched from my kitchen window, I was grumpier than they were. Just days before, I'd spoken with an adolescent who'd escaped a UM household. His stepmother woke him at five every morning to do chores while she attended UM videoconferences, worked on its Expression Program, and practically starved her kids. Non-cult books, television and music were banned from the household, and when the father began talking about humans evolving into eleven-foot-tall extra-terrestrials, and told his son that if he didn't behave Esoterically, he would attract entities that would rape the women and girls in the household, the boy fled to the home of a relative, leaving behind siblings he feared he may never see again. His guardian, who'd accompanied him on the call, gasped as he told me, and I reassured her that what he was saying was consistent with other accounts. He hadn't told her or anyone before because he'd been punished for dissent in the past; food and other necessities withheld, and his guardian had received legal threats when she questioned the Eso-parents. He feared she might be subjected to reprisals.

The police were trudging up the stairs. UM was publicising its 2016 Girl to Woman Festival, to be held again in January at Lennox Head. It went against all my instincts, but I was determined to stick to my plan to avoid blogging about it and sending out notifications. Social media images revealed that the first Festival was worse than I could have imagined, and included activities not mentioned in the advertising. A photo showed a 'Healing Tent' with the Brides of Serge in Universal Medicine t-shirts performing their hands-on routine on women. One victim had three pairs of hands on her. The 'True Beauty Tent', meanwhile, was decorated with pink and magenta tulle curtains, fairy-lights, and flowers, and inside, the Esoteric Breast Massage sorority painted lipstick, nail polish and eyeshadow on primary schoolers. The girls then attended a selfie photo workshop, and Emmalee Benhayon taught them how to make perfumed body cream. Sarah Broome posted that about three hundred bodies showed up, with images indicating they were UM supporters. Adults greatly outnumbered kids, and a significant number were men.

My contract was running inexplicably late and I just wanted to get it signed and get on with my life. I offered the detectives seats at my kitchen table, but the meeting was brief. Only one spoke and he did so sternly. There had been thirteen police complaints against me so far. It was quite serious, he said.

I shook my head wearily and interrupted. 'But you're not here to lay charges.'

Prickling, he replied, 'what makes you so sure?'

'Because I haven't broken the law.'

lxix Poor bastard

September 2015, a reader found an announcement on Facebook and commented on my blog: 'Those UM scouts must watch this site so carefully. No sooner does Esther say what would Natalie know about "Sex bomb" etc. etc. and presto Natalie is engaged.' Serge's understudy was set to wed a strait-laced young Englishman, Conor Turley, and my delighted twin, Pranic Princess, couldn't help but comment: 'OMG it's all making sense now — they'll put the Esoteric thumb screws on him to change his name and he'll be CON BENHAYON LOL'.

My readers and I wondered if the wedding night would be webcast to the faith-full, and Princess added:

> She was SINGLE BY CHOICE five minutes ago. Can't wait until the poor bastard finds out she's a SEX BOMB purely for promotional purposes, and that sexiness is all 'in the eyes', nothing to do with actual sex... My prediction: it'll last until the second she doesn't get her way — he'll be tarred an animal, a detractor and full of carcinogenic male energy, but not until after the wedding, which will be #crowdfunded.

Natalie-Con registered their marriage in Lismore later that month, and announced a wedding celebration would be held in England in November. Within six weeks it was cancelled. The marriage was over.

lxx Baby carpet

Early November 2015, I was staying with relatives in Brisbane, a mother and her small children, and all were asleep when I flicked the light in the guestroom to find a visitor lying motionless in the doorway; a baby carpet snake. They don't move fast, but I didn't want to let it out of my sight. I'm no wildlife handler, but tiny geckos sent the other adult into shrieking fits. The snake coiled back. I would have to act quickly. A few years before, I'd caught a tree snake inside my mother's house — not big and not poisonous, but a fast mover, and in a rushed pursuit, it slithered into a bedroom that was stacked with artefacts Mum couldn't throw away; baskets, boxes, toys and chairs. I couldn't risk losing it in there, so I dropped to my knees and looked for something to pin it down. As I grabbed a folded pillowcase from a laundry basket, it reared and darted past me, and I goalkeeper dived across the carpet and grabbed it with the pillowcase, clutching until I got a hold behind its head, my mother providing commentary from the hallway. It was a beautiful creature, greenish black, soft, velvety and warm. More terrified than me, it lashed about and wrapped itself around my forearm. Released in the garden, it shot through the ferns out of sight.

The small python was bigger and the hallway beyond was dark and spacious with a lot of open doors into adjacent rooms to confound a search. I moved slowly to take a cover off a pillow, and remembering my phone in my pocket, I shone its flashlight into the snake's eyes. It coiled back, and using the pillowcase as a clumsy glove, I grabbed it behind the head, but botched what should have been a simple manoeuvre to pull the case inside out and bag it. The poor thing got distressed, whipping around, urinating and emptying its bowels, and I worried I was crushing it.

The mother woke when I was trying to unlock the front door, one-handed, to take it away, but the little ones hadn't stirred. Hailed as a hero to friends and family, I didn't see it as heroic. Plenty of people would have simply picked it up. A bigger snake of a different species would have been something else entirely. I didn't do it because I wanted to, but because it had to be done, and I was the most capable coward on hand. Two days later, back home in Byron Shire, I was served with Benhayon's defamation claim.

One late afternoon in his private Eden, Hayes said something that captivated me. I was weary of the strain, of never being able to relax or properly grieve, and was toiling to envision the well-rounded characters that

I might internalise to usurp the despot and the bootlicker within me. What did they look like? What would they say? Hayes began to talk about his comfortable home, his teeming garden, his loving companion; his sanctuary from the war-zone of modern existence. I'd seen his partner on the beach one afternoon at sunset, the breeze lifting her long hair as she romped with their terrier on the wet sand. The idea was that the home you make and the people you keep close are a reflection of what's going on inside you, regardless of outer circumstances. The sun had dropped low and the light in his consulting room was fading. His little dog dozed on the rug. 'Everyone has a right to a conflict-free self,' he said.

The words were like a cool drop of water on an overheated soul. I jotted them down. The idea felt intoxicating and alien. Imagine, I thought, living in peace.

lxxi McIntyre v O'Regan

The two day trial of McIntyre versus O'Regan began at the Supreme Court in Sydney, December 2015, the day before the initial listing hearing of Benhayon versus Rockett. In challenging their mother's will, lawyers for Sarah McIntyre and her brother Seth advised them to plead that it did not adequately provide for them. The lawyers were reluctant to plead that Benhayon had unduly influenced Judith, saying it was difficult to prove and would increase their financial risk by lengthening a trial.

As executor of the estate, Benhayon's pet lawyer, Serryn O'Regan, hired a specialist barrister to go after the siblings. The first assault came when O'Regan's pick successfully stopped Sarah from putting any of the emails from her mother's inbox into evidence. Sarah had previously forwarded me an exchange between Benhayon and a few of his valuable followers.

Serge Unimed   Tue, May 13, 2014 at 3:50 PM

To: Paula Fletcher, Nicola Lessing, Christoph Schnelle, Ingrid L, Judith McIntyre

Cc: Anne McRitchie, Natalie Benhayon

Hi All,

As you all know I have a policy to not disclose those who donate money to UM. I do not have to explain it too much. It will suffice to say that it is not in the best interest of the donor to receive the direct force of group or personal jealousy. To the donor it can cause serious harm as through the jealous person great astral energy will vent its fury. Anything that can advance the dissemination and accessibility to the Ageless Wisdom receives the personal ire of the Dark Lodge. Of course the DL know who the donor is but they need the jealous conduit/channel to send through their evil.

No ifs or buts on this one as it is too serious to tamper with.

It is an unfortunate situation as we all deserve to be named for our contributions. But on this particular subject, and it being about money (kidney energy); an energy most have squandered over lifetimes, it is a very sensitive subject.

with love, Serge

The barrister argued that the emails were improperly obtained because Judith had given Sarah her password, but had not granted explicit permission to read them. Tom, when he found out about that ruling nearly a year later, held the opinion that as direct and authentic evidence, a minor indiscretion in obtaining them should not have prevented their use.

Scrubbed Benhayon had poked himself into a dark business suit and tie. We caught our first glimpse of each other in over ten years in the corridor outside the court where he was surrounded by a cluster of cultists, including Alison Greig. When he clocked my wide smile, his gaze was glacial. The seer hadn't seen me coming. The McIntyres, meanwhile, had made *The Sydney Morning Herald* aware of the case, and in the small courtroom I sat beside journalist Tim Elliott at the rear of two rows. O'Regan, wearing a cheaply tailored, silver silk suit, was perched at the bar table, looking like the Arcturan lawyer who fell to earth.

The estate's counsel raked over thirty-four year old Sarah's income, savings, superannuation and expenditure. Sarah didn't know the value of Judith's assets until she'd died. She'd never intruded into her mother's affairs, but she'd hoped her inheritance would help her buy a home in Sydney where she'd grown up. One of the most expensive cities in the world, Sydney's median house price was one million dollars that year, but SergeCorp's barrister waved around property listings for two-bedroom flats twenty kilometres west of where she was renting, priced under seven hundred thousand. 'I suggest you'd be able, with the estate's current provision, to put a deposit on an acceptable hovel in Woop Woop,' was the inference.

In a sworn affidavit, Sarah's brother Seth stated that his mother had asked him how he'd feel if she left the majority of her estate to Universal Medicine, and he'd replied that spirituality should not rest on money.

> I said that I believed that she should deal with her money with respect to how she had come into the money herself, which was through inheritance over the last four generations, and that if she wanted to give back to Universal Medicine she might consider doing things to help cancer patients rather than giving such large amounts of money to them directly. I encouraged her to pay in proportion to the services received, even generously, but with rationality.

He'd had concerns about Judith's prior financial generosity to gurus, beginning with the Siddha Yoga movement, until, to his mother's shock, its original leader, Muktananda, was accused of assaulting followers. Next it was her charity to the Sydney based New Age goddess. Seth told Judith that he thought she was being duped.[83]

The questions he faced are too defamatory to reproduce, even though he answered them in the negative. Typical of UM's Taliban-style moralising, I half expected UM's barrister to interrogate Seth on whether he listened to rock and roll music or wore tight pants. Like Sarah, he was calm, reasonable, and intelligent, and had no dispute with their mother. They'd told her they were uncomfortable with UM's influence, but were otherwise on good terms.

The trial, the first I'd observed, was a useful introduction to forensic smear tactics, where two honest, down to earth people had the minutiae of their personal lives pored over at the instigation of grasping bigots. Serge's email exhorting secrecy was sent ten days after Judith signed her final will and four weeks before she died, while she was receiving in-home palliative care from a roster of Benhayon butt-kissers.

In her reply to the email, Nicola Lessing, the wife of Judith's financial advisor, Christoph Schnelle, said Benhayon's entreaty made 'complete sense energetically', and described it as 'enormously loving'. She promised she hadn't told anyone about donations and vowed to maintain confidentiality. It was gaunt Nicola that lurked behind Tom during the defamation trial.

Serge's insistence on anonymous donations meant that nobody apart from him and his management could know how much he was reaping. Yet, there sat silver-plated O'Regan, primly passing documents to their hired attack-artist, while his wowser peanut gallery cheered his grab for a dead woman's assets. 'Just look at this racket,' I whispered to Tim in disgust.

lxxii New exposés

I would have closed my practice anyway, but my cyber-employment contract never materialised. A company director persuaded the firm's owner that they could hire a roomful of researchers in South East Asia for what they'd be paying me. I was contemplating my next move when I got served, and the litigation wiped out all chance of starting a new career.

As soon as I launched a crowdfund for my legal bills, the Sons of God attempted to sabotage it, reproducing their Serge-loving testimonials and defamatory slurs in the comments on the crowdfund website, but it's unlikely UM's spammers made any difference. Over three years, I raised a fraction of Natalie's haul for the TV career that flopped before it began, but it was enough to get me started and keep me alive. Serge's champions seemed to believe the litigation would deter me from continuing the exposure, and Rebecca Baldwin's husband, Simon Asquith, blogged his pity for my feeble finances, expressing pre-emptive disappointment that he would not get to see the truth come out in court.

I renewed my scrutiny, however, and went deeper. If I hadn't been sued, for example, I might not have discovered records showing that the Australian Tax Office had revoked the College of UM's endorsement to receive tax-deductible gifts. No reasons were made public, but the ruling was finalised the month before Benhayon filed his claim. The charity's six hundred thousand dollar Fiery Building Fund subsequently evaporated. 'Where'd the money go?' I tweeted at board member Alison Greig. 'Have you informed the donors?'

The amount of work involved had deterred me previously, but I quickly learned to produce videos to upload to YouTube: a series of talks with audio excerpts from Benhayon's recorded lectures, allowing my growing audience to hear, many for the first time, the madness from his own mouth. Filmed in my living room, my vlogs became proof of life for anxious supporters, and they conveyed to cultists that it was not an evil wraith before the camera, but ordinary, no-budget me talking through the workings of a crooked business.

UM's Brotherhood professed to welcome the trial, but they underestimated the pranic lust for vindication. The financial and logistical challenges for my defence were potentially insurmountable, but through my video talks, I could at least show that they did not frighten me. That was probably the boldest act of blasphemy of all.

lxxiii The sphinx

Identified to the court as a teacher, practitioner, author, and life-coach, besuited Benhayon played the affable counsellor to stricken Judith, as if dairy-free butter wouldn't melt in his mouth. Sarah and Seth's lawyer, however, tendered a chart identifying the Universal Medicine crew who'd assisted in making her final will. O'Regan was executor, solicitor Paula Fletcher, acting for both benefactor and beneficiary, drafted it, and Charles Wilson played counsel for the estate until he was shunted for the high-end pro. Esoteric Breast Massager, Elizabeth Dolan, was Judith's guardian and in-home palliative care nurse; UM permanent fixture, Christoph Schnelle, was Judith's financial advisor; and Mary-Louise Myers witnessed the will with omnipresent Désirée. When asked if those named were UM members, Serge, who would never let semantics get in the way of a big payout, answered, 'we don't have any members.' When pressed, he said, 'we respectfully refer to them as students'.

The barrister for the McIntyres read through an incomplete list of his businesses and properties, and Benhayon surprisingly denied ownership of the extensively renovated Unimed Brisbane property, despite its title showing his fifty percent share through one of his front companies. The McIntyre's lawyer didn't pursue it, but when Tom revisited that answer in 2018, the bloke who knows everything in the universe said he hadn't been aware that he owned it. He'd held the title since 2010. The purchase price was nearly two million dollars.

Judith gifted Benhayon eight hundred thousand dollars in cash five weeks before she died, transferred three days after UM's management held her hand as she signed her final will. Serge told the court that he put the funds toward over a million dollars' worth of renovations to convert the cold storage nuthouse into his windowless, soundproof, commercial temple. He also said the next largest single gift he'd received was six hundred thousand dollars, but was not asked for further information. The cross-examination ended too soon, having barely touched on what should have been thrown at him.

Smug little Serge came off the dais and moved toward the public gallery. Wealthy supporter, Anne McRitchie, shifted her bottom in the front row to make room for him, but he made his away to the row along the back wall, squeezing past a couple of observers to where Tim Elliott and I sat. A littering of journalistic paraphernalia; notebook, papers, and phone, lay on the seat between us, and on my other side was one vacant seat between me and Seth's partner and other members of the McIntyre family. Serge smiled and spoke to Tim, 'can I sit here?'

'No mate,' Tim answered gruffly. 'This seat's taken.'

Benhayon then made to step over my boots to wedge himself between me and the McIntyre family. Perhaps I could have pointed out the free seats in front and told him that seat was taken too, but I got up, moved between him and the family, poked my thumb to the warm cushion and said, 'you can sit there.'

The next witness was another beneficiary of Judith's will, her housemate Ingrid, also a cancer patient who went on to author a blog, 'How to have fun while preparing to pass over' in which she praised Serge, explained how to pre-purchase a cardboard coffin and advised readers to leave a list of assets, accounts, and passwords for one's executor — no doubt one of UM's experienced professionals. The article featured a photo of her no-frills casket standing on end against a wall, with Ingrid inside, waving cheerily.[84] Judith left her over three hundred thousand dollars toward the purchase of her Goonellabah home on condition that the residence was used to care for other cancer patients, but Ingrid acknowledged that no others had received cared there in nearly two years since.

Ingrid and the late Judith were in the photo of Serge's fundraising tour that was yanked from the Fiery Building Fund website when the Charity Commission began its inquiries. They were surrounded by psychologist Caroline Raphael, GP Jane Barker, Paula Fletcher, Christoph Schnelle, Nicola Lessing, Désirée again, and barrister Charles Wilson hiding behind a pole, or impersonating one. Ingrid told the court that she and Judith had also travelled to a UM retreat in Somerset and were impressed by the conference barn bankrolled by the European flock. She said Judith wanted a hall of similar quality in Australia.

I'm not a hefty build, but sitting beside Serge, my legs had at least triple the meat on them. I told Reverend Millikan how he'd remained motionless until the end of the hearing day. 'He was like the Sphinx,' I said. 'It was as if he wasn't breathing.' Tim and I scribbled and scratched and fidgeted on either side of him. 'Do you think he was trying to be intimidating?' I asked.

'Oh, he would have BELIEVED it,' David crowed. 'He would have thought he was ANNIHILATING you with his STILLNESS!'

The judge chose Christmas Eve to deliver his finding that there wasn't enough evidence to support the McIntyres' claim that Judith did not adequately provide for them in her will. He'd heard no evidence that Benhayon was a crook. A couple of days later, Tim's report made *The Sydney Morning Herald's* front page, and it became one of those stories that continues to resonate, making international news, and infuriating people far beyond those who've had the misfortune of crossing Unimed's path.[85] The dismissal of the claim meant that Seth and Sarah received two and hundred and fifty thousand dollars each from an estate that was valued at over two million dollars. Judith's bequest and gift to Benhayon totalled one point four million dollars.

lxxiv Rouge

The True Beauty tent at the 2016 Girl to Woman Festival was bigger, staffed by more of UM's over-groomed women, and its tables were loaded with cosmetics. Photos showed much younger children receiving makeovers, with the clinic receptionist applying makeup to a toddler. It was midsummer, the rouged-up girls were mostly dressed in shorts and little tops, and Natalie taught them a True Movement routine to an Esoteric hymn, which they performed onstage for the grown-ups and UM's cameras.

The festival also launched another front targeting kids: Natalie's 'Sexual Education and Life Foundations for Youth' or SELFY, was put forward as a provider of sex education for kids, and its short-lived website and Instagram account displayed photos of devotees' adolescent daughters. At the festival, an array of UM women cheesecake posed with the SELFY brand and logo. Michael Benhayon's next wife, Kelly, was captured True-Sexy pouting with three lipsticked primary schoolers.

The more I thought about UM's proliferating red flags, the more I was convinced that Benhayon brought his legal action to deter me from scrutinising, among other things, UM's targeting of women and girls. The cops showed up in September and Benhayon filed for defamation in November, as if trying to get police to carry out their stand-over tactics was management's last ditch before the litigation plunge.

'This is not a police matter,' I said to the detective, who refused to confirm that the complainants were UM promoters. 'I know they are,' I said. 'I don't post about anyone else.'

'You've said some strong things about these people,' he grumbled.

'That are true,' I said, 'or opinions based on facts.'

'It sounds as if you've read the law.'

'Of course, I have,' I said. 'I'm publishing within it. It's not even a civil matter, but that option has always been open to them.'

I felt sorry for the detective in a way and offered to show him documentation of UM spamming authorities with complaints, but he had better things to do. As he and his offsider lumbered back to their car, I imagined thirteen of UM's most precious whingeing at him. I'd tried to reassure him by telling him I was blogging less, I was sick of them too and was trying to move on. 'All of their objections,' I said, 'it's all bullshit.'

He gave a bitter puff. 'It *is* all bullshit,' he mumbled as he walked away.

lxxv Palliation

> Death is but a new beginning in the heart of the true servant.
>
> Serge Benhayon[86]

Simon Asquith, a UM audiovisual contractor, was one of Judith's volunteer palliative careers, and his UM FACTS blog, 'The blessing of Judith Mcintyre's life and death', was a beatific write-up of the exemplary community that rushes to the deathbeds of wealthy divorcees. Before praising his employer and devoutly laying the boot into Seth and Sarah, accusing them of failing to spend time with their mother in her final stages, he wrote that he hardly knew Judith before leaping at the call to help. On my blog I questioned whether he would have wiped a dying woman's backside if she was penniless. Was the blessing of a rich woman's death a leg-up UM's hierarchical ladder?

Asquith's barbs contradicted Sarah McIntyre's unopposed evidence that from the initial diagnosis onward, she'd made time to travel the eight hundred kilometres from her home to be with her mother, and that they'd grown closer. Esoteric social climbers taking over Judith's home couldn't have made it easy, and according to Seth's sworn statement, his mother

> didn't want any strong emotions around her. It felt odd and I felt uneasiness about it as I just wanted to leave everything and go to be with her, but she kept wanting me to come at certain times that didn't always work for me due to my schedules with my children and work.

He visited as often as he could, speaking with her nearly every day by phone.

In the deathbed video produced by Asquith's wife, Rebecca Baldwin, Judith doesn't mention her children or grandkids, but fleetingly describes her life before UM as 'complicated', with 'so many entanglements'. In a segment titled, 'How to have fun while dying' she beamingly describes her palliative pampering. 'I've got all these expensive French creams, and people put them on me and I lie here and smell them. Yes, there's an amazing amount of pleasure and joy being in this bed.'

For Judith, Unimed made good on its provision of self-loving choices. The child in all of us would love to have undemanding servants at our beck and call, smiling all day and saying yes; just as the child within wishes that every experience was joyful and to insulate itself from all emotional discomfort. It's difficult to deny the appeal of such a luxury death.

We may never know what Benhayon promised her in those 'free' weekly counselling sessions, but he reneged on his offer to Rita of an Esoteric rebirth as his grandchild. Well after the birth of Michael and Emmalee's two children, he announced to a congregation likely unaware of her bequest, that she'd resurfaced in Germany as the infant daughter of a low-rung believer. It was too late for Rita to get her money back. Just before the McIntyre case went to trial, Benhayon tellingly paid eight hundred thousand dollars for fifty acres of gently rolling hills among the nut farms of Tregeagle, renovating the existing homestead supernaturally quickly. After his win, he spent another million dollars constructing an Esoteric McMansion on the same allotment.

In the film, Judith restates her belief that she'd created her cancer, and speaks of 'the ease that life starts to take as you really care for yourself first'. The irony that her volunteer carers were engaged in thankless prostrations to her guru was lost on her. She left behind no evidence that she'd interrogated the controversies surrounding him, or that her special treatment was not afforded to the majority of his Sons of God. Toward the film's end, Judith says, 'I love the clarity that I have and that I don't feel any issues with anyone and that allows me to really enjoy each moment.' All that mattered was that she felt good. The silver-tongued swindler organised her physical comfort and told her what she wanted to hear. Her new religion absolved her of reckoning with her selfishness; that the price of her self-indulgence would be paid by her kids.

lxxvi Henry

Lance ran a defence fundraising ad in the Byron Shire Echo every second week in the early months of 2016. It didn't raise a cent, just a few inquisitive phone calls, some to warn me about Benhayon's powers. A woman told me that her friend had confronted Serge and accused him of being a fake, and he'd responded by causing the friend to collapse and fall ill. 'She didn't doubt him enough,' I said. David Millikan had asked me before Seven's cameras if Serge had special powers. 'No,' I answered. 'He has special techniques.'

I persuaded Lance to pull the ad, arguing we could use the money for my bills instead, but he forgot to cancel it, and a fortnight later, I received a call on a Friday afternoon from an elderly man with an American accent, Henry di Suvero. He gave a frank opinion of the litigation. 'That Benhayon, he's a fraud!'

Henry was a retired barrister, and if not for Lance's slackness, I might not have received his crucial referral. 'Call Tom Molomby,' he said. 'He's a silk, a Senior Counsel.' The two worked from the same chambers in Sydney, and Tom had a record for getting disadvantaged clients out of extreme predicaments, even getting murder convictions overturned. Henry knew people who were caught up in Universal Medicine and he urged me to call his old friend immediately. 'What time is it?'

'Uh, it's about ten to five.'

'Call him right away!' he said. 'He catches the five forty-five bus.' He told me to get off the phone. 'You don't want to miss him.'

My call reached an answering machine and a mature radio voice that smoothly announced, 'You've reached Tom Molomby…' I jabbered an unrehearsed briefing. 'I'm being sued by a cult leader for defamation…I'm flat broke…' About an hour later, the silk returned the call. He had a firm, slightly stern manner, and a skill good lawyers have of getting the information he needed quickly, without saying much. I did not sugarcoat my situation. 'I wrote strong stuff about Benhayon, not just in that blog, but in a lot of blogs before that — hundreds of blogs. I realise that might sound a bit mad. I've always called him a cult leader, I called him a sexual predator, I've insulted him, called him a sleazebag, called him fuck-face and told him to fuck off, made fun of his height…'

Tom waited until I'd finished. 'Yes,' he said with a rising inflection. His speech was measured. 'Henry is quite right, this is the sort of case that interests me.' He spoke with the melodic diction of an important person, an elder statesman, and I tried to form a mental image of him; wearing a suit, behind a big desk, surrounded by law books. I didn't want to get excited, but Henry emailed to say that Tom was delighted at the prospect of taking on Serge, 'even thinking up some cross-examination on the spot!'

I distinctly remember Tom's final question during that first conversation. 'Tell me, does this plaintiff have money?'

'Oh yes,' I said. 'He has money — ill gotten money, but plenty of money, property worth millions.'

'Ah, good,' he said. Rather than work pro bono, Tom drew up a contingency agreement, meaning he'd bill the plaintiff if I won and Benhayon was ordered to pay my legal costs.

After Lance cancelled the ad, I'd still get random callers warning that Benhayon's evil energy could do terrible things to me. Their concern was genuine, and their fear was real, but as with all conspiracy phobias, the basis for it was not. Believers in mysterious cabals, or meddlesome spooks misidentify the sources of their anxieties: the real social inequities, and dull old greed, incompetence, and corruption of those in power that make life difficult for so many. Benhayon's threat was not his hocus-pocus, but his mendacity, callousness, and unscrupulous manoeuvring of money and manpower to cover up his underhanded activities. That now extended to manipulating the judicial process against me. I thanked one caller and assured her I wasn't worried about Serge's supposed sorcery. 'Besides,' I said, 'how do you know I haven't put a hex on him?'

lxxvii Inquisitions

'…years of vile accusations with no results… there will be no wrong doing found as all investigated complaints have met with our very high levels of integrity…' That Benhayon quote, published on UM FACTS, was parroted by his disciples *en masse*: Unimed has no victims, the trolls have no evidence, no wrongdoing found. It's unlikely their defamatory mantras convinced anyone outside of the group, however. Persisting with them, long after evidence to the contrary was made public, they were trying to persuade themselves.

When my complaint about psychologist Marianna Masiorski's Benhayon promotions went before a Professional Standards Panel of the Psychology Board of Australia, late 2015, the panel agreed substantially with me. Masiorski's listing on the AHPRA registry was updated with a statement that the Board had imposed conditions on her registration for twelve months, and she was required to meet with an approved supervisor monthly, and to permanently remove her articles from the *Medicine and Serge Benhayon* website.

Rosie also achieved some vindication. After a four year process and a public hearing, a Professional Standards Committee of the Medical Board of New South Wales, were 'comfortably satisfied' that Dr Samuel Tae-Kyu Kim's conduct, 'as well as being significantly below the relevant standard,' was also 'improper and unethical'. He was found to have inappropriately referred her for Esoteric treatments without disclosing their lack of evidence base, or his links to Universal Medicine and its associated practitioners. He was also censured for failing to refer Rosie to an appropriate specialist for conditions outside of his specialty, and for improper prescribing. Dr Kim received an official reprimand, was ordered to undergo professional supervision for a year, have his treatment files audited, and was prohibited from making referrals to complementary practitioners without seeking a second opinion from an approved physician. Rosie also brought a civil case against him, but that settled out of court, subject to a non-disclosure agreement.

Although the Medical Council hearing took place on planet Earth, the doctor appeared to be in orbit elsewhere, telling the Committee that Esoteric Chakra-puncture had both been devised by Serge sixteen years earlier and had origins in ancient Egyptian times. It was an internationally recognised therapy, he said, but agreed that Universal Medicine was the only organisation that practices and teaches it.

The Committee also found him to be a model of UM's Esoteric integrity:

> Dr Kim's evidence was not always clear or coherent... At times Dr Kim did not appear to be a reliable witness... he appeared to prevaricate or respond to questions in a tangential manner. For example, he attempted to minimise his association with Universal Medicine by challenging questions [about it]...[87]

He told the panel that he suspected Rosie was colluding with a campaign to defame and discredit UM.

Journalist, Josh Robertson, covered the outcome for *The Guardian*. Despite Dr Kim making a written admission to the Council that he'd engaged in unsatisfactory professional conduct, UM FACTS portrayed the accountability process as akin to an Inquisition/crucifixion. I had nothing to do with Rosie's complaint, but the Sons of God made fresh calls to have me jailed, and Alison added, 'If we take a stance other than this we are in effect aligning to every pogrom and genocide that has ever occurred.'

lxxviii Joelle

I didn't feel good about issuing a subpoena to Joelle. I'd resolved to only call willing witnesses, and I didn't blame her for getting cold feet, but she'd initially agreed to give evidence, and we needed her. Fortunately, when she appeared via video link from Queensland, the court saw a vivacious woman in her thirties who seemed relaxed. Through the first two weeks of the trial, while her former tennis colleague pouted in the public gallery, the witness had gotten a suntan spectating at the US Open tennis tournament at Flushing Meadows.

In 1998, the year Joelle turned fifteen, Benhayon approached her mother, Dinah*, offering to coach the talented player in his 'elite' live-in programme, saying he'd prepare her for the professional circuit. His fee was one hundred and fifty dollars per week. Dinah agreed to it, but for Joelle it was an unpleasant experience. In court, she recounted a rule that the doors in the Benhayon household had to be kept open.

'Which doors did that mean?' asked Tom.

'So bedrooms, bathrooms and the rooms that we were in, I guess.' Joelle added that Serge gave the reason that 'everybody should be able to come and go from the rooms and not shut the doors.'

'Did that apply to the bathroom?'

'Yes, from what I remember, yes… We shared a bathroom at the back of the house, myself and the kids, and Miranda.'

'So when you had the shower, what position was the door in?'

'The door couldn't be closed — so ajar, but not closed.'

'What about when other people had showers in that same room?'

'The same thing,' she answered. 'The door just had to be not closed.'

Louise halted when reviewing Joelle's statement during one of our pre-trial conferences. 'What kind of joker invites a fifteen year old girl to stay and won't let her close the bathroom door?' she asked.

Smark's cross-examination was short. 'It's fair to say, isn't it, that your recollection of these events isn't particularly strong at the moment?'

The witness replied without hesitation. 'I do remember that because I do remember the conversation around it, and there's things that I do remember clearly.'

'When you say it was a rule, who do you recall saying this rule to you?'

'It was said by Serge to me and the family... it was a rule that everybody just knew that you don't shut the doors in the house.'

Serge and Deborah Benhayon denied that such a rule existed. In the witness box, Deborah embarked on a long, unprompted explanation that as a mother of four she needed to manage the household so that it had a 'strong rhythm... so that things had a flow and everybody knew the boundaries...' and her kids were responsible for waking themselves for school and sports training '...so your bedroom — everything, the bedroom doors were closed.'

I had a little whinge that Tom could have pressed Joelle for more evidence. She'd told me that Miranda was unfriendly and had drawn a line down the centre of their bedroom and barred her from crossing it. She was surprised to learn that Serge and Miranda had married, because as far as she'd seen, Miranda was the one infatuated with Benhayon back then and was obsessed with trying to impress him — similar to the pattern among Benhayon's admirers to this day.

Joelle found the household regimented, under Serge's strict control, with Miranda doing a lot of the housework and ordering the kids around like a second wife. Deborah worked full-time, and seemed 'normal', and she noted that Serge argued frequently with Miranda and Simone. She recalled Deborah accusing Miranda of going into her room and going through her belongings, and she heard no mention of any other live-in tennis pupils. Miranda, by then, had resided with the family for at least two years, and the younger girl saw no sign of contact with her parents during the time she stayed there; not even a phone call. Miranda had no peer-group friends either, and the Benhayon family did not socialise.

The girls trained from early morning and underwent distance education while Benhayon's kids attended school and Deborah went to work. If Joelle had not been there, Serge and Miranda would have been alone together through weekdays. She saw no evidence of an intimate relationship between them, but said that the pair went off together at times, telling her to make her own way to the tennis courts. Joelle was the second person to tell me that Serge had Miranda listening to audio cassettes — some sort of personal development talks, but neither knew who the speaker was.

As his new pupil had expected, he was a tough fitness coach, driving the girls to practise at local courts and then making them run home, or to run until they couldn't run anymore. On a few occasions, he drove them to a court at an isolated residence a few times, but the occupant was never at home. The girls would also help coach younger pupils at his morning and afternoon tennis lessons.

Aside from Joelle's increasing discomfort with the interpersonal tensions, Benhayon would not allow her and Miranda to snack between meals, and he restricted their diets, cutting out dairy. She was constantly hungry, and the soy products he gave her didn't agree with her. He also refused to allow her to return home on weekends, claiming that would interfere with her training. On hot nights, he stopped her from using an electric fan in the bedroom.

Dinah was uneasy about the arrangement, and when Joelle called her and asked to come home, crouching under a table with the phone so she wouldn't be heard, her mother got straight in her car and drove three hours from Queensland to collect her. Benhayon was out when she arrived, and she bundled her daughter and her gear into the car and fled. When she called to say Joelle would not be back, Benhayon told her she was making a mistake.

The mother was alarmed to learn of the rule about the bathroom door, and Joelle and Dinah's accounts diverge from Deborah's. Dinah said that the unusual layout of the house made the shower stall in the bathroom visible from the living room. Deborah countered that there was a sideboard along the adjacent wall that blocked the line of sight.

Dinah and Joelle would occasionally glimpse Serge and Miranda on the competition circuit after that. Miranda would play her matches and the pair would leave without interacting with anyone. It was another pattern that did not change, with observers at UM retreats reporting that the Benhayon family did not mingle with the flock. Occasionally they would join them at some staged celebration, but only at a degree of distance. Another contact who'd known the family a long time said that Serge had always dominated, and that he was an excessive disciplinarian. If one of his children misbehaved, all of them were made to stand and stare at a wall for hours.

Miranda's parents were never seen at matches either. Other parents told Dinah that Benhayon had approached them wanting to coach their kids, but they were suspicious and thought that he pushed pupils too hard. A local mother who noticed Miranda being made to continue training with severe blisters said she was afraid to intervene because she'd heard Benhayon had made legal threats to a coach who'd questioned his dealings with his most talented charge. The woman described teen Miranda as ground down. She'd observed her sitting alone one day courtside, eating lunch out of a plastic lunchbox. It looked to be a rice salad and Miranda was counting out the grains and eating them one by one.

Part III

Ash

lxxix Interruptions

I could only get a few words out before the judge would interrupt. It was the morning of the fifth of May 2017, I should have been at a three year old's birthday party, and I'd made my first blunder of the hearing. The plaintiffs had filed two applications for orders, I'd asked for an adjournment of one, and told the judge I was willing to argue the other, but I should have asked to postpone both. I probably looked every bit the internet lunatic, alone at the bar table, no supporters in sight, opposed by a seven-foot-tall barrister. Beside Charles Wilson was a curly-haired, grey-faced solicitor in prissy business attire, with two togged-up plaintiffs and Alison Greig seated behind them. A woman I didn't recognise observed from the rear of their side of the public gallery.

I looked a fright. I'd woken from three hours of sleep to find a blood vessel had burst in my right eye, turning it deep bloodshot. I'd been up until three that morning drafting submissions and an affidavit with one hundred and twenty pages of exhibits, and I'd dressed in jeans, boots and a blue linen shirt, to show that I wasn't pretending to be any sort of professional. It was a two-hour drive to Brisbane during an aggressive peak hour, I'd parked in a city parking lot I couldn't afford, and shouldered my daypack with three copies of my affidavit to line up at court for a Justice of the Peace to notarise the copies.

My submissions were a carefully organised argument, and I hoped to persuade His Honour to stop UM's legal geniuses from vandalising my defence. Team UM had filed the applications at the Brisbane District Court and listed the hearing just three days earlier. The judge's Associate emailed Paula Fletcher and me to inquire how much time we'd need in court. Fletcher replied that the argument would take less than two hours if I had a lawyer, but 'if Ms Rockett is self-represented it is difficult to estimate.'

I replied to both that the plaintiffs had refused to negotiate the hearing date: 'I did not expect that I would have to represent myself on the application to strike out the contextual truth imputations, which is a complex and wide ranging argument. I am not adequately prepared... If I'm granted an adjournment of the strike out application, argument should take less than two hours.'

Tom was busy, but when I got through to him, he advised me not to feel pressured by my lack of expertise. He said that most judges respond reasonably to litigants who sensibly and logically state their case and assured me I'd be all right. He hadn't been in court with Smith and me three months earlier, however, and this was an unknown judge looking at me askance. I began to state my argument as calmly and as rationally as I could, but His Honour would not let me finish a sentence.

lxxx The cupboard

> We've got delicious fruit we say is good for you when in fact it is a poison to the body.
>
> Serge Benhayon[88]

In England, Graham's concerns for his seven year old daughter, Lara, were deepening. She was compulsively reading ingredients on packaging, had stopped eating foods she'd previously liked, including bananas and other fruits, and was anxiously insisting that family members would have heart attacks and die if they ate bread. Lara's GP told her parents that their daughter was developing an eating disorder and affirmed that she was not allergic to any of the foods UM restricted.

Graham and his mother were also concerned that the child was suppressing normal emotions — not reacting, for example, when given birthday presents. She wore one of Serge's healing symbols on a bracelet, and she drew it on bits of paper that her father found in her school bag and coat. Fixated on UM's rituals, Lara would only walk in an anticlockwise direction on visits to the grocery store, and she burst into tears, protesting that they would not reincarnate, if her Dad stirred the pancake batter clockwise.

Lara's grandmother, Leonie, observed that Fran and the child needed constant contact and validation from each other. When staying with Graham, Lara continually phoned her mother for guidance on what she was allowed to eat and do, shutting herself in a cupboard during calls. It was less a relationship between a responsible grown-up and her daughter than a smothering dependency where the mother's emotional state was about as mature as her child's.

It took years to work through the Family Court, but Graham secured orders protecting Lara from UM. A court-appointed social worker reported to the judge that UM's worldview could confuse a child and hinder her ability to form healthy relationships. The orders barred Fran from taking Lara anywhere near Unimed and from discussing its doctrines with her. No sooner were they handed down, though, than Fran chose to ignore them. She kept up her regular Esoteric healing sessions, and her attendance at UM events, and when Graham raised her recalcitrance, she denied involving their daughter in her Livingness habit.

A few weeks later, she took Lara to The Lighthouse.

lxxxi Claim 2.0

Benhayon had just expanded his defamation claim, in September 2016, when Joelle messaged that he'd materialised at her workplace. A couple of weeks earlier, Winston Churchill, latterly known as Simone Benhayon, had shown up at the Gold Coast sports store where she worked. Pretending she was shopping for trainers, Simone acted surprised and struck up a conversation in which Joelle mentioned that she'd soon start managing a homewares store. 'My first day he was in here with Miranda at nine a.m. I was creeped out, it was too much of a coincidence.' The Esoteric royals showed up in a big white Audi and made a few purchases, while another staff member covered for Joelle, who hid out back. 'I'm super intimidated by him and the feeling I got was overpowering,' she said.

'It's not a coincidence, the fucking bastard,' I replied. Her name was mentioned in documents I was required to hand over under disclosure rules, and Joelle had listed her workplace on her public Facebook profile. 'Trust me, he has no special powers…the fucker won't know what hit him when I bring this defence and the media.'

Weeks later, though, that confidence was shot. I was out of money and my defence was in doubt. Although Tom had just come on board to help, I also needed a solicitor willing to work for no money. Some busy Sydney lawyers tried to find one for me, but UM's second defamation claim wiped out any chance of that.

The plaintiffs in the Queensland action were UM psychologist Caroline Raphael and UM FACTS team member, Ray Karam, a whiny ex-police officer who owned a health food shop in Ballina, and was married to Matt Sutherland's ex-partner, Sarah Baldwin. With UM's customary Christmas cheer, Fletcher filed in Brisbane over nine hundred kilometres from Sydney, on the twenty-second of December 2016 and served their claim on the Friday afternoon before the break. At the end of November, we'd filed a ninety-five page defence to Benhayon's expanded claim. Fletcher knew most lawyers had finished work for the year and would not return until well into January, and Queensland's civil procedure rules were not exactly festive, requiring me to file a defence within twenty-eight days.

I'd just arrived in Brisbane that Friday to celebrate with family and was lunching on my eighty year old mother's veranda when I noticed a large car crawling up the street — a white, late model Audi. No, I thought. Benhayon preached that Audis are the most Esoteric of makes, causing some of his flatterers to go into major debt in their quest for automative godliness. Still, I doubted it, and with veranda rails and trees partly obscuring my view, I stooped as it passed to glimpse a pair of skinny arms at the wheel. Again I thought, no. But it made a U turn and on the second slow pass I got a good look at the underfed Esoteric at the wheel, looked him straight in the eyes. It was one of Serge's shrivelled defenders who would lose half his body weight if he passed wind. Damn him if my mother's place wasn't booby trapped with dog-gates and fences and latches and Escheresque staircases, I would have been down there with my phone, filming the stalker. I would have made him an internet star.

lxxxii Hidden assets

It was Smith's idea to challenge the jurisdiction of the Queensland defamation claim. He confidently figured the case might go away if it was transferred to Sydney, so I scraped together funds for him to travel to Brisbane in February 2017 to argue it. No one I knew thought Raphael and Karam's claim was anything more than an attempt to disrupt my defence to Benhayon's action in New South Wales. They were suing me for criticising their public promotions of UM, claiming I'd defamed them in an email I'd sent to Ballina Shire Councillors, and six tweets. Moon-eyed Benhayon fan, Ray Karam, was running for a council seat and the mayoral ticket in a shire that he didn't live in.

Round-faced Raphael showed in court in a floaty white polyester jumpsuit as if it was a garden party. Someone had stuck a suit on scrawny Karam, Paula Fletcher played backup for Wilson, and Alison Greig hovered. She'd just married the lurching barrister,

Smith estimated a two hour, straightforward argument to the effect that running the case in Brisbane put me at a major disadvantage. None of the parties resided in Queensland, there was already a related proceeding well afoot in Sydney, my legal team was there, and the plaintiffs were business and property owners, whereas I'd spent every cent I had defending the Sydney action and was demonstrably deep in debt. But the hearing spilled into a full day of Wilson's high-pitched bellyaching, and the first sign that things were going badly was when the dour judge glanced at my pleadings to the Benhayon claim and said, 'Some people call the Catholic Church a cult.'

With that, Wilson was off, calling me a religious bigot and a troll. By then he was listed on the UM FACTS website as one of its authors, and the bulk of his legal argument replicated its allegations that I was a malicious bully. He asserted that the Sydney action was not related, despite imputations in both claims about Benhayon and his cult, and the fact the three closely associated plaintiffs shared the same legal team, themselves part of said cult. Wilson argued, contrary to everything under the judge's nose, that my publications about Raphael and Karam were an unrelated personal vendetta.

Judge Dour* frowned along, but what really did me damage was Wilson planting a baseless suggestion that I had 'hidden assets'. Despite tendering a sworn affidavit declaring that I was broke, Wilson speculated that the fact that I still had lawyers representing me a year into escalating litigation meant that I had a stash of funds somewhere — a trust fund, a share portfolio. Smith dramatically overestimated our chances of winning, but there was nothing wrong with his performance. All he could do was argue that 'the plaintiffs have produced no evidence for that allegation your Honour' over and over. We, on the other hand, had evidence of the plaintiffs' professions and assets, but the judge got it into his head that I had money somewhere and began to repeat it himself — supporting the theory that if you throw around enough bullshit, some will stick.

The judge was also sold on the argument, admittedly their strongest, that the Brisbane court was more convenient to the parties. It was geographically closer and easier to get to. We were beaten badly in that fiery baptism into Team UM's Queensland strategy, and terrifyingly, Wilson told the judge that Fletcher had made inquiries on possible trial dates. A backlog in Sydney's Supreme Court meant Benhayon versus Rockett could not go to trial until the latter half of 2018, and he proudly announced an intention to have the Raphael and Karam trial heard in Brisbane at least a year ahead of it — not just leapfrogging the Benhayon claim, but putting me under pressure to comply with heavy obligations in two jurisdictions with different procedural rules. Only days before that Brisbane hearing, Justice McCallum had ordered Benhayon and me to give discovery of documents, a contentious process even when opponents behave reasonably. She'd granted me six weeks to complete the task.

At the end of the hearing, Judge Dour threw out my jurisdictional challenge and ordered me to pay the plaintiffs' costs. The Esoterics wafted out of court in a cloud of smug exultation. Exhausted, Smith and I slumped into a conference room overlooking the rail lines of Roma Street and the bright parklands behind it. He spelled out the consequences. Aside from the obligation to file a defence within weeks, that bad day in court would come with a bill of forty-five thousand dollars. There wasn't enough in the kitty to pay Smith's half, and it was neither possible nor feasible to borrow more.

I stared over the treetops and the sloping lawns where children were playing. A day-long thrashing that ends in ruin hurts like not a lot of things hurt. It wasn't panic or despair or regret, but the stark apprehension of unrelenting hardship for the foreseeable future. Smith started mumbling about an appeal, but that made no sense to me. 'I can't cover these costs,' I said in a rasp.

He then delivered the final wallop. 'They're going to bankrupt you,' he said.

lxxxiii Default

Heath's name also appeared in my disclosed documents, and not long after Joelle was graced with an Esoteric visitation, his ex-girlfriend, Ellen, emailed him with questions about his role as a defence witness. She wanted to chat with him because UM's lawyers were asking whether he intended to suggest that Serge was a predator. Heath declined.

I was startled by UM's approaches to defence witnesses, but Tom wasn't concerned, seeing we'd held our own. His mind was on the Queensland claim, and he suggested it might be best to let it go. 'Why go to all the trouble of putting in a defence?' he said. 'Let it run its course — let them go through the motions of applying for a default judgment...'

I grunted disapprovingly, 'they'll get costs though...'

'It's up to you... but you have nothing. If you can't pay, you can't pay.'

'They'll bankrupt me…'

'Oh, I don't know…' he said, 'they won't get anything out of the claim; you can't unsend the email, and you said yourself that you don't care if the tweets are taken down… Your time is better spent focusing on your defence of the Benhayon case…'

The first time I met Tom in person was in October 2016, after Benhayon had tripled his claim. Our few brief emails and phone calls had been curt and business like, but our first conference ran to two hours, his indulgence of time so unexpected I had to interrupt our conversation to get to my next appointment. I first laid eyes on him in the chambers foyer, with its twenty foot ceilings and its towering shelves of law books; a tall, fair, balding man in his late sixties in a white business shirt, beige pleated trousers and white sneakers. He was distinguished, yet genial, and he approached, chin down, with springing short steps and a surprisingly amiable smile considering the trouble I was in.

Our meeting ran the range of topics in Benhayon's case. Daylight streamed through the tall, north-facing windows overlooking Martin Place. I surveyed his bookshelves; law tomes interspersed with a selection of novels and dozens of non-fiction volumes in English and French, including at least four on the Dreyfus case, and several books he'd authored. Vintage circus posters adorned the walls, matching his Ferris wheel; an illusionist sawing through smiling woman in a hinged box, and a flying French belle on a trapeze. Above the sofa was a large poster of the charcoal and graphite Archibald Prize winning portrait of David Gulpilil by Craig Ruddy.

We talked a lot about Judith McIntyre. Benhayon's new pleadings included an imputation that he'd unduly influenced a cancer patient to get her assets. 'Don't get me wrong,' Tom said, 'the sexual allegations in this case are extremely serious, but when you think about it, cosying up to a dying woman and persuading her to overlook her family to give you her money…' He drew breath. '…you could argue it's nearly as bad.'

He often agreed with my view when other lawyers hadn't, and when he learned that Health Care Complaints Commissioner Pehm had asserted that it would be difficult to determine that Benhayon's clients had not consented to indecent touching, he objected with the same reasoning I'd used three years before: 'If a person is deceived as to the reasons for the touching, it's not consent.'

In drafting the amended defence, three times the size of Richardson's original, I worked directly with the silk. I didn't have the money to pay Smith to act as go-between, despite his grumbling. The day before filing, Tom and I probably spent eight hours in phone consultations; Tom in Martin Place, and me at my desk in my Byron Shire flat. The lawyer usually hand wrote his documents, scanned them, and emailed them to his typist, but I took over typing for my case.

What I hadn't appreciated before was that a good lawyer isn't just a good talker, but a good listener. Tom really listened. He didn't rush or interrupt, he absorbed knowledge like a high powered sponge, and he could recall fine, critical details that lesser minds miss, often the exact words in the precise order they were put. He was extremely generous with his time, explaining precedents and points of law to untrained me. If I proposed an amendment or a new angle for my defence he always explained why he thought it wouldn't work, but he also listened carefully to my dissenting arguments, sometimes changing his mind when he heard my reasoning, more often changing mine. Like most lawyers he'd seen cases end badly when the system malfunctions, the corrupt and powerful prevail, or a client proves flawed or fragile.

My readers reacted to the Raphael and Karam case pessimistically. Lance shared Tom's view that it was not worth mounting a defence, but to me a default judgment in their favour would green-light injunctions against my publishing, and more claims seeking to take my publications down. 'They'll get orders and they won't stop until everything's gone...' I said.

Tom didn't think it would be that easy, but my strategy was to surrender nothing, put Team UM to as much work as they put me. He wasn't troubled if we disagreed, and remained supportive, agreeing to represent me in Queensland, depending on his availability. I steeled myself for more defamation claims, and told him that no matter what they brought or where they brought it, I'd be giving it back, in spades.

lxxxiv 860

I'd start to speak and the judge would stop me.

'As I wrote in my email to your associate, Your Honour, I'd like to seek an adjournment of the application to strike out…'

'One thing at a time,' he said. 'The non-disclosure application is first. We'll see how that goes.'

I held up the sheaf. 'Your Honour, I'd like to hand up this affidavit. It's…'

'Hold on, you can't just hand up affidavits at hearing. Any affidavits should have been filed before today.'

I frowned. Wilson had handed up a last minute affidavit from Paula Fletcher at the February hearing. 'Your Honour, at short notice…'

'Does the affidavit pertain to the application before the court?'

'Not the first item, but for the adjournment…'

'Hold on to your affidavit… and you may sit down Ms Rockett. I'll hear from Mr Wilson.'

UM's counsel gave a longwinded outline of the plaintiffs' application for orders and referred to the affidavits of Raphael and Karam. The judge turned to me. 'You understand the plaintiffs have filed affidavit evidence…'

From my seat at the bar I answered, 'yes, Your Honour,' and hurried to stand. 'I have objections to the affidavits.'

The judge, a fair skinned balding man around fifty, with dark brown eyes, raised his eyebrows. 'Objections?'

'Yes, your Honour, at paragraph…'

'Which affidavit?'

'Mr Karam's, the second plaintiff...paragraph, um, um, six, or four, to six, maybe three to six, are irrelevant to today's argument, and they're prejudicial.'

The eyebrows shot up again.

I laboured on. 'The allegations here that I'm a liar and a troll have no relevance to a non-publication order, your Honour, and the um, material, about the plaintiff, Mr Karam's, um, marriage and the...'

'Mr Wilson?'

Wilson rose.

'You may sit down Ms Rockett. Stand when you address the court and when I address you.'

'Yes, thank you your Honour. I beg your pardon.'

Wilson embarked on a speech about my malicious campaign against his clients, two respected members of a religion falsely tarnished by blah blah blah and Ms Rockett has a vicious vendetta of trolling and this impermissibly large defence of one hundred and fifty pages reads more like a blog than defence pleadings with all these stories, and they're nothing more, scandalous hearsay, therefore the fact that Ms Rockett is a troll makes her an unreliable...

His Honour had sharp eyes and a sharp tone. 'Stop calling her a troll,' he said. 'That is a label, it's not evidence.'

Wilson persisted. 'Your Honour, Ms Rockett is being sued in New South Wales in a very big trolling case...'

The judge cut him off. 'Stop calling her a troll. I'm striking out those paragraphs the defendant objected to. They're not relevant; they're opinion, not evidence.'

I lost the argument, however. I'd named a couple of children in my defence pleadings and in applying for non-publication orders, Wilson demanded that the entire defence document be sealed in the court file so that journalists or other observers could not access it. He added that a single mention of the children in over a hundred pages of diverse particulars warranted an order that the trial be held in a closed court.

Tom disagreed, and the only solicitor I could get hold of agreed with Tom, saying that at most, just that part of the defence could be sealed. His Honour, however, overruled. 'We don't do that,' he said. That brought Wilson to his feet to witter about putrid allegations and besmirching children, to which the judge turned to me with a scowl. 'Why on earth would you identify children in a case like this?' he said.

I rose. 'As I referred in my written submissions your Honour…'

'You have written submissions?' said the judge.

'You have written submissions?' said Wilson.

I'd emailed them to judge's Associate and Fletcher that morning, and luckily had printed copies. 'Your Honour, I did not name those children lightly. You will see footnotes in my submissions referring to the defence particulars of truth. The Universal Medicine organisation poses very strong risks to children, and those were factual particulars of a serious threat of harm.' I explained the advice I'd gotten, that the court could seal that page of the defence.

He softened slightly. 'Look,' he said, 'that's not how our registry works.'

I couldn't risk annoying him further and apologised. 'If I'd known that I would not have contested it.' He offered me a choice of consenting to strike out the paragraph identifying the kids or he would grant the non-publication order. Having plenty of other evidence to rely on, I agreed to strike it out. With that, Wilson suggested that the judge should order me to file an amended defence.

His Honour sighed with irritation. 'The last thing this court needs is more paper!' He dangled his bulging copy of the defence over the bench. 'Just cross it out.' Frizz haired Fletcher then spent the next twenty minutes colouring in the paragraph with a biro so that it could not be read. But Wilson began carping and cavilling about the form of the orders until the judge was seething and there were only twenty minutes left. I no longer needed to ask for an adjournment on the second argument. The judge adjourned it and cracked to Wilson, 'at the rate you move, you'll need a full day.'

He found a listing date before another judge about three weeks away, but I had no idea whether Tom would be available. He'd mentioned that another lawyer in chambers might help, but I didn't know who that was. When I'd expressed a foreboding that Team UM would list hearings without negotiation, he'd said, 'oh no, they can't do that.'

Wilson then began a cryptic discussion with the judge, and I became distracted. My mind drifted to the identity of this mysterious, helpful barrister at Tom's chambers. I'd probably reached the limit of anyone's cognitive performance after a two-hour drive in peak hour, and a fraught two-hour stab at self-representation on three hours of sleep. Next thing I knew the judge had called a short adjournment and was strolling toward his chambers giving me the side-eye.

What I'd missed was that he was allowing me ten minutes to contact counsel to check their availability for hearing. I began sorting my papers until Fletcher prompted, 'Are you going to call him?'

'What?'

The UM cluster glared at me and Raphael and Greig sniggered with scorn. Fletcher explained, and exasperated, I repeated what I had put in writing to her five times that week: 'He's in court!'

She whined a reply. 'Call his clerk!'

'He doesn't have a clerk.'

The judge scanned the characters before him as he stepped back to the bench. I knew I looked bad. Wilson got up and sneeringly spoke for me, that Miz Rockett was unable to reach counsel. 'She tells us he's a Senior Counsel who has no clerk,' he sniffed. All I could do was explain what I already had to pig-headed Team Esoteric. I did not try to explain that my high profile lawyer manages his own diary and has never owned a mobile phone. Wilson and company probably deliberately listed on the Friday on the odds that Tom was appearing in Justice McCallum's weekly defamation list.

The judge questioned me about my lack of solicitor — Smith was history. Litigants don't ordinarily interact with barristers, relying on solicitors to liaise on their behalf, so I had to explain Tom's direct access brief. His

Honour then listed on the date Wilson requested and warned that I'd be unable to use the same excuse again. Turning to the plaintiffs, however, he gently suggested that they consider mediation or some compromise with me. I nodded emphatically. The plaintiffs were claiming two hundred and fifty thousand dollars each in damages, but the nature of the imputations and extent of publication meant that even if they won, any award of damages would be minuscule. I couldn't pay it in any case. 'There's no money in this claim,' said the judge. 'This could drag on for years, and at best it'll be a Pyrrhic victory. No one gets anything out of these cases but lawyers.'[89]

Wilson scoffed at the suggestion. 'My clients won't settle,' he replied before moaning about 'malicious damages', and complaining that I hadn't complied with a number of his clients' demands. He boasted that they intended to seek more court orders against me before the next listed hearing, confirming that they would keep calling hearings on the flimsiest of premises without negotiation. I needed help, and although the judge didn't like me standing without being addressed, I rose and asked if I could hand up my affidavit. I had to go for it.

'Your Honour, Mr Wilson has indicated that he intends to seek further court orders in the next few weeks, possibly at short notice. On the tenth of March, Justice McCallum handed down discovery orders in the Supreme Court of New South Wales in Benhayon versus Rockett. I am under obligation to comply with those orders. Ms Fletcher and Mr Wilson are also representing the plaintiff in those proceedings, who is under similar orders. I was given six weeks to comply, and I'm running about a month late.'

The judge's mouth was open, on the verge of speaking, but he was listening. I pushed on. 'On March twenty-fourth, as you see, I filed a comprehensive defence to this action, requiring considerable work with counsel.' I was still holding up the document. 'This bundle of annexures to my affidavit, one hundred and twenty pages, is the letters I've received from Ms Fletcher in the five weeks since. I've been bombarded with threats that the plaintiffs will seek orders with respect to numerous demands. They've demanded I produce for inspection about one thousand documents, pursuant to rule two hundred and twenty two within fourteen days; applied to strike out forty contextual truth imputations; and this is a sixty page letter with eight hundred and sixty requests for further and better particulars they say they require within fourteen days as well…'

The judge's mouth remained open.

'…and refusing to extend me reasonable time to complete any of them, which I'm endeavouring to do. I would like this evidence here at court to show that it is not humanly possible for me to keep up with this volume of demands while I'm subject to pre-existing court orders in another state, and if they insist on calling hearings without negotiation.'

It came out fluently, but the judge was unable to do anything. 'You can't hand up that affidavit,' he said. There was no condescension or irritation in his tone. He spoke carefully. 'I can't take it, not under the scope of today's applications.' I lowered my hand and the sheaf clumped onto the bar table.

'What you can do,' he said, 'is file it in the registry, take it downstairs and file it, and then it's there if you need to call it up.'

'Okay,' I nodded. 'Thank you.'

The hearing was over, and the judge got up to leave, but before he reached the door he turned to look me one more time in the face, deep into my crimson eyes.

lxxxv Human shields

According to Raphael and Karam's statement of claim, only one person had read my email; Ray's mate, David Wright, a gnomish former science teacher who dressed neck to toe in black and happened to be mayor of Ballina. The mayor had phoned Karam to assure him that he didn't believe a word of it. A competent lawyer would have advised their clients that any potential award of damages would be negligible if the only person who'd read the alleged defamations took no notice of them.

I wouldn't have bothered email Council if Karam didn't have a decent chance of getting elected. He'd headed Ballina's Chamber of Commerce, and on Twitter, he'd posted photos of himself hobnobbing with National Party parliamentarians. A snap with Federal MP, Kevin Hogan, was captioned that they were 'great mates'. Karam was also backed by UM's media team, who relentlessly flogged his credentials as a former cop, even though he'd never ranked higher than constable in his relatively short police career.

Ray tweeted photos of himself embracing Serge and Michael, with the comment: 'Some may call him a friend — I call him family @sergebenhayon #brothers', and the connection drew negative reviews from New South Wales police officers who contacted me. Early 2014, Karam and Caroline Raphael had conducted training days for staff at Northern Rivers police stations, but the arrangement ended abruptly. His former colleagues were also uneasy about Ray talking up his police career in his roles as a Girl to Woman Festival organiser and presenter, and the way he seemed to mimic Benhayon's cheesy appearance.

My email to Councillors laid out Karam's enlistment to the UM FACTS team that had singled out local resident, Rosie, in their slurs. Development applications for the Hall of Ageless Wisdom also went before Council, where permission to increase student numbers at Serge's 'approved educational facility' was voted down due to road safety concerns. I questioned whether Karam, who lived in Goonellabah, thirty kilometres from Ballina, was running to represent the shire's constituents or whether he was representing the interests of Benhayon and UM. Karam went on to deputise for Benhayon at Council meetings, and the Girl to Woman organisers published a photo of David Wright at the 2017 Festival; Ray with his arm around the pink faced, black-clad mayor. The group's love-bombers served as Karam's campaign volunteers, schmoozing into the shire's caravan parks and retirement villages to tout their fiery candidate.

Tempting as it was to leave him to the bloodsport of local politics, I couldn't gamble on Karam gaining influence, and his review of Benhayon's *The Way It Is* spoke to his suitability for the role.

> I have never really read books and was that way from very young. I was always one to read part but never finish them... At first this book confused me but at the same time it seemed like it made sense... To say this book has changed my life would be an understatement... I read this book back to back three times and it seemed like each time I was reading a new book.

That volume's teaching that the Four Lords of Form control human consciousness via their army of discarnate spirits probably did change his life, just not in the way he wanted to believe.

Fervent Unimed promoter, Caroline Raphael, contributed blogs on UM websites and advertised herself as a 'registered Esoteric Practitioner' alongside her credentials as a registered psychologist, and as an assistant facilitator at Benhayon's healing workshops. Matt remembered her attending one he went to in 2007, and she was regularly photographed at UM events since. With that record, it's difficult to buy that she was concerned about her reputation, yet she claimed I'd harmed it by making negative inferences about her professionalism.

To me, Raphael and Karam were two of Benhayon's human shields, throwing themselves into my path as I pushed for meaningful scrutiny of their idol. As adults, they could wear responsibility for the consequences, but **UM FACTS** continued to publish testimonials from kids, shoving the fifteen year old daughter of The Lighthouse proprietors, Simon and Janet Williams, onto the propaganda frontline. In praising Serge, the youngster stated that she'd been a regular houseguest at Chez Benhayon since the age of two, and she and other teens were named as authors of seriously defamatory material about me.

Their blogs also revealed what they were led to believe about themselves. The young woman Heath saw trailing Serge at a workshop wrote: 'Without Universal Medicine, I would be out partying, drinking and sleeping around, because I would know no differently.' Others attributed their sober behaviour to 'being so close to Serge and his family.' UM followers seemed fine with Benhayon supplanting parental authority and undermining the youngsters' ability to think for themselves. Its zealots were willing to exploit children to vouch for their gutless guru.

lxxxvi Sergeant Eric

A month after Detective G* (for Grumpy) clomped up my stairs, Ray Karam and other unisex Brides of Serge tweeted at the NSW Police Force Twitter account whingeing about a campaign of stalking and online bullying. Naturally, I replied with a suggestion that they stop wasting police time. 'Tried to have you arrested?' Alison Greig tweeted in retort. 'Rockett your imagination running wild — just like your sexual abuse stories.'

An imputation in Benhayon's claim, however, that he'd engaged in bullying to stop me exposing his inappropriate behaviour with children, allowed me to subpoena New South Wales police for documentation. About thirty Eso-luminaries, Mystic Dentist Rachel Hall included, made criminal complaints about me in 2015. Alison and her clairsentient colleagues were also unaware that a significant leak from the compound yielded in-house communications organising to pressure police into prosecuting me.

One of UM's most dogged fibs was that 'Serge never tells anyone what to do', but messages posted from June 2015 on one of UM's password protected forums revealed he'd led the Esoteric vigilantes:

> know this, Esther Rockett her mentor Lance will meet with their crimes in more ways than temporal law will see fit. You do not make such deals with the astral and for one minute hope that you can simply walk away free of the pranic karma that awaits.

That was followed by considerable input from a ten-year acolyte who dared not identify himself publicly; a serving officer in the South Australia Police, Sergeant Eric Walsh. Walsh fielded questions about the Australian

Cybercrime Online Reporting Network (ACORN), a complaints portal operated by the Australian Federal Police, and the first inquiry was from a devotee who wanted to make a complaint '…even if my name is not used yet in the bullying, attacking my brothers and UM is attacking me.' Upper-crust British film director, Otto Bathurst, offered to send a four thousand word complaint.

'As many as possible should be going the full hog on ACORN. Flood Eric's inbox and let's get to it,' Benhayon replied.

Sergeant Walsh posted a two page instructional on framing my publishing as personal threats rather than criticism of UM promotions, urging complainants to express fear for their safety:

> the fear of answering the phone, double locking the door, checking your rear view mirror as you drive…hiding your identity, no longer having the confidence to speak to strangers… If in doubt run it past me - as Serge said — hit my inbox…

Serge added:

> This is Gold, Eric…Let's make Esther and Lance 'famous' with the police… As you all know these horrific attacks and lies have not stopped me or brought me down but that will not stop me from saying it is a crime. I have done my full police report, have you?
>
> Keep reporting her. It will work.

Ray Karam left a message offering to help, and Paula Fletcher was amongst it, replying with her Universal Law letterhead and questioning why so few of the faith-full tweeted links to 'our FACTS blog. In fact I encourage it.'

At some point after he'd visited me, Detective G, a thirty year veteran of the force, notified the Esos that no criminal offence could be identified, and the case was closed. But Sergeant Eric Walsh, the congregation's financial advisor, Christoph Schnelle, and others, refused to accept it, instigating a flurry of emails that copied in complainants and lawyers, including doctors Malatt, Szramka, Minford and Kim; psychologists Masiorski, Mooney and

Raphael; Chris James, Otto Bathurst, Wilson, Fletcher, Greig, and O'Regan. Walsh wrote:

> [Detective G] is determined to make this an issue of Esther Rockett vs UM - which it is not… ER is deliberately and maliciously targeting individuals…
>
> There is and continues to be a real threat of physical assault occurring — and this is directly attributable to Esther Rockett's conduct and actions — and nothing else.

In another two page missive he gave instructions on grilling the detective.

> Don't be persuaded that this is a Civil matter or that her conduct is supported by Freedom of Speech…
>
> You will need to state… That you have and continue to be traumatised, threatened and intimidated as a victim.
>
> You will be stating that you expect to be informed about the nature of the conversation he had with Esther regarding you.

However, when Walsh proposed a federal charge for the crime of 'using a carriage service to menace, harass or cause offence', Paula Fletcher replied that section 474.17 of the *Federal Criminal Law Act* was only used when there were 'serious threats of harm…or where a carriage service is used to transmit child pornography etc.'

Despite that, Schnelle encouraged the pack to recalibrate their energy to assert themselves as 'pillars of the community… threatened by a malicious troll.' He circulated a list of questions for interrogating the officer and said he would make a complaint to the Police Ombudsman, alleging misconduct on the part of Detective G.

lxxxvii Non-publication

During that short adjournment, before Fletcher rudely interrupted my downtime, the unknown woman in the back corner got up to leave. Wilson shouted at her. 'Where are you from?!'

She scowled. 'I'm the court reporter for the Courier Mail.'

His voice remained raised. 'You can't leave the courtroom! You can't report this, we have a non-publication order!'

'You can't tell me what to do,' she snapped back, and left.

Gangling Wilson pivoted to me. 'Tell your friend she's prohibited from reporting…'

I cut him off. 'I don't know her.'

'…bringing the media to a non-publication hearing…' He continued to mutter and sputter about trolling and lying and media bias as if the UM FACTS website had been rolled up, bleating, into an ill-fitting suit.

I let him carry on, before interjecting sharply. 'Knock it off Charles, you've got no evidence.'

Behind me, Greig, Fletcher and Raphael began cackling like Macbeth's witches; the mocking laughter persisting a little too long. Wilson shut up, but continued to glare at me, eyes watering with what looked like panic, or might have been offence — whatever it was, he was in a state.

Beyond the judge's dais were twenty foot walls of glass that gave generous glimpses of sky, filling the room with natural light. At the corner of the ceiling was a security camera, and I remembered that courtrooms are full of mics. I pictured the judge with his feet up on his desk watching the show. It made me feel a bit like Jane Goodall, cutting through the jungle to encounter the UM species in the wild; to see firsthand that their irrationality was not feigned.

lxxxviii Front foot

Fletcher kept heaping her legal love letters on me, and Tom read a lot of them. Those related to the Brisbane action comprised senselessly urgent and largely unnecessary demands, while those for the Sydney case dodged and stalled on Benhayon's compliance with Justice McCallum's discovery orders. Barristers are not permitted to carry out the work of solicitors, but Tom could advise me to reply with reasons for contesting any demand. 'Write all your letters as if they will be read by a judge,' he said. That way, I could demonstrate to the court that I had attempted reasonable negotiation.

But Tom was semi-retired and had an unkind habit of trotting off on long vacations without permission. Thankfully, Louise Goodchild joined my team soon after my bareknuckle Brisbane hearing against Wilson. Her office was twice the size of Tom's, with two solid walls of bookcases, a large, antique, leather topped conference table, and space for her clerk Madeline's station near the door. 'You can play golf down there,' Tom said. Louise's caseload, however, was huge.

If legal brevity was a sport, Louise would be an Olympian. Her every word was a sharpened spear. I sat up straight when she spoke, measured my replies, and never dozed off. She spared nobody, and I'd witnessed her merciless cross-examinations of an unflinching Tom on his strategies for my defence. If his explanations were not to her satisfaction, she would turn up the blowtorch, but if it was a good answer, she'd melt into a cheeky grin, and say, 'oh well, that's all right then,' and I could resume breathing. Out of the robes, Louise was a classical music loving softie who couldn't wait to get home to her two excitable pooches, and her giggle was as disarming as her forensic skewerings.

But as an extremely busy barrister, she didn't have time to read or advise on Fletcher's screeds. So when Tom took his four month sojourn, this amateur solicitor was on her own: cramming statutes and procedural rules and drafting detailed letters and schedules. I spent precious hours fruitlessly trying to find stand-in counsel, available at short notice and willing to work for no money, when Fletcher persisted in listing hearings without negotiating hearing dates. Matthew Richardson had offered to help where he could, pro bono, as had a high profile Sydney Senior Counsel, but barristers of their calibre were never available at short notice. A Brisbane not-for-profit organisation, LawRight, tried to help my search.

Louise was not available until a few days after the next listing but Fletcher refused to adjourn to a date to be agreed between counsel. The court had not set a timetable for the Queensland claim, so Team UM's hastiness was unwarranted. Thinking Wilson might be more accommodating, I copied him in to an email appealing to common sense, and when he hit reply, it came to both Fletcher and me. 'She's had help I gather,' he began, with Ageless astuteness, but he advised the solicitor not to relent and to keep nagging me to seek representation other than my retained lawyers.

> This is a tough call. IN the end, I imagine that Rockett will come up, represent herself and seek the adjournment. Will she get it, probably, but I can't be certain. Energetically, we need to not dig in out of reaction, but also to see that if we yield and consent to an adjournment that we do so on the front foot.
>
> Love Charles

I addressed my answer to both, confirming that I was preparing to apply for an adjournment, and I recommended that they stop wasting time trying to get their stories straight and relist while a mutually agreeable date was available.

> I note that you are determined to remain on the front foot regardless of the merits of your argument or the claim. That is plain. Leading with the chin as well, it appears.
>
> I also suggest you read my correspondence carefully… Clearly no judge wants unrepresented litigants fronting court when they have counsel able to appear.

Wilson's next reply dropped the Esotericisms and requested I delete his reply, claiming it was subject to legal professional privilege. I was familiar with professional privilege, and knew its limitations. The privilege belongs to the client, not the lawyer, and only covers communications created for the dominant purpose of providing legal advice pursuant to the administration of justice or the provision of legal services. Shifty listing hijinks are neither. I filed it under 'dirt'.

lxxxix Lookout

Hostilities continued apace. Lance paid Louise's airfare to Brisbane to sort out the next hearing, her finesse ensuring that I was not penalised for failing to keep up with Fletcher's wishlist. The Esoteric lawyers, however, kept up their unreasonable demands and a bitter campaign of resistance to Benhayon's discovery obligations. He'd been ordered, for example, to turn over all documents that recorded him offering advice or guidance to his devotees, procuring donations and unpaid labour, arranging juvenile sleepovers or organising to harass me, and had publicly bragged of answering hundreds of emails from students per day, yet he yielded a pitifully tiny and carefully curated collection. Fletcher claimed he and his employees were in the practice of deleting all emails and attachments as soon as they were read, and had thus disposed of years of pertinent communications. It was an unusual way to operate a business and a suspicious way to prepare for litigation.

He also pushed back on turning over unpublished audio of his workshops and EDG meetings. My witnesses had seen recording equipment at every event and meeting, but Benhayon whinged that they only existed as a mass of unlabelled digital recordings too huge and oppressive to sort out. Digital files are simple to order by production date, though, and a UM escapee told me it was unthinkable that they were uncatalogued. As his founding revelation suggests, Benhayon was the consummate anal retentive.

On it went. Mid 2017, Esoteric Women's Health shopped its Girl to Woman show to Tenterfield, but this time a school principal and the head of a local child welfare service thanked me for my notifications. Sarah Broome expressed her gratitude by posting an **OFFICIAL STATEMENT REGARDING TARGETING & HARASSMENT OF THE FESTIVAL & COMMUNITY MEMBERS** to Facebook, encouraging anyone who heard from me to 'contact your local police'.

In the interim, Nick Farrow tried to resurrect the *Sunday Night on Seven* report on UM, with journalist Matt Doran. We now had footage of Serge in Way of the Livingness event videos that UM published in a subscription package, but Nick wanted to record the feted 'World's Teacher' undergoing proper questioning. Benhayon again refused an interview, so another ambush was carefully planned on the only date left in the year when it was guaranteed he'd surface in a public space, entering his Level One healing course at the Lennox Head Community Centre in August.

Nick was concerned he might not show, that he might get others to run the course, but if I understood nothing else about the premium poser, I knew he'd never relinquish a chance to grace a stage before adoring customers. On the mornings of the workshop, I waited, discreetly, along the route to the venue to make sure, and to alert the crew when he was on his way. Minutes after he passed on the Sunday, chauffeured by Natalie, one of our lookouts called. The Audi pulled up outside the Community Centre and out jumped Channel Seven. My friend was laughing as the camera crew surrounded it. 'Serge won't get out of the car.'

xc Fiftieth

Without a solicitor, I had no access to facilities available to professionals. Where solicitors are able to file documents online in seconds or minutes, I had to apply to the registrar for permission and then rely on regional snail-mail, taking up to eight weeks to get sealed copies back from the registry. My subpoena to New South Wales police had expired by the time service copies came in the mail, and had to be reissued.

Meanwhile, in Sydney, my father's health was declining. He'd been hospitalised many times over previous years. His partner had died the year before, he had no family in the city and he needed help with some errands, so I planned to drive there to give him a hand once I'd cleared a few tasks. I could get the subpoena reissued while in town. I'd had to sell my car to pay Smith after our court loss earlier in the year, but luckily my brother bought it and lent it back to me, otherwise I don't know how I would have managed the trips between Brisbane, Sydney and home, two hours in one direction and ten hours in the other.

Excitement of the Lennox Head rumble over, I got back to work. Nick was delighted with the footage. Matt Doran questioned Benhayon as he skulked into the venue, where his minders drew the curtains and the workshop seemed to go ahead. The camera crew waited all day to catch him when he left, but at some point the self-described 'world renowned philosopher' was smuggled out, probably in the glove compartment of one of the Audis. Encouragingly, Nick said that only a couple of dozen attended the workshop, and my lookout reported that they were all familiar faces, no new inductees. At his peak, Benhayon would get over three hundred to the Level One course.

But during the following week, my father fell gravely ill, and wasn't responding to medical interventions. Organs which had been on the blink for years were failing fast and he lost consciousness. The medical team told me he would not survive. Having power of attorney, I was responsible for the final decisions around his care.

Shortly after receiving the call that my father was dying, I received one of Fletcher's odious letters notifying me she'd be listing a hearing in Brisbane the following week. She warned that if counsel was not available within a fortnight she'd list without further notice to me, which was an improvement for her. Thankfully, LawRight had found a couple of busy Brisbane barristers willing to help, but I called, messaged and emailed them explaining the situation with my father, and got no reply. That meant dealing directly with Fletcher. I had no option but to inform her of my father's impending death, that I was about to drive to Sydney, and that I'd been unable to reach counsel. Expecting she'd accuse me of faking my father's illness, I explained that I could not get a medical certificate until I reached the hospital. Privacy regulations prevented the hospital from sending one via email.

> I request that you do not list any application for hearing until after we have held my father's funeral... Please note that I do not give permission for you, Mr Wilson, or the plaintiffs to disclose or share any information about this personal matter, including my father's medical condition, to any party other than my counsel and the court... I will inform you when we have arranged a funeral date. I request that you do not trouble me with unnecessary correspondence until I have done so.

Fletcher replied that afternoon. I read her email at a pit-stop in Coffs Harbour. A nurse had just phoned to ask how far away I was. Dad's breathing was failing.

> We look forward to receipt of the medical letter as offered and the name of your counsel for our counsel to liaise with. Otherwise we are awaiting instructions.

It was the twenty-fifth of August — my fiftieth birthday.

xci The certificate

'I've never seen anything like this,' Louise said on hearing Fletcher wanted the medical certificate. 'They don't need that. They need to leave you alone for a few weeks.'

Dad died on Sunday when his doctor was not on duty, meaning I had to travel across Sydney on Monday to get the letter. I'd spent two nights in his room in vigil. When I sent it, I informed Fletcher that I was sorting out my father's affairs and helping arrange his funeral, to be held in Brisbane, and repeated that I did not give permission for information on the circumstances to be disclosed. Counsel in Brisbane still hadn't replied, so I asked for her patience until I could reach them. Again she hassled me for their contact details, saying that Wilson wanted to organise a 'mutually convenient listing date', clearly excluding me from any convenience. She repeated her threat to list for hearing if I didn't fall in with her timetable, adding:

> It is not open to you to unilaterally to impose upon, or enforce against our clients and our firm, a gag on the disclosure of information contained in your emails of 25 August 2017 and 28 August 2017…

When I replied on Wednesday with contact details for Brisbane Queens Counsel, Rob Anderson, I made another appeal:

> My father's funeral is to take place later this week and I request that out of normal human decency and respect for my family that you do not badger me with unnecessary correspondence until next week.

At three in the afternoon of my father's funeral, Fletcher emailed me a thirty page letter. It was a reply to a lengthy list of gaping deficiencies in Benhayon's discovery I'd sent her seven weeks earlier. Filled with defamatory accusations and insults, Fletcher's missive read like an Alison Greig spray on UM FACTS. When events a few months later prompted me to blog about Team UM's vindictiveness around my father's death, a number of supporters contacted me out of concern for my wellbeing. All I could say was that I expected it. That's what cults do.

I caught the train to the hospital on the Monday to get the doctor's certificate. Returning through the city, I collected my subpoena from the court. Later I'd travel to police headquarters at Parramatta to serve it. Needing to scan the medical letter, I dropped by chambers. Tom was still away and Louise was out of town, but Louise's clerk, gentle Madeline, came to greet me. She had big, green, searching eyes and the first thing she said to me was sorry about your Dad. I opened my mouth to thank her, but no words came out, only sobs.

xcii Rob

The ultra-modern District Court in Brisbane is all gleaming metal, glass, and blonde wood, but ruddy-faced Judge Tory*, who several times mentioned he was nearing retirement, displayed the Australian flag on the dais alongside the Union Jack. When the court officer called, 'all stand!' he added a rousing 'God save the Queen!' I braced for the worst.

It was September 2017 and a fortnight after Dad's funeral. I'd never met Rob Anderson and had to giggle when he sauntered out of the lift in a perfectly cut double breasted suit. The QC was everything Team UM was not — professional, friendly, kind, handsome, youthful, successful, and smart. Rob and another barrister, Amanda Stoker, had answered LawRight's appeal, but Amanda was on maternity leave with her fourth child.

Rob was a practised defamation barrister whose clients included shock jock Alan Jones, and then Prime Minister of Australia, Malcolm Turnbull, who was defending a defamation action brought by mining magnate Clive Palmer. Pleasingly, Rob told me that Raphael and Karam's claim would require a trial of at least six weeks, and no judges were available for such a large block of time for at least a year, until after the Benhayon showdown. I put it to Rob frankly: 'This case will never get that far.'

'I must say these interlocutory arguments in defamation seem such a waste of time and money,' Judge Tory grumbled as Wilson rose to begin his address. 'Most of these cases settle.'

'There's no chance the plaintiffs will settle,' was Charlie's endearing rejoinder.

Wilson then handed up his submissions, and the judge immediately exploded. 'Do any of you people read the practice notes?!' he shouted, brandishing the document. 'Written submissions are to be no more than four pages!' Charlie's were thirty. With that, Judge Tory ripped the first four from the staple, hurled the remainder over his shoulder, and the papers fluttered through the air, landing beside the Union Jack with a plop.

xciii The can

The *Sunday Night on Seven* report was shelved again. Nick spent weeks negotiating with defectors who were vacillating about going on camera. I could understand the refusals of those who feared being cut off from family still in the group, but the remaining two were especially aware of Unimed's risks to kids and risked nothing at all in coming forward.

I was losing patience with gutlessness. Nick had produced reports in warzones, and on international organised crime and terrorist groups, where people risk their lives to speak out, but he said it was easier to get them on camera than Benhayon's former clients. Perhaps the insecurities that Serge exploited to entrap them in the first place were responsible: emotional fragility and New Age self-centredness. To me, UM's enormous hazards overrode personal anxieties. If the fear was about litigation, we all doubted

Benhayon would take on a major television network. After all, Serge didn't sue *The Sunday Telegraph* for publishing my account of the ovarian reading.

The Lennox Head footage stayed in the can. Matt Doran asked Benhayon to step out of the car to answer some questions, but the Ascended Master refused and called the cops, laughing fiendishly as the fiery trio waited inside the Audi, filming the TV crew on their phones. A patrol car from Ballina eventually appeared, and when Serge opened the car door, the mic caught his words to the officer: 'They told us they would send a squadron down.'

Ballina command had two cars on patrol that Sunday morning for the entire district. The unruffled officer replied, 'well, here I am,' and added, 'what's the complaint?'

Benhayon was no longer smiling and his voice went quiet. 'Uh, we're not allowed to get out of the car…'

'Yes you are, Serge,' said Matt Doran. 'You're more than allowed to get out of the car.'

UM's guiding light spoke meekly to the cop, 'would you escort me?'

In coat, gloves and scarf, Benhayon made his way toward the centre, trailed by his offspring holding up their phones. Matt stepped beside him pummelling him with questions, and Serge turned imploringly to the officer, who moved away and told him, 'Just walk inside. If you don't want to answer, don't answer.'

Matt got up close. 'You're a cult leader, you run a money making cult. Where does all the money go?'

Benhayon was silent. 'Nothing to say sir?' said Matt. 'You have so much to say. You've built a career out of saying things and you have nothing at all to say?'

The guru muttered to the reporter as he as he scurried indoors: 'I've got you on camera, and your *lies*…' Serge was projecting again. We could say the same about him.

xciv Tory

Judge Tory was hearing a continuation of Raphael and Karam's application to have large chunks of my Queensland defence struck out, which had stumbled at two prior court dates. Although we came ready for a fight, Rob Anderson could not have spoken for more than five minutes of the three and a half hour hearing. The wizened judge, however, kept Wilson on his feet, quizzing him on defamation basics and letting him waffle on with submissions that even I knew were hopeless. At first I was nervous that Judge Tory might not be up to scratch on defamation law, but His Honour would contradict Wilson's prattle periodically, making me wonder why he didn't cut him off earlier. I turned to Rob, who'd eased back in his chair and was twiddling his pen, and whispered, 'What's happening?'

'I don't know,' he said. 'I'm not sure why he's making Charles work this hard.'

In fact, the old guy was extremely sharp on defamation law. One o'clock came and Wilson proposed a lunch adjournment, but His Honour told him to finish his submissions, prodding him for another forty minutes until his arguments sputtered to an end and he collapsed in his chair, arms dangling, legs stretched out, practically panting. Although His Honour had ruled on parts of the application as it progressed, and overwhelmingly in my favour, he said that he was unable to decide on the remainder, and invited further written submissions. Suddenly convivial, he added: 'There's no hurry, gentlemen. You see, I have a vast backlog of reserved judgements and this is not among those of priority. It's unlikely I'll get to it until next year.'

It was wonderful news. A reserved judgment would pause the Brisbane proceedings for months, derailing Team UM's plans to disrupt my Sydney defence with mock-urgent demands. As Rob and I smirked at each other, though, I caught a sudden movement out of the corner of my eye — a dark presence, a fast moving shadow, swooped from the public gallery to Wilson's side. Alison Greig, in black, had launched from her pew to wag her finger and mutter feverishly to her near prostrate husband. Jaw set, she retreated as Wilson sprung to his feet and addressed the court. 'Your Honour, the plaintiffs abandon their remaining objections, we'll accept Your Honour's ruling if it may be handed down immediately and we won't require reasons…'

'Oh!' said Judge Tory brightly, and hastily dictated orders dismissing most of Team UM's application.

They'd been flogging that strike-out attempt over three hearings and four months. Dropping its remnants so readily confirmed their real motives.

xcv The scrap

Litigation on skates was the next twelve months, a knuckle-mashing procedural roller derby without brakes. Tom called it the judicial equivalent of a jailhouse scrap; 'rusty razor blades at five paces'. The lack of mandatory case management in the Brisbane courts gave Team UM rein to play the jurisdictions off one another, careering between aggressive threats to call hearings in both states; and passive aggressive stalling on compliance with orders and procedural rules. If the tactic was to create masses of unnecessary work, it was a Glorious success. I was constantly fending off unjustifiable demands, including for irrelevant documents the plaintiffs were not entitled to — most particularly seeking to identify the UM critics among my contacts. Fletcher also listed hearings in Brisbane without negotiation on eight occasions.

An upshot of not having the caution and expense of a solicitor, though, was the freedom to become the aggressor. Tom and I prepared to seek further court orders to compel Benhayon to hand over documents, and I gave Fletcher notice that if he didn't produce them within a fortnight, we'd apply to Justice McCallum as soon as possible. Two weeks later, of course, she replied that he needed more time to ponder his reply, and Tom said there was no choice but to give them another week. When Fletcher eventually came back in November merely repeating previous refusals, the delay tactic had bought them two months. Justice McCallum had no listing dates available until February 2018.

But in the intervening weeks, Team UM amended the Queensland pleadings substantially, meaning I had to comprehensively renovate my defence. Fletcher also barraged me with ultimatums and served me with a summons to appear at a hearing in Brisbane, a preliminary step in enforcing payment of Raphael and Karam's costs for the jurisdictional massacre before Judge Dour. The summons required me to produce every document about my income and expenditure for the previous five years, including copies of fees agreements with my lawyers, my legal bills, loan agreements, bank statements, tax returns and years of accounts from the business I'd closed two years earlier. They also wanted a copy of my father's will. I'd already complied with a demand to file a sworn statement of my financial position, which showed I had nothing but debts, was surviving on a thin, irregular stream of donations, and was expecting no windfalls. Clamouring for money, however, was a sacred Esoteric ritual, and I had to threaten to seek a ruling of abuse of process when Fletcher refused to list on a date when Rob was available to appear.

I'd still get random callers. A woman told me that as a youngster she was inducted into a cult where she was sexually abused, yet when I offered condolences, she was dismissive and changed the subject. She said that Benhayon had tried to rope her into UM but she'd been suspicious. She also wanted to say that she sensed from my blogs that I was — she hesitated — 'pretty angry'.

'You don't think I have good reason?' I said.

'Sorry,' she said, 'I'm just worried about what it might be doing to you.'

I asked that she consider the alternative. 'It'd be a lot worse for me if I was somehow unable to act.'

Another caller reported that his UM ex-wife told their little daughter that her father was possessed by supernatural snakes. The mother used to cleanse their child after access visits, performing a hands-on exorcism before she'd let the kid in the car. He said he'd donated twenty bucks to my defence, which unfortunately came with his advice about the 'energy' that came through my social media posts. 'You're too aggressive,' he said and recommended I consult a friend of his, a healer and teacher, for instruction on more peaceful communication.

'Does she have litigation experience?' I asked.

'Uh...'

'Thanks for your suggestion,' I said. 'I'll give it some thought.' I hung up.

xcvi Alan

Typical of Team UM, they'd listed a fifteen minute hearing on obtaining information to facilitate the payment of the costs order, but it went for three hours. Wilson used the opportunity to cross-examine me before a disinterested court registrar about every cent that rapidly transited my bank account, down to what I paid for petrol and rations per week. It was the first time UM brought an audience to court too. Mystic Dentist, Rachel Hall, and Sam Kim's mirthless looking wife, Jasna, plumped in with de facto UM FACTS team member, black clad geriatric, Alan Johnston, who sat with Alison Greig, the pair taking notes on laptops while the others stabbed at their phones.

Wilson read out the names of family and friends who'd lent me cash, and their home addresses, and questioned the nature of my relationship with each, telling me, 'Speak up, Ms Rockett, you're addressing the court.' I obliged by dialling the volume to a notch below a shout. Knowing the contents of documents I'd had to turn over were confidential unless given in evidence, Serge's servants dipped their heads, taking down the information. Alan an occasional commenter on my blogs who never hung around to answer questions, had recently visited to suggest the litigation would give me a 'reality check', adding that he knew where I lived. He and his fellow parasites were now noting where my family and friends lived as well.

With no solicitor and counsel busy, I'd had no advice to prepare me for my first stint in a witness box, but my answers were instinctively blunt, except for the laugh out loud exchange in which Wilson asked if Tom was a published author. 'Uh, yeah.'

'Has he advised you on getting a publishing contract?'

'Ba ha!'

Or an advance from a publisher?

I laughed harder, Rob stood to object, and Wilson started clucking, so I shout-laughed over the top of them. 'No! There's no publishing contract, ba ha!'

Had I been paid for my statements to the media?

God no. Wilson's addled mind was wedged in conspiratorial fairyland.

As the questions wore into more personal territory, the registrar's young associate became uneasy. Leaving his post, he moved to each of the spectators to tell them to switch off their phones, as required under Queensland court rules. But for people who'd made a special trip to watch me get harassed over my inability to pay a bill, they looked remarkably lethargic, except for pasty forty-something Caroline Raphael, who was very perky indeed. At one point, I thought Alan's wife, semi-conscious Josephine Johnston, was about to careen off her seat. Complexion green, eyes narrowed, her posture was diagonal, listing away from her shrunken husband, who tapped at his keyboard with two fingers, chewing gum.

Wilson then started on my father's will, which Dad, bless him, had left me out of.

Are you a beneficiary?

No.

Why not?

Rob stood. 'Her father's intentions have nothing to do with whether she has the means to pay the order.'

Wilson replied. 'The defendant's father's intentions are evidence of her poor character and prove that she is an unreliable witness.' The registrar frowned and told him to move on.

Knowing Wilson and company would broadcast those aspersions publicly was one factor that prompted me to blog about Team UM's behaviour around my father's death. Ordinarily, I'd never go public with such private matters, but it was better to get the facts out ahead of UM's vile libel. I wasn't the only member of the family Dad had overlooked, but we'd all felt that his partner deserved whatever he had left, and no one expected his younger companion's departure would precede his. Nuance in interpersonal relationships is lost on the hearse chasers of Team UM, though. The surviving beneficiaries were three of my brothers, and Wilson asked, 'have you considered challenging the will?'

I shook my head in disgust. My father had been dead three months. Rather than explicate my views on creating conflict with my siblings to pay for Wilson's sorry legal services, I cut to the point: 'There's nothing to get.' I spared the court my father's low opinion of UM too. He'd needed no persuading that I was in the right and described the lot of them in anatomical terms readers might guess.

Next, Wilson climbed onto his high horse to whinge that I'd redacted names of donors from the documents called for in the summons, and argued that I should produce the copies unredacted. Rob objected. My supporters had made donations on condition of confidentiality — I'd assured them of it on my blogs. It was also clear from the evidence before the court; ledgers and bank statements, that there were no regular payments that would warrant an order to garnish the small amount of money that came in. Yet Wilson insisted that his clients needed the names in case there was some mystery benefactor they could sue to pay my bills, impervious to Rob's argument there was no legal basis to do so.

Cross-examination over, the registrar called a short adjournment, and Rob and I remained at the bar table as UM's circus carried on around us, the Sons of God poncing about as if they owned the courtroom. Triplicate copies of my financial documents had become shuffled during the hearing, and as I sorted them, a dark shape moved unexpectedly before me, between the bar table and the bench, where members of the public didn't usually venture. Weedy Alan, dressed neck to toe in black, was pacing out a slow stalk, toes slightly pointed, nodding his chin and clenching his buttocks as if trying to contain a fart. It occurred to me later that he and his greenish wife had probably paid His Holiness for Esoteric Walking lessons. Eager to squeeze every cent out of his subscribers, Benhayon ran classes in the 'modality', leading indoor laps of the Hall of Ageless Wisdom for thirty dollars per head, and instructing his students that they must never walk and think at the same time.

Alan circumambulated the courtroom, anti-clockwise, like a wind-up Esoteric, and then popped up behind me with Raphael and Karam to pester Rob about my redactions. Leaning on a bench, he griped, 'and the numbers don't add up.'

I swivelled sharply to confront him. 'Why were you looking at my financial documents?' I said. 'Are you a lawyer?'

Alan straightened his slouch and his gum caught between his teeth. 'I'm on the legal team,' he squeaked.

'Who is he?' said Rob. Alan, who resembles a Sopranos figurine, is a property developer, Benhayon fan-boy and an Esoteric feminist, who'd courageously put his name to a review of the beneficial effects of Esoteric Breast Massage on his wife. The group dispersed, I returned to sorting my papers, and Rob turned to watch them. UM was probably his first cult. 'They're moving in for a group hug...' he murmured. 'Look, look...' He nudged me, 'now it's back rubs.'

They'd formed a prayer circle, cum pep talk, limp arms around each other, Greig stroking Wilson's back. 'Ugh,' I cringed and returned to my papers as Rob chuckled.

When the registrar resumed the hearing, he ruled in the plaintiffs' favour, ordering me to hand over the names of my donors. I was stunned, and so was Rob, who continued to object but got nowhere. At the behest of Wilson, the registrar also ordered me back to court for cross-examination on the results. For years I'd made every effort to protect my contacts from exposure, and now a minor official, who barely seemed awake, was ordering me to out a bunch of them without any valid legal reason.

The court adjourned and we sank to our seats.

'Oh fuck,' I said breathlessly to Rob. 'What am I going to tell them? Oh fuck…'

The lawyer looked around uneasily as UM breezed out of court, and reminded me quietly that the room was miked.

'Oh fuck,' I gasped.

xcvii Summons

Wilson muttered during the hearing about pursuing costs enforcement in the coming weeks — indicating I'd be gifted a third summons for Christmas, and they'd list more hearings in January to pursue a debt they knew I couldn't pay. I was less troubled that they were taking steps toward bankrupting me, however, than I was by them timing the aggressions to disrupt my preparations for the February hearing in Sydney. Wilson was also lusting to win further costs orders against me to increase my debt.

The only way to halt the costs action was to petition for bankruptcy myself, but that would end my crowdfunding. Under the law, all gifts or donations to an undischarged bankrupt must be surrendered to pay debtors, which would leave me with no income at all. Tom called a bankruptcy lawyer in chambers for advice, but they saw no way around it, except perhaps to organise supporters to buy food for me and pay my rent and bills.

Rosie and her husband, Bart, were already dropping off care packages, and my mother would send me home with a box of groceries when I visited. Doubting my supporters would commit to regular payments, I came up with an alternative. The law allowed a bankrupt to earn taxable income up to fifty-five thousand dollars per year before the trustee could garnish it. I was already registered as a sole trader, so I blogged notice to my supporters that I could no longer take donations; they could pay me for my journalistic services instead — my ongoing blogging about Unimed.

I petitioned for bankruptcy as soon as I could, but the regulator can take a couple of weeks to make it official, which meant I had to obey the summons. Rob was not available, so again I contended with UM's legal scarecrow alone. The registrar did not look any more alert than the week before, but I was better prepared, and this time only the plaintiffs, Alison, and grumpy Jasna lumped into court. Fletcher remained in Mullumbimby, so Raphael and Karam joined Wilson at the bar table, Caroline taking notes on her laptop. I addressed the court by referring to the procedural rules. 'I submit that I provided all required information prior to these summons, and it clearly showed that I do not have the means to pay the order. The plaintiffs have obtained no information through these summons that could facilitate payment, and further cross-examination will not do so either.'

Wilson, however, reckoned he had 'new evidence', so the registrar allowed him to call me back to the witness box. Charlie's smoking gun was a copy of a Facebook post from my legal defence page, dated months before the Queensland action, in which I'd made an appeal for donations and invited donors to join a mailing list for fundraising updates. Wilson wanted to know why I hadn't produced the mailing list.

'Uh, I never got around to putting it together.'

But Wilson bludgeoned away, implying that I'd not produced all the relevant documents. When I answered that I'd been too busy responding to Fletcher's legal spam to compile a list, Raphael, whose laptop tapping had grown increasingly agitated, stopped typing and squealed in open court, 'Liar!' And again, 'Liar!'

She roused dopey Karam, whose attendance seemed purely ornamental, and the slouching registrar, who'd been slowly swivelling in his chair, straightened himself somewhat. 'Ah, Miss,' he said with a frown. 'Miss, please be quiet.'

Then Wilson started. The defendant has committed perjury! She's a liar, something something contempt of court et cetera. He waved the long forgotten Facebook post, waffling that it proved the existence of some secret font of wealth and on and on. Spittle might have flown if he had any body fluids.

'No, it doesn't,' I said.

Eventually he calmed down and moved on to the list of names on my unredacted donations ledger. Fortunately, I hadn't used many full names, and quite a few donations were anonymous. Over two years I'd received around thirty thousand dollars in total — piddling beside Natalie's takings to make her a sexy TV star, and the nearly six hundred thousand in charity money that had vanished from cult's College accounts under the watch of the bloke interrogating me and his missus. They refused to answer my public questions as to where it had gone.

Either way, all evidence proved I was existing on a pittance, scrimping every dollar. Still, Wilson began to question my relationship with each donor. Who is Leonie Jones*? She's a friend. Where does she live? In England. How long have you known her? A couple of years. Have you communicated with her? Yeah. How? On the phone. Why does she donate to your legal defence? She thinks Universal Medicine are a mob of predators. Who is Joe Dale*? He's a friend. He's made several donations hasn't he? Yes, every time Universal Medicine annoys him he gives me money.

When he started on the next person, I turned to the bench. 'Registrar, I object, this questioning is irrelevant…'

Wilson erupted. 'She can't object! She's a witness on the stand!'

The registrar began to show signs of life. 'Yes, she can.'

'She should have arranged for legal representation if she wanted to make objections!'

'Mr Wilson, she's entitled to represent herself.'

I continued my appeal. 'This kind of questioning about donors' relationships with me doesn't get us any more information that could bring about payment of this debt. Nothing produced or said in these hearings is capable of proving anything further to the information I provided to the plaintiffs months ago. I do not have the means to pay…'

The lights seemed to come on at the bench. 'What are these donations?' the registrar asked. God knows why he was so disengaged, and why he hadn't read any of the filings, but perhaps in ordinary enforcement proceedings he didn't have cults abusing the process to extort information about their critics.

I explained that I was being sued in two states by plaintiffs who are part of the same occult religious organisation Wilson belongs to. I'd started a crowdfund to help pay my legal bills, but could no longer afford a solicitor, and was not eligible for welfare payments, so now it was helping to pay my living expenses. 'I'm seventy thousand dollars in debt,' I said.

The lights were on. 'You ran out of money?'

'Yes.' I sighed. 'I've provided sworn statements to this court saying so for nearly a year… If Mr Wilson continues this questioning, which is not even about my ability to pay, we'll be here all afternoon again.' The registrar was awake. 'It's a long list of names…'

He upheld my objection and I returned to the bar table for closing submissions where Wilson began huffing and puffing his accusations all over again; perjurer, liar, and so on. He concluded as I expected, by seeking an order that I pay the plaintiffs' costs of the whole charade.

My turn came. 'Registrar, Mr Wilson has produced no evidence for these allegations…'

Seated to my right, Raphael screeched again: 'Liar! You're a liar!'

Startled, I turned to find her in as much of a lather as Wilson had been when he went all wild eyed.

The registrar blinked and repeated, 'Er, Miss, please be quiet.'

I continued. 'Going back to my opening submission, registrar, I can't pay the costs order. I have no assets or significant income. I filed a sworn statement to that effect well in advance of these summons. These hearings have obtained no information that could facilitate payment. We didn't need to be here. The plaintiffs should not receive an award of costs.' The registrar ruled in my favour.

In hindsight, I should have filed for bankruptcy before the hearing of the first summons. It didn't take a seer to predict how UM would use the ledger after Wilson tendered it. I emailed supporters and blogged about the mischief as soon as I got home, and added a YouTube clip of the London Cello Quartet performing Radiohead's 'Burn the Witch' and its searing vocal, 'we know where you live.' One donor reported a spike of three hundred or so views of her LinkedIn profile that evening. Another was verbally attacked by her Esoteric relatives during the family Christmas gathering — accused of colluding with an anti-religious criminal troll.

The victory came at a cost, but on exiting the courtroom, I found Team UM in an unhappy huddle in the lobby. Spiteful Wilson raised his voice as I passed. 'What would Senior Counsel think of that kind of behaviour?' He got beat, by me; an untrained, unrepresented bankrupt, and all he could do was fantasise about me getting my bottom smacked.

Caroline's outbursts were also a promising sign. 'It was sensational,' I told Tom. 'Pity there was no audience to catch it...' I was entertaining a fantasy of my own, that Caroline or the others would go off like that at the trial. 'Can you imagine?' I said. 'The jury will love it.'

xcviii Unpacking

Nine women are perched on a row of bar stools at the Hall of Ageless Wisdom before a hushed congregation. Intently focused, exuding gloom, they read from a copy of a Benhayon sermon. The red wall looms behind the monthly rite, and Serge sits onstage at the end of the row, following the text, smirking. The mic is passed to a woman in a bright green dress who solemnly reads, 'A spirit looks very much like the pictures we have of aliens, an image they do not like us to know about…'

Serryn O'Regan is in the line-up in a lacy off-white dress, staring downward into the near distance, her mousey shoulder length hair hanging lank. When her turn comes, her voice is grim. 'A spirit has no nose, though in that known to us location they have a small crevice which is not used to breathe, but to take in all that is not Astral. Hence it can be colloquially said that spirits have a muzzle for all that is truly divine and aligned to true evolution… It is said that a spirit can smell a son of God, or a reclaimed and evolved human being from a mile away.'

'Fact!' says Benhayon. 'Have you ever been smelt?'

The Way of the Livingness sermon video was recorded in February 2017. Subscribers accessed recordings on demand; sermons, forum presentations and music performances, some of which ground on for hours. The readers changed each month, but the content was the same drivel Benhayon had convoluted in new and unimaginative ways since 2000. After the sermons, he'd hold a forum where his students passed the mic around and affirmed their dedication to his Way.

A detractor pact had taken out a subscription to capture the content for family court proceedings. I was so desensitised to UM's madness, however, that it wasn't until a young father phoned me in tears, saying, 'that's the mother of my children on that stage,' that I realised the recordings' power to expose the group. Few outsiders had seen what went on at events.

Another woman takes her turn to read, pronouncing slowly, 'Spirits have a mid-grey coloured thin body, long fingers, they are all equally nine feet tall and have no feet.'

A newly bankrupt defendant with any sense, fighting two Esoteric legal actions with a lengthy trial nine months away, might have gotten on with her massive workload, but I had to consider that my defences could fail, halting my publishing, and that all of my work could be taken down. My bankruptcy came through before Christmas, and I saw the week following as my last window to tackle one of my most compelling exposés to date, my *Unpacking Universal Medicine* series of YouTube documentaries.

Again, someone with more sense would have quit when their laptop clapped out in the middle of the public holidays, but I switched to my small, ten-year-old spare, and kept going from morning until late to produce five films in under a week. 'Do you have to?' said Tom and Louise when they heard of the project. As always, the answer was yes.

The women on stage read on in their stilted way. 'It is an old tip or skill that, if you are seeing an image that is in discarnate form, be it Moses, Jesus, Mary, a ghoul, or a demon or a loved-one; if you look down towards their feet, chances are that they will either disappear or their real appearance will be revealed.'

Serge chips in: 'So that's what you teach the kids at night if they're seeing ghosts and ghouls and nightmares, whatever, just teach them to look down at their feet. They go. Simple!'

As I was cutting my documentaries, I sent copies of the source recordings to Tom, who spent 'many loony hours' picking out excerpts for my defence. They also gave him an understanding of the way Benhayon might behave under cross-examination. The silk's preparations were well underway. We'd identified four main topics among the allegations I needed to prove: sex, money, cult, and a combination of quackery and the occult, which Tom labelled, 'voodoo'. Those became the strands of Benhayon's cross-examination.

'When I teach people to pass over,' Benhayon says, 'I could easily teach them to look at feet as they pass over so that they don't get stuck in the Astral plane. The problem is the spirits can also create feet...' Beside him sits a registered nurse, a chronic believer. Her mouth falls open. A collective gasp is heard from the gathering. Serryn O'Regan, sitting two stools away, is motionless, knees together, copy held with both hands in her lap, still staring into near space.

'But they all look so normal,' said Tom's partner Janet, a filmmaker, when she saw some of the presentations. Mature-aged, middle-class white women comprised the majority of the congregation. Some dressed like O'Regan in their Sunday frocks, but others were in sandals and pedal pushers as if on a trip to the shops.

Perhaps it was that footage that inspired one of Tom's most critical points of attack. He made a chuffed announcement during one of our conferences in early February. 'I've got it,' he said with a naughty grin and a glimmer in his eyes. 'My opening question for his cross-examination.' He delivered it as he planned to seven months later. 'Old Pythagoras won't see that one coming.' Louise offered ebullient congratulations, and of course I wholly approved, but I could not feel the buzz that my lawyers were sharing. I didn't spoil the moment by saying what I felt: we had to get there yet.

xcix Everest

A well-intentioned relative gifted me clairvoyant consult soon after Benhayon filed his claim. None of the psychic's predictions were accurate, but she was a kind hearted person and her simple words of encouragement stayed with me. 'This will be your personal Everest,' she said. 'Whatever happens, you must keep going. Just keep going.'

That became the mantra I woke to every morning as trial preparations intensified into 2018, propelling me out of bed, to breakfast, strong coffee and a boundless vortex of work. Just keep going. I'd always been tidy, but now I couldn't concentrate if there was mess or smears or dust in the house and I'd scrub mercilessly before I could start. Motivation ran like lava, channelled into lucid productivity and ruthless focus on accuracy, but my habit of extreme multi-tasking delivered undesired side effects: working on defences, blogging, tweeting and cooking all at once, many dinners were served burnt.

Just keep going resounded as I pushed through each task and surveyed the jagged peak, echoing with each truculent demand from Fletcher. UM's persistent acts of bastardry fuelled my defiance, seven months to trial, counting, calibrating each productive minute, aware that only rage could spur me to that summit. I'm not the most robust animal, but found myself pacing my flat, or pounding up the beach, never time to stop; seething, scheming. Matt Sutherland came around most days to walk me, often appearing as a goggle-eyed Lord of Form at the kitchen window, startling the stuffing out of me, and I exacted revenge by never letting him dawdle. 'Hop to Duckie!' I'd say, and he'd generously bear my railing as we trotted along.

At times he'd stir me on, rasping like Marlon Brando, 'Grind their bones into the dust!'

Often in the shower, scrubbing and plotting, the fury would boil over and I'd step out, dripping and wet headed, preoccupied by tactics and injustices, and growl from my guts, knees bent in a kung fu stance, and I did not hold back, because that was the physical preparedness I needed to get me to trial. Fortunately, the primal roars, shouted expletives, and burning odours didn't trouble my neighbours. Byron Shire residents are used to women who bay with the wolves.

But the pressure before the February hearing disturbed my sleep. UM piled on legal demands and threats and takedowns as I was preparing for our interlocutory tussle against Smark. I'd be so exhausted after my carbonised dinner I couldn't wash dishes or take a shower and would collapse into bed, to wake sharply at two in the morning, mind motoring. Rather than waste time trying to get back to sleep, I'd get up, clean up and get back to work, sometimes until seven or eight when I'd eat. After breakfast, the fatigue would overwhelm me again and I'd sleep for a couple of hours, but thankfully those periods of disturbance didn't last.

As narrator in the Unpacking UM videos, I was the antithesis of True-Sexy, deliberately without makeup, needing a hairdresser. Such luxuries were not within the budget, and despite filming in midsummer, I was vampire pale. Dramatic inspiration was never in short supply. Every fortnight, Universal Law ran an ad in the Byron Shire Echo with a photo of Cameron Bell and Paula Fletcher posing at a desk, hands clasped, doing an impression of professionalism. Every glimpse of that image provoked an incandescent rage that flared hotter after my father died and zombie Team UM went clutching at his casket. It inspired a ritual where I'd collect the paper, scissor out the ad, take a lighter, and set fire to it. 'A plague upon your houses,' I'd mutter, as I watched it turn to ash.

c G2W 2018

The mic is passed to Anita and James, a well off middle-aged couple from suburban Brisbane. Blonde coiffed and carefully maquillaged Anita begins: 'I was just going to share from the physicality of a woman's body from, you know, the position of the cervix…' She smiles proudly. 'And even in intercourse when the man is actually touching the cervix that is an incredible power that is felt by the man, and it's a complete surrender.'

The video cuts to Benhayon onstage in black suit trousers, shiny leather shoes and a pastel pink business shirt buttoned at the cuffs. It's September 2017, a week after Judge Tory tossed Wilson's submissions over his shoulder, but Serge is animated. Perhaps it's the subject matter, and the thrill he gets from pretending at expertise, or perhaps it's the intoxication of having a rapt, albeit stupefied, audience. The cloistered stage at the Wollongbar Hall is where he feels most alive. 'I know you guys make love,' he says to the couple. 'If the man does not surrender, you can't make love; James, correct?'

Tall James with a gangrenous complexion, takes the mic. 'You cannot describe what it's like to fully surrender in the act of making love to anything else. It's just so beautiful as compared to all the other releases and the stuff that used to go on. It's a moment to be shared by everybody.'

When I used the footage in 'Unpacking Universal Medicine: Mystifying Sex', it certainly was.

'It's atomic,' says Serge.

To be clear, it doesn't concern me if adults want to discuss their sex lives with webcast church gatherings of hundreds, recorded for publication. But a boy of about twelve or thirteen was clearly visible in the row behind Anita and James — a foster child of one of UM's lifers. I cropped him, and any other children out of my films, but the source footage shows him and another adolescent boy helping to pass the mic around. Younger kids' voices are heard in the background.

Not to be outdone, Serge begins to brag, 'I've shared with the men's group that my orgasms are inward much more than they are outward, and that I orgasm like a woman every time I orgasm, as much as I do as a man, and often more as a woman than I do as a man.'

The dim foster parent is a few rows away chewing gum. Waiting for the mic, the boy sits very still, he blinks, his chin drops, his face turns pink. Onstage, Dr Maxine Szramka, Neil Ringe, Professor Bill Foley, and Associate Professor of Sociology Rachel Lynwood, sit on stools, listening intently with blank acceptance. Benhayon's on a high. 'It's the most amazing, spectacular thing that happens inside your body and you don't even care what's happening outside. What we call ejaculation is secondary to what's going on on the inside and the explosion that goes on in the body.

It's an amazing…when you orgasm as a hermaphrodite, the orgasm is quite spectacular.'

In the same recording, he's seen stalking clockwise around his audience, defying his own superstitions, riffing on social expectations of women to be 'a good mother or a good slut'. 'A slut was good when you lived in Maroubra,' he says. 'If we knew who the slut was, that was a good girl to go after.' During the morning's sermon, with a row of women onstage, the bogan messiah conflated everything that doesn't align with his teachings with violence, saying, 'just having a conversation on the Astral level is a violation'. Feeble applause breaks out as he likens criticism to terrorist bombings and acid attacks, and adds, 'wait til we get to rape, ladies, then you can applaud, and I'm wearing pink for you…' Children were subjected to a whole day of that, with the organisers, patrons and 'role models' of the Girl to Woman Festival present.

I'd rushed to get Unpacking Universal Medicine published before the 2018 Girl to Woman Festival, and my supporters were gobsmacked by the films. Within days, however, UM's audio-visual contractors, Jonathan and Rebecca Baldwin, and Simon Asquith, used bogus copyright complaints to have them taken down from YouTube. I issued counter notices but the platform took weeks to restore them.

That year's festival was advertised widely as a springboard for female 'empowerment'. One unsuspecting young mother became apprehensive, however, when she was asked on entry to sign a photography waiver allowing the organisers to use images of her pre-schooler. When the Esoteric happy-clapping began, she realised the Festival was run by 'some weird, cheesy church'. When her daughter was offered a make-over, she began to freak out.

The waiver cleared the event's management to use images of children for promotional or 'internal purposes', whatever that meant. 'There were a lot of cameras,' the mother said. Esoteric Women's Health broadcast a livestream of the Festival's concert — girls invited to dance onstage to Michael's raucous band, with Simon Asquith strumming, Miranda doing her best on vocals and True Sexy Natalie prancing about. Visible in the recording are five devotee photographers with professional equipment; four of whom are blokes, and hanging about stage left, pointing a whopping telephoto lens at little girls, is Alan the Esoteric Breast whisperer. I blogged the screenshots.

That was the fourth annual Festival, and I always studied the social media images to see who attended. A defector reported that management instructed followers not to photograph or publish images of certain cult personalities at events, but a livestream is difficult to curate. In the final minute of the footage, at the end of the performance, near backstage, is a clear shot of a flyweight male in a pastel pink business shirt, worn untucked, buttoned at the cuffs.

ci UQ

On a UM website, Dr Maxine Szramka referred to herself as 'an astute physician' who'd seen 'miracles in Medicine' as everyday occurrences among Unimed students. She was on the faculty of the University of Wollongong and publicly identified as a medical advisor to the Esoteric Practitioners Association. 'I have seen people's chronic pain not just managed, but resolved. Cured, permanently,' she stated, before asserting that it 'rarely occurs in Conventional Medicine'.

At a Way of the Livingness forum in 2015, Szramka described all in attendance as 'a living walking miracle'. She claimed to have gotten younger in the ten years she'd been knocking around with UM. 'I've not aged,' she said, and 'so many people in this room [are] incredibly young, vibrant, vital and enormously healthy…There's nothing like this in any of the medical journals.'

In early 2018, however, international medical journals were blessed with three Esoteric research papers. One, the findings of a 'cross sectional survey' of four hundred and forty-nine female 'participants' in Universal Medicine, boldly concluded that they 'claim substantially lower levels of illness and disease than in the general Australian population.' The survey was conducted in 2015 via an online questionnaire.

The lead researcher and author was Christoph Schnelle. Detective G's bugbear was a PhD student in Bio Statistics at the University of Queensland (UQ), and the other papers were preliminary studies for hospital trials of Esoteric Connective Tissue Therapy (ECTT), another Benhayon invented modality. They didn't mention the premise that connective tissue circulates the light of God throughout the body to expel prana — Serge says so — but the researchers admitted that they were not permitted to run the trial in Australian hospitals. They sought out, instead, a cooperative private hospital in Vietnam, not far from UM's annual retreat venue and the tailor shops that stitched up the sage's shirts. Schnelle's co-authors included Szramka, Minford, Marianna Masiorski, NHS human resources consultant and former Esoteric Breast Masseuse, Jane Keep, and two ECTT practitioners, Kate Greenaway and Steffen Messerschmidt, who worked at Unimed clinics.

Of the requisite declarations of conflicts of interest, one paper said, 'none declared'. The other stated that the researchers 'attend Universal Medicine events' and that none had 'received any funding, reimbursement, instruction or direction of any kind from Universal Medicine or its affiliates.' Schnelle, a tall, snowy-haired duffer, whose alpine peak popped up in images of UM events going back years, declared that he'd 'received ECTT for back pain in May 2016. No other competing interests exist.'[90] UM promoters' agility in switching from hysteric exaggeration to radical understatement was truly dizzying.

Schnelle didn't declare that his wife, Nicola Lessing, was company secretary of Benhayon owned marketing firm Unimed Living Pty Ltd, or that the couple were believers in Benhayon's user-pays religion, or that they'd corresponded with the Ascended Master about keeping financial gifts to him secret. Schnelle got the projects past his PhD supervisor, UQ's Research Ethics Committee, and the journal's editors, without disclosing the extent of the authors' UM involvement.

Pushing my legal work aside, I notified the head of UQ's School of Public Health and the journal editors with evidence of the authors' longtime UM involvement. The University commenced an investigation of possible academic misconduct, and Josh Robertson, now at ABC television news in Brisbane, went to air with a report that found two more UM peddlers, Drs Sam Kim and Amelia Stephens, on UQ's medical faculty. The research team were also appealing for forty thousand dollars to fund the Connective Tissue Therapy study.

At the Hall of Ageless Wisdom in July 2015, around the time UM conducted the online survey, Szramka told the congregation, 'every single person in the world wants what we've got…to feel amazing, to feel vital, to feel incredible, to feel healthy…'[91] One might surmise that she was suggesting how participants might make their responses. At another event a few months later, Dr Szramka urged the students to do more to spread Universal Medicine to the world. 'We're actually abusing others by not sharing this,' she said.[92] She'd also been all in on the police complaints around that time, replying to the call to fill Sergeant Walsh's inbox. 'I'm loving the way that you pin evil Eric,' she wrote, 'these criminals have nowhere to go with you around!!' The majority of those involved in the phoney research had reported me to the cops and were recipients of the email exchanges about pursuing Detective G.

But a dissenter appeared within the Way of the Livingness videos in early 2017, contradicting the survey findings and more accurately describing what was conspicuous in UM's sluggish exemplars: Serge himself. He described outsiders' criticisms of the UM student body:

> They hug for too long. They walk too slow. They're all getting too thin because they think they can just eat one meal like Serge does. They've all got depleted iron levels because they don't commit to life. They have issues of lead poisoning… Mercury readings are off the scale.[93]

Benhayon had boasted that he slept three to five hours per night, only drank water or cucumber and spinach juice, and existed on one meal per day of vegetables and fish. If followers were emulating him, the mercury toxicity might have resulted from overdoing the fish. Other complaints observed among the students were symptomatic of disordered eating — fatigue, mood, and digestive disturbances, and the cessation of menstrual periods in relatively young women. High profile dietitian, Rosemary Stanton, also drew attention to the 'extremely low' body mass index reported in one in six of the surveyed Brides of Serge. 'Hardly the sign of a healthy diet,' she said.[94]

Benhayon also gave it away when he berated his dazed audience for not keeping up with his amazing insights. As his readers struggled through one of his sedative sermons, he told them that the energies of his teachings are 'way too far in the future...beyond the current form of intelligence,' and warned that their health was set to deteriorate from failing to keep up. His students' substandard fieriness was 'calling in energy' to attack them, and he predicted hormonal imbalances until 'hardly anyone has periods anymore', as well as exhaustion, inflammatory disorders, and mercury levels 'through the roof'.[95] All would be their own fault; nothing to do with his life-threatening pronouncements.

Soon after the UQ research scandal broke, a contact reconfirmed the risks of Benhayon's dietary lunacy. A patient critically ill from malnutrition was rushed to the emergency department of Lismore Base Hospital, and subsequently airlifted to Brisbane for intensive care. The law prevents me from identifying him and those directly responsible, but he had an uncommon name, well-known within Universal Medicine. The patient was a nine month old infant. He'd been unresponsive, close to death.

cii Privacy

Josh Robertson went to air with another UM related report within a week. The New South Wales Privacy Commissioner had published a finding that Dr Sam Kim had broken medical privacy law. The breach was discovered in 2017 when Lance's new GP found an unusual diagnostic letter in his file. Lance had consulted Dr Kim in 2010 for a lung infection, and the respiratory specialist's letter gave a detailed and rather inaccurate opinion of his patient's general health, but most alarmingly, the specialist had signed off with a smiley face stamp and the words, 'Copy to: Serge Benhayon, Director of Universal Medicine'.

Lance flipped. It was the first he'd heard of it. Dr Kim denied to the Commission that he'd not obtained consent to share it with Benhayon, and argued that there was no evidence of harm done. But the Privacy Commissioner found the medico had breached the Health Records and Information Privacy Act, noting that doctors are required by law to obtain written consent before sharing medical info 'for a purpose other than the purpose for which it was collected'. Dr Kim had no such consent on file, and Lance told the authority that if he'd been given the opportunity, he would have refused it. The Commission also noted that it was unclear why the doctor provided a summary of 'what appears to be the patient's entire medical history to Mr Benhayon.'

Sam Kim proposed to resolve the complaint with an apology and by undertaking to comply with his privacy obligations, but only on condition that Lance agreed to release him from liability. Lance refused, but aside from official advice to Dr Kim to comply, no penalties are available under Australian law. A civil claim for damages was possible in theory, but without legal precedents, it would be a test case mounted at Lance's expense. The investigation did not probe whether other patients' private information was forwarded to UM's leader.

It was not the only breach of privacy covered in Josh's report. I'd published a guest blog in 2017 by a former Benhayon disciple. We disguised his identity, giving him the name Olga, and I encouraged him not to reveal his whereabouts — not even the country he lived in. Having strictly adhered to the Way of the Livingness austerities over several years, Olga's health deteriorated until he descended into acute panic attacks. None of his Esoteric practitioners detected his breakdown or that he was dangerously malnourished. None recommended that he consult a doctor. They performed their useless 'healings', and took his money instead. 'I wanted to be dead rather than alive for every single second in the final few months,' said Olga.

At his lowest, he reached out to one of UM's demigods, who blamed his distress on inadequate Esoteric commitment. At that point, Olga allowed his family to take him to hospital, despite his fear that evil pranic energies would kill him there. When his father told him he was proud of him for agreeing to medical treatment, he replied, 'wait and see. In a day or two you'll get a call that I've died for unexplained reasons.' During the week he spent in a locked ward, he asked his doctor, 'if a fairy appeared in a puff and offered to fulfil your wish to die immediately and painlessly, would you take it?'

None of his UM Brothers visited or expressed concern in the three months he spent in the facility, or afterward. Blood tests revealed that he was suffering from severe malnutrition, and he was diagnosed with schizophrenia. Mandatory reporting laws for his profession meant his mental health diagnosis ended his career.

After I published his firsthand account, Olga started his own blog about UM and identified his general location where there's a small but pathologically loyal cluster of Benhayon fanatics. In April 2018, UM FACTS retaliated with a blog: 'Sources with pseudonyms: "Olga"'. Its spineless authors, who'd railed against detractor pseudonyms for years, published anonymously under the moniker 'The UM Facts Team'. The thrust of the four-thousand-word smear was that my sources are unreliable because one was diagnosed with mental illness, and the FACTS pack posted Olga's full name, his diagnosis, his location, the name of his girlfriend, who was a former UM follower, and photographs of both of them.

Withholding identifying details, ABC News published his response: 'Finding UM's article was shocking. My privacy in respect to that diagnosis is very important. I'm worried about not finding a job because of that.'

Asked for comment, UM's outspoken spokesbods Alison Greig and Charles Wilson were struck silent, but Queensland's former mental health commissioner, Lesley van Schoubroeck, provided a statement:

> It's entirely inappropriate for any organisation, particularly one purporting to be a health organisation, to publicly reveal identifying information of anyone's diagnosis… It's certainly the case that people with schizophrenia suffer stigma and discrimination in the workplace and in the community.

Olga's hospitalisation ended his UM involvement. It was his first and only psychotic breakdown, and in the intervening years he never relapsed. That led me and others to suspect he may have been misdiagnosed. Ros Hodgkins, the head of an Australian nonprofit organisation, Cult Information and Family Support, told me she'd seen it many times: involvement in a high demand group leading to a mental breakdown, often with psychosis and suicidal ideation. Many, however, make a full recovery when they exit the group. It may have been an acute stress or trauma induced psychosis, but mental health professionals, who are often unaware of, or misunderstand the environment the patient has come from, do not readily make the connection. Olga's doctors were not told that he'd been in the group or of the teachings that dominated his life.

So much for 'Universal Medicine has no victims'. Outing Olga was payback; Unimed revealing its malicious innermost — what its degenerate hierarchy would do to vulnerable clients if they spoke out.

ciii Breaches

Some might call it unassailable optimism, others might call it obstinate delusion. Either way, after narrowly missing out on a Ballina council seat, Ray Karam sought National Party preselection for the state seat of Lismore. When that nosedived, he ran as an independent candidate for the federal seat of Richmond, where twice as many voters ended up voting informal than voted for him. Determined to outdo him, Dr Maxine Szramka sought preselection for the Liberal Party in former Prime Minister Turnbull's seat of Wentworth, and finished sixth in a race of six.

In the interim, a Way of the Livingness delegation appeared before a Federal Senate Inquiry on proposed Freedom of Religion legislation. Wilson, Greig, Dr Rachel Hall, and Dr Amelia Stephens, complained to the Senate committee that the UM community were victims of religious vilification and that their persecutors should be jailed. If I'd had time, I'd have made my own on submission questioning whether undue influence, misleading advertising, defamatory mobbing, exploitation, and molestation, are considered religious practices.

Encouragingly, the group's expansionary zeal was gaining new opposition. When residents of Lismore and Frome attempted to share Josh's news reports to local Facebook groups, UM supporters harassed admins with complaints and legal threats. Certain business leaders and opportunists chummy with Lismore Chamber of Commerce head, Deborah Benhayon, posted defensively: never mind the scandals, Unimed were 'great clients'. But because no one could be sure who was an Esoteric and who was not, locals became increasingly suspicious of each other, fearing they'd be sued for speaking ill of UM's covert Brotherhood.

None of the animosities curtailed UM's community incursions, however. Members of another support group for breast cancer patients, all of whom were undergoing treatment for advanced disease, revolted when its facilitator Sarah Broome brought in Universal Medicine practitioners to deliver a sales presentation to the group. When the local manager of the not-for-profit blew off the womens' concerns with 'we don't discriminate against people on the basis of their religious beliefs,' a member called to ask whether I thought the women could be sued if they asked Broome to stand down.

I'd been preparing evidence for trial that Serge Benhayon is the head of a group that preys on cancer patients, and calls like hers made me feel like my hair was going to burst into flames. I didn't know that Broome worked for the organisation, and I dropped everything and notified its national chain of management, astounded that the members had been put in that position. The organisation had already had a scandalous brush with UM when all or part of a seven hundred thousand dollar federal government grant was squandered on UM's 'body awareness education'. The government refused to release further details on the grounds it might damage the not-for-profit's reputation, but Benhayon admitted to trousering the public cash.[96]

Sarah Broome was gone within twenty-four hours, along with a couple more UM promoters on staff, but Broome, with Rebecca Baldwin, Simon Asquith, and others, continued to work for the publicly funded Positive Adolescent Sexual Health (PASH) Conference while serving on Serge's media team and running the Girl to Woman Festival. When notified, PASH's management also spun the religious discrimination excuse and did nothing.

All of it increased my workload. Ideally I'd have continued my therapy with Hayes, who probably would have waived his fee, but amid that cram of litigation and controversy, there was never time. Another whale migration passed where I couldn't spare thirty minutes to sit in the dunes, and had to content myself with watching for breaches on hurried late afternoon beach walks, eyes on the sea. There was no time to absorb the loss of my father or to be with loved ones, and I missed them, like I missed Laurie, and not being there for him when I should have been. But not wanting to compound my family's stress, I avoided discussing the war.

Consequently, they weren't aware of what was at stake, the pressure I was under, and why I couldn't visit Brisbane as regularly as before. 'You might as well have joined the cult,' said one relative.

It was a fair point. The financial loss was just one part of the gnawing personal cost. I was disappearing into combat; there was no me anymore, just a struggle. I set out to trap a cult, and got caught in the same snare. Near explosive passion had propelled me to the battlefront, and panicked Serge's soldiers, but as the rigours intensified, the fury was displaced by robotic focus. No longer capable of expressing grief or wrath, I had equivalent incapacity for pleasure. I'd become like a cultist and I wanted to speak with Hayes. I needed to tell him that this was never how I wanted to live.

civ Stew

The evidence against Benhayon was scattered among thousands of documents on my hard drive and I was the only fool able to locate it. Student notes and witness accounts indicated that the strongest material lay in audio recordings, but finding it meant listening to countless hours of dross — time I did not have. I tried to outsource, but the one volunteer I judged to have the time, patience and intestinal fortitude to handle it, and could trust with the confidentiality requirements, interrupted my work a few minutes into the first recording with outraged messages about what he was hearing. Within half an hour, he'd resigned, citing mental health reasons. Nursing friends through a Benhayon triggered meltdown wasn't factored into my schedule.

I hadn't foreseen becoming homeless either. Supporters were just covering my rent, but in April 2018 I was evicted by a landlord wanting to renovate, leaving me unable to afford a new lease and my rental bond swallowed by the bankruptcy trustee. Like Esoteric clockwork, an investigator from the bankruptcy authority also informed me that an anonymous complainant had alleged that I'd failed to disclose financial gifts. I was required to turn over all my financial information again, and told that if the regulator classed any of my meagre income as assets they would confiscate every cent in my account, which would leave my rent in arrears, bills unpaid, and no money to move my belongings into storage. When I explained the situation, I asked the officer, 'and how am I supposed to eat?'

'Those are the regulations.'

That complaint went away too after I produced the paperwork and could demonstrate through my blogged announcements that support for my journalism since my bankruptcy was taxable income. Besides, by the time the investigation concluded, there was nothing left to confiscate.

One Friday afternoon in April, I was drawing up briefs for expert witnesses David Millikan and Professor Dwyer, half-packed boxes strewn around me, when Tom called. He'd just won a big trial, and the solicitor he'd worked with, Stewart O'Connell, asked what he was up to next. 'He says he wants in,' Molomby told me. 'He's willing to represent you in the Benhayon case…with your permission of course.'

With those words, I was borne aloft, floating, flying on a heady cloud reminiscent of hope. It was a pleasantly tingling, vertiginous sensation — unlike the flaming head feeling I'd grown used to — and it rendered me temporarily speechless. Within moments, however, I snapped back to my default. Stewart worked at O'Brien Criminal and Civil Solicitors with the principal Peter O'Brien, a well-known advocate for disadvantaged clients brutally mistreated in the Northern Territory youth justice system. Stew was a veteran of the criminal courts and was developing his defamation practice, often representing First Nations' clients defamed by media outlets. He was willing to work on a contingency basis, knowing he'd only be paid if we won and were awarded costs. It was a major financial risk for a small law firm.

'Does he realise what he's getting into?!' I said.

cv The long game

Hayes would have approved. When my whole team conferred with our expert witnesses in Tom's chambers in the first week of May 2018, I realised how much I'd upgraded the lead characters in my externalised psychodrama. It was not until I was within pinching distance of Stewart, though, that I was prepared to believe he was real. A sharp, likeable solicitor in his early forties, he had a youthful smile, sparky green leprechaun eyes, and he wore a silk tie emblazoned with an Aboriginal design. Faint traces of red, central Australian earth could be spied in the upper soles of the Darwin-born lawyer's boots.

Stewart was accompanied by paralegal Meri Ayala, a model of elegance and calm efficiency who transcribed our meetings, typing at lightning speed. The Spanish born lawyer spoke better English than most native speakers, and Tom showed off by bantering in her mother tongue. It was novel to be around high achievers in spacious suites in the heart of Sydney, who listened when I spoke and took my suggestions seriously. Tom went further, introducing me to colleagues as 'the celebrity defendant', saying that no client of his had ever worked so hard on their own case. Even I was impressed.

But the unwieldy case was well advanced, and there was never time for a full briefing. I still hadn't compiled our evidence, and if I didn't get it into a form my lawyers could access, all our efforts could come to nothing. That's where UM's disruptions achieved what they'd calculated, keeping me, and then us, so busy with procedural nonsense, I could never properly hand over. As a result, too much of our direction depended on me.

Justice McCallum had also set us a challenge by limiting the trial to three weeks — not enough time to prove over fifty diverse allegations. Tom said that the handful around Judith McIntyre's bequest would ordinarily comprise a trial in itself. 'With all these topics to cover, we're not running one trial, but a number of trials in one.'

Her Honour's ruling on the February argument remained reserved as well, with no indication of when she might order Benhayon to hand over relevant documents. Tom and I were so pushed in our preparations for that hearing that the silk was speed-stapling my hastily shuffled exhibits in the chambers library ten minutes before the court officer cried, 'all stand'. While an array of lawyers assured me I was in good hands, I'd never seen him perform in court, and although his dark suit transformed him from the cuddly gent into the stately senior lawyer, I wondered if the plaintiff's counsel might be more wily. Tom had the sharp eyes of a fox, but with his tall build, long nose and equable temperament, he was more like a bloodhound to dyspeptic chihuahua Smark.

I was greedy for every bit of material we could extract from Benhayon, but Tom told me not to be concerned if he didn't seem to argue hard for further discovery. He was sure, based on our written submissions, that Justice McCallum would give us enough. Playing the long game, he banked on the plaintiff's minders attending court. Serge stopped attending interlocutory arguments after Matthew Richardson's win, sending human shields instead, and Tom said he didn't want to look too flash as the trial approached. 'We don't want them to see me as much of a threat.'

cvi Chambers

Tom impermissibly took a three month holiday from May 2018, not returning until a week before the trial. Louise and I conferred, but concluded that any attempt to unlawfully detain him would not succeed, so his penance was to have me parked on his chambers' sofa for a fortnight before he took off. Again, though, he flattered me, allowing me to work in one of chambers' vacant offices when he had meetings. He and I went to the same Japanese takeaway each day where he'd order salmon *nigiri sushi* or a salad, and a yellow fruit drink in a bottle. He never drank tea or coffee, and there were no crystal decanters on his bureau, or hip flasks in the top drawer. After lunch he'd produce his toothbrush and excuse himself to 'go polish my smile.'

Homelessness at least relieved me of the burden of rent. I became a litigation nomad, commuting between hearings in Sydney and Brisbane, my borrowed car packed to the windows. I slept in a ten year old's bedroom in Sydney's northern suburbs, while the young fellow moved uncomplainingly to an inflatable in the spare room, beside his guitar, and after Tom left, I continued preparations at the family's dining table. Grateful as I am that my friends fed, housed, and tolerated me over two months of hair tearing legal preparations — they failed, however, in their duty to keep me warm. Theirs was one of those cold, dark Sydney homes, and worse, they were of British stock. My health idiosyncrasies have made me chronically hypothermic (although not quite as reptilian as the Benhayons, it seems), and below certain temperatures I cannot stay warm unless I'm in motion. In sheepskin boots, and multiple layers beneath my pink fluffy robe, I strove through sedentary work, my extremities like ice, and over a couple of weeks, my fingers swelled with itching, aching chilblains until the skin painfully cracked at the joints.

When she saw the state of my hands, Louise gave me keys to Tom's office and a security pass, another display of trust and generosity that strained my reality tester. I spent the hour-long train commute productively working through audio recordings, crossing the glistening Sydney harbour in dazzling morning sunshine, and returning under city lights to Benhayon's bent narrations on exorcising entities or supernatural snakes. Tom's chambers were warm and quiet, and taking in the view over Martin Place, I bragged to friends, 'I have the most salubrious office of any bankrupt unemployed person in Australia!'

It was the sort of set up that Louise Hay reckoned might manifest if I kept up my daily affirmations. She might have said all was well in my world.

But I had enough sense not to get comfortable. For all Tom's compliments, I could rely on the courts to smack down any inflations of ego.

cvii The playbook

Lara's anxieties escalated as her mother, Fran, ignored the court orders, and kept the child immersed in UM's Kool Aid. Graham felt the only way to keep her safe was to return to the Family Court to seek full-time care, proposing that Fran only have time with their daughter on strict condition that she abide by the judge's previous ruling. Lara's new court-appointed social worker reported that the girl was growing apprehensive of Graham and resisting contact with him because he didn't share her and her mother's beliefs, and concluded that Fran's Universal Medicine involvement was actively harmful and risked alienating the child from her father. No sooner was the report released than Fran made a second allegation of sexual abuse against her ex-partner, which, again, she would never substantiate.

In ruling on Graham's application for full-time care, the Family Court judge rejected the abuse allegations and determined that Fran's UM involvement was the sole source of the family's problems. He found Graham sincere in wanting to protect his daughter, and made a finding of parental alienation, yet he refused to grant him full-time care. The judge merely restated the existing orders meant to protect Lara from UM, and added stipulations that Fran consult with a dietitian, and seek professional support to disconnect from the group.

The mother, however, continued to deny responsibility, and with his contact with Lara diminishing, and no confidence that his ex-partner would comply, Graham appealed to England's High Court. The appeal ruling was published, and a pranic parent who read it asked me if UM was issuing a script to mothers in family disputes. Benhayon's blessed meddlers seemed to have a well-thumbed playbook and provided coaching as well. Lord Justice Jackson of the Appeals bench observed that Fran described her ex as 'controlling and abusive', 'obsessed with her involvement with Universal Medicine' and had accused him of online stalking. Detractor parents were labelled identically, regardless of their behaviour, and a number contended with false accusations of sexually abusing their children.

Graham's appeal was backed by the court's social worker, who recommended that he be granted full-time care with a provision for Lara to have supervised contact with her mother — but only on condition that Fran make a full break from UM.

cviii The rails

If Team UM had a pre-trial game plan it was this: three months out, they would fire a new barrage of arbitrary court applications at me in two states, list a bunch of hearings simultaneously, and have me running back and forth between Sydney and Brisbane like a headless bantam. That way, when Justice McCallum handed down her ruling on Benhayon's outstanding documents, which included his tax returns and searchable electronic copies of his texts, I wouldn't have time to examine them properly.

Fletcher lettered me the plaintiffs' intent to list three hearings in Brisbane in June that could have been heard in one, and listed the first just days away, while applying in Sydney to strike out more of my Benhayon defence. Rob Anderson was deep in lengthy trials, and Amanda Stoker had quit practice to take up a federal Senate seat for the Liberal party, but thankfully, Rob found a reader, a newly admitted barrister, Mei Barnes, to help. Still, getting Fletcher and Wilson to narrow the Brisbane nonsense down to two hearings wasted days of our time, and in the end, Raphael and Karam's threats to seek further orders against me were empty. After the first hearing, no listing was available until the end of July, and they dropped all their applications at the last minute, after weeks of unnecessary work.

It might have been a misstep, but I pushed ahead with my own discovery application against Raphael and Karam at the July listing to seek documents I believed to be relevant to proving the allegations. The Queensland plaintiffs had emulated their guru's Esoteric diligence by deleting relevant emails, and I figured that getting court orders or a reserved judgment against them for other insufficiencies, it would keep them off my back during my final weeks of preparation for the Benhayon trial. Mei represented me, and I stayed at my mother's home, where the milder winter and the warmth of her household mutts helped my chilblains to heal.

Our day in the Brisbane court commenced promisingly with a grouchy judge hoisting the court's file onto his bench, reams of paper overflowing from an archive box. When he opened by remarking that 'this case is well and truly off the rails', I strongly agreed, but His Honour appeared to blame me. UM's nine-foot-tall barrister pitched forth with the usual 'troll, cyber-bully, religious persecution' song and dance without any resistance from the bench, and whinged that my bankruptcy made me an unfair opponent because I had 'nothing to lose'. Mei and I therefore spent an excruciating day before an oppositional judge, who, making rulings as the hearing proceeded, gave me a fraction of the orders I'd sought, and ordered me to pay Raphael and Karam's costs, adding twenty to thirty grand to my debts.

The next day I began the drive to Sydney with one of my mother's care packages. She and Rosie always included toothpaste, deodorant and soap. Perhaps they were trying to tell me something. Mei, at least, notched up four combat hours in the litigation trenches, and His Honour's orders prevented Team UM from pulling further disruptive stunts in Brisbane for the next month. Still, I didn't trust them not to call some hearing or other in Brisbane in the middle of the Sydney trial. On planet Earth, the trial of one party in one jurisdiction would normally pause legal proceedings in another, but this lot was from Planet Serge.

cix Adjudicators

Of all Benhayon's applications in the month or so leading up to trial, there was one that I was genuinely nervous about. Over two years earlier, I'd elected trial by jury, but Serge waited until the last minute to apply to have his claim heard by a judge alone. We didn't know which judge we'd drawn in the Supreme Court lottery, but I'd banked on members of the public being better adjudicators of Benhayon's reputation. A worst case scenario would put us before a Judge Dour, or a Judge Grouch, or one with the unworkable slant of the Health Care Complaints Commissioner, Kieran Pehm. Another consideration was that overworked Supreme Court justices commonly took a year to hand down trial rulings, usually hundreds of pages of reasons. Juries are not required to give reasons, so their decisions are expeditious and less susceptible to appeal. A jury trial was more likely to bring finality.

However, on the day of the argument, Louise was sick with a fever, so Stewart had to stand in. I worried that he wasn't adequately briefed. Benhayon's guided missile, Kieran Smark, would argue that the evidence in our case was too technical and scientific for jurors and would require prolonged examination of documents. We'd counter that the proceedings were not complex; a jury most suitably represents the interests of the community; and an expeditious outcome best served the interests of justice, particularly where the plaintiff's operations have an impact on many hundreds of people.

Smark gave Benhayon his money's worth. It's a three week trial, Your Honour, and we have four expert reports of a highly technical nature. It's too difficult for a jury to digest the material with all the other evidence in that timeframe. The defence has sought access to hundreds of hours of recordings for example and numerous textual publications and will be requiring the jury to work through copious materials.

Stew was alone at the bar table. I scribbled a note and passed it, then another. He was on his feet giving it back — on the contrary, Your Honour, the defendant wishes to avoid overwhelming a jury. She intends to use short excerpts of materials, and some items of evidence go to proof of more than one imputation. There will be no prolonged examination of documents. If it were a judge only trial, Your Honour, both sides may be more tempted to tender a higher volume of evidence under the assumption that a judge is better able to consider large amounts of complex material. The time and complexity consideration, we submit, favours a jury trial.

Smark tried another one. The medical report by Professor Dwyer is twenty-three pages and of a highly expert nature, and the sixty page appendices of material attributed to my client is equally lengthy and difficult.

'Not at all, Your Honour,' said Stew, 'we take you to the report.' He glanced at me, patted the chair beside him, and I shifted to the bar to quickly locate excerpts that showed that Professor Dwyer's report was not only easy for a layperson to read, but that Benhayon's source material was anything but technical:

> Everyone who is in psychosis can read their therapist inside out... Put them in hospital, they know the doctors back to front. They know the nurses back to front. They can read them. Their powers of reading are very very very accurate, at a certain level.[97]

Smark then argued that the content of an expert report on the religiosity of Benhayon's 'philosophy' was too intellectually subtle for a jury, too 'esoteric', so I opened the defence particulars of truth, put my finger on one of Benhayon's quotes on religion and slid the binder across the table. Stewart took Her Honour to the subparagraph:

> Let humanity rot. Let them choose their own way. You wanna choose a rabbi, then you can choose a rabbi. I am telling you now the rabbi will give you far worse energy than your cancer will ever give you.[98]

One of Justice McCallum's eyebrows twitched. I hoped we'd won, but she reserved her ruling for a week. Louise kicked some Smark butt during those pre-trial arguments, but Stewart was also quick as a whip. Out in a chilly southerly breeze in Queens Square, I told him and Meri how pleased I was with the hearing. 'We're all over it, Esther,' he replied.

He'd even mucked in with Justice McCallum's banter after the argument. Her Honour was headed to the United States on a 'Thelma and Louise style road trip' with her family, she said.

'Let's hope Your Honour's holiday doesn't end the same way as the movie,' Stew rejoined. A little glint of light bounced off his teeth as he smiled. Everyone in court laughed, oh ho ho and ha ha ha, and I smiled along, but all I cared about was my jury. My jury.

cx Cult experts

At the beginning of August, Fletcher handed the Queensland case over to Serryn O'Regan, probably to focus on Benhayon's. Wilson, however, disappeared from Team Serge, replaced by a non-Esoteric Sydney barrister, Nick Olson. I'd just filed an amended defence to the Benhayon case, and Smark may not have been aware of the extent of Wilson's UM involvement until he read its added details of Charlie's directorship of the College charity and his roles in the McIntyre case and as a UM FACTS Team stalwart who'd publicly laid into me and other UM detractors. His pointy head also stuck up like a lightning rod in video evidence from Church of Serge services.

Soon after, Meri tried to serve a subpoena to the College of UM by emailing it to its directors, Wilson, Greig, and O'Regan, but they refused to acknowledge service, so I had to hire a process server to hand it to them in person. Fletcher returned the favour with subpoenas to an array of my contacts demanding all their correspondence with me and any document in their possession that mentioned UM or Benhayon. That's where having a fleet footed legal team on the ground was invaluable. Serge's proxies, surly Natalie, sour Alison, and scowling Alan, watched on in courtroom 12C as Louise despatched all UM's pre-trial arguments in the lead up, and had all their subpoenas thrown out. Her Honour would not allow such an invasion of privacy based on a 'fishing expedition' for items of dubious relevance.

Just three weeks before kick-off, Justice McCallum handed down the discovery orders that gave me Serge's tax returns, his investment trust documents, and other goodies. Her Honour also gave me my jury. She didn't accept that they'd have too much reading. Benhayon versus Rockett was 'a community values case', she said, and added that a jury would bring to bear 'the moral and social standards that they share with the community at large.'[99]

But the judge had some additional observations on expert testimony. I'd assumed the simplest way to prove UM was a harmful cult was via an expert report. David Millikan had no trouble concluding that the plaintiff has all the characteristics of a cult leader.

> There are numerous occasions when the language used to describe Benhayon sounds as if we are hearing about Jesus...
>
> He has an outrageously elevated view of his own importance. He is hostile to all alternative explanations of reality but his own. He envelops his followers in an illusory world which allows no scrutiny or examination. He is operating in an organisation where no one can call him to account. If the history of religion tells us anything it is that unrestrained authority is incorrigible.

Team UM, however, commissioned Reverend Gary Bouma, an Emeritus Professor of Sociology and Associate Anglican Priest, to make a report in reply, disputing Millikan's definition of a cult. They also commissioned a UK academic, Dr Joscelyn Godwin, to argue that Benhayon's Ageless Wisdom belonged 'within a recognised current of religious and philosophical thought', but because UM's experts based their reports on a limited collection of Benhayon's doctrinal statements, and were not supplied with material about the organisation's controversial activities, Louise and I planned to get both thrown out at trial as irrelevant.

In my studies I'd come across sociologists who minimised the danger of cults by casting them as fringe-dwelling New Religious Movements, and characterised objections to them as questions of religious acceptability. Such dismissiveness can be expected from those who study such groups rather than investigate them — selectively focusing on beliefs and rituals and overlooking antisocial behaviours and impacts. Many cults are not religious at all, such as Keith Raniere's personal development enterprise NXIVM. Others are counterfeit religions, cynically deploying doctrines that exclusively benefit their leadership. If such scholars scrutinised the extent to which groups plunder followers' assets, engage in deceptive and coercive practices, shun dissenters, harass critics, exploit disciples for unpaid labour, endanger children and the infirm, and cover up sexual abuse — they'd reach very different conclusions that might challenge their bias toward 'religious freedom'.

Justice McCallum read the expert reports and couldn't see how Benhayon's concordance with Theosophy was relevant to any of the allegations. She'd limited us to a three week trial because the costs of a lengthy hearing would be 'vastly disproportionate to the interest at stake'. But what she said next tripped the light switch. 'There's a real question here of the utility of taking up hearing time on two theologians arguing about definitions. You have a jury trial. Most members of the community don't need an expert to tell them how to recognise a cult.'

It was so obvious when she put it that way. The call was mine to make, and I did it immediately — forestalling what Her Honour flagged as potentially confusing academic quibbling. Most members of the public might not be able to articulate what makes a cult, but they know one when they see one; and as far as cults go, Universal Medicine was one of the cultiest.

David was understanding when I broke it to him. He'd put a lot of work into his report and would have been an entertaining witness, but the decision to cut him rendered Bouma's reply redundant. Dr Godwin's also took the shuttle to Sirius.

cxi Reasonableness

Two weeks out from trial, my lawyers should have had every document related to our defence pleadings at their fingertips, but my workload was overwhelming and I'd made no progress in compiling them. At least I'd found a trustworthy person to work through the remaining recordings. Only Olga could tolerate Benhayon's most perverse garbage. I worried it might reignite his trauma, but he'd heard it all before, and was out of work and wanted to help.

Ten days out from trial, I was busy cutting over two hundred audio and video clips. We'd only play a fraction in court, but I needed a selection of Benhayon's greatest hits to give Tom plenty to choose from. When I realised I couldn't possibly get them all transcribed in time, I sent out an SOS, found four volunteers, and was drawing up transcript templates near midnight when Riz boiled over. He burst into my little room, crying, 'Stop! Stop this! Go to bed! Go to sleep!'

'I'm fine.'

'You're working yourself to death!'

'Don't be silly.'

He stood in the space between my trestle table desk and my bed, pleading. The gap was just wide enough for my chair. Riz was on a career sabbatical and going through a torturous and well medicated relationship breakup. Staying with him worked for both of us because he was not used to living alone and not particularly good at it, and his small apartment in Sydney's inner-west was closer to court than my friends' well appointed fridge in the north. His bachelor pad only had one bedroom, though, and a houseful of his anxiety.

Secreted in a glorified cupboard that real estate blurbs call a 'media room', I had a camp mattress on the floor, and my office piled on top and below two small tables. At the end of each working day, I'd push in my chair, make an about-face, drop to my haunches, and roll into bed.

'I sleep. Look, I've got to get this done, there's no one else to do it.'

'This is insane!'

'I can't throw away six years of work against these pricks by failing to get the evidence together for the trial.'

Riz was sweating and his voice was breaking, 'I don't want to come in here and find a corpse!'

I shooed him away. Riz hadn't witnessed the hours I'd kept over the past year. Preparations had intensified, but I was used to pacing myself. Either way, I didn't have time to focus on his state of mind. Each day I half expected the axe to fall. The guardedness borne of sudden deaths, near deaths, and bad days in court, manifested, not as jitters, but icy hypervigilance. Riz's building was secure enough for witness protection, and I kept my location secret, making sure I was not followed when I left chambers or got off the train. But my real fear was that Benhayon could drop his claim. I told my team that I would not settle, I wanted our evidence on the public record.

Tom opened his war room on my fifty-first birthday, the day after jetting in from his Astral travels. To keep the SC away from barristers constantly bailing him up for a chat, we set up in his home's expansive kitchen while Janet was still away. It got me out of Riz's thinning hair, but came with the fresh hell of Louise prodding me to get all our proposed evidence into a tender bundle within days. When she cast her eyes over the heaping mess of folders and papers on Tom's dining table, and asked, 'when is this going to be sorted out?' I rounded on her like a flea-bitten terrier.

'When you stop giving me jobs to do!'

On our second day in the kitchen, the lawyers prized me away from the mess to draw up a timeline of the facts and events that led me to publish the blogs and tweets within Benhayon's claim, and all my attempts to get UM brought to account. An hour passed of my recounting. Two hours, and the more I remembered, the more Tom and Louise's faces lightened. They were learning for the first time of the extent of my complaints to authorities, and all the contact I'd had with people with concerns about the group. There'd been no time to go through it all previously. 'She could sweep this on reasonableness,' Louise said with a cool smile.

I blinked, not grasping what she was saying.

'Your section thirty defence,' said Tom, easing back in his armchair. 'Qualified privilege. The defence allows you to make minor errors or misinterpretations as long as you were publishing to readers with a legitimate interest in the material, and the way you went about it was reasonable in all of the circumstances.'

I sighed with impatience. 'Bloody oath it was reasonable. I thought that was obvious.'

Louise gave her inimitable giggle. We'd pleaded section thirty to all imputations. 'We could clear this whole thing,' she said to Tom.

I frowned. 'You didn't think I'd win?'

cxii The admiral

Tom worked amidst his own clutter at a smaller round table beside the French doors that overlooked his garden, easing the pressure, as the week progressed, in his unflappable way. 'There's no need for a tender bundle,' he said after a couple of days. 'We don't want to drown the jury with all this. We'll just tender documents as we go, and if copies aren't ready, Meri can bring them later.'

The silk never grew impatient. He quietly read through the recording transcripts in one morning and marked those he wanted to use. He wrote his examinations of each witness in his notebooks, longhand, with no errors and no crossing out. Beginning with Serge, he worked through each theme of the cross-examination, calling for documents as he went. What do we have on this? What do we have on that? Oh, just one of the tax returns will do…At junctures he'd cheerily announce, 'Well, that part's done…'

Serenity began to settle with the admiral at the helm, but Tom knew that he was cutting it fine with only a week of preparation time after long flights from a distant timezone. He'd calibrated a routine for dealing with jet lag by taking strategically timed naps until his body clock normalised, and he'd dedicated the week to trial preparation, with just one engagement at its end, an annual talk he gave at the Bar Association for newly admitted barristers. I was alone in his kitchen late that Friday morning, printer whirring, when Louise called. 'Tom's in hospital,' she said. He'd collapsed during his talk.

cxiii Colours

We were driving into the shopping centre when Louise phoned on the Saturday morning. She was delighted that Riz had bullied me into a shopping trip. He'd seen what I planned to wear to trial and would later say that the fact sales assistants consulted him and not me when I tried on clothes, was proof my dress sense is hopeless.

Louise spent Friday afternoon at Tom's bedside, leaving him briefly to come to his house as he awaited test results. No one had a clue why he'd keeled over. He had no history of it, but was recovering well and complaining about not getting through his speech. Louise and I began a differential diagnosis, surmising that a combination of jet lag and overwork can't have helped. She stalked to his fridge and conducted a forensic examination of his pantry, which we both declared understocked. 'What is this?' she said, holding up a large bag of puffed grain of some sort. 'Don't tell me he's living on this.' She examined it closely, 'whatever it is…'

I recalled the two weeks I'd spent with him in May where he'd eaten salmon sushi nearly every day, washed down with his mystery yellow fruit drink. 'Everything he eats is orange!' I said. Despite witnessing him eat decent lunches and dinners all week, we ruled, on minimal evidence, that he wasn't taking care of himself while Janet was away. It was nonsense of course, and Tom's son told us as much when he visited that weekend. He and his fiancé had been checking in all week and had made sure the silk was properly exercised, rested, and fed.

Discharged from hospital on the Friday evening, the SC's test results showed no abnormalities, but Louise told me to clear out, concerned he might wear himself out if he started chatting about the case. He'd been plotting all afternoon from his hospital bed. 'We have to make sure he rests,' she said.

Earlier that afternoon though, she'd paused the pantry audit to make a sober observation. 'I might have to run this trial.' Her eyes darted away and then back to mine. 'I'm not ready.' It was the first time I'd seen Louise daunted, and I suggested we cross that bridge when we came to it. Later I stopped to consider what we'd need to do to if Tom had to bow out. I did not doubt she would rise to it, but we'd have to pull some long hours.

As Riz drove into the mall carpark, she'd called to suggest that I leave it until after lunch to convene at the war room. We weren't to get Tom excited by starting too early on the case. She had a message for Riz too: 'Tell him,' she said, 'colours. Nice colours. Friendly colours. Innocent colours. No black. We don't want you dressing like a troll.'

'When do I dress like a troll?'

Riz, in the driver's seat, shrieked with laughter.

Part IV

The Scales

cxiv The genius

Taking the jury to my crescendo blog, Smark read aloud, "'Just how many girls have stayed in that household? And lived with them as well?? And why?'" By September 2018, that post had been visited about four thousand times. 'When you're called to account for the sort of allegations where you call someone things like "sleazebag guru" you're using the sort of allegation which calls for a very high level of proof,' he said.

Introducing his client, Smark stated that Universal Medicine was neither a cult, nor socially harmful, but an organisation that gives people spiritual comfort. He announced that the plaintiff would call as witnesses Doctors Malatt, Minford and Szramka; his daughters Natalie and Simone; Judith McIntyre's beneficiary, Ingrid; Lance's ex-wife, Anna; Neil Ringe, Neil Gamble, Rebecca Baldwin, Sarah Baldwin, and the now eighteen year old Williams child who'd blogged in his defence at fifteen. 'At worst,' said Smark, 'ordinary people would think Universal Medicine is harmless.'

The journalists barely touched their keyboards during most of Benhayon's biographical testimony. If his statements about his schoolboy days were true, perhaps the bullying triggered the nuclear-powered ego defences that blasted his grandiosity through the stratosphere. Excelling at sport was a means of coping with his 'tremendous insights' about people, he said, and by the time he dropped out of high school, he'd 'represented the State in athletics and representative soccer, representative cricket, and representative rugby.' Likewise, his talent for tennis was so prodigious that he was invited to start coaching at fifteen and was exposed to 'some of the best tennis coaches in the world', although he did not name them.

The gifted one said nothing about his failure to coach a single pupil to the professional ranks, or his habit of driving away those with promise, or about burning out the object of his most intense focus. Miranda put down her racquet while still in her teens and never played tennis again. Of his commercial failure in the early nineties, he said that his coaching business was 'very healthy', and the trouble was a contract dispute, contradicting his 1995 statement to the bankruptcy court blaming bad weather. Smark didn't raise his bankruptcy or the toilet revelation and its lovely backing voices, but Benhayon spoke of an experience, in March 1999, soon after his thirty-fifth birthday, of profound stillness. 'I just deepened back into the incredible amount of joy that I had in my body...' he said, adding that it gave rise to Universal Medicine and the suite of healing modalities that came to him in an 'instant knowing'. Before us was an under-exalted genius on a mission to make his bliss and clairsentience available to all; a devout and philanthropic sage forced to relive childhood trauma by a cruel bully.

Each day, as more evidence came out, I felt a certain triumph, but remained wary he could still abandon his claim. Shortly after shopping with Riz, where my sartorial disadvantage relieved him of several hundred dollars, a calm settled properly on me. Perhaps what kicked in was akin to what athletes experience when they're 'in the zone'. My team worked late each night at the war room, but I would sleep soundly from the moment I was horizontal until my alarm woke me. In waking hours, I was alert but unflustered, driving in peak hour traffic to the city each morning and driving Tom home each evening, sticking to the speed limit, focused on the road and my mirrors, determined that no mishaps would disrupt my defence. The primal war cries of months before had cooled into a clinical relentlessness, and I had years of UM's bootcamp to thank. Tom quipped that they'd driven a steamroller over me so many times, flattened me so repeatedly, I could not get any flatter. I just slipped under the rollers and kept going. Riz didn't fare so well. After a couple of hours observing in the public gallery he fled Sydney and checked into a health retreat.

Under Smark's questioning, moist eyed Benhayon told the court of reading my crescendo blog for the first time. 'The intrusion,' he said, 'and the raping of my integrity, the raping of my…'

'How did you feel about it?'

His answer was met by a delicious hail of press fingertips on keyboards: 'Well, you feel raped.'

Each witness had to pass me to reach the witness box, and that morning, every pair of eyes in the room followed His Holiness as he made his crab-like way down the narrow passage between the wigs and the public seats. As he approached, I searched his face, and about a metre from me, he lifted his eyes to meet mine with a wrathful 'I'm-going-to-get-you' look. Rosie, who observed from the row behind me, said, 'he looked as if he wanted to deck you.'

The glare suggested he was confident, but he'd just passed the SC who was placidly girding to take him on. Benhayon swore his oath and perhaps he really did think I'd be intimidated, but the look he got back was not from an impostor who'd hidden for years behind lawyers and minders and little girls. It was from a hardened frontline fighter; a stare that seared through his seemingly invincible hubris. 'You have no idea what you're in for,' I thought.

cxv The silk

Benhayon leaned forward earnestly as he neared the end of his evidence in chief. 'You feel the intrusion that is ongoing, the onslaught, and you feel the impact of the onslaught, because I feel things at an energetic level, I feel the forces that are trying to intrude.'

'The allegations that you say are carried by these publications,' said Smark, 'are they true?'

'Definitely not.'

'Why did you start these proceedings?' was Smark's final question.

Benhayon lifted his chin. 'Obviously to protect my reputation, but most of all because it's one of my principles, that we should have a fair and decent society, and that this type of behaviour should not be allowed.'

Smark sat. Tom rose in the silent court and opened his notebook on the lectern. He took a fob watch from his waistcoat pocket and laid it on the bar table. There was a clock above the witness box, but he did not glance at it through the cross-examination. He kept his eyes on Serge. Back straight, squarely facing the plaintiff, the silk opened in his broadcaster diction with the question he'd waited six months to ask: 'Mr Benhayon, in the time you've been in this courtroom since Monday, have there been any discarnate spirits in the room?'

Serge blinked, and his head twitched. 'Any?'

'Discarnate spirits...'

'Yes, there has,' Benhayon blurted before Tom could finish.

'...a phrase I'd suggest you've used in your teachings.'

The plaintiff recomposed. 'Yes, there has been actually.'

'When were they here?'

'They come in and out all the time.'

'Are there any here now?'

'Yeah, there is — there are, sorry.'

'Where are they?'

'They, they stand in this room.'

'Yes, but where? Would you point one out to us please?'

'You can't see them.'

'Can you see them?'

'Can't see them.'

'But you know they're there?'

'I can sense them.'

'Without seeing them, you sense them? Is that what you say?'

'That's correct.'

The keyboards were silent. Everyone but the silk and the plaintiff was silent. A non-Esoteric stillness had descended on the court.

Tom pressed. His tone was measured, but firm. 'How many are here now?'

'I never count them.'

'Could you do so now?'

'I beg your pardon?'

'Could you now do so please?'

Benhayon's tenor remained steady, his face straight. 'I never count them.'

'But I'm asking you to do so now.'

'I don't count them.'

'Is that because you can't count them?'

'No, because…'

'Because you don't really see them or detect them?'

'I can detect them.'

'How many are there?'

'I don't count them.'

'Please count them now.'

'It's not something I do.'

'Can you do it?'

'I could if I wanted to, but it's not something I practise and it's not something I'm allowed to do.'

'Would you please do it now?'

'I cannot do it.'

'You just said you could do it in the previous answer.'

'By virtue of what allows me access, I cannot break that rule.'

'Whose rule is that?'

'The rule of my soul, the rule of our connection, the Ageless Wisdom.'

'That's a rule you've made up for yourself, isn't it?'

'No.'

'You said earlier "The spirits have come and gone" in this court since Monday.'

'That's correct.'

'When did the ones who are here now come?'

'Happens everywhere, all the time, not just in this room.'

'No, but I'm asking you particularly about this room where we all are and we all can experience.'

'Have they come in? Sorry, can you ask the question again?'

'I think you answered my earlier question that there were some present now.'

'Yes.'

'But you couldn't or wouldn't count them.'

'That's…'

'Do you remember that?'

'That's correct.'

'Now I'm asking you, when did you first detect the presence of those spirits that you were talking about in that answer?'

'You feel them coming in, when they come in, and you feel them leave and new ones come in. You can feel it all the time.'

'Yes, but…'

'Constantly.'

'…my question is, when did you feel them come in today?'

'There are some that were present when I walked in, and particularly when you walked in.'

'Present already, do you mean?'

'Present when I arrived, yeah, and particularly when you walked in.'

'Have there been any periods in this court when you've been here, since the start of the case, when there were no spirits in the court?'

'No, always.'

Tom paused to glance at his notebook. 'I want to pass to another topic for the moment.' He paused again and returned to the witness. 'Are there any spirits close to you right now?'

'There are.'

'Which side of you?'

'Particularly on my left.' To Benhayon's left sat an elderly court officer, eyes half closed, then me on the end of the first row of the public seats. Tom had walked into court that morning with me and the rest of our team.

'On your left?' said Tom. 'Can you give us a clue of how many there might be, even though you're not counting them, like an approximate number?'

'No number.'

'No number, and there are some on your right?'

Benhayon wisely said no. To his right was Justice Lonergan and her Tipstaff.

'None on your right but some on your left?' said Tom.

'Yes.'

'If they were corporeal, could you reach and touch them?'

'Possibly.'

'Are they close enough for you to reach and touch?'

'Possibly.'

The report in *The Sydney Morning Herald* that afternoon began with the line, 'It must be among the most arresting opening questions ever uttered in a cross-examination.'

I'd like to imagine that I could have wrangled Benhayon if I'd made it to trial without my legal team, but in those first minutes Tom had shown that he was worth every thread of his silk. From decades of trial experience, he knew how to take a bullshitter by the horns. Nevertheless, Benhayon had performed better than I thought he might. He'd held his nerve.

cxvi The returns

'As a result of having been bankrupt for three years, you had no substantial assets or savings in 1998 at the end of that bankruptcy period, did you?' said Tom.

'Correct.'

If the trial's primary focus had been financial allegations, Tom might have quizzed him on how a rural tennis coach and his wife managed to accumulate assets so quickly after discharge from a conjugal bankruptcy, but the challenge of trying so many allegations in limited time meant Tom had to skip over questionable occurrences and strictly minimise our evidence. Under Smark's examination, Benhayon claimed that he'd treated eighty percent of his healing clients for free since 2010 — which former followers found about as plausible as Patanjali's sojourn in Atlantis. Tom, however, went to Benhayon's 2016 personal tax return where the guru declared his taxable income was around one hundred and ninety thousand dollars. Miranda's was one hundred and seventy five thousand that year, and Serge confirmed that Miranda contributed one hundred and fifty thousand dollars to her superannuation fund in 2017.

Molomby followed with a close examination of the proprietor's status as sole shareholder, director, and trustee of the elaborate network of companies and trusts connected with the Universal Medicine business. In 2015 he'd acquired a fifty percent shareholding in Evolve College, a nationwide business formerly known as The Australian College of Massage, owned by two devotees, Robert and Deborah Wild. Whether he'd bought in, or they'd donated half their business, we don't know, but the company began offering a course in Esoteric Chakra-puncture, and tax documents revealed that the College turned over several million dollars per year, yielding Benhayon nearly half a million dollars of its annual profits.

The 2016 tax return for Benhayon's main clinic and events business revealed turnover of about two million dollars, with a declared net income of nearly nine hundred thousand dollars. That did not include UM's European income — and no documents accounting for his overseas trade were provided to us. The Australian income was paid into the Universal Family Trust, from which Miranda, Natalie, Michael, Curtis, and Curtis's wife Isabella each received a distribution. Natalie received the most at one hundred and thirty thousand, Miranda got one hundred and twenty, and Curtis got the least of the offspring at sixty thousand. Benhayon paid himself fifty thousand and the residual four hundred thousand was paid to another of several investment trusts that he controlled. The trust distributions were paid on top of each family member's wages for working in the business, while Deborah Benhayon earned a salary as the corporation's financial controller. 'So really the whole of your extended family gets their living from Universal Medicine?' Tom asked.

Serge conceded, but his answer was somewhat more tentative than when he'd aired his expertise in courtroom spooks. Tom then read out an inventory of Benhayon's real estate assets — an outlay of over eight million dollars for the properties he currently owned, and all had significantly appreciated following extensive renovations at an untold cost. The jury were given photographs of the well maintained Brisbane, Wollongbar, Goonellabah and Tregeagle addresses, as well as images of large homes owned by the Benhayon dependents, Deborah included. The Unimed Brisbane Clinic, half-owned by Serge, was bought for almost two million dollars, but when asked how much was still owed on the mortgage; how much it had cost to renovate; and how much his followers had donated to the purchase and upkeep, Benhayon's instant knowing had deserted him. Tom assisted by presenting a document that showed donations to the Unimed Brisbane mortgage between 2011 and 2016 came to two hundred and seventy thousand dollars. Another showed that Benhayon collected one hundred and eight thousand dollars for his Hall of Ageless Wisdom ambitions in one financial year ending in 2012. Those gifts were made to his businesses.

Moving to bequests, Benhayon affirmed that UM cared for people afflicted with serious or terminal conditions, sometimes at Unimed House. The silk then asked about Rita, who'd left Serge her half of her home. 'While she was still alive, you suggested at a meeting of your students that she might be reincarnated as your grandchild, didn't you?'

'I played around with the idea, yes.'

'Well, to be more precise about it, you suggested, didn't you, that she might come back as your son Michael's child?'

'Playfully I said that, yes.'

'After she died, however, you told your students that she had in fact been reincarnated as the child of a woman living in Germany, didn't you?'

'We don't, I don't use the word "reincarnated" but yes, words to that effect.'

Questioned about Judith McIntyre, Benhayon acknowledged that she was recovering from breast cancer when she began attending sessions with him. 'You believed that she, like Rita, would be reincarnated?' said Tom.

'We all reincarnate,' Serge replied.

'And you were doing your best to give her whatever advice would assist her, weren't you?'

'That's correct.'

'When I say "advice" I mean teachings of yours that would assist her?'

'I shared the science so that they can make their own decisions.'

Asked to clarify what he meant by science, the plaintiff sneered, 'reincarnation is a science'.

'Is it taught at universities?' said Tom.

Benhayon halted. 'I beg your pardon?'

'Is it taught at universities?'

'Not yet,' he said.

cxvii Science

My job was to look out for missteps in Benhayon's testimony where we might catch him out. Yet, for the first few hours, my eyes, and those of the jury, were as much on Tom as they were on the plaintiff; back and forth, back and forth — the best tennis match we might ever see.

We knew nothing of the four jurors except what we could deduce from their appearances. It was an exercise in profiling, but our panel gave me confidence that I'd made the right call in fighting for one. The two men and two women, with an average age of around forty, were mature and attentive, and if it's possible to look intelligent and come across as non-crackpots, they did. None were as glow-in-the-dark white-skinned as ninety-five percent of Benhayon's congregation, either, which made them potentially more awake to UM's racial uniformity, visible in event videos and in the public gallery, which smacks of cultishness, and which whites are often blind to.

Each day Justice Lonergan gave the jury strict instructions that they were to rely only on evidence put before them, and that conducting their own research could result in a mistrial and a charge of contempt of court. They were reminded not to look at news reports or social media and to avoid discussion of the trial with anyone other than fellow jurors, and Her Honour told them it wouldn't be fair to anyone involved to draw on information that was not tested before the court.

Delving further into bequests, Tom raised the judge's remarks in the McIntyre's family provision case. 'He said this, didn't he: "The evidence points strongly to the conclusion that the deceased attributed her peaceful and content state of being to the teachings of Mr Benhayon."?'

The plaintiff agreed and added that the judge 'honoured the deceased person.' Not once in his testimony did he utter Judith's name.

Tom continued to question him about providing teachings to his benefactor to assist her in her next life. 'Because according to your view of reincarnation what a person does in one life can affect what happens to them in their current life or their future lives?'

'It can.'

'You have said to your students, haven't you, that if someone leaves their money to their children, they will have bad kidney energy in their next life?'

Benhayon paused. 'Not like that.'

'No words like that?'

Serge's mouth did something unusual. It shut.

'Do you recall telling your students this, in 2008, ten years ago: "Now, if you are leaving an inheritance to your children, the way that they then spend the money affects you in your next life"?'

Benhayon confirmed that it was still something he taught.

'You were telling your students in 2008, weren't you, if they or anyone left money to their children that could inflict them with unfortunate consequences in the next life?'

'I wouldn't use those words but the science teaches us to be responsible with our money.' He conceded that he'd told his students that bequests to Universal Medicine, as long as they were made unconditionally, would bless them with fiery energy in their next life.

'Do you accept this,' asked Tom; 'that what you were saying to your students on this topic could easily have had the effect of deterring them from leaving money to their children and causing them to leave it instead to you?'

'Definitely not.'

'You told them to Mrs McIntyre, didn't you?'

'Not quite. She got the whole science, not just the, the small part that you're identifying.'

'You were trying to do the best for a woman who you thought was going into a new life; right?'

'That I know was going into a new life.'

'A woman you know is going into a new life and according to your knowledge if she did the wrong thing in her will that could injure her in her next life; correct?'

'I taught the science and she made that decision.'

With that, Meri cued excerpts from recordings of the 2008 EDG meeting at which Benhayon described donations to Unimed as investing in 'the true work of the Hierarchy on Earth', and hypothesised around Kate Greenaway making her will. 'If I've lived all this life doing great work and creating my money esoterically, if I invest that wisely, that's going to give me a platform from which it feeds me fire in my next life.'

He spoke of the consequences of leaving money to relatives who might use it in pranic ways.

> All of Kate's good work gets dragged in her next life because of this constant drain on her kidney. She's in her next life saying, 'How come things don't work for me?'... Have you ever had that feeling you're running into brick walls and so forth? It means that you've done an imprint that is still alive today, that has a pranic emanation that is holding another and stopping them from being in their soul.

He also preached the dos and don'ts of leaving assets to him.

> ...if you leave in your will, 'I'm leaving my money to Universal Medicine, but I want it used to help those who cannot afford courses, to use the money I leave behind to be able to pay for the courses', you're in prana...
>
> Because you've put a lineal condition on spherical energy. Because if you identify us as the place of Hierarchical truth, then that trust will transfer itself to the spherical nature of what we represent. Therefore we will know how to best use it.[100]

cxviii The clown

When Tom asked him if he thought it appropriate to give graphic sex talks in front of children, Serge was unapologetic. 'My job is to make it very real, what's going on in society, otherwise people get cushioned. They need to know what is truly going on,' he said.

The jury then watched the video of the Way of the Livingness forum where Anita shared her feelings about the position of her cervix during sexual intercourse, and Benhayon talked of his spectacular experience of orgasm as an 'hermaphrodite'. The plaintiff confirmed that the boy seated behind Anita was aged about thirteen at the time. 'He looked a bit stunned, didn't he?' said Tom.

'I don't think so. It's one of the most beautiful presentations you could receive at that age, and I wish I would have received it and not spent all those years doing what I did as a male until I discovered how to truly make love to a woman.'

'Mr Benhayon,' said Tom, with a weary tone, 'I'm not talking about that, or the suitability or otherwise of what was being talked about for mature adult discussion. I'm talking about doing it in front of a thirteen or fourteen year old.'

'Do you know what kids get up to these days on a mobile phone, at the age of eight, and what they're able to see on a mobile phone?'

'Is that your justification for doing it?'

'No, it's my justification to teach them or to do a presentation of what is possible, as opposed to what everybody has been regurgitating generation after generation, and the miscarriages that occur in relationships.'

Tom then called for audio from the Couples Workshop Lance had attended with Anna, in which Benhayon gave advice on how women could seduce their partners. He told them to say they'd bought a stunning new dress and recommended they make the partner sit on the bed to cushion their fall. The audience is heard laughing. 'So he sits. She goes in and says "I won't be long"…goes in wherever; you can go in the closet, you can go under the bed… The point is you're being playful. You come out naked.'

Lance had looked around the room at that point and noted that he was one of very few who was not amused.

'The guy's… CPR… He's got an erection like he's never had before… or the woman's turned on like she's never been turned before — wet to the bone, if it's two girls.' The laughter is uproarious.

You can milk it, you can keep them there for an hour. It'll be the longest erection he'll ever have. Keep him there…What turns the guy on more than anything else is not a woman that's forward; that's only a guy that's looking for relief will look at that, cause he's looking for… it's better than a jerk off. So he's looking… sorry kids… but he's looking at just to get a release, right?[101]

Tom returned to the plaintiff and suggested he'd been performing for laughs, 'like a comedy club clown'.

The guru's expression soured. He whinged that the lawyer was taking him out of context; that he was all about invigorating stale relationships. Tom challenged that there was no justification for going into such crass detail in the presence of children.

'The children were in a separate room unless they wandered in,' said Serge.

'Do you remember just at the end of it you said, "Sorry, kids." You knew there were children there, didn't you?'

The plaintiff's reply was quick. 'I must have caught a child in the corner of my eye walking back from the childminding room at that time and at that moment I got caught, yes.'

'Just one? But you said "kids"?'

'Well, there were kids in that room, yes.'

'Could they hear you in the room?'

'Usually not.'

'You wouldn't have been saying sorry to kids who couldn't hear you, would you?'

Benhayon denied that children were present through the whole routine, but the next day, Tom handed him an attendance list for that event and others. I'd had to wrestle Fletcher to get them. The lists revealed the names of adolescents who'd attended his unsavoury presentations, those Lance had seen among the audience, and the silk had the guru confirm their ages. He called for more audio.

cxix The Outsider

Serge Benhayon is delusional. Serge Benhayon is dishonest. Those were two of the allegations I needed to prove. In the blog I'd referred to him as a self-styled messiah, and I told the court that it was delusional to think that UM's public hostilities did his cause any good. The question of whether he believes his own bullshit is not simple to answer, though. David Millikan insisted that he does, that he'd convinced himself that he'd conceived a profound universal philosophy with all the answers. But Esoteric Breast Massages? Cursed bequests? A revelation on the dunny?

A barrister in training and former army chaplain, Mark Burton, who joined our team to assist at trial, reminded us that Martin Luther, and other religious figures, recorded fairly vivid scatalogical epiphanies. 'This realisation was given to me by the Spiritus Sanctus on this cloaca in the tower', Luther wrote of his inspiration for the Protestant Reformation, adding that he 'felt totally newborn' afterward, 'and through open gates I entered paradise'. It was arguably a better review of a bowel movement than Serge managed.

Still, I doubt an individual who sought so aggressively to quash exposure of his deceit really believes his own bunkum. Robert Lifton describes Donald Trump as a grandiose solipsist, a generator of his own reality, capable of believing and disbelieving his own lies simultaneously. Truth is only of value to such characters when it serves their interests, which is rarely. Without integrity or merit one can't profit from the truth. Their overblown sense of entitlement is the only genuine conviction they have, and they use dishonesty, bullying, and the confident 'charisma of certainty' to gain the wealth and power they crave.

Our problem was cracking Benhayon's persuasiveness in court. During preparations, Tom would stop at some tidbit of Esoteric logic and rehearse a challenge. On a quiet afternoon in chambers, he found an excerpt where Serge told his students that they could not rely on knowledge, they could only rely on feeling, but when most of them said to him, 'oh yeah, I can feel that', they hadn't actually felt it at all. 'I'll tell you when you can feel it,' he said to the group, 'because sometimes it's not even a release for people to feel until it is released for people to feel.'

'Ho!' scoffed Tom. 'How does he know when it's released?'

'He's got direct access to the Hierarchy,' I said, imagining his answer.

'But who says so?'

'Well, he does,' I said, 'but how are we going to prove he's not hearing the voice of heaven.'

Tom frowned. In the next part of the sermon, Benhayon claimed every sacred or classic text, in fact, everything ever written, except for his own stuff, is a re-interpretation that has been channelled to mankind by dark Brahmanic Lords. That included all versions of the Christian gospel, Patanjali's *Yoga Sutra* and the *Bhagavad Gita*. 'Unless you get the exact word of the messenger, which is very rare… Very few writers have been free of Brahmanic energy. Therefore it's very difficult to get the exact meaning of things.'

'Preposterous,' said Tom. 'What about Socrates?'

'A bastardisation, probably, if you ask His Nibs.'

'How does he know this?'

'It's the same problem,' I said. 'You might win a rhetorical argument, and if it were a judge only trial, a judge would probably see through it, but before a jury, we don't know. They might find it too subtle, or lose interest, or get confused, but in the worst case, they might be persuaded that he genuinely thinks he's receiving spiritual inspiration. Even if they don't believe it themselves, they might find him sympathetic. The real worst case would be if he converts one or more of them.'

Tom put the paper down and rubbed his chin.

'I think don't give him the opportunity to go down the metaphysical rabbit hole,' I continued. 'He'll have some spherical answer — he'll go off on tangents — maybe he'll look a bit crazy, but unless you rein him in, he might take control the same way he does at his meetings. He knows how to use confusion to run rings around people.' The image of Szramka, Professor Foley and Neil Ringe on stage with him, silent and blank faced, came to mind, with Benhayon pacing around them, boasting of his hermaphroditic superpowers. 'We risk getting lost in the abstractions, like his followers have.'

It was not that I doubted Tom could out reason him, but we needed the jury to reach unanimous conclusions. Irrationality is an unfair and unpredictable adversary. Trump exemplifies it; weaponising confusion and obfuscation to divert attention from matters of real importance — from his corruption and incompetence — to achieve dominance. 'We need to pin him down on what is concrete, no matter what he throws back.'

Tom listened pensively. I wasn't sure if my reasoning had come out coherently. 'Do you know what I mean?' I said. 'Where you become so conditioned to the awfulness of something that you lose the sense of how awful it is?'

To an extent it had happened to me, where I was so desensitised to Benhayon's statements I'd underestimated their impact on people new to his rot. 'If we put too much focus on his meaningless words, the jury might lose the sense of what he's done, his actions; they might be persuaded he's the victim; that he merely has some eccentric rationale; that he's been misunderstood.'

Tom knew what I meant; that we couldn't risk the jury losing any sense of Benhayon's cutthroat absurdity and its real consequences. 'There's a passage in The Outsider,' he said. 'Do you know the book by Albert Camus? The murderer waits in his jail cell, and to console himself he thinks back to something his late mother had often said…' The sun had moved westward, the dazzling noon light no longer glinting on the chambers' windows. I knew the book.

Tom finished his thought. 'His mother used to say that over time one gets used to anything.'

cxx Leonardo

To prove Benhayon was both delusional and a bullshitter, Tom had to prevent him from using the witness box as a pulpit, and demolish his assertions about the nature of knowledge. Serge had railed against all thoughts, ideals, and beliefs as psychic sabotages of the Lords of Form, and preached that the only way to salvation was by connecting with the Ageless Wisdom and the Light of the Soul through unthinking, unemotional feeling.

The silk always took care to quote his exact words. 'You say, don't you, that we have all had two thousand three hundred previous lives?'

'At least.'

'At least? Now, how do you know that?'

'I access the Ageless Wisdom to know that information.'

'How did you come up with that figure?'

He answered that his innermost stillness connected him to an ageless energetic imprint that translated into conscious knowing, and so on.

'How do you know that that's right?'

'You can feel it.'

'So it's correct, isn't it, that in terms of your teachings in Universal Medicine, we have only your own certainty in your feelings as the guarantee of their truth?'

'Correct.'

Pressed for details about his past lives, he said he'd been a woman in the immediately previous. Followers would have understood that was Alice A. Bailey. Before her, he'd been a man, but said he knew little more than that.

The barrister persisted. 'Of how many of your previous lives do you know something?'

'I would probably say I know very little of my entire catalogue and I know a little bit about some of them.' A scant recollection of two lifetimes had exhausted his feeble imagination.

Tom kept his tone even. 'Have you ever said to your students, "I know all my past lives and I can connect to the details"?'

Benhayon cleared his throat. 'As a summary I can say that, and it will be a true declaration, but you're asking specific details of past lives and I don't have that because I've never inquired about it.'

'When you said, "And I can connect to all the details" what details were they?'

'The details that are what needs to be corrected and what needs to be advanced and also what needs to be confirmed.'

'Are you making this up as we go along?'

'No. It's in my teachings for nineteen years.'

Tom then read out a quote from his March 2016 sermon: 'I know all my past lives and I can connect to the details. I know how to do it. I don't use memory because you can't remember them. Human consciousness can't remember them but you can energetically feel them.'

'That's correct.'

'Do you recall in another sermon in September 2017 saying this, "One of the greatest lies that we all carry is that you can't remember your past lives when, in fact, you can." Did you say that?'

He answered quickly. 'I agree with that.'

'That means, doesn't it, that you can remember your past lives?'

'We can all remember our past lives or have access to our past lives. We choose not to. It's not convenient.'

'Now, how do you know that you were once Leonardo?'

'I can access the Ageless Wisdom,' he said.

'Is he a member of the Hierarchy?'

'Definitely.'

'But he's also incarnated in you, is that right?'

'We could say that. The essence that was in that life is today in this body you see before you.'

'Do you really believe that?'

'I don't believe it actually, to tell the truth,' Benhayon said haughtily.

Tom stopped and gave a slight shake of his head. 'You don't believe it?'

'I know it,' said Mr Self-Satisfied. 'I have a knowledge of what I am and what I am not. I don't have to believe in something when it's energetically confirmed.'

After moving through a few more topics, the lawyer called for a sermon excerpt in which Benhayon referred to his wondrous philosophical system:

> there has never before on earth been anything that has been put together that answers everything… Take it apart, yes it looks weird, Astral plane, Four Lords of Form, reincarnation, autism, Karma, you know, it looks easy to pick on if you take it apart and pick a piece and surround it. Put it all together and nothing, no stone has been left unturned. Nothing has not been explained. And everything, everything correlates.[102]

Tom continued. 'In giving that presentation, you were advancing things that you thought would lead people to accept what you were saying, weren't you?'

'I'm presenting an opportunity to listen to something that could possibly be the truth and for them to put it to the test.'

'You say to listen to something that could possibly be the truth?'

'It's, it's, well, I believe it to be the truth.'

As soon as the words were out, Benhayon gulped. I smiled.

Tom reiterated his answer. 'You believe it to be the truth?'

'I know it to be the truth,' said Serge, but it was too late.

'Are you correcting the terminology there?' said Tom.

'Yes.'

'To fit the evidence that you gave earlier about not believing in what you teach but having this other affinity with it, is that right?'

Benhayon didn't answer.

'A bit of a quick correction made on the run there, wasn't it?… A bit of a slip?'

'I know it to be the truth.'

'So, when you just said now, "believe it", that was getting it fundamentally wrong, wasn't it?'

'For me it is, yes.'

cxxi Sirius

Tom summarised, 'You say, my teachings can't be attacked, can't be examined or analysed piece by piece, because they only make sense as a whole. That's what you say, isn't it?'

'Yes, as Plato warned us, you can't treat the part, you've got to treat the whole. If we treat the part, we're going to be in trouble. Same thing.' Benhayon seemed to think that name-dropping Plato gave him an opening. 'Isn't this what this cross-examination is all about? Aren't you taking extracts and picking on them, without testing the whole? Have you asked me how I live, how amazing my life is?'

'No, I'm not asking you that. I imagine you've got a very long answer.'

'But I'm living proof of my teachings.'

'You've published ten books?'

'Nineteen years of presentations, and ten books.'

'Hundreds and hundreds of hours of recordings?'

'Yes.'

'Indeed, you have so many recordings of so many sessions, that your lawyers said it was unreasonable for them to have to provide them all to us, didn't they?'

Again Benhayon's mouth closed. As the journalist Matt Doran had said to him a year before: 'You've made a career out of saying things and you have nothing to say, sir?'

'And they provided only a selection, isn't that right?'

Benhayon claimed not to know what his lawyers had told me. Personally, I'd be troubled if my legal team did anything on my behalf without my explicit instructions, but I doubt anyone believed his answer.

Tom moved on. The jury had heard recordings in which Benhayon claimed to have told the toilet chorus that 'everything is upside down, we've been robbed, we've been stolen, lied to'; that professors of medicine need thirty years of science to tell them what he could get in one minute; that spirits are nine feet tall and have no feet. Next was a recording of Benhayon stating that moving one's elbow has 'an enormous impact on life on earth and also on the cosmos... Whereas in other planets they don't have arms and legs...'

'What other planets are you speaking of?' Tom asked.

'There's life in other planets.'

'No, that's not quite what I asked you. What are the planets you're speaking of? Mars?'

'Sirius,' said Benhayon, and added Regulus, Aldebaran, and Antares. His instant knowing didn't distinguish between planets and stars, apparently. He also informed the court that some of earth's inhabitants are angels and archangels, former residents of those celestial outposts that have incarnated here to 'help us return to who we truly are.'

'Have you ever been on Sirius or any other of those stars?'

'No.'

'In any of your two thousand, three hundred previous incarnations?'

cxxii Haley

Mostly, the jurors stayed prudently blank-faced through some of the most challenging evidence. That included Esoteric Healing workshop audio where Benhayon talked about a hypothetical fourteen year old girl who started to 'want male energy' as her breasts began to grow, and her father stopped showing her physical affection.

> ...no girl likes sleeping around. Fact. They only like it when it's satisfying the emotion that needs to cover the hurt. But the reality is that the first disharmony that they get is actually vaginal. And the vaginal walls harden because they know they're having sex and they're not being made love to by the boy that is just scoring a release and a trophy to tell his mates.

> The disharmony is the fact that you are inbuilt to make love and the moment you are not making love your body hardens to have something inside you, intercourse…

Mid-sentence, Benhayon referred to a girl in attendance, Haley, getting her 'first lesson in the real birds and the bees.' The audience laughed and he went on, claiming that the vaginal wall hardens 'to go through with that act', and that the vagina contracts, resulting in 'displaced hips'.

At the same workshop, he discussed alcohol and drug users picking up entities that 'hook into' kidney energy.

> So let's say you have a partner who drinks. Well every time you sleep at night with that person, you get drained energetically by the entity. Not by your partner, but by the entity that's in the partner. Fact.

> … as a man — my children can't tell me what to do — I'll go out and smoke pot. I'll come back in and just have dinner with them. Well, I'm not just having dinner with them. Whatever I've picked up is going to affect my children. If I've picked up an energy that loves sex then that entity will be sexual with my children. If I picked up an entity that wants to grow strong, then that entity will want to take kidney energy from my children.

> For example, if I had an entity that was sexual, it could, while I sleep at night, totally innocent, it leaves me at night, and it goes and rapes my daughters while I sleep. Now, I have no idea that happens because I have a heavy sleep (let's say — I don't, but, let's say I did), and then ten years later my daughters have issues around sex or they've got issues around hardening of the vagina or something like that, or they sleep a different way because they could sense that they were visited at night. All of that from the father that just said it's okay to smoke pot because it's organic.[103]

Toward the end of the recording, as he handed out attendance certificates, the maestro read out Haley's full name and referred to her as the youngest level one participant. 'How old are you Haley? Eleven. Awesome. All the way from Perth just to do the course.' Again, when questioned, Benhayon insisted that the subject matter was appropriate to discuss in front of kids.

'You don't think it might have any adverse effects on them?' said Tom.

'If we don't mention it, it will have a worse effect on them.'

'And are you the sole judge when you make one of these presentations as to whether it is suitable to ventilate in front of an eleven year old?'

'I do my presentations, people attend, they pay their money. The rule is if they don't like it and in time they leave, they get a full refund with no questions asked. Those people paid money to come to my presentation, they know I'm outspoken, they know what I present; they know what I'm about.'

'I'm not talking about whether it's appropriate for most of them, I'm talking about children, do you understand? Children?'

Serge maintained that he would not hold back, and the lawyer noted that it was too late to ask for one's money back. 'They've copped it already, haven't they?'

Our tireless opponent answered that he'd rarely been asked for a refund. The Senior Counsel then asked whether he'd conducted any medical surveys to establish that young women's sexual experiences could cause hardening of their vaginal walls.

'No, but from an energetic point of view you can feel that — you can feel when a woman's body has closed down.'

'Have you done internal examinations on women?'

'Never.'

'So you've never done any physical investigation on which you've based that proposition?'

'I don't have to, because you can feel it energetically.'

cxxiii The appeal

> Imagine if you are five years old and you hold love in your heart naturally, because it's not really polluted, I mean unless there's been a sexual abuse case, but most kids at five are still holding on to what they truly are...

Imagine if you relate that energy to the way your parents live, and if you expressed yourself and said, 'Mum and Dad, you guys are not love.'

Where do you go with that? You can't. You can't walk up to Mum and Dad and say, 'the reality is Dad, when you come home sometimes, I don't want you to touch me.'

Imagine if the five year old was given expression, the ability to actually communicate. Imagine if a seven year old girl hung on to their clairsentience, which is the ability to feel energy and communicate it. And she said, 'Dad, every time you drink, I feel stuff on my anus or my vagina. I know it's not you Dad, but from you there's energy that I can feel all over me, and the truth is, I don't like you coming near me.' ...As kids they're going, 'yeah, it's true, we can feel these things.'

Serge Benhayon, The Study of Esoteric Medicine, 2011[104]

When a frustrated Graham appealed to the High Court to be granted full-time care of Lara, Fran applied to have his appeal dismissed, arguing that the court-appointed social worker's recommendations that she break from Universal Medicine were in breach of Articles Eight to Ten of the European Convention for the Protection of Human Rights, namely her rights to privacy; freedom of thought, conscience and religion; and freedom of expression. She again repeated her allegation that the father had sexually abused their daughter.

Graham had tendered a sizeable evidence bundle to the Family Court, including David Millikan's expert report, but the diatribe above was not included. That was in a subscription recording that his followers were known to listen to repeatedly. I didn't come across it until after the High Court made its final determination in 2021. There would never be enough hours in a day to trawl Benhayon's ocean of muck. Fortunately, the court's social worker had learned enough to conclude that Fran would not be able to extricate herself from UM without genuine commitment and significant therapeutic support.

The appeals panel of England's High Court agreed, finding that the Family Court judge had erred in failing to make adequately protective orders. Yet, to Graham and Leonie's dismay, the High Court Justices were also reluctant to rule on full-time care of Lara, and gave Fran yet another chance to comply with orders she'd only ever flouted.

cxxiv The bodyguard

Tom once told me about a mischievous defence lawyer who trolled prosecutors at a long running criminal trial by planting a bulging binder marked SURPRISE WITNESSES on his side of the bar table. The folder was stuffed with scrap paper. Courtroom 12C had no solicitors' tables, so I had to sit at a trestle table awkwardly placed in the front row of its cramped public gallery. Sitting behind it put me too far from my lawyers to give instructions, and it was a trip hazard if I needed to get up to speak with them, so I chose to sit beside it, at the end nearest the witness box. Seeing Serryn O'Regan stationed in the seat behind me, I placed the copy of my subpoena to the College of Universal Medicine, that she'd tried to dodge service of, on the table, practically under her snout, and left it there to remind her and her Brothers of what was coming.

In the meantime, the High Priest or his enforcers had decided that his faith-full court attendants should try to look intimidating. Whatever effect they intended, it was obviously orchestrated. At every break, Benhayon's cheer-squad exited ahead of the legal teams and lined up on either side of the courtroom doors. My team would thus exit to an Esoteric guard of dishonour; the Benhayon dependents, Hamish Broome, the Johnstons, Baldwin, Lessing, Greig, and whoever else straggled along, glaring at us with all the gluten-free menace they could muster.

Tom had instructed us not to discuss the case within the court precinct — all discussions were to take place in the private conference rooms adjacent to court or in chambers, and sure enough, as we left court at lunch or the end of the day, UM believers were stationed along the exit route. One or two would enter the elevators with us, treating us to the sight of Tom towering over Micheal Benhayon, casting his eyes slowly from the top of his greasy pate to the toes of his scuffed shoes. A Broome or a Johnston or a cluster of Benhayons lurked behind pillars on the ground floor, and one or more would pass us on Queens Square and overtake us on Phillip Street, dropping their investment in slow motion Eso-walking for a swift stride.

'Are they trying to scare us?' I asked the team as we scoffed our sushi and salads at Louise's leather topped table. 'Or eavesdrop? But what good is that going to do?'

Louise had a better explanation, which covered the way they were positioned in the public gallery as well. 'It's a spell,' she said, 'a pattern. Like those symbols. They're configured in the court to energetically interfere with our case.' It accounted for Alan Johnston's butt clenched stroll on the wrong side of the bar table in Brisbane, and O'Regan at it in the corridor — arms rigid, chin lifted, slight stoop with each measured, point-toed pace. Benhayon would walk the same way in his videos. A few of us had a go at mimicking the gait.

If it was supposed to frighten us, they must have felt demoralised when my legal team seemed to get bigger every day. On day one it was just Louise and Stewart with me for jury selection. Day two we were joined by Meri and Tom. Around day four, we took on Mark Burton, who was joined in the second week by another reader, Ronny Chen. The visual was magnificent; the penniless defendant showing to trial with two robed and wigged barristers and a wall of suits. Ronny and Mark took the seats at the trestle table, and Stew and Meri tagged on the bar table beside Louise.

Our team weren't alone in noticing UM's courtroom efforts either. A journalist friend of Jane Hansen, Deborah Cornwall, loudly remarked, 'there's a bit of an atmosphere in here,' and Justice Lonergan seemed alert to it: sheriffs came by several times in the first few days to peer around the public gallery. In the second week, over the days I gave evidence in the otherwise still courtroom, Simone and Michael Benhayon would squirm in their seats as I answered questions, grimacing and grinning like delinquent primary-schoolers; craning their necks, widening their eyes and baring their teeth to try to catch my eye. Every time my glance caught Alan, too, he was staring contemptuously at me over his reading glasses, probably in anticipation of the 'reality check' he reckoned I had coming. Justice Lonergan often had her eyes down, taking notes, but her staff on the bench must have noticed. I mentioned it to my team.

'Should we raise this with Her Honour,' Louise asked Tom; 'that the plaintiff's family appear to be attempting some sort of interference?'

Tom turned to me, 'Are you intimidated by it?'

'No,' I said. I looked to Louise. 'Are you?'

'No.'

'There's no need to raise it then,' said Tom.

That's not to say I wasn't cautious. Mark Burton often walked with us to and from court. With his attentive posture and military bearing, Louise affectionately dubbed him my bodyguard. I didn't fear UMers, but was wary of them pulling some disruptive stunt, some set-up, so I chose not to move around the court building alone. Fortunately, Mark was able to attend almost every day for the three weeks of witness evidence, and he'd escort me to the facilities on the floor below for bathroom breaks.

Perhaps Justice Lonergan, if she was aware, thought similarly to Tom, but ultimately, there was a good reason for letting the displays go without mention. The jury had the next best vantage point to Her Honour's, slightly elevated, with a view of the whole room, and the plaintiff's family were seated near them. The court was examining allegations of UM's cultism, shunning, and bullying, and the Esoterics' performance was, if anything, helping my case.

cxxv Public benefit

Justice Lonergan gave Tom permission to sit while examining witnesses if he was tired, but he stayed on his feet through his cross-examinations of the plaintiff and his witnesses. It was not until I began my evidence in chief in the second week that he took up the offer — during my convoluted recollection of attempts to bring UM to account. We had to get the evidence out, as dull as it was, but Tom looked wan. I worried he was flagging, but he pepped up after a night's sleep, and tendered the documents from the charity authorities.

The first letter from the UK Charities Commission verified its compliance action against the Sound Foundation. The next letter confirmed the ACNC's action arising from Klaus's investigation. The Australian Commission allowed the College of Universal Medicine to remain registered as a charity on condition that any lease arrangement with Benhayon 'must include comprehensive protection of the College's equitable interest in the property'. It included a requirement that the Hall of Ageless Wisdom 'be used solely for the purposes of the College, and will not be used by any other entity.' In other words, the regulator required formal assurances that Benhayon could not financially benefit from the lease deal, and prohibited him from operating commercial activities from the same building. I wanted the charity deregistered for having zero public benefit, but at least that rort had been officially foiled.

Happily, the Mystic Dentist and Caroline Raphael trudged to Sydney to join the no-wrongdoing-found chorus that day. Tom tendered a copy of a thirty page ruling by the Australian Tax Office, a document obtained under the subpoena to the College, and read some excerpts onto the record. Soon after Klaus commenced his ACNC investigation in 2013, the ATO began its own, examining the College's eligibility to receive tax-deductible gifts (DGR) for its school building fund (SBF). In February 2015, the tax office ruled that the College had not satisfied the conditions. Its management failed to separate its bank accounts correctly, for example, meaning public money was flowing to a non-public fund.

> This finding is indication that the safeguard of public money is threatened and it is also an indication that the DGR money for school building purpose is potentially able to be used by CoUM for other purposes.
>
> Therefore, the responsible persons of CoUM acting for a qualifying body breach due responsibility and obligation as public trustee…

Three of the responsible persons were in court for the fun — unsmiling O'Regan, Natalie Benhayon and Alison Greig. It was a pity Wilson, Désirée, and the other board members hadn't come along.

> Consequence.
>
> As CoUM is not entitled to a DGR endorsement for a school building fund operation, its DGR endorsement of CoUM is revoked retrospectively from 25 August 2011.

The tax office also found that the Fiery Building Fund could not be authorised as a School Building Fund because the College did not meet the authority's definition of a school. The Ageless Wisdom warehouse did not meet the criteria for a school building either. So much for classing it as an 'approved educational facility' in development applications. It had never been approved by anyone but the cult. The authority ordered the charity to transfer the nearly six hundred thousand dollars from the gift fund to another charity or institution entitled to receive tax-deductible gifts, and under that process, the money made its permanent exit from the charity's accounts. When I tweeted questions to Alison Greig over two years earlier asking where the funds had gone, the operators hurriedly published a statement claiming that the College had voluntarily requested, in October 2015, that the ATO revoke its DGR endorsement. The ATO had, in fact, handed down its ruling eight months prior to that; nothing voluntary about it.

The tax office also had a special message for Serge and his philanthropy brides.

CoUM and its founder or related parties are not allowed to generate or set up another DGR entity for the purpose of being a recipient to receive the balance of the fund money mentioned above.

A ledger of the charity's tax deductible donations went into evidence too; a document that raised more questions than it answered. Despite UM's fiery fundraising campaign, the six hundred thousand dollars in proceeds came from only twenty-seven donors. I would have thought that the incentive of tax deductibility would have attracted more from a zealous community of seven hundred that was constantly hustled for cash. One donor, businessman Stephen Ninnes of Brisbane, threw in three hundred thousand dollars. The remainder were familiar names: Neil Gamble donated fifty thousand; long-lens Alan and Josephine Johnston put in another fifty; Caroline Raphael, sixty thousand; Rachel Hall, forty thousand; Dr Sam Kim, nearly five thousand; and Dr Jane Barker three thousand. But a lot of well-off devotees' names were absent. No Greenaway, Schnelle, Lessing, Malatt, Mooney, Wild or Szramka, or other devotee doctors, accountants, business executives and practitioners who publicly beat the drum for the Benhayons and their shonky school. We heard no courtroom outcry from Caroline this time either.

Tom quizzed the plaintiff about his public allegations that I'd made baseless complaints. 'Well, they got her nowhere,' said Serge. The ATO document revealed that the charity planned to pay him eighty thousand dollars in public money per annum to rent the Converys Lane nut facility, but Benhayon denied the College abandoned the agreement. 'I decided to not pursue it myself actually,' he told the court. 'I didn't know anything about what was going on in the background.'

'You don't know then,' said Tom, 'whether or not any action was taken by the ATO as a result of Ms Rockett originally approaching the Australian Charities and Not-for-profits Commission. Is that correct?'

'Correct.'

'So you wouldn't be able to say, if she made such a complaint, that it was baseless, would you, if there's the possibility that the ATO, in the end, took some action as a result of it?'

Benhayon sniffed. 'In lay terms I can say that it was baseless.'

cxxvi Rolf

Smark apologised. Justice Lonergan spoke again. 'It might not have been the answer you thought would happen.' A ruby-haired woman in her late fifties, with a porcelain complexion and green eyes, she presided with a firmly reasoned but unintrusive bearing.

'I withdraw that and I shouldn't have said it that way. I accept that.' Smark turned to me. 'Please excuse that, that was discourteous.'

Discourteous was not how I would have described his interrogation. He'd attempted to isolate what Benhayon said during the ovarian reading from what he did, laying his hands on my abdomen above where he said my ovaries were situated. The barrister continued: 'You accept, I suggest, that this fishing exercise, as you've styled it, did not amount to an intentional indecent touching. It may have amounted to other things but it didn't amount to that; do you accept that?'

I frowned again. 'That would depend.'

'I suggest to you it's even further short of making Mr Benhayon a sexual predator who had preyed on you; do you accept that?'

'I reject that.'

Arguably, Benhayon and crew had made it easier for me by giving evidence before I did, but my testimony felt pedestrian compared with theirs. I was concerned that we might lose the jury out of sheer boredom, but had to maintain dull composure.

'It's nothing like the sort of conduct that years later you would come to understand that Rolf Harris had engaged in, in terms of sexually assaulting girls and women, is it?'

Rolf was always going to make an appearance. That reference still had my lawyers clinging to their wigs. 'That's drawing together two completely different things,' I said.

Smark read from the crescendo blog, '"SergeProp claims with confidence no one will come forward because 'there are no victims.' Rolf Harris had no victims either until two years ago." Now, as at this time, 2014, you knew that Mr Rolf Harris had been recently convicted of a number of charges of indecent assault?'

'Yes.'

'So what you were suggesting was that the readers should draw a comparison between the position of Mr Harris and his victims and the position of Mr Benhayon and his victims? That's what you were suggesting, wasn't it?'

'No.'

Smark was carefully reading around the point I'd made in the blog and I'd already affirmed under Tom's questioning. In preceding paragraphs I'd written about the harmful actions of the cult as a whole, Benhayon and his FACTS outfit included, and his flock's public denials of the harm.

'But the context of "victims" here was, wasn't it, victims of Mr Benhayon, that's the person who you are referring to in the immediately preceding section, do you agree with that or not?'

'No.'

'Weren't you seeking to bring to readers minds that the complaints that you were making when you said that you'd been preyed upon in Mr Benhayon's treatment room were comparable to the complaints of victims who had been preyed upon by Mr Rolf Harris?'

'No.'

'Do you accept, looking at the matter now, that ordinary people could reasonably read it that way?'

'No.'

Smark flipped through the blog, referring to lines where I'd discussed Benhayon teaching people to touch the genitals of sexual abuse victims, and girls as young as ten staying unaccompanied in his home. 'And then you say you knew his current wife moved into his home at age fourteen against her mother's wishes, do you see that?'

'Yes.'

'You were suggesting that he had had a sexual relationship with his current wife when she was underage and living in his home? That's what you were suggesting, wasn't it?'

'No, I was suggesting exactly what's written on the page.'

'Then you say this at line six, "My claim that Benhayon is a sexual predator is not false." So you were saying Mr Benhayon was a sexual predator, weren't you?'

'Yes.'

When I stated Serge was a sexual predator, it was based on my experience of him pressuring me into the ovarian reading, and on the manual images. At no point did I accuse Benhayon of indecently assaulting me. Lismore Police had told me in 2012 that they didn't think a prosecution was possible. When they called me in to give the second statement, just weeks before I authored the crescendo blog, they were still unsure. Prosecutors ultimately opted not to pursue charges because they were not confident they would result in criminal conviction. I'd avoided making allegations of assault because I was uncertain about how the act would be viewed under the law. The manual images, to me, were clearly molestation, but otherwise, sexual predation doesn't always extend to physical assault.

That was the essence of the legal predicament I was in. Because I'd discussed the facts of Benhayon and his cult's sordid behaviour with women and children, raising legitimate concerns in the public interest, I was being tried like a criminal — harassed, bankrupted and dragged through the courts. Most disturbingly, I could lose my case if a clever lawyer hoodwinked the jury into believing I'd made allegations I had not. If he succeeded in confusing separate allegations, and convinced them that my intentions were improper, he would defeat my defences of reasonableness and honest opinion.

Smark also referred to an interrogatory answer I'd given about another serious allegation. I was required to give a sworn, written, yes or no answer, to whether, at the time of publication, I believed it was true that Serge Benhayon had an unlawful sexual relationship with Miranda after she moved into his home at age fourteen. I'd answered no.

'Do you recall that?' said Smark.

'That's the answer I gave.'

His tone was derisive. 'But you did believe it was true didn't you? Your answer should have been "yes", shouldn't it?'

'I didn't know,' I said. 'When you answer an interrogatory you can't say, "undecided".'

It struck me as odd to be grilled over whether I believed an allegation was true when I couldn't possibly know the facts unless I'd witnessed them myself. Then again, UM exemplified the inclination to believe all sorts of things without a semblance of proof.

When Tom took the jury through each of my publications, he asked what I'd meant in various key passages. 'Then in line nineteen you said, "Just how many girls have stayed in that household and lived with them as well? And why?" What were you getting at there?'

'Well, it was known by then, and admitted on the Universal Medicine Facts website, that young women regularly go to stay in the Benhayon household.' Miranda, Joelle and Haley were some of the girls I was aware of at the time.

'Why did it matter to you to ask this question? What was the point of asking "How many girls have stayed in that household?"' said Tom.

'The point is that there were so many red flags at that time, so many indicators of suspicious behaviour. There was Serge Benhayon having himself photographed molesting somebody, putting his hands on somebody's genitals and calling it a healing for sexual abuse; his, and his community's denials of any impropriety, refusing to acknowledge any concerns about that; and denying the anatomical locations; the whole problem with misleading conduct; their attacks on critics; and knowing what we know about him speaking about sexually explicit subject matter in front of children; all these bogus therapies, putting his hands all over women's torsos — to me there were just so many things wrong here that it was natural to ask the question, "How many girls have stayed in that household with this person whose conduct is so problematic?"'

Across the court, Benhayon was gazing at Smark's back. Paula Fletcher was eyeing me with habitual disdain. Simone Benhayon had her head cocked and teeth bared, eyes bulging at me. 'And where he's vigorously defended by these zealots that follow him,' I continued, 'publicly compromising themselves, professionally and otherwise, to tell lies about these practices and about these behaviours.' My gaze travelled across the gallery to Miranda and Josephine's matching cat's arse pouts, to Alan glowering over his glasses, and to sallow and expressionless Alison Greig and Serryn O'Regan with their dismal eyes on me. 'To me, it was a good question.'

Smark did his best to frame my Rolf Harris comment as accusing Benhayon of sex offences against underage girls, removing it from its context relating to victims' fear of speaking out about a revered personality. Tom had read out the preceding passages about the cult's harassments of me and others, and had me explain them. The jurors were given binders to hold documentary evidence, including copies of several UM FACTS articles. They'd read UM's assessments of my character. 'They made these adamant assertions Universal Medicine has no victims,' I said, 'based on this assumption that because no victims had come forward, there are no victims. So what I was referring to was this well-known fact — and well-known through cases like that case of Rolf Harris, which was a perfect illustration of the way that victims behave — victims don't necessarily come forward, or can take decades. UM followers can't possibly know if there are victims or not. That's a completely invalid argument.'

I had to trust that the jury would see through Smark's conflationary gymnastics. It might not have hurt to reiterate that by the time I published the crescendo blog in November 2014, I'd come forward, as had Matt

Sutherland and Rosie. Others had complained anonymously on my blogs and the Cult Education Forum about an array of harms. Anyone attacked and defamed on UM's websites was one of their victims. But it occurs to me now that in the witness box, despite all that had gone before, I was not thinking of myself as one.

cxxvii C. B. Fry

At lunch on Friday of the first week, Louise encouraged Tom to wind up Benhayon's cross-examination. 'He's too comfortable up there,' she said. 'Too cocky.'

I saw sense in the suggestion. We couldn't risk the jury getting used to Serge's blarney. The Senior Counsel wasn't convinced, but he'd been in hospital just one week before, and as he pushed through the afternoon, he turned pale and his voice broke up, yet Benhayon's cross-court backhands remained as vigorous as ever.

A review of the trial transcripts over the weekend, however, re-energised the lawyer, and he locked on something from early in Smark's questioning. I was so numb to Benhayon's bombast I'd missed it. Monday, Tom took him back to his evidence about getting a job at fifteen as an assistant tennis coach. 'How much time did you invest in that job every week?' he asked.

'It required five hours to six hours on a Saturday, and sometimes after school.' Questioned further, Benhayon said he trained on weekdays and competed in tournaments every two or three months over his last two years at school. He dropped out at the end of year eleven as his coaching picked up.

'You said in your evidence that by the time you left school that you had "represented the state in athletics and representative soccer, representative cricket, representative rugby."'

'The equivalent to State level, yes,' he agreed, but quickly corrected to say that he'd competed at state carnivals in athletics, and although he was selected for the state soccer team, he didn't end up playing for the state. 'But I played in the state selection,' he said.

'Did you mean you'd represented the state in cricket?'

'No, sorry, I didn't play for New South Wales, but I was selected in the rep sides that…'

Tom stopped him. 'No, I'll give you the chance to tell the Court what the actual facts were in a moment. Did you mean you represented the state in rugby?'

'No.'

Tom then drilled down on each sport. Benhayon explained that he'd made it to the state athletics championships — competing with other athletes representing zones within New South Wales. That his event was the long jump could not have been more apt for a compulsive exaggerator prone to rhetorical leaps.

'You see, that wasn't representing the state, was it?'

'No, correct.'

'Would you agree that the understanding that people would gain from the words "representing the state" is that in some way you were representing the state of New South Wales against people from other states or another state?'

'That's correct.'

The questioning continued for at least ten minutes in that fashion. Tom asked him about soccer and his alleged selection for state trials. 'If it was under sixteens, it would have been the same year that you started your assistant tennis coach job, wouldn't it?'

'Yes, my second year into it.'

'Could you fit all that in?'

'Yes.'

'Did you do soccer training?'

'Only what the team demanded that I do, twice, two nights a week.'

Benhayon then answered that he played club cricket on weekends when he was thirteen and fourteen, and later for his high school team.

'Where did you go towards representing the state?'

'I got selected to play representative cricket in the local, in the region,' he said. He couldn't recall which region. Despite being selected, 'I chose not to play...Not to proceed.'

'But that's nothing like representing the state in cricket, is it?'

'That's correct.'

Rugby was a similar debacle. 'I played rugby union for the school and rugby league outside of school,' said Serge.

'Did you represent the state in one or other of those two?'

'No.' Again, the story was that he attended the trials to play for a regional league team but chose not to participate. 'The coach outlined...'

The barrister stopped him. 'You don't need to explain why. You were actually quite a long way from representing the state in any of those things, weren't you?'

'Yes.'

Tom played it absolutely straight, but I knew how much he was enjoying himself. 'It was, therefore, not true to say, "I already had represented the state in athletics and representative soccer, representative cricket, representative rugby." That wasn't true, was it?'

'Technically no, correct.'

'When you say "technically no"...'

'Well, it's incorrect to say that.'

'For someone to say that of four sports, well, almost puts them up with the level of C. B. Fry. Do you know him?'

'No.'

Molomby became more lively. 'You're a sporting person? C. B. Fry? English cricketer? First to hit six successive centuries in test cricket and he also held, would you believe, the world long jump record. Now, it's putting yourself into the big league, isn't it, to say you represented the state in four separate sports, do you agree with that?'

A few weeks later in his closing address, Tom would say to the jury, 'in answering questions to Mr Smark, not under pressure, when he had the opportunity to say what he liked to set up his case and make himself look good, what did he choose to say? A complete lie.

'When people tell that sort of lie, it's often a natural curiosity to say, "Why would he say that?" I'd suggest your experience would lead you to know that mostly when people do that sort of thing, it's because they've been doing it forever and getting away with it and what happens is they get into a situation where somebody is watching a bit more closely than usual or just knows a bit more than usual and they get caught.'

cxxviii The intrusion

Goonellabah's arbiter of everything female didn't deny that I'd had healing sessions with him, as I expected he might. He said I presented as 'a demoralised woman... a straightforward case,' and described the technique he used on me as 'an application of kidney energy, a kidney boost... I rolled her over, she lied on her back, fully clothed of course, and then I proceeded to do a technique that applies both hands just over the lower abdomen, and incorporates the uterus, and I rotated very gently anticlockwise with both hands.'

'And before you placed your hands there, did you tell her where you were going to place your hands?' said Smark.

'Yes.'

Asked to recall our conversation, Benhayon said he explained 'the compromised energy that I could feel in that area, and the depth of intrusion that she had been abused by her guru in Japan.'

'Do you recall asking her any questions?'

'Yes. Did she feel in any way, shape or form intruded, or had she had, to the best of her knowledge, any form of intrusions, whether it be abuse, sexual or that nature, because her body was definitely registering compromise, and there was a shutdown in the woman's body.'

My lawyers steadily took their notes. No hint of a grimace or noise arose among the jury or observers; an indication of how distant the court is from any normal social situation. Serge was always going to make up a story, but even I thought he'd come up with something less incriminating. For years, UM FACTS alleged the ovarian reading never happened, yet he was divulging an intent, not just to fish for a history of sexual trauma, but to simultaneously place his hands on my lower abdomen in the region of the uterus. I'd taken the statements about 'a man in your life' in the context of my reproductive organs as implicitly sexual, and now, in his own evidence, he was saying that he'd grilled me about sexual abuse.

Two days later, Tom questioned his version. 'You said to her, "Today I think we should do an ovarian reading," didn't you?'

The plaintiff returned with a line used in UM FACTS' denials. 'No such modality existed back then.'

Tom was unmoved. 'Whether the modality existed or not you see I'm asking you about what you said. That's what you said, isn't it?'

'No.'

'She said, "What is it?" And you said, "I'll be getting some information from your ovaries."'

'Definitely not.'

'You do have a method of getting information from people's ovaries, don't you?'

'We do an energetic reading on any part of the body we put our hands on, yes.'

'That includes ovaries, doesn't it?'

'It includes the entire uterus area, yes.'

'Let's just talk about ovaries, if we may. You do have the ability to get information from someone's ovaries, don't you?'

'The energetic state of being of that area in the body, yes.'

'You said, "You don't know what it is, it will really benefit you"?'

'If a client doesn't want something it's not done, but she didn't say it. She didn't say she didn't want it and I'm not saying that I did what you're saying I did.'

'Did you have any clear memory of this session really?'

'I have a very good recollection, but not exact, obviously.'

'You've told the Court you do thousands and thousands of sessions. This one was in 2005, and when did you first know that Ms Rockett had any complaint about this; in approximately what year?'

'She came and saw me through a mutual friend.'

'Did you think I asked you that?'

'Sorry. My apologies.'

'I'm asking you a time indication and you want to give me a whole other story.'

'My apologies.'

'You do that often, don't you? It's a technique you have in answering questions to actually talk about something that you weren't asked about at all, isn't it?'

'I should have waited.'

'You didn't, again, answer my question, did you? It's a technique you have in answering questions to talk about something that you weren't asked about, isn't it?'

Benhayon didn't speak.

'I think you could answer that one, yes or no, or is there a very big story behind it?'

'No.'

'Did you say to her, "When you were five years old a man in your life let you down"?'

Benhayon claimed he didn't recall any of the details I'd recounted, and that he knew exactly what he'd said to me.

'See, at that time you had engaged in reading women's ovaries, hadn't you?'

Again he denied it.

'According to your teachings if you placed your hands or your fingers or whatever it is you need to use on or near someone's ovaries, is it possible to get information about their ovaries from that?'

'Yes, it is.'

Tom asked if he'd ever done it, and Benhayon recalled commenting on someone's ovaries for the first time around 2009.

'So you have at some stage done readings of ovaries but you place your beginning to do it about four years or five years after the session with Ms Rockett?'

'Yes, and it's only, it's only occurred very rarely.'

Tom called for audio of Benhayon presenting to his Esoteric Developers in 2010.

> The ovaries themselves, the ovaries of a woman are stillness. They don't have any motion whatsoever. And yet when I started putting my hands on people, or women, back in ninety-nine when I first started, I found myself with my hands in situations where the right ovary is so hard and so lifted off the body because of this constant motion that the woman is in, and then the left one is shrivelled and contracted.[105]

Benhayon confirmed that he was referring to the year 1999.

During our debrief in Louise's chambers later that day, I got a message from my friend running the 'Benhayon v Rockett Defence News & Updates' Facebook page. A woman named Pina* had contacted the admins to say that she'd been in a treatment room with Benhayon. 'I too felt he was inappropriate during a session…' she told them. She was willing to provide a sworn statement.

I didn't have to do anything except get her contact details. From being the person who wore all the hats for years, to having a top notch legal outfit swing into action on my behalf felt deliciously luxurious. Stewart was on the phone to her within an hour.

cxxix Anatomy

Smark had commenced my cross-examination before the lunch recess. Nearing the same point the following day, I was struggling to suppress impatience. 'Do you accept as a general matter that the presentation of this blog to ordinary people reading it was alarming?' he asked.

'Alarming might not be the word that I would use.'

'What word would you use?'

'Concerning.'

'It was concerning, that is, the overall way in which this blog was presented was one which would cause concern in ordinary readers of it?'

'The content is of concern, not the way it's presented.'

He flapped his hand at an image I'd used at the top of the post — a sculpture by British artist Kevin Francis Gray; '…that would be concerning, wouldn't it?'

'The use of… *art*?'

'Yes.'

'An image?'

'A woman covered in…' He shook his head, abandoning description, '…and her face draped?'

Philistine, I thought to myself. 'Sexual abuse tends to be a concerning issue wherever it occurs,' I replied. The sculpture was exquisitely carved from fine white marble, so smooth and glossy it reflected light. It was a figure of a young ballerina; face downcast, draped and somewhat bound in a delicate cloth, rendered in the luminous stone.

'What I'm suggesting is that in the words you chose and the images you included and the way you expressed yourself, you knew you were going to increase the concern in the reader, not decrease it, quite apart from the content. Do you agree with that or not?'

'To decrease a reader's concern about a culture of abuse this broad would be irresponsible. I think this is appropriate. The tone is appropriate for the kind of problem we're talking about.'

'You know that one of the matters that's raised in this case is whether your conduct in publishing this material is reasonable in the circumstances, don't you?'

'Yes.'

'Do you accept that you expressed yourself in strong language in the first matter complained of?'

'Strong language for strong subject matter.'

Smark didn't blink. 'You're agreeing with me?'

'Strong language for strong subject matter,' I repeated. Perhaps he wasn't familiar with the Hippocratic adage, 'extreme diseases call for extreme remedies'.

'Can I suggest that you often expressed yourself in a forceful way so that you were stating things as a matter of fact; do you agree with that?'

'I think you're making a generalisation and unless you are willing to point me to each example, then I can't answer.'

'It was a brilliant reply,' Tom said to me later. At the end of the previous day, after two hours of Smark's questioning, I felt that I'd started awkwardly with stumbles and stammers. I was not excused from the witness box until after the jury had retired and as they filed out and the rest of the court relaxed and shuffled about, I glanced to where Louise, Meri and Stewart were gathering documents and Tom waited in his seat, maintaining his decorous composure before Her Honour. But as soon as he caught my glance, the solemnity vanished, his eyes twinkled and he gave the kind of smile an indulgent parent gives to a precocious but entertaining child; a tilt of the jaw, a lift of the brow, and the corners of his mouth turned down. My evidence had not come out perfectly, but the look told me I was surviving. I just had to hold on for as long as Benhayon's gun dragged it out.

Smark directed me to a paragraph in the blog where I'd challenged UM's denials of the positioning of Benhayon's hands. 'What I suggest to you is that this is an example of you choosing terms that are designed to inflame the ordinary reader; do you agree with that?'

'You will need to point out exactly what terms.'

'In that example you refer to the young girl's anus; a term you use elsewhere in relation to these pictures; do you agree with that?'

I could no longer conceal my impatience. 'Anus?' I repeated.

'Yes, it's a term you used to describe part of what's been depicted, you say, in these photos; do you agree with that?'

'That Serge has his hand on a young woman's anus?'

'That's what I'm asking you, you used that term?'

'It's an anatomically correct term.'

'I didn't ask you that. I'm asking you only if you used that term and if you agree with it?'

'I used that term.' My eyes were fixed on him. It was difficult to believe he thought the line of questioning would help his client.

'What I'm suggesting to you is that you chose to style it in that way because you were seeking to elicit concern and alarm in your readers; do you agree with that or not?'

My frown was unmoving. 'No.'

Smark kept clawing up his chain. 'I appreciate as this blog shows there was some back and forth about how one describes the body parts in question…'

'How one locates anatomical parts.'

He referred to the photos in my blog showing the 'Transmuting Sadness' technique, with Benhayon's hand pressed to the backside of a very petite, jeans clad young woman lying face down on the treatment table. The palm of his adult sized hand was on her lower posterior; his other grasped the back of her neck. The accompanying text from the manual referred to palpating the 'sacrum'. I'd explained to the court in my evidence in chief that Benhayon's fingertips rested on the girl's sacrum, but the palm and heel of his hand were much lower. Over two years earlier I received a swift reply from Matthew Richardson after I'd emailed the photos to him for the first time. 'How old is that young girl?!'

'That's what I'm being sued for,' I wrote back, 'asking that question.'

Benhayon had made a sworn interrogatory admission that the young woman was Simone Benhayon. Although her face was visible in other images in the handbook, she had her eyes closed, and looked twelve or thirteen. Benhayon said that he was unsure when the photos were taken, and guessed 2002, meaning she was sixteen or seventeen.

'It would be perfectly ordinary to refer in ordinary language to where the hand is placed as being on her bottom, wouldn't it?' Smark continued.

'You could say that,' I said, 'but his hand is on her anus. It's the anatomically correct location. His hand is on the midline of her bottom and the heel of his hand is located directly above her anus and appears to be pressing it as well.'

'She's wearing clothes, isn't she?'

My hackles rose. 'Yes, she's wearing clothes.'

'His hand is on the part of the body that would be considered or could properly be referred to as her bottom; do you agree with that?'

'Her bottom, yes, if you were being polite and not quite anatomically precise.'

'That's a term you would use to describe where his hand is?'

'I could have described it as the bottom, but I prefer to use anatomically precise terminology, especially when we're talking about something that I consider to be totally inappropriate.'

'If we're going to a level of precision, the anus, your term, is actually the orifice, isn't it?'

'It is.'

'It's the sphincter at the end of the alimentary canal?'

My eyes narrowed. 'It is.'

'It's not the buttocks?'

'No, it's not.'

'Buttocks is an anatomically correct term, isn't it?'

'It is.'

'She's clothed, and in order to come into contact with her anus she would have to be unclothed, wouldn't she?'

'Not necessarily. He's pressing his hand to her anus through her clothes.'

'You have no idea, do you, from looking at the picture what degree of force at all is being applied by the hand depicted?'

The edge in my voice was razor-like. 'His hand shouldn't be there at all.'

'My question to you is this: you have no idea, do you, from looking at the picture what degree of force is being applied by the hand in the picture? Are you able to answer that question?'

I still find it hard to believe a clever lawyer would pursue that line of questioning. Perhaps he was merely acting on instructions from Benhayon and his scatter-brained enablers. 'Yes, I am actually, because the crease in his wrist, the way that the wrist is angled, appears to me to indicate a degree of pressure.'

Smark's retort was tinged with sarcasm. 'Do you have any training in determining from wrist angles what degree of force is being applied through a hand?'

My voice rose. 'I've worked on bodies for nearly twenty years!'

With that, Smark snapped his face toward Justice Lonergan so sharply he probably sustained a whiplash injury. 'Is that a convenient time for the lunch break?' he said.

He did not return to the topic after lunch and wrapped up the cross-examination within an hour. On my release, my team conferred outside the courtroom before Serge's followers trooped out. Only Stewart was smiling. 'Well I did say, Esther,' said Tom, 'that no one gets through a cross-examination without taking some hits. And shall we say that Kieran dealt you a few bruises?'

I understood why Tom, having spent decades on the Phillip Street battlefront, wasn't blustering about my evidence, but I didn't quite agree. 'Maybe,' I said, 'but I dished out a few of my own.'

cxxx Universal Medicos

Dr Anne Malatt had the walk of a woman who'd listened a little too intently to Serge's teachings on self-loving choices. In her late fifties, with freckled brown skin, curly black hair and hazel eyes, she glided into court in a bias cut black dress with a pert Mona Lisa smile. Benhayon's cross-examination had run over schedule, so she'd had to wait a couple of days outside the courtroom. Maxine Szramka was also lined up to give evidence, but unfortunately Eunice Minford was dropped from the witness list. Perhaps Smark had read her UM FACTS article promoting Benhayon's commercial exorcism services.

> Serge Benhayon has made general observations about the possible impact of entities upon mental health, including schizophrenia, depression and suicide...
>
> The fact is that Serge Benhayon has been presenting on the reality of entities, their effects and how to remove them in a way that makes them a normal part of life.[106]

We were ready for all of them, having gathered their bent statements from UM publications. Aside from her magical thinking treatise about cancer, Malatt had encouraged followers to 'surrender' to Benhayon's preachings. She also claimed to exist on a similar diet to her idol; lamb, fish, greens and a small amount of nuts, seeds and 'low sugar fruit'. If reduced to one meal a day, it was the ultimate anti-aging diet, a Glorious express route for getting closer to God.

Malatt minced into the witness box and after some brief biographical questioning about her medical career, Smark asked when she'd first met the plaintiff.

The opthalmologist smiled serenely. 'I met Serge in 2001.'

'Did you go and see Serge?'

'I did, yes.'

'What sort of services or interaction did you have with him?'

Tom stood. 'I object.'

Justice Lonergan appeared to have expected it. 'Yes, well…' she said, and asked the witness and the jury to leave the courtroom, as was the rule for arguments on legal points. The back and forth on Tom's relevance objection took all afternoon and continued the following morning. Smark did most of the talking and Her Honour engaged in some of the arguing before making her ruling.

Smark argued that the doctor would give evidence of the positive impacts of UM on her personally, preempting evidence brought by my defence witnesses that UM is a dangerous cult that pushes harmful claims and therapies. He summarised her evidence to the effect that Benhayon did not discourage Malatt from having medical treatment for cancer, and that she didn't see any pressure tactics deployed by the group. The specialist also intended to give evidence about UM's benefits to her lifestyle, that she might use to advise her own patients.

Her Honour replied, 'That seems to be, if I may say in my experience, a context where doctors ought not express their personal views.' Among Justice Lonergan's specialties as a lawyer, prior to becoming a judge, were clergy abuse, and medical malpractice.

Tom argued that Malatt's evidence had the potential to mislead the jury. In short, producing witnesses to say that UM was not harmful to them did not prove it was not harmful to others. 'That in principle is really no different from somebody who's accused of assault calling a busload of witnesses to say, "We've all known him for twenty years, he's a lovely guy and he's never beaten us up,"' he said. 'It's not relevant to the particular thing alleged…I'd submit she's not entitled to be talking about the effect on other people — and the effect on herself is, well, restricted to herself.'

Tom was also concerned that Dr Malatt's evidence about her professional practice in relation to UM verged on expert evidence. There was a formal process for tendering expert reports and Team UM had not served us with any from medical witnesses. Her Honour agreed. 'It wouldn't be permissible,' she said, 'for evidence, in effect, in response to matters raised by Professor Dwyer, to come in the back door.'

Justice Lonergan ruled to uphold Tom's objection, and published her decision, seeing it would apply to other witnesses on Benhayon's roster. 'To show that something is "cult-like" and that some people follow the leader, there is no requirement that every member or every follower or attendee follows or has their life affected. One only has to show that some did.'[107]

Tom had argued a similar rationale for defence witnesses. A cult did not have to harm all its members to be considered dangerous.

Her Honour recalled the jury and had Malatt return to the witness box to be formally discharged. On hearing that her moment in the spotlight was over before it had begun, the doctor's eyes widened, her nostrils flared, and her head tipped back slowly and then forward until her forehead almost collided with the bench. Justice Lonergan turned to the jury to dismiss them for the morning break when Malatt rose from her seat, winked at Tom and made a reasonably loud comment that was difficult to make out over the judge's address.

The doctor sashayed off the dais as the court rose and Her Honour exited. My lawyers murmured to each other. Stewart, at the bar table, turned to me with eyebrows raised at the scandal. The remark had come to the attention of Her Honour's Associate and Tipstaff, however, who approached my team to ask if they'd heard what Malatt said.

Sharp eared Stewart told them: 'She said, "well played, Sir."'

cxxxi New Era

About the gurus, spiritual teachers, etc —

At the moment, the world is easily fooled by anyone who is soft, nice and seemingly calm...

> Come 2012, people will see that these people are not so calm, that there is an agitation in them as well, that what they are doing is not real and that they are only protected from the realities of life which makes them not as erratic as most people.
>
> But give them the slightest semblance of what it is like to live in reality, and they will be caught, on camera, by their followers and others…
>
> So many more gurus and teachers will be caught out and exposed and their greed and self-motivation exposed.
>
> Serge Benhayon, 2011[108]

Herbert Kane kicked off the New Era in January 2012 with his humble inquiry on the Cult Education Forum. News outlets also began their exposure that year, followed by me. Six years later, a couple of friends volunteered to run a Facebook page to update supporters with the press reports on the trial, and Herb messaged them during Benhayon's cross-examination to say that he was nearly bursting with tension, scouring the internet day and night for news. He wrote that the trial felt like

> [our] first chance to have some real fight back… some real, in public for all to see, exposure of UM that will live on in the public record for ever… Lordy does it feel good to hear the SC going for Benhayon and saying what we all say and think, in a court room.

In some ways, Universal Medicine got lucky in that media organisations were so cash-strapped that reporters could only attend sporadically, and missed many critical moments. One that didn't slip by, though, was the airing of a recording of Benhayon's views on disability.

> Nero, he used to put the Christians to death and all of that, is still today autistic. Still today incarnating as an autistic child. Still. Almost two thousand years and he's still incarnating in autism.
>
> All autistic people are incarnates of former authority abuse, and powerful abuse over others. As are Downs Syndrome, as are spastic or any other disabled child. They are former incarnates of corrupt politicians, corrupt generals, army people, dictators, or just your local councilman who is abusive and gains at the expense of others.[109]

That material generated a mass of angry social media posts across the country, and Lismore paper, *The Northern Star*, reported criticism from the town's former mayor, Jenny Dowell, who described the comments as appalling, and deeply insulting to people with disabilities and their families. 'I think they would be offended and upset,' she said, adding her concern for Lismore's reputation as a city.

I had, in fact, blogged Benhayon's abhorrent teachings on that topic several times in the previous five years, including his claim that the apostle Judas's betrayal of Christ saw him reincarnated into many lifetimes of disability. Those posts were only read a few hundred times each. The plaintiff's New Era court action ensured his repugnant views were broadcast to an exponentially wider audience. At last they were receiving the universal pillory they deserved.

cxxxii Defenders

By the time Malatt flounced into court, Justice Lonergan had already pulled Fletcher up for nodding at her client and mouthing words to him while he was under cross-examination. On return from the break, she warned the public gallery and future witnesses that interjections about evidence or rulings could be considered contempt of court, particularly if heard by the jury. She told 'those in the back row' that it was not acceptable to convey to witnesses what was going on in the courtroom, either, as she'd learned that Malatt had been receiving updates as she waited in the foyer.

Some on my team quipped that the doctor had been flirting with Tom. The silk received a huge bouquet of flowers during the lunch break, and UM's madness had impaired my reality tester so severely that I believed Stewart when he said they were sent by Malatt. My wits weren't completely dulled, though. I was wholly disgusted by the doctor's antics. Contempt indeed; she'd gone into bat for a predatory scam artist, and said, 'well played Sir,' as if the trial was a game.

She fully deserved a forensic dressing down for promoting UM, but the court was right to deny her the chance to unduly influence the jury, and the plaintiff's witness list halved after Molomby won that argument. Szramka, Ingrid, Rebecca Baldwin and the young Williams were dropped. Simone and Natalie Benhayon were also cancelled and joined Rebecca and their other UM Brothers brooding in the public gallery.

The next witness was Neil Ringe, who was slightly suntanned, and slimmer than he'd been in UM's videos. Tom made another relevance objection when Smark asked Neil whether I'd given him acupuncture treatment in 1999 when he'd visited my Sensei's clinic in Japan. Neil had complained of a sore lower back and Smark wanted to ask him if he'd undone his trousers so that I could work on his abdomen and lumbar area. He said that the answer 'might be thought to bear some similarity to some techniques for which the plaintiff has been criticised.'

Justice Lonergan answered, 'Except Mr Ringe doesn't have ovaries.'

Tom withdrew his objection, though, and there was nothing in the question. Neil answered that it was a standard treatment, and that he did not feel uncomfortable when I treated him. Otherwise, he said that he only remembered me complaining about Serge in the context of expressing 'reservations about the capacity for energetic reading of the abdomen.'

Given his turn, Tom asked, 'You have been given a reading on the Universal Medicine initiation scale by Mr Benhayon, haven't you?'

'I have.'

Neil admitted he'd had no cause to recall our conversation about the ovarian reading until Team UM had asked him to earlier that year, and he couldn't recall any communication with me for several years until that conversation in April 2005. But we'd met several times in the preceding months, including when I sat beside him at Serge's Patanjali channelling performance. I didn't get the impression that Neil was lying, he just didn't remember.

Next was Neil Gamble, the retired casino boss who'd publicly commented that the real men of Bangalow should show Lance what happens to 'bully boys'. In a suit jacket and business shirt, he looked as comfortable under court examination as he might at a board meeting, and under Smark's examination he said UM's gargantuan content mill, unimedliving.com, which advertised Benhayon as 'The World's Teacher', was his idea, as were the online videos branded 'Unimed TV'. 'Serge deserved a global audience,' he said, and he'd personally funded the website beginnings, and remained a coordinator of its hundreds of unpaid contributors.

But Tom opted to keep the questioning brief. A wealthy business leader's endorsement risked elevating the jury's opinion of the plaintiff, he told my team. Gamble, who lived in Sydney, agreed that he'd attended a considerable number of UM events, including five or six Vietnam retreats in six years, and estimated that up to two hundred and fifty students had attended each.

'You have had a reading of your initiation scale from Mr Benhayon, haven't you?'

'I have.'

Lance's ex-wife Anna was markedly less sure of herself. Tall, well dressed, and with a neatly styled blonde bob, she sat alert and blinked a lot. Smark chose to focus on her relationship with Lance, labouring Team UM's misapprehension that I was bringing Lance, Matt and Heath to say that Serge had broken up their relationships. It's not something I ever claimed, even if it would be difficult to argue that UM was not a contributing factor. My witnesses had other valuable evidence.

Anna's workshop habit began in 2005. The couple had been together off and on for twenty years before they married in 2007, and moved from Sydney to the Bangalow area. Their daughter was born the same year. They divorced in 2012, and Anna said that she'd always been the instigator of the couple's breakups. Like Sarah Baldwin, who gave evidence later, she predictably described her ex as bullying, abusive, and aggressive.

Tom's cross-examination, however, focused on the changes to her lifestyle as her UM involvement deepened. When asked if the couple still had their music collection and books when they moved to Bangalow, she said that she'd gotten rid of some when they made the move, 'and Lance was always making fun of the books I had, so I cut them back.'

'I suggest to you at some time you got rid of some music and books and instead you put reproductions of works by Leonardo da Vinci on the walls?'

Her body stiffened. 'Sorry, can you repeat that please?'

'You know Leonardo da Vinci? Have you heard of him?'

She looked startled. 'Yes.'

'Mr Benhayon is the reincarnation of him, isn't he?'

'I don't know that as a fact but I…yeah.'

'Have you never heard that?'

'Yes, I have.'

'That's not a secret in Universal Medicine, is it?'

'No, I saw it in the newspaper. Yes, I've seen it before.' The pace of her speech fluctuated. Benhayon had admitted to the Leonardo claim in the media in 2012, in Way of the Livingness recordings since, and Anna seemed unaware that he'd also admitted it in court.

'You've only seen it in the newspaper?'

'No, I've heard it, but it's, it's not spoken about.'

'It's not spoken about? It's well known, isn't it?'

'Well known to who?' said Anna.

'Among people in Universal Medicine,' said Tom.

'That what?'

'That Mr Benhayon is the reincarnation of Leonardo da Vinci.'

'I don't really know about what other students feel.'

'You see, you had some degree of respect for Mr Benhayon?'

'Yes.'

'You read in the newspaper that he was the reincarnation of Leonardo da Vinci. Do you regard that as a bit unusual?'

'I believe in reincarnation.'

'So what did you do when you were at your next meeting of Universal Medicine? Did you ask something about that?'

'There was a lot of other things in that newspaper article that wasn't true. There was a lot of lies printed.'

'I suppose the Leonardo da Vinci one, if you'd never heard of it before, you didn't know whether that was the truth or a lie, did you?'

Anna pursed her lips, her eyes darting from the barrister to somewhere in the near distance.

'Isn't that right?'

'Isn't what right, sorry?'

'Well, if you hadn't heard of it before, and your first knowledge was reading about it in the newspaper in an article that you say had a lot of lies in it, you couldn't know whether the claim that Mr Benhayon was the reincarnation of Leonardo da Vinci was a lie or not, could you?'

'I felt it could be a possibility.'

When asked if she'd changed the music she listened to, she answered: 'I started listening more to Glorious Music that I really liked. I didn't listen to hard rock and pop anymore, I was a mother with a young child. It wasn't appropriate.'

'Did you say "Glorious Music"?' said Tom.

'To some music... yeah, some different music.'

'I just missed the word you used and I'm simply trying to find out what it was and what it means?'

'It's just the name of a record company and I like them. I just really enjoyed listening to the music.'

'You actually avoided saying the word "glorious" again, didn't you?'

Anna blinked. 'No, sir.'

'You didn't say the word "glorious" again, did you?'

'I've got nothing to hide if that's what you mean.'

'The fact is, Glorious Music is a record operation run by Michael Benhayon, isn't it?'

'Yes.'

'It puts out music which you understand to be clear of pranic energy, doesn't it?'

'It's music that I like to listen to.'

'Where did you get it?'

'I don't know, probably at a Universal Medicine event.' She hurriedly added that she used to play The Wiggles for her daughter.

'Is there pranic energy in The Wiggles?' said Tom.

'I don't know. I don't know what you're talking about. She loved it.'

'You've never heard of pranic energy?'

'She loved it.'

It took another five questions for Anna to admit she viewed prana as bad energy. All the while Tom's tone remained that of an amiable grandfather. 'If behind the scenes one of the people connected with The Wiggles turned out to be taking drugs, would that have an effect on whether there was pranic energy in The Wiggles' music?' said Tom.

'Well, yeah, because if someone's taking a lot of drugs then that's probably not a good thing. I wouldn't like to know that my child is listening to music where someone is addicted to drugs.'

Anna gave a marvellous impression of an evasive cult member, and provided a lot of useful answers in that fashion. Yes, she knew other UM members who had Da Vinci prints on their walls; she'd heard of a book burning at Cameron Bell and Paula Fletcher's property but she'd not attended personally; yes, she used healing symbols near her bed and listened to UM recordings in bed when she had time; yes, she'd been to a UM couples workshop with Lance at Lennox Head in October 2011.

'You remember there were a few children at that workshop, weren't there?'

'I think there were a few, yes.'

'Now, you were going to various counselling sessions throughout this period, weren't you?'

'Yes.'

'A psychologist called Caroline Raphael, for example.'

'Yes.

'You went to see her on a number of occasions?'

'Yes, and I wanted Lance to go along too.'

'After those sessions you sometimes spoke to him about your marriage being "convenient and loveless", didn't you?'

'Yes, it had gotten that way.'

Tom moved to 2012, when UM received its first media scrutiny. 'Did you tell your husband that people told lies about Serge Benhayon and Universal Medicine because they were jealous of Serge and they didn't like hearing the truth?'

'That's possible, yes.'

'You did accuse your husband of being behind some media article, didn't you?'

'I did know he was behind it because he had stolen emails of mine from a private email and had published them in there, so, yes, I do know about it and he was behind it because how else were those emails that were taken without my approval and published for everyone to see.' Tom did not correct her. No emails were ever published. The jury had copies of the articles in question and would have seen no mention of Lance or Anna.

'These were emails, were they, between you and Mr Benhayon?'

'They were private emails he stole off my computer.'

'Were they emails between you and Mr Benhayon?'

'Yes.'

'In which you were speaking to Mr Benhayon about your marriage, weren't you?'

'I wasn't talking to him about my marriage, I was talking to him about what had happened since I had returned from the retreat and how volatile things were.'

'You wrote to Mr Benhayon by email seeking guidance from him about what you should do in relation to your separation, didn't you?'

'I wasn't seeking guidance, I was sharing with him more so, like you would a friend.'

'Sharing with him?'

'I had a counsellor, I didn't need to be counselled, I just was sharing with him the situation.'

'You wanted to talk to him about it, didn't you?'

'Yes, because he always spoke highly of Lance and I know that he would offer me a way through and to support him and, and like for us to move forward in the relationship.' She appeared not to recall that Benhayon's reply accused Lance of channeling, sabotaging her glory, and lying.

Tom reminded her of a short reconciliation after the couple's initial breakup. 'You asked him back, he came, and you told him you were uncertain about UM and you wouldn't attend events for a while.'

'Yes, because there was a lot happening and he was behind a lot of these lies and false allegations… It was an incredibly stressful time for me, I was extracting myself out of a domestic violent relationship and I thought I was very responsible, I felt terrible about what was happening when all the lies and attacks being directed towards Serge and his family and I felt like my only way of trying to improve the situation was to give him a chance, even though deep down I knew it probably wouldn't work because he was so blinded by things. He said he had absolutely nothing to do with anything and in that moment I knew he was deeply lying, which wasn't uncommon.'

'Then you gave an interview, didn't you, to *A Current Affair*?'

'I did.'

The one occasion on which Anna's name appeared in the media coverage of UM was in that television report, when she went on camera to defend Serge. Lance, who has a different surname, declined an interview. It was Anna and UM that persisted in publicly naming them both.

'Did you send emails some time later to your husband saying that your lawyer had advised you to get an Apprehended Violence Order if he persisted in bullying you about your involvement in UM?'

'My lawyer never advised that. I had such abusive emails and I was scared for my safety, I went to the police.'

'Did you have a lawyer at the time?'

'I don't know if I'd engaged a lawyer, no.'
'Did you ever have a lawyer around that time?'
'Yes.'
'And who was that?'
'Paula Fletcher.'
'Is that the lady who is in court here as Mr Benhayon's solicitor?'
'Yes.'

Tom asked Anna if she'd published a blog about Lance on a UM website, criticising him in terms she'd ventilated in court. 'I was bringing the truth,' she said.

'Indeed, you did apply in the Court for apprehended violence orders against your husband, didn't you, in 2012 and 2014?'

'Yes, two, on advice of the police, yes.'

'Yes, and both applications were dismissed, weren't they?'

'Yeah, but it doesn't mean it wasn't real.'

cxxxiii Dwyer

'The only time I mention conventional medicine is when I praise it,' was another Benhayon answer to a Smark question. He'd always gotten around quackery accusations by insisting that his Esoteric modalities were complementary to medicine and that he'd never discouraged anyone from seeking medical treatment. Tom, however, raised a quote from his book, *Esoteric Teachings and Revelations*: 'Do not let your doctor/physician/practitioner or the like advise you on good health and/or clean living if they do not look and feel the whole of what they espouse.'[110]

Benhayon asked to see the book, and while it was being fetched, Tom questioned his stance on immunisation. Serge answered that he was 'pro-choice', adding that when his clients asked him whether to immunise, he told them that his children and grandchildren are. Tom called up another recording.

> If your kid is stuffy nosed, is down, is not sleeping well, don't get immunisation. Because they're not strong enough to cope with it...

> The problem with parenting is they go and get the immunisation because the doctor says it is a certain age rather than actually checking where the kid is at. And there's a third factor in here and that is feeling whether that child needs that immunisation...You can be pro-immunisation and say, 'no I don't feel to immunise'...

> ...if you immunised the kids out of fear it means that you're relying on medicine to look after you.[111]

The Healer's Healer prevaricated as hard as he could, saying that he was only talking about the timing. He seemed more uncomfortable at getting chipped for undermining medical advice than when questioned about inappropriate touching and airing his sexual quirks in front of kids. Tom took his copy of the seven hundred page book and pointed out the title page inscribed 'By Serge Benhayon and the Hierarchy'. Are you satisfied that is a book by you and the Hierarchy?'

'Yes, it's my book.'

Tom then stayed on the lines disparaging medical advice for about ten solid minutes, in which the best the plaintiff could do was accuse the lawyer of taking them out of context. The problem was, they appeared in the tome as a short axiom. No other context was available.

'Universal Medicine, as a name, suggests that the organisation has something to do with medicine, doesn't it?'

'Yes, but not conventional medicine.'

Benhayon also conceded that UM's workshop consent form required those who attended a five-hour workshop to provide the kind of details that would be requested if they presented to a hospital emergency department: their entire medical history and current medications. 'We want to cover all bases, yes,' said Serge.

'Universal Medicine is not equipped to deal with major medical issues, is it?'

'No.'

'So you have no valid basis to ask for this whole spread of information sought here, have you?'

Benhayon swallowed. 'Where are you coming from?'

Tom didn't blink. 'I'm not sure I'm coming from anywhere,' he said. 'I'm just here. You might be able to tell me about other people who are here as well, but I think you know what my question was, don't you?'

Serge answered that 'if something happens, we want to make sure we know what possibly could be happening' in case the Esoterics needed to call for real medical help.

'Do you have any reason to think that people might take a turn at any of your events?'

'It hasn't happened, but it could.'

The jury were given time to read Professor John Dwyer's expert report before he was called to the witness box. His opinion was unambiguous, that untrained Benhayon 'lacks the knowledge and skills to provide clinical advice and perform procedures claimed to alter pathological states.' From his perspective as an immunologist, it was dangerous to propose that people ignore medical advice and attempt to feel whether their child needs immunisation. In general, he found that UM's healing services expose people to physical and psychological harm, give false hope, and have the potential to delay patients from seeking effective treatment. He also wrote of lifestyle advice that would cause people to avoid positive enjoyments and endanger family dynamics, and of financial harm that comes from wasting money. He was critical of Benhayon's patient blaming that undermined empathy, loving relationships, and women's notions of femininity, as well as the 'cruel concepts' that form 'basic tenets of the cult', regarding disabilities, sexual abuse as punishment, and mental illness resulting from demonic possession.

Of all the witnesses, the professor was the last I expected to show signs of nerves. The curriculum vitae attached to his report ranged to forty-six pages. He'd been Clinical Dean of the medical faculty at University of New South Wales, tenured Professor of Medicine and Paediatrics at Yale University, and held numerous posts on international medical boards and committees. But in the witness box, he got the pages of his report out of order and had trouble finding one of the paragraphs. Louise was permitted to help him unshuffle them. At nearly seventy-nine, he was nearing retirement.

During cross-examination, Smark raised the professor's statements about the potential harm of UM's activities. 'Whether or not harm actually results in the case of a particular person depends on the choices and acts that a particular person makes; would you agree with that?'

'No, I wouldn't agree with that, with due respect,' the expert said firmly. 'Because especially in a clinical situation where someone is seeking help and is vulnerable, the natural human reaction is to trust the person that you're seeking advice from. You may, therefore, be very much influenced by what they tell you.' If Professor Dwyer had been nervous, he was no longer. Or perhaps what I took as nerves was earnestness; he was still maintaining the rage. 'So we're not talking about an equal partnership in terms of the clinical outcome here, and I think as a doctor for fifty years or more I've been very conscious of the fact, over the years, that one has to be very careful in a therapeutic situation, because people naturally have an inherent trust in the person they're seeking advice from.'

Smark reworded the question, as if that might yield an answer that relieved Benhayon of responsibility for conning his clients. 'Whether or not harm occurs in a particular individual, in a particular circumstance, will depend upon the particular steps that that individual takes; do you agree with that?'

'Well, the steps that individuals take may, in a specific situation, have been determined by their accepting the advice given by the practitioner that they're seeking help from,' said the professor.

It didn't come up in court, but an unexpected highlight of his report was found in his CV, under non-professional interests. From 1960 to 1963 the professor had represented Australia in International Collegiate Tennis. He'd been a better and more decorated tennis player than Serge.

cxxxiv Versions

Under Tom's cross-examination, the plaintiff admitted that he had no medical evidence for claiming the Deeper Femaleness technique could help sexual assault survivors. He also acknowledged that the hands seen in the manual images were his. 'The hand in the lower photo is over the woman's perineum, isn't it?'

'Just above, yes,' Benhayon replied. Asked by Justice Lonergan to clarify for the jury what he meant by the anatomical term, Serge said, 'Energetically it's between the anus, and for a woman up to the pubic bone, and for a man to the shaft of the penis where it protrudes and it comes out as an appendage — the area in between,' he said.

When Tom questioned how many survivors he'd used it on, he guessed it was less than a handful, but added, 'let's go with five.'

'How much did you know about what had, in fact, happened to them?'

'Only what they told me.'

'Yes, but how much did you ask for?' said Tom.

'They came with a condition and I asked and they said they got raped and I don't need to ask details.' Asked if he'd followed up in the months after the sessions, he answered that 'in all cases they were able to reintegrate with their body, which is a very horrible thing that happens after a rape, a woman is disassociated with her body.'

'But you are basing your whole statement, here, "great for cases of rape recovery" on your experience with four or five people, is that right?'

Shifting in his seat, Benhayon agreed that he based his assertions on his understanding of energy, not on any professional assessments.

'Did you ever consider that somebody who had been through the sort of trauma that a rape victim can suffer might actually be very deeply traumatised in a way that's not at all evident to ordinary observation?' said Tom.

The plaintiff's reply was indignant. 'What I would like you to do is repeat the question.' Aside from the moments where he claimed he felt raped by my publications, it was the most emotional he became. 'Because my mind wants me to address this issue that you're raising once and for all so that the court does actually hear where I stand with this…' He raised his chin. '…and all we're doing here is playing games with a very, very, very serious condition and all you're doing is trying to pin me to become some sort of mad man with this.'

Tom waited.

'…when you understand rape from an energetic point of view, it is very, very horrible what gets left inside people by way of configuration and in the way they are, therefore, later able to communicate or have a relationship with their body…'

Tom took him to another page in the manual. 'This paragraph has something rather like what you've just been saying in your evidence, "A great example of this is a woman or a man experiencing rape and not having it cleared energetically." That's what you've just been talking about, isn't it?'

'That's correct.'

Tom took him to another page showing his hands on a woman's pelvis. The accompanying text claimed the technique could also clear the energy of rape. 'Now, this book we're looking at came out in 2007? Is that correct?'

'2002.'

'It was revised, wasn't it, in 2013?' It took prolonged exertions against Fletcher to get all versions of the manual in the weeks before the trial.

'Yes, all the textbooks undergo that throughout the years.'

'It's true, isn't it, that the revision that happened in 2013 removed all these references to rape? Is that right?'

Benhayon answered softly, 'yes.' He moved to examine the copy. 'Is this the… have you got…'

'No, this is the earlier version.'

'If that's what you say,' he said, regaining his pomposity, 'and I don't have the proof in front of me, I would say, yes.'

'That was because of Ms Rockett's complaints that were starting to be ventilated. You realised that what you had in this book about rape was a bit touchy, and you'd be better off removing it?'

Benhayon sneered his answer: 'Yes, it was a very sad moment for me to do that actually, but that's the nature of cyber-abuse, isn't it?'

'Well,' began Tom, 'this case is not for you to ask me questions, Mr Benhayon. I might have some interesting answers. You removed those references to rape because you realised that you could be vulnerable in relation to them, didn't you?'

'I removed them because they would be desecrated, because the sacredness of the technique was lost by the distortions that were being perpetrated by your… the defendant.'

Tom asked Meri to project a page from a level four Esoteric healing manual onto the video screens. It was a clear shot of the plaintiff with his fingers pressed to the pubic area of another woman, Miranda Smith. Benhayon confirmed that his hand was on her perineum.

The headline in *The Sydney Morning Herald* the next day read, 'Spiritual healer accuses barrister of trying to paint him as a madman'.

cxxxv Deborah

Contacts had described Deborah Benhayon as quiet and mousey. Some said she seemed 'nice'. Petite, with pale skin, blue eyes, shoulder length blonde hair swept up into a loose knot, and with her narrow, dark rimmed glasses and neck scarf, she looked more suburban bookkeeper than upper-rung management of an occult quackery corporation. On the witness stand, however, she planted her backside on the chair, squared her elbows on the bench, put her mouth close to the microphone and eyed Tom like a pugilist.

She gave Smark the long, unprompted explanation for keeping bedroom doors closed in the family household twenty years before. She also told the court that she and her ex were on very good terms. Serge, in his own evidence, had been so gushing about their continued relationship one wondered why he'd ever ditched her. 'In 2002, it was a parting that was based on pure love,' he said. 'Since then, that love has only got deeper and deeper and grander and there's never been a time where we haven't deepened our love for each other.' Deborah wasn't in court for that rhapsody, but Miranda was. He didn't say anything about her.

After Deborah gave evidence, she attended the trial every day until its end, usually sitting behind Miranda, and only occasionally accompanied by her most recent husband. She appears in nearly all the press photographs of the Benhayons on their way into court, often walking closer to Serge than his latest wife. Her ex-husband's talent for spherical obfuscation had rubbed off on her too. Tom had to do some interrogating to extract that the firm's financial officer agreed with Serge's teaching that money comes with an 'imprint' of energy, but she resisted questions about its voodoo hitting the kidneys. Further coaxing revealed that she used healing symbols, but she denied using them to clear prana.

'Is Mr Benhayon the reincarnation of Leonardo da Vinci?'

Elbows glued to the desk, hands tightly clasped, Deborah squinted. 'No.'

'Have you ever heard him say he is?'

'No.'

'You have had a reading on the scale of initiation of Universal Medicine from Mr Benhayon, haven't you?'

'Yes, I have.'

Sarah Baldwin gave evidence immediately before Tom opened the defence. Later that day, when my stint in the witness box commenced, Sarah and Ray Karam took the seats behind Tom, in my direct line of sight, Sarah draping herself over her gaunt husband, resting her head on his shoulder as if they were on a matinee cinema date. Rosie said she felt like telling them: 'Get a room.'

Sarah pre-empted ex-fiancé Matt Sutherland's evidence, and she faithfully crammed a dazzling array of slurs into the relatively short examination. She said she was introduced to UM around 2000, at eighteen or so — likely by her devotee mother. Matt and Sarah met in 2005 and their 'volatile' six year engagement broke up in 2012. By the time she'd finished her evidence, she'd portrayed the chap who'd taken me on leash-free walks as such a lazy, hopeless, dishonest, sex-crazed, anti-social oaf that she'd damaged her own credibility by ever associating with him.

Tom managed to get out of her that she had not allowed their children gluten and dairy products since they were born, but he cut the questioning short, choosing not to quiz her about Da Vinci, healing symbols, or whether she'd had her initiation level read by the master. He described her as a firecracker and thought it unlikely she'd yield much sense. Her account of the couple's breakup and how extremely hurt she was, and how the relationship had 'eroded' her delicate self, peaked with convulsive tears; blub, blub, blub.

Everyone watched patiently as she wept, all faces straight except for the one in the hot-seat close to Tom. After Benhayon had finished his evidence, greyish waif Nicola Lessing was replaced by a roster of strategically placed Sons of God, ensuring specially selected characters sat in the unavoidable line of sight of the witnesses under examination. Rebecca Baldwin was stationed there for sister Sarah's performance, and I glimpsed matching tears rolling down her quivering cheeks — risky outpourings from parishioners who believe emotions are the cause of all disease. It's unlikely lasting damage was done, however. As the questions continued, the sisters' tears dried quickly, leaving no trace.

cxxxvi Sisters

Where the Benhayon worshipping Baldwin sisters were perfect jewels of solidarity, Sydney based Esoteric practitioner Michelle Crowe gave the court a taste of the affections UM enthusiasts show toward family members who don't share the passion. Michelle practised in Sydney's leafy northern suburbs, describing herself on her website as an EPA accredited practitioner of Universal Medicine therapies, and Team UM called her to answer evidence given by her estranged sister, Odette*. The two had not communicated in over a year.

A working Mum in her late forties, Odette told the court of her growing concerns about Michelle's UM involvement, recalling a conversation they'd had when she was helping paint her sister's treatment rooms. Michelle said she was studying toward a qualification, but would not give a straight answer to the question, 'qualified as what?' Michelle is a breast cancer survivor and Odette worried about her strange diet and her belief that her cancer was caused by emotional problems stemming from a relationship breakdown. Michelle forbade wine from her household and made a point of telling her sister that she energetically cleansed herself with candles and clearing symbols after visits to Odette's home. She placed healing symbols under her little son's bed.

The Esoteric sister practised UM's bogus healing on clients with serious conditions, including cancer, charging one hundred dollars per hour. Tensions boiled over when Michelle performed Chakra-puncture on

Odette's adolescent daughter without seeking the mother's permission, but the relationship properly ruptured after Odette visited her sister to try to explain why she thought she was being misled. 'I said to her, "I'd just like you to look at the big picture and just make sure that you understand what you're doing, what you're getting into and how it is affecting our relationship and other relationships" and she said that I didn't understand and to get out of the house.'

In the witness box, the Esoteric Practitioner had nothing charitable to say about her sister and said that the two had always argued. She claimed her brother in law, Steve, tried to come between them, but Michelle didn't know that Steve had spoken to me years before about his concerns for her, describing her as a 'great bird' and mourning her transformation into a rigid fundamentalist. Odette's distress prompted him to call because he didn't know who else he could speak with or what to do to console his wife. The three had been close, and he missed the sister-in-law he knew.

With long blonde hair and glasses, Michelle also looked like any middle-class working mother. Once she was done denigrating her sister, Tom asked if she'd heard Serge say that spirits are nine feet tall and have no feet. 'Do you accept that?' he said.

'Yeah, I accept that.'

He asked her about her training in UM modalities, Esoteric Connective Tissue Therapy and Chakra-puncture. 'You said that after you'd done the fifth level you got some accreditation?'

'Yes.'

'Who is the accreditation from?'

'The Esoteric Practitioners Association.'

'That's run by Mr Benhayon, isn't it?'

She frowned. 'I'm not sure if it's actually run by Mr Benhayon, I think it's an independent association.'

'Do you know who is behind the Esoteric Practitioners Association?'

'Well, yeah, it would be the Benhayons, I think, that would have set it up.'

'It's Universal Medicine, isn't it?'

She acknowledged that the accreditation is not recognised outside of UM. Yes, Michelle used the house clearing symbol to clear prana from her home and the people in it. Yes to Da Vinci prints in her treatment room. No, she'd never heard Benhayon say that he's Leonardo's current avatar, but she thought it was probably true that we've had at least two thousand lifetimes each. Yes, she would describe some of her clients as sick people, and no, she had no medical qualifications, but was an accredited AcuEnergetics practitioner. On investigation I found that AcuEnergetics was a trading name for some Reiki-like hocus-pocus in which the practitioner closes their eyes, hovers their hands over their customer, and charges them for it.

'I've also got a Diploma in Chakra-puncture with...' Michelle said, and hesitated. 'Yeah, with a college.'

'With?' said Tom.

'It's in a — yeah, a diploma.'

'No, but with whom?'

'Evolve College.'

'That's a business that Mr Benhayon has an interest in, isn't it?' said Tom.

'No, not at all.'

'Not at all?'

'Not that I'm aware of, I don't think so...not that I'm aware of.'

'I would suggest to you,' said Tom, 'that via another organisation he has a fifty percent shareholding in that, have you never heard of that?'

'No.'

'How did you get to Evolve then? Who directed you?' said Tom.

She seemed surprised by the questions. 'You studied Chakra-puncture with Universal Medicine and then somehow Universal Medicine suggested to you to go onto Evolve, didn't they?'

'No, they didn't suggest it.' Michelle floundered, as if searching, as Anna had, not for the factual answer, but the right thing to say. 'I found out through another colleague of mine that it was being offered and it's a completely... it's completely independent, as far as I'm concerned.' But she had to know that Evolve's staff was stacked with UM devotees, including Serryn O'Regan. The College's brochures were filled with the glossy smiles of UM's volunteer promoters, and the one for the Chakra-puncture course featured photos of the Benhayon family stabbing each other with sharp metal objects. She added that the financial outlay, which I knew to be up to seven thousand dollars for the course, was less than what she'd forked over to train in AcuEnergetics.

I believed her when she said she didn't know Benhayon owned half of the College business or that he'd cashed in twice from his students repeating the sham Chakra-puncture course. I believe that she didn't understand what genuine accreditation is. She turned out to be a useful surprise witness for the defence by representing the hundreds of students Benhayon and his management misled. Unfortunately, however, she's gone on to charge customers, some with serious illnesses, for worthless therapies; proving herself to be, like many cultists, both a victim and a proponent of the scam.

cxxxvii Past energy

After Sarah Baldwin and Anna's evidence, the jury would have been forgiven for expecting Lance and Matt to lumber into court in gravy stained Bonds singlets, grunting obscenities and leering at the women. Instead they saw two regularly showered blokes with combed hair and collared shirts who gave calm and thoughtful answers. Matt was crucially able to tell the court that about two hundred students were instructed in Deeper Femaleness at the workshop he attended. He then gave evidence on the impact of the Way of the Livingness on his young family. After Matt and Sarah's breakup and throughout Sarah's marriage to Ray Karam, they shared care of their two primary school aged sons, with Matt having them most weekends. The boys' learning and behavioural difficulties were a constant concern, and they would wake at four each morning and wouldn't go back to sleep. He knew the Karams kept Esoteric hours, but it wasn't until the school principal called the parents to a meeting that he learned that the kids were arriving at school exhausted and unable to concentrate. The principal also took Matt aside and told him that the younger son was so hungry she'd had to buy him food. 'She'd been doing it on a regular basis,' he said.

I'd seen the boys eat well at his home. Chef Matt is a big guy and always put plenty of food in front of them, but he'd underestimated Sarah's UM adherence. We were out on a walk when he told me about that meeting. He was reeling. 'Didn't the kids tell you they were hungry?' I said.

The boys were aware of their parents' disagreement and avoided discussing the Karam household. Matt assumed they didn't talk about it because they wanted to avoid conflict, so he didn't pressure them. On an outing after the school meeting, though, he bought his seven year old a cream bun, only for the child to run off with it and hide. Matt found him crouched behind a wall, crying, clutching the contraband, saying he didn't want his brother or step-siblings to see him with it in case they dobbed him in to the Esoteric parents.

Under cross-examination, Sarah denied that the school had informed her that the boys were underfed, but Matt told the court that the school must have alerted child safety authorities, and an officer from a neighbouring region was assigned to the case because the child safety office in Lismore had UM zealots on staff. Smark had nothing to touch it with. In questioning Matt, he could only hone in on his quarrels with Sarah to try and discredit him. Matt agreed that he probably swore at Sarah in the heat of their final breakup and thought it possible that he'd called her the biggest nightmare he'd ever met in his life. Benhayon's barrister then questioned him about the couple's parenting and money pressures, and Matt said without hesitation that they were difficult circumstances.

'Did you find social situations sometimes a bit taxing?'

Again his answer was unreserved. 'With the group, with her family, I just got to the point where I couldn't be around them, cause all they talked about was "Serge said this, Serge said that". It was just like you were either in the club or you weren't in the club. If you asked any questions challenging his beliefs or anything like that, they were, you know, kind of hostile.'

Lance too held his ground in the witness box. 'Anna was complaining constantly of being tired,' he said. 'Of having diarrhoea, being lethargic, and she actually looked it. I mean, the colour of her skin changed. I remember about seven o'clock in the evening her eyes would be hanging out of her head.' He told of her throwing family and other photos into the trash, including those of her deceased sister, but he'd not known of any conflict between them. Anna had mumbled something about 'past energy', but she stonewalled when asked why she was behaving that way.

Conjoined Sarah and Ray Karam were in the eyeline seats during Matt's evidence. Odette was treated to a view of her unenthusiastic brother-in-law beside Natalie Benhayon; and Anna sat there during Lance's turn. She too ended up with tears streaming down her face as he answered questions about the bitter end of their marriage. The seating arrangement, by then, had to be obvious to the jury. Matt told me that the panel smiled and nodded to him as he gave his evidence, and I saw them do the same with Odette. After the plaintiff's lineup, and five days of me, the jurors were probably relieved to hear from relatable inhabitants of planet Earth.

In his closing address, Tom told them that my witnesses came across as decent, fair-minded and level-headed, and that they all showed a degree of sympathy for the state of those they were formerly close to. 'They did not present as vindictive or trying to score points, or trying to put them down here,' he said. 'Now, I have to say, regrettably, the plaintiff's witnesses presented a bit of a contrast to that, and seemed to be wanting to take every opportunity they could to stick an arrow in or to launch a criticism.'

cxxxviii Multi-prong

According to another Sergileaked email, before the trial, Benhayon had a 'multi-prong plan' to out 'Rockett, Lance and whoever joins them like Dwyer and Millikan as akin bodies and activities that resemble if not emulate the Ku Klux Klan and the Nazi regime.' Among the proposed prongs was a 'dedicated section' on the Unimed Living website, outing the detractor KKK alongside gluten free recipes and Esoteric Breast Massage reviews; plus a book penned by telephoto Alan; the cult's 'own naming names page — journos galore'; and

> Blogs and tweets labelling and naming those who are part of the supremacy in Australia…
>
> Again — NO REPLIES — incubate, begin writing and spawn a tsunami ready to flourish after judgement at trial or post trial if only a judge sits.

It explained the courtroom presence of Sarah Broome's UM worshipping journalist husband, Hamish Broome, with Rebecca Baldwin and Alison Greig trying to look busy at their laptops, and it closed with an Esoteric salutation:

> Delete email if necessary.
>
> With Fire,
>
> Serge

Another prong must have been a defamatory audiovisual extravaganza planned for Unimed TV. Clayton Lloyd and ghost-pale Jonathan Baldwin began loitering around the court steps with SLR and video cameras every day that I gave evidence. But the Brotherhood weren't comfortable when caught on the other side of the lens. At lunch breaks, for fun, David Millikan photographed the Esos as they dribbled out of the courthouse. The Reverend neither wanted nor needed the photos, but he prankishly recounted how an unhappy Alan Johnston jeered through his chewing gum, 'your report was a piece of shit! And so are you!'

The Esoteric encroachments went too far, however, when Michelle Crowe was called as the final witness. Odette and Steve remained in court to observe — the only defence witnesses to do so, and took seats a vacant chair away from O'Regan. Odette, however, became restless as Michelle claimed that the only reason her sister and Steve were upset with her was because they weren't allowed to guzzle liquor at her birthday party. 'That's not true,' said Odette, a little too audibly. I turned and shook my head, encouraging her to stay quiet to avoid a reprimand from Justice Lonergan.

As Michelle continued her evidence, her sister became tearful. Behind me, a movement caught the corner of my eye and I swung my head to catch O'Regan's thin, black trousered leg extending sideways, spider like, followed by her black trousered behind, into the seat beside the defence witness. Steve, on Odette's other side, leaned forward and made a low sound and as I kept my eyes on O'Regan, her spindly black hindquarters made the reverse movements to her original post.

Getting up, I put my pranic posterior between the two women. 'You have to be quiet,' I whispered to Odette. 'Don't interject.'

Steve had told O'Regan to get back to her seat, and her vacuous shadow continued to hang behind me for two more weeks, blunting her psychic daggers on my thick Astral hide. Unlike the propaganda rabble who fought Benhayon's battles unpaid, she had obvious money. She'd purchased Serge's former home, with its vestal birdbath, for a million dollars, and drove a late model black Porsche Carrera (another make sanctified by Sergio), yet Judith McIntyre's professional executor had no discernible career outside of UM. She'd been CEO of Evolve College for a period, then its general counsel, and she held a solicitor's practising certificate, but her business address was her Goonellabah home.

As we left court one day in the fourth week of the trial, a black Audi saloon pulled up on Phillip Street, chauffeur driven by one the group's women. O'Regan climbed in the back, and was spirited away like an etheric Lady Muck.

cxxxix Symbols

'Ha!' Tom laughed when he first glimpsed Benhayon's healing symbols. 'We'll have some fun with these.' He liked the zany blue splotches so much that he kept the cards as souvenirs, but not before asking Justice Lonergan's Associate if she'd like one to keep her desk safe from bad energy. The Associate coyly declined.

The postcards still retailed for seven dollars fifty apiece. Benhayon had never bothered to get the preprinted address lines removed, but a Désirée designed love-heart with wings took the space for the postage stamp. Tom presented Reading Symbol 1 to the court, describing it as a 'scattered design' that reminded him of Picasso's *Guernica*, and he asked the artiste if the cards had origins anywhere else. 'Like inspired by Picasso?'

Serge answered in the negative, but I doubt he knew Picasso's war painting from Monet's *Water Lilies*. He said the reading symbol could clear the flow of energy and could be placed inside books to cleanse their 'excessive headiness'.

'Say I put it under a book for a while,' said Tom, 'then I take the book with me on a holiday two hundred kilometres away but I leave the card behind, does the card still work or not?'

'It would have an effect, yes.'

He offered another hypothetical. 'If you post this card to someone, does it clear the energy of all the other letters and things cluttered around it in the postman's bag?'

'I would like to think so,' said Benhayon, 'but maybe no. I don't know, I've never considered it.' His 'instant knowing' was on pause again.

The lawyer moved to music, and the Esoteric aesthete affirmed that the doctrine that '..music is ten times more damaging than food poisoning if the music comes with pranic energy', applied to all kinds, whether it was classical, jazz, or reggae, and that the prana comes from the lifestyles of the composers, musicians, engineers and producers. Tom asked if a recording of a symphony orchestra with over one hundred musicians could infect him with prana.

'Correct.'

'Because of pranic energy coming from one member of the orchestra?'

'No.'

'How many members of the orchestra do you need?'

'You'd have to have a little more than half for it to be what we would call a pranic imprint.'

'If it's a string quartet how many do I need?'

Benhayon's eyeballs shot toward the ceiling momentarily. 'Three.'

'You just made that up then, didn't you?'

Again, the guru insisted his balderdash was based in the Ageless Wisdom. 'I know where it comes from,' he said. 'That's why I'm willing to do what I do, even though it's publicly unacceptable and uncomfortable, but I do it.' The clairsentient would never acknowledge that inviting public derision was not compatible with aggressively litigating to protect his reputation.

cxl Pina

Like Joelle, Pina gave evidence via an audiovisual link from Queensland. She was about fifty, wore glasses, her dark hair in a bright hair-tie, and she smiled broadly when Tom confirmed her full Italian name with immaculate pronunciation. She testified that she visited Benhayon in 2006 at the rooms beneath his house. Her husband waited for her in the waiting room. She told Serge that she was recovering from cancer, and he performed his hands-on routine while she lay on her back. 'I do recall,' she said, 'the stages where the hands started to go to the lower abdomen and it's like a bubble of memory that I do have of that session. He did say words to the effect of, "I am feeling that you have been a victim of sexual abuse".

Pina had mentioned nothing to him about her sexual or reproductive history. 'I do remember I was a bit taken aback and then he said, "Can I heal that area? Can I manipulate your" and it was "pubic bone". I believe they were the words, "Manipulate your pubic bone for healing".'

'What did you say to that?' said Tom.

'"No!"' Pina was emphatic. 'I was quite shocked and it was quite a defiant "no" and I recall that there was kind of a change in the whole atmosphere of the room and then I don't recall much, but the session finished and I left that room.' She told her husband what had happened as they left, describing the experience as creepy.

Pina confirmed that Benhayon's hands were on her lower abdomen when he tried the line about sexual abuse. When questioned, Benhayon said he had no recollection of her or her visit. During the break after Tom announced the name of our new defence witness, I found a gaggle of grim-faced Brides in the court's foyer surrounding a worried looking Miranda, murmuring about something on her mobile phone. They'd googled Pina's name and had enough brains between them to grasp that she was going to be a credible witness. They had no means to pre-emptively get to her or label her a troll.

Smark asked Pina if she'd made any complaint to an official body or the police. 'I didn't know what to do with that information,' she said, 'because I felt it was — even though it was a request — it was an inappropriate request. What did I do with that? Was that part of the healing? And so I did keep it to myself for a few years. I did mention it to my adult children only a few years ago.'

Pina firmly denied Smark's suggestion that she may have misremembered the part of the consultation concerning her pubic bone. 'It's always been in the back of my mind, and it's been a memory that to me is quite fresh… it was like a bubble of a violation that I didn't know what to do with and it has been very clear in my mind that few minutes particularly.'

'Wasn't Pina a terrific witness?' said Tom when the team returned to Louise's chambers at the end of that third Friday of the hearing. He was upbeat, despite his fatigue. Odette and Michelle would follow, and then his closing address. Madeline brought him one of his yellow drinks, but he stayed on his feet, still in his robe and wig. 'I've rarely said this at this stage of a trial,' he told us, 'but things are going remarkably well.'

I didn't disagree, but I could not feel the same enthusiasm. Tom remained buoyant to the end, but seemed to sense my cheerlessness. One day, when he and I arrived at court after everyone had gone in, he tried his own version of Esoteric Walking in the empty corridor. His was a stooped, cartoon villain version, with long strides, eyes rolling, knees and elbows bent, and claw-like hands grasping the air as his robes trailed the floor. 'Someone will see you doing that,' I said, 'and then you'll have to defend your own reputation.' His pricelessly rare performance was wasted on my humourless riposte.

Yet, despite my narrowed emotional range, I'd been moved by Pina's evidence. That vindication, spoken aloud in the most public of forums, plunged me into a deep sorrow that she and others had to endure Benhayon's vile behaviour. I knew he had a routine for preying on women, cold reading them as sexual abuse victims as an opening for his perverse conduct. Thankfully, one more woman had confirmed it under oath; as disturbed by it as I'd been. Her evidence also went toward proving that he preyed on cancer patients.

Women reluctant to come forward told me of incidents going back to the early days of his healing sham. A survivor of sexual assault said that Benhayon began working on her pelvis without telling her what the healing session would involve. As he pressed, he claimed that the energy of the perpetrator and of her former partners was lodged in her uterus and causing disease, and that a miscarriage she'd suffered was caused by an evil entity inside her. For years she'd believed it, to her prolonged distress.

Another woman who'd consulted him for help with a musculoskeletal ailment became increasingly uncomfortable as he worked on her. She said he was sweating as he palpated her abdomen, eyes closed. He told her that she had an entity residing in her reproductive area and that a 'male force' in her life had mistreated her from the age of five, but when she refuted his suggestion that she'd been sexually abused, he told her it had happened during a past life; that she'd been a small child and that the man had a large penis.

We may never know how many clients, of thousands Benhayon got his hands on, were subjected to similar ploys. His training manuals indicated that sexual abuse survivors were part of his target market, and one of the recordings Tom selected to play for the jury was an excerpt from a 2012 Benhayon spiel:

> Let's say you did something like rape, which is pretty horrible. And you get jailed, hopefully. If in your jail term you come to your senses and you say 'I can't believe I did that, I forced myself onto someone, I've ruined that person, I've left my energy inside them,' it's going to be a seed that stays forever in them. If it's not cleared it becomes a cyst, a fibroid, or possible endometriosis, possible infertility, for as many lives as that seed remains in there without it being removed. Thank God for esoteric healing.[112]

cxli Uncle Jim

> Let's say for example I have a niece or nephew that I fantasise over, and here I'm bashing myself saying, 'come on don't do that, don't do that', but I would never touch them, yeah, because I fear I'll go to jail — that's the only reason. The fear of going to jail prevents me from touching them. But I don't deal with my issues and I still hold a fantasy. When I'm in control I go, 'stop that, that's silly, don't do that'. But when I'm low and I'm weak I'll go into the fantasy and play it out. Later I might feel guilty. Are you with me? Okay.

Those were the words Heath heard Benhayon say at the 2011 healing workshop. Olga suffered hours of recordings to locate them. The jury also heard a recording where Benhayon said that karma is great medicine, and that children who are molested were sex offenders in a past life.

A couple of weeks into the trial, the elder of the two women jurors came to court on crutches, her leg in a cast. We expected she might ask to be excused from the remainder of her duty, reducing the jury to three. Yet, she attended every day until the end, despite her mobility difficulties and appearing to be in considerable pain. The injured juror was the most expressive of the restrained panel. She'd frown or squint and tilt her head during the evidence at times. Through the Uncle Jim audio, she covered her mouth with her hand.

> During that playing out [the niece or nephew] feel the energy, and it's happening energetically to them, just not physically... You don't need to be molested. A child knows when there's a feeling that way towards them, but more so if that feeling or that intention or the fantasy is incessant...
>
> Now let's go to the person who holds that fantasy. Because if I said, 'Uncle Jim, you know you're raping your niece.' He'll say, 'Don't be ridiculous, I've never even touched her, I just hug her, I...'
>
> 'Uncle Jim, you know energetically you're all over her.'
>
> Now let's assume he confesses. And you [sic] say, 'look, I can't get it out of my mind. I can't help it. I don't know what happens. Something comes over me. When I can control it, I can stop it, other times it overcomes me, I just go there.'
>
> Just like porn, no different, only this time it's with his niece.
>
> What we don't realise in those instances (and here I am, I can teach you this because I know what is really going on, take advantage of me), it's not just Uncle Jim.

Benhayon said that spiritual entities feed the fantasy to Jim.

> They feed you at your lowest time... The entity that gave you that, then goes out to rape the kid, which takes their kidney energy. In return they bring you the satisfaction of being with that kid and then they bring home back to their body your life force and the kid's life force. And then they grow strong on that. The problem is you can't grow strong on anyone's energy,

> you have to keep doing it… And the Lords of Form assign these guys to you, to us, so that they can keep working on our weaknesses…
>
> Even worse than Uncle Jim, even worse is the person who in their mind cannot believe this is true, because they are fed that it's not true…
>
> Why can Uncle Jim have fantasy over healing? Or has had fantasy in the same way in a past life over another? It can't happen to an innocent child.

Under Smark's questioning, Benhayon defended the photographs of his inappropriately placed hands by arguing that all of us are able to sense who is a danger to us. According to his spherical logic, women would be able to feel it if he was a predator, and not allow him near them. I guess that didn't apply to me. 'A woman senses a man's approaches at a bar,' he said, 'and will know that he's a sleaze — everybody has access to that sense…We, as a young child, we can walk into a house and we know which rooms feel safe or not.' In the real world, however, the problem of grooming is the opposite. The perpetrator is often a person who is trusted, and nobody senses at all.

The Uncle Jim diatribe continued:

> It can't happen to an innocent child. So if you feel it, if you feel it all over you, you don't have to have it had done. That means that you've done it to others.[113]

Kids were at that workshop too, and again Benhayon defended expounding on 'energetic rape' to them, a concept Tom suggested they may struggle to understand. 'If they've experienced it, they know it,' Serge said. 'They don't have to understand.' He repeated his line that they're paying customers attending by free will.

'Indeed,' said Tom, 'and perhaps the proposition that as long as you're a paying customer, if you're a child, it's okay to turn up and get a bit of discussion of rape shoved in your face.'

The grubby guru was blasé. 'If they are, they know what they're there for. They know what they're doing. That's why they're there.'

I heard the Uncle Jim speech for the first time, late at night, at my mother's desk, just six weeks before the trial. Each time we uncovered disturbing material, a sober resolve crystallised within me: Benhayon's words needed to be heard in a courtroom.

It can't happen to an innocent child?

cxlii The storyteller

Asked by Smark to explain his teaching on 'energetic responsibility', the plaintiff answered that 'everything that we do and touch comes with a quality of vibration that can potentially harm or heal another person.' He offered an example:

> If I do pornography, and I don't, but if I did, and I did it in a private room and nobody knew about it — I'm talking legal stuff, nobody knows about it, it's my private domain; when I hold a baby, that energy comes into that baby, whether I like it or not, because it's part of my being. Therefore even if the baby is fully clothed, there is a sexual intrusion on that baby that can be registered.

That was the first day of the trial, not even two hours into the plaintiff's evidence in chief. Justice Lonergan's Associate, working before the bench, stopped what she was doing when he said it. Frowning deeply, she peered across the court, scanning every face at the bar table and beyond. It was never going to be an ordinary trial.

The jury were given names of children who'd stayed in Benhayon's home unaccompanied by a parent or legal guardian. We'd won court orders compelling him to provide a sworn statement in which he'd listed fifteen children aged ten to seventeen who'd stayed between 1995 and 2015. Twelve were girls. The three boys were over sixteen. Several girls had lived with the Benhayon family for more than a year, with one staying for three years from the age of fifteen and working full-time as receptionist at the Goonellabah clinic. The list was limited because Benhayon excluded his kids' peer group friends who'd visited for sleepovers, whose names he said he had 'no reason to recall'. It was an odd distinction to make, but Tom didn't pursue it.

But the SC did raise Benhayon's recurring line about children viewing pornography. He'd referred to it several times while giving evidence, volunteering it where it was irrelevant to the questions. 'That's a theme that you're somewhat repetitive about, isn't it?'

'I have to contextualise what you're distorting,' said the plaintiff.

'Well, I'm only talking about how much you talk about it,' said Tom, 'because you talk about it a fair bit, don't you?'

'I present the realities. We have to get responsible.'

The lawyer called for an audio extract from Josh Robertson's 2012 interview with Benhayon. The journalist laughed when I told him that Serge had produced his own recording of the interview in discovery. Josh had gained permission to record and was not aware that his interviewee was recording him. 'We didn't see any equipment. He must have been wearing a wire,' he said.

Josh had asked Serge about his bankruptcy, as well as the financial operations of his College charity, and the plaintiff had diverted to raving about his fixations.

> Child pornography is out of control as we know. The kids are doing porn on their mobile phones as young as nine and twelve. Some of the obscenities that they're being involved in like splitting, girls getting made to bleed and things like that.

He told Josh that families confided in him like a pastor.

> You get to hear stories that aren't discussed at dinner tables. Things like splitting, it was something that I was shocked when I first heard that. But when I started asking and they said, "Yes. I've heard of that. That's what's going on. And it's not just in any school…"

The journalist interrupted: 'Splitting?'

Benhayon continued.

> It's where older boys go with younger girls and the game is to make them bleed. So that they can boast that the girl was bleeding. They try and put

three fingers up there or sometimes boast the size of their penis if they split them with their own penis that sort of thing.

Josh spoke hesitantly. 'Okay. That's news to me.'

'Yeah, me too, when I first heard of it,' said Serge. 'Plus they film each other doing sex with their phones and that sort of thing.'

I won court orders to obtain the recording of the EDG session where he'd alleged 'splitting' was perpetrated in Goonellabah on girls between ten and twelve years old, but Team Benhayon claimed it was not in his possession; consumed by a rogue bonfire perhaps. As late as 2016, his followers continued to blog the tale as an example of the Astral world's depravity. EDG notes and other recordings were also riddled with Benhayon's references to kids viewing porn and engaging in sex acts.

He was on the back foot when Tom questioned him about his 'gruesome' descriptions, less ready with his answers, and I'll never understand why he wasn't better prepared. I'd described that material in my pleadings. Tom thought I'd given him too much notice of what we would throw at him, but I reasoned that if Benhayon was going to settle before the trial, it was better for me if he did so sooner, and more likely if he was forewarned of the case against him. I'd also blogged about his 'splitting' yarn in 2013 — asking similar questions to those Tom put to him. Smark must have warned his client how such utterances would come across. It led me to ask David Millikan whether Serge had a crucifixion complex, but the Reverend put it down to pig-headed arrogance and garden-variety stupidity; the plaintiff having convinced himself he knew better than his first-class lawyer. It seems he didn't contemplate that surrounding himself with yes-artists and refusing to countenance criticism might result in decisions that would come back and belt him.

'When you were asked about it,' said Tom, 'did you make any detailed enquiries to find out precisely where it was happening?'

'I did, actually.'

'And who was involved?'

Serge said he had stopped short of asking who was involved.

'Did you alert any authorities to the existence of this?'

He said he notified a school teacher at one school.

'What about child welfare authorities, or police?'

'Well, I passed it on to the school teacher to take care of it, because I only heard it from one parent and it wasn't happening to their child, so I said it had to be reported to the school teacher, and I did, and the school teacher said that they were aware of it.'

'So you had only one person's name to pass on as a potential source of information to maybe chase the problem to its source?'

'As a concerned parent, yes.'

In his closing, Tom said to the jury, 'If you had the care of a child, whether it was your own or someone else's, would you be happy to entrust it to Mr Benhayon? Would you let him tell some of his stories to that child or not?' He was more expressive than during his examinations of witnesses. His tone was scathing. 'Of course not,' he said.

cxliii Formalities

'I say to you Universal Medicine is a scam.' That's how Tom began to sum up the evidence. Earlier that day, he'd played to a full house, and had argued that a number of the defamatory imputations in Benhayon's claim were not conveyed within my blog and tweets. At the morning break, however, UM's sentries were absent from the exit for the first time in four weeks. In the corridor, a patient looking Smark, bewigged head slightly bowed, held the door of a conference room open for a subdued Serge, and followed him inside.

When court reconvened, Benhayon and Miranda were gone, and as Tom's address continued, residual Sons of God skulked out one and two at a time. We'd swapped sides with Benhayon's team to be closest to the jury,

O'Regan opting not to lurk behind my new seat, and Serge never came back. Natalie took his place beside Fletcher through Tom's closing, and David Millikan said she looked tragic and lonely, eyes bloodshot and swollen. The following week, she was gone too, and through Smark's closing and until the end, Deborah Benhayon accompanied his lawyers to court, trailed by the adhesive Alan. I hadn't properly appreciated until the trial that she was the real deputy in Serge's dirty commerce.

At the end of that fourth week, an acquaintance spied the extraordinary ordinary plaintiff at Sydney airport, an oversized bald bodyguard accompanying him home. The jury commenced deliberations on October fourth, the end of the fifth week, and Tom, again without permission, took off with Janet on a holiday to Japan. Smark plunged into another trial. No one could guess how long the jury would take to reach unanimity on more than two hundred questions, and the following week gave nervous onlookers plenty of time to second guess the process. Matthew Richardson was one of the hand-wringers, voicing doubts over my preference for a jury trial, and even Louise was rethinking, speculating that Justice Lonergan might have been more favourable than the jurors whose decision we did not yet know.

'Knock it off,' I said. 'You lawyers worry too much.'

'It's a fraud,' Tom continued in his closing address, 'and Mr Benhayon is a fraudster and a conman and I will be showing you that in his own words.' The silk explained how people are attracted to scams, acknowledging that a lot of problems the guru raised were genuine, and that's how he appealed to a range of people, including the very vulnerable. 'Some of them are desperate for answers and they come and if someone is offering them what seems like the right answer, they follow on, they join up.'

The jurors were more relaxed after Serge's cheerleaders cleared out, more inclined to smile and nod, and I'd wager that no matter what they thought of me and my case, they liked Mr Molomby and had warmed to his authoritative but personable bearing — the kind anyone would want in an advocate for their case. I was in no hurry for them to return. Their deliberations were the first real days off I'd had since the previous

Christmas, prior to producing my Unpacking UM films. On the public holiday that week, Riz and I took the ferry to Taronga zoo and found ourselves identifying with the chimpanzees shambling around their enclosure, picking at each other's fleas. On the Friday, the jury considerately sent a note to Justice Lonergan to say they'd have their answers by noon, Monday, October fifteen.

'There are people out there with real problems,' Tom told them. 'The issue is the solutions he offers.' On the imputation that Benhayon engages in bizarre sexual manipulation to make money for his business, he said that 'it's pretty obvious that everything he does is aimed at making money for his business, and the evidence suggests he's been very successful at that. "Bizarre sexual manipulation" though? What he did to Ms Rockett was manipulative, saying those things to try to get information out of her. A lot of his sexual circus, the hermaphroditic orgasms, some of the things he said about love and relationships, that sort of thing — what's it there for? It's there to somehow influence people in their behaviour and obviously to incline them towards him and his scheme of things.'

The silk emphasised that consent obtained by deception is not real consent and argued that Benhayon was deceiving people by saying in substance '"I have this magic. I have this voodoo I can do on you and it will make you better." That is conning people into agreeing and that's not a real consent.' He added, 'it is very clearly proved that Mr Benhayon intentionally indecently touched Ms Rockett during that consultation in 2005.'

The only UM presence in court by then was glum Natalie with Fletcher, O'Regan, Alan, and another stalwart or two. Who knows how the other delicate souls would have coped with the Senior Counsel sealing our case? 'Where does the money go?' he continued. 'The money all goes to Mr Benhayon. The whole extended Benhayon family lives off Universal Medicine. In analysing it, you'd have to say that on the deck of the good ship Benhayon the money is sloshing around ankle deep.'

Into the second day of his two and a half day address, as he covered the examples of the plaintiff's mendacity, Tom came to the question, 'Is Mr Benhayon crazy? Does he really believe it, or is he a crook? You know I'm saying he's a crook, because — think of it this way — a crazy person lives in their craziness. They really believe that's their real universe. A crazy person doesn't slip, as Mr Benhayon has done several times, out of their crazy world into the real world.'

The lawyer returned to his question about healing symbols bumping around in the mailbag. 'He just hadn't thought whether or not it would clear all the other mail. But according to his position he doesn't have to think about it, he just gets it from The Ageless Wisdom, with no thought at all. That slipping between the two worlds, that's the mask slipping, and he's back in the normal world thinking up the story. So another fuse gone with the Ageless Wisdom. Perhaps the Ageless Wisdom is showing its age...'

Throwing off at Benhayon's incoherent oratory style was standard among UM's detractors, but Tom credited our adversary as a highly experienced public performer, used to being before an audience, and able to 'keep the words flowing very effectively'. The lawyer recounted a catalogue of his fibs; his denial of conducting ovarian readings, and pretending kids weren't in the room during his sex talk, but boasting of his sporting achievements was an occasion on which the plaintiff had lied to his own lawyer. Tom referred to the point in the cross-examination where he suggested that none of Serge's claims about representative sport were true and received the answer, 'Technically no.'

'Now, where's the technical about that?' The silk paused and fixed the jury with his fox-like eyes. 'Not Mona Lisa anymore, huh? Mona Liar. The person who sat opposite you in the witness box and lied his head off was not Pythagoras or Leonardo da Vinci, it was Serge Benhayon, conman from Goonellabah. That lie was told in exactly the same way as he gave all his evidence, and one of the things that means is you cannot judge whether someone like that is telling the truth or telling lies by how he does it, because he does it all the same seamless way. The lies come easily, you only catch them when you've got some real ammunition to do it.' Tom reached his summation: 'You cannot believe a word he says.'

The jury kept their promise and bang on midday on Monday, the message came that they were ready. In court was a line-up of reporters and a row of observers, none I recognised as associated with UM. Only Deborah and Alan showed up on Serge's side. It was an unceremonious procedure where the jury foreman handed the sheaf of answers to the court officer, who passed them to Her Honour. It was expected the parties and the judge would need at least an hour to check them for errors or omissions and analyse the outcome as a whole. The court staff made copies so that each side could inspect them, with an appointment to reconvene after lunch. Tom was still on holiday, so led by Louise, we did not look at the answers until we'd reached the privacy of chambers.

'All stand!' said the court officer. Justice Lonergan made her exit, the door closed behind her, Nick Olson bundled his things and Louise flew for the door, beating him out. Meri and I scrambled behind her, and trotted, practically running in her wake as she strode up Phillip Street, answers in hand, robes billowing; clerks, construction workers and cops quick-stepping out of her way.

Toward the end of Tom's address, he asked the jurors to review copies of my complaints to regulatory authorities. 'They are well presented, they are thoughtfully written, they are carefully researched, they are responsible in their tone and their attitude and respectful of the authorities that they're directed to. They are really well done...' His words were a humbling balm. 'She was raising these issues with them in an impeccable way. Now, that's a real sign of what her approach was overall.'

At chambers, Louise darted up the steps and held the lift for us, muttering about slow coaches. The second the elevator doors closed, her eyeballs were on the document, a raise of the eyebrows, a frown, a tentative smirk, another frown, a flip of a page, the lift doors opened and she shot out, Meri and I scampering after her. Halfway along the corridor she pushed the document back at me, pointing to a troubling finding on the first page. The jury had found that imputation 3(a), that Benhayon had intentionally indecently touched me, had been conveyed by my blog. 'Oh shit,' I said, my hopes plummeting. I never believed that meaning could be gleaned from that publication, and I'd maintained that if the jury found that it was, they were not on my side; we'd be cooked.

'Ms Rockett has, in these publications and in the vast bulk, if not all, of her activity, of which you've got very ample evidence, acted reasonably and responsibly, and one key thing I haven't mentioned so far — with no possible benefit to herself,' Tom told the court. 'She has done this in the public interest with only the risk of it damaging her, as it obviously has. Public benefit, the importance of these public issues has been her flag right from the start, and she's achieved a number of significant things; those regulatory authorities that took action, and the recognition that she's got from Professor Dwyer, for example.'

'You'd think they'd try harder to not look like a cult,' Louise commented after the UM contingent trickled out during the early hours of Tom's closing argument.

'You wait,' I said to her. 'They'll all pile back in for Smark's summing up.'

'They wouldn't be that obvious would they?' she said.

Greig, Baldwin, the Johnstons, and other devotees who'd exited the court a few days before, streamed back in for Smark's final swings at the troll. Stewart sat beside me as Smark reiterated that the targets of Benhayon's hands were fully clothed, and argued that as a society that practices religious tolerance we shouldn't mock beliefs we don't agree with, as the defendant had in deliberately intending to harm his client. He topped that with an assertion that the plaintiff was neither mad or bad. 'I suggest to you that when you look at Mr Benhayon, as imperfect as he is, exaggerating his sporting achievements… you still don't conclude that he's either of those. You would conclude he is a man of strong, unusual religious beliefs that he is seeking to teach and spread…' Ten minutes into Smark's address, Stewart began to fidget and check his phone. Twenty minutes in, he stood, buttoned his jacket and said he wanted to get back to the office to tie up loose ends. Benhayon wasn't delusional or a con artist, according to Smark, just religious.

It wasn't that I was confident during the jury's deliberations, I was resigned, and willing to wait. We'd thrown everything at it — there was nothing more we could do. Only once did I become properly anxious, waking suddenly one night, wheezing, with a panicked thought that the jurors might buy Smark's argument about religious belief, and conclude that the plaintiff was merely quirky and ultimately harmless. In daylight hours though, with a clearer mind, I estimated that they were too intelligent for that. The court would convene briefly at the beginning and end of each day of deliberation, and whenever the jury room door opened, Louise caught glimpses of a whiteboard and a flip chart; binders open on a table peppered with highlighters and pens. They were going about it professionally.

The panel maintained their inscrutable composure as Smark over-stretched an argument vital to his client's case: 'You do not prove, or you do not have to accept proof, that someone is dishonest — that is generally dishonest, has a dishonest character — because they've told one lie. You know that Mr Benhayon has told one lie at least… Why he did it? Who knows. Does that support a general allegation of dishonesty?'

Stewart messaged from his office. 'I couldn't listen to it,' he texted. 'After five minutes, I knew you'd won.'

I wasn't so sure.

Louise rifled the pages as she strode, her finger landing on another finding as she reached her chambers where Madeline waited on her feet. 'They found that imputation 3(a) was proven true,' she said.

'Oh shit,' I said somewhat more breathlessly. We'd proven the ovarian reading was intentional indecent touching.

Finalising, Tom said, 'Mr Smark, I've got no doubt, will say to you something about freedom of belief, freedom of religion. The real issue in this case is not freedom of religion or freedom of belief, it's freedom to criticise and bring to account people who propagate bizarre and cruel and dangerous ideas and exploitative practices and that is what Ms Rockett has been trying to achieve from the start…'

Restrained as he was, there was note of triumph in his tone, and while his posture was always steady and upright, he seemed to stand taller. 'If Mr Smark is going to say there's freedom of religion, I'll say, sure, but there's not freedom of fraud. And that's what we're talking about here.' He repeated the word with all the gravity that Henry di Suvero had applied over two years before, 'fraud.'

After lunch we returned to court for an anticlimactic formality. Her Honour made no announcements or comments on the jury's answers. No one found any anomalies among them or raised objections. Justice Lonergan thanked the jury for their service and dismissed them. They rose, and without looking over to the bar table or public gallery, left the court, and dispersed back into the anonymity of Sydney's throngs. It was only Deborah with Nick Olson now, and as soon as the door closed behind Her Honour, those last remnants of Team UM vanished into the ether.

Less hurried, Meri, Louise and I gathered our belongings. Again, just a few members of the public were in court, and the row of waiting journalists looked a little stunned. They were yet to receive the jury's answers. 'Should I?' I said to Louise.

She gave the nod.

I faced the press and told them, 'I won.'

Epilogue

cxliv The verdict

The journalists seemed startled. Perhaps they weren't sure whether to believe it. 'I've had some pretty significant wins on the defence of truth,' I told them.

The jury found that sixteen of Benhayon's claimed imputations were not conveyed by my publications. Those, therefore, were eliminated, and did not require a defence. Of the forty-three imputations found to be carried, the following were proven true:

1. Serge Benhayon had intentionally indecently touched his client Esther Rockett during a consultation in his treatment room.
2. Serge Benhayon had intentionally indecently touched a number of his clients in his treatment room.
3. Serge Benhayon instructed students at Universal Medicine training workshops to touch the genitals of victims of sexual abuse.
4. Serge Benhayon has an indecent interest in young girls as young as ten whom he causes to stay at his house unaccompanied.
5. Serge Benhayon is the leader of a socially harmful cult.
6. Serge Benhayon is the leader of Universal Medicine, a group which to his knowledge, engages in misleading conduct in promoting the healing services it offers.
7. Serge Benhayon is the leader of Universal Medicine, a group which to his knowledge, makes false claims about healing that cause harm to others.

8. Serge Benhayon as the leader of Universal Medicine exploits the followers of that group through his false and harmful teachings.
9. Serge Benhayon is dishonest.
10. Serge Benhayon is the leader of Universal Medicine, a group which to his knowledge preys on cancer patients.
11. Serge Benhayon engages in inappropriate conduct towards women.
12. Serge Benhayon dishonestly promotes fraudulent ideas of karma for self-gain.
13. Serge Benhayon engages in bizarre sexual manipulation to make money for his business.
14. Serge Benhayon is a hypocrite because his Esoteric Healing has death as its goal.
15. Serge Benhayon has persuaded followers to shun loved ones who won't join his cult.
16. Serge Benhayon denigrates life and glorifies death.
17. Serge Benhayon is the leader of a socially dangerous cult.
18. Serge Benhayon is the leader of a socially harmful cult, which to his knowledge had engaged in dishonest healing practices.
19. Serge Benhayon, the leader of Universal Medicine, had exploited children by having them vouch for Universal Medicine's dishonest healing practices.
20. Serge Benhayon has engaged in bullying to stop Esther Rockett exposing that he is guilty of inappropriate behaviour with children.
21. Serge Benhayon is guilty of inappropriate behaviour with children.
22. Serge Benhayon is not a fit person to hold a Working With Children Certificate.
23. Serge Benhayon vilifies people with disabilities.
24. Serge Benhayon is the leader of a socially harmful cult that is paternalistic to women.
25. Serge Benhayon is sexually manipulative of his cult followers.
26. Serge Benhayon preys on cancer patients.

27. Serge Benhayon exploits cancer patients by targeting them to leave him bequests in their wills.
28. Serge Benhayon is a charlatan who makes fraudulent medical claims.
29. Serge Benhayon swindles cancer patients.
30. Serge Benhayon was to inherit the bulk of a follower's million-dollar estate as a result of his exercising undue influence on her.
31. Serge Benhayon is the leader of an exploitative cult.
32. Serge Benhayon is engaged in a healing fraud that harms people.
33. Serge Benhayon makes bogus healing claims.
34. Serge Benhayon is guilty of exploitative behaviour.
35. There are reasonable grounds to believe the plaintiff intentionally sexually preyed upon his client Esther Rockett by administering an "ovarian reading" during a consultation in his treatment room.
36. There are reasonable grounds to believe the plaintiff had intentionally sexually preyed upon his clients.
37. There are reasonable grounds to believe the plaintiff had intentionally indecently touched a number of his clients in his treatment room.

Just one defence needed to be upheld for each publication for my case to succeed. The truth defences prevailed for fifteen of the eighteen publications in issue. The honest opinion defence succeeded for seventeen publications, and the defence of statutory qualified privilege succeeded for all publications, that is, the jury found my publishing of all of them was reasonable in the circumstances.[114]

Tom's less is more approach to evidence — tendering only short excerpts of the Benhayon's materials — was a masterstroke. The jury didn't need to hear every mad thing Serge had spouted — just enough — and therefore experienced the antithesis of cult conversion. Spared the love-bombing, they received a distillation of his lies, self-contradictions and grubby behaviour, under rigorous questioning, and could not be misled by the mass of pseudo-spiritual padding that enveloped his dross.

Interestingly, they found that I'd proven that Benhayon is dishonest, but not that he was delusional. 'You did too good a job of arguing that he's a con-artist!' I mock complained to Tom. It didn't matter in the final reckoning because they found that I had a reasonable and material basis to form such an opinion. And Serge's defeat ensures that he can never sue anyone again for saying he is any of the things found to be true. I'd proven that he's the universal predator, and he'll wear those findings as a cloak of infamy as long as he lives. As Justice Lonergan remarked in a post-trial ruling: 'It was, for the defendant, a comprehensive victory, and for the plaintiff, a comprehensive defeat.'

'Cult Leader Cops Rockett' was the headline in *The Northern Star*.

cxlv Lara 2020

Nothing could be more Esoteric than stubbornly denying three separate court findings that Universal Medicine is a harmful cult. Ruling on Graham's applications for full-time care of Lara, the UK Family Court made its own finding in 2019, affirmed in April 2020 by the High Court. Lord Justice Jackson of the High Court's Appeals bench had no illusions about the manipulations deployed by Benhayon's ilk, writing of Fran:

> She now approaches the arrangements for Lara on the basis that she knows best and that the father is someone from whom Lara is to be protected. She views Universal Medicine as a vital and benign entity. She has not begun to understand the substance of the judge's findings and the concerns expressed by others. That is how cults work.[115]

The Family Court judge had remarked that the findings of fact in Benhayon versus Rockett were such that no reasonable parent could ignore them. Yet Fran did. He found that she had not read the ruling or taken any interest in the evidence that led to it. Still, he'd stopped short of changing the shared parenting arrangement, stating his reluctance to disrupt the bond between mother and daughter.

At the High Court hearings, at risk of losing access to her child, Fran reiterated all her denials and accusations. Lord Justice Jackson noted that it was 'particularly striking that [the mother] should promote suspicions about the father, despite the lack of any evidence, when she is at the same time impervious to proven allegations against Benhayon.'

On Fran invoking the European Human Rights Conventions, the Appeals panel ruled that the freedom to manifest one's beliefs is still subject to necessary limitations to protect the health, morals, rights and freedoms of others. 'In matters of religion,' wrote Lord Justice Jackson, 'as in all other aspects of a child's upbringing, the interests of the child are the paramount consideration…The mother's rights to protection from coercion and to freedom of belief do not confer upon her the right to harm others.'

Yet, despite their ruling that the Family Court judge had failed to protect Lara, the Appeals Justices also gave Fran one more chance to sever ties with UM, and deferred the final determination to another hearing in June 2020 before the High Court's Family Division. By then, Graham was desperate. He told me of his fears that Fran might succeed in her persistent delay tactics, and that he couldn't cope if proceedings went on much longer. The courts kept returning Lara to harm, and his relationship with her was deteriorating by the day. Britain was in pandemic lockdown, and the ten year old was resisting contact. On the days that she did stay with him, she lashed out with temper tantrums and tried to run away from home.

Fran was far from the only UM believer to disregard the court judgments. Simone Benhayon, in a letter to her swim school clients, aired denials typical of those circulated by UM's subscribers. Omitting mention of the success of my truth defence, and the thirty-seven allegations proven by her father and his supporters' own words and behaviour, she wrongly asserted that I'd only won on an opinion argument, 'meaning if she believed it, it's accepted…' Even the opinion defence required me to have a proper material and rational basis for my views.

Unsurprisingly, defectors report that Serge blamed everyone but himself for his failure, telling his congregation that they were at fault for being in the wrong energy. The majority of his followers still cling to the cult, irreparably sullying their own reputations by continuing their association.

Fran squandered her last chance. At the final hearing, High Court Justice Williams found that she'd made no genuine effort to break from Unimed. She'd done nothing to disabuse her daughter of her UM beliefs, or toward undoing the damage to Graham and Lara's relationship. His Honour said: 'How can this child begin to move closer to her father when she still believes he lives outside "love"?'

He granted Graham full-time care, and prohibited contact between Fran and Lara for a period of weeks, to recommence only under professional supervision. The mother was barred from resuming her parental role until she'd thoroughly disentangled herself from UM's influence.

Graham understandably describes Fran as brainwashed — and I've struggled to find a more suitable term for such destructive extremes of irrational devotion. Despite his encouragement, she made no attempt to reunite with their daughter for nearly three years. The legal proceedings cost the father sixty thousand pounds, even with pro bono assistance in the later stages.

These sad events were not a problem of 'religious freedom'. Fran's were not acts of spiritual piety, but the mindless sabotages of a hostage to underhanded coercions; her cognitive capacity so damaged that she was incapable of making decisions in her child's best interests, or her own. Yet, she was only one of many cult parents who sacrificed the welfare of their kids for the shonk they worship like a God.

cxlvi The road trip

Justice Lonergan awarded me indemnity costs — the highest possible award — on the grounds that Benhayon unreasonably rejected my offer, over two and a half years earlier, to settle the case. She noted an 'apparent appetite for public humiliation of the defendant' in his refusal, and added that his own settlement terms suggested that his intention in bringing proceedings was to coerce me into falsely incriminating myself, and 'to censor further exposure and criticism of his controversial activities, rather than for the purpose of truly remedying asserted damage to his reputation.' Serge and his benefactors therefore paid Smark, Nick Olson, and my lawyers for every hour they spent on Team UM's futile stalling tactics and ill-conceived applications. Benhayon paid my legal team nearly one point one million dollars.

During the costs argument, Justice Lonergan took issue with Fletcher's 'disgraceful' correspondence around the time of my father's death, describing it as 'at best, unprofessional and most discourteous' and 'at worst, bullying and harassment'. The timing of the letters, their insults and their phrasing suggested 'that the solicitor who authored them had a lack of independence from, or objectivity about, the litigation.'[116] She called a special hearing to examine the circumstances, and Tom called Fletcher to the witness box, where she testified that the letter she'd signed and sent on the day of my father's funeral was mostly authored by Charles Wilson and Alison Greig. Her Honour referred the incident to the Legal Services Commissioner and following an investigation, Fletcher was officially reprimanded for unsatisfactory professional conduct and fined fifteen hundred dollars. The Queensland Bar Association did nothing about Wilson.

The Queensland claim also took the shuttle to Sirius. Raphael and Karam settled by vacating all costs orders and forgiving my debt. Some polite letters from my lawyers also saw the whole UM FACTS website and all the cult's defamatory articles taken down. The authors and publishers, including Serge, published retractions and apologies to me, but it would take another year to get my bankruptcy annulled and clear my debts. No compensation was available to me for the time I spent working on my defences or for lost income, and the costs to me were such that I may never recover.

Priced out of living in the Byron Shire, I began a long homeless road-trip as I put this story down — an attempt, perhaps futile, to exorcise the cult from my life. Despite submitting the court's findings and the evidence from the trial to authorities, no action has been taken to curtail Benhayon's predatory commerce. Unimed continues to operate and recruit, only more secretively, and its leadership are wealthier than ever. It's slipped back under the radar.

After the trial, I kept a promise to Tom to help thin out the mountain of paper that threatened to avalanche him at his desk, and as we worked, he volunteered his own ageless wisdom. He sensed that I'd been steamrolled one too many times and he advised that I shouldn't be surprised if I went through a range of emotions in the times ahead, and that others may not understand. 'When you've had an experience like you've had, it can be like getting out of jail,' he said. 'Yes, you're free, but you've paid for it.'

I'm not so sure I'm free.

His words were more helpful than Hayes', who urged me not to waste time, to enrol in a law degree right away. Suffice to say I opted to write my memoir instead. Even if I had the stomach for law, I'd probably end up just as broke representing underdogs and buried by student debt. Hayes should have picked up that I came to him in a raw new skin, smeared in the ashes of my old life. What I needed more than anything was a hug.

Charles Wilson told judges that I was not a fair opponent because I had nothing to lose. But someone who obeys the commandments of an empty charlatan would say that. Someone indoctrinated to fear their own humanity, who can only feel purpose when mouthing the words of the mob, will never comprehend what was at stake. The drive to prevent suffering is far from nothing. If there was one marked personal benefit, it was the allies I gained, from all walks of life, and to have, forever in my memory, the indelible voices of those who carefully examine all sides — to be able to ask how would they view this? How would they argue this? How do I? Even

Matthew Richardson apologised for his naysaying, but I wouldn't hear it — he helped keep my belly to the dirt. 'Spirits in the courtroom,' he muttered, with a shake of his head. 'I've never heard anything like it.'

Some months after the trial, I visited Reverend Millikan's mountaintop home, where the breathtaking views over the forested slopes of Kangaroo Valley might tempt a person to believe a God does exist. He gave me a tour of his 'free range' vege patch, stepping through the weeds to show off his dwarf fruit trees. 'They're the way of the future, Esther!' he sang out as he took a miniature peach tree in both hands. 'Small trees, full-sized fruit — you don't have to climb.'

He cooked a trout lunch and opened a bottle of posh bubbles, congratulating me on the 'stone-cold' way I'd 'dismantled the little rotter', and while I'm pleased some saw it that way, the undercurrent of protectiveness was an altogether different temperature. 'This is on Serrrrge!' he proclaimed as the cork bounced off his hand-hewn rafters. The award of costs meant he was paid for the expert report that went on to help Graham and Lara, and it allowed us to toast Benhayon seething at buying us a bottle of pranic pop.

Stewart was always optimistic he'd be paid, but Louise and Tom both said that they'd never expected it. When I reminded the silk of his question during our first conversation about whether the plaintiff had money, he gave his little laugh. 'I wasn't thinking about whether or not I'd recover my fee,' he said. 'What I saw was a defendant of scarce means in a fight against someone much wealthier. I didn't know whether you had a good case or not, I took it on because I wanted to make sure you got a fair trial.'

I'm ashamed that I'd not been properly awake to the fact that Tom really was the anti-Serge. Nothing the lawyer said or did indicated he was motivated by anything but justice. Having worked that way for decades without fanfare, most people would never recognise that the polite elderly man riding beside them on the five forty-five bus might be the fellow who gets their wrongful conviction overturned. Generous, always, he complimented me on my resilience, and I said that I think that the world is an unfair place. I strongly feel that we should use whatever we can spare to help those less able and less resourced.

'You know,' he said, 'that's exactly the way I feel too.'

Key, perhaps, to my foolhardy resilience was knowing that no amount of wishing or rituals or toil guarantees anything. In his Esoteric fantasy, Wilson probably believes my lack of faith is as pitiable as my penury — nothing to lose. But to know that the axe can fall at any time, that winning is as random as any other iteration of fate, and to use everything you've got to push for justice anyway, is not nothing — it's power. I like to think that's an understanding that Tom and I share. Still, the silk's estimation of fairness may have differed to mine. Of course Benhayon and his cult versus Rockett was never going to be a fair fight. We were never evenly matched. I was always going to beat them.

Afterword

- Benhayon and associates have made no public acknowledgment of the Supreme Court findings.
- After the trial, UM added a notice to its event advertising that attendance was restricted to persons eighteen years and older. The group has since withdrawn all event publicity. During the coronavirus pandemic, UM cancelled its overseas events, but continued to webcast its services from the Hall of Ageless Wisdom. Benhayon's followers publicly opposed coronavirus restrictions and vaccines.
- All UM events previously held at Tytherington's Sound Training Centre have been moved to secret locations.
- Simone Benhayon resigned her directorship of the Sound Foundation Community Care Charity at the end of September 2018, before the end of the Benhayon versus Rockett trial.
- In October 2018, Ballina Shire Council banned UM from hiring its venues. The Girl to Woman Festival was cancelled indefinitely.
- Sarah McIntyre released email messages between her mother, Benhayon, and Paula Fletcher, to Australia's ABC News. Benhayon had written to the dying woman that the Astral was trying to play with her money, and that her children were trying to destabilise her and invoke her sympathy: 'it is all an attack on the funds that will help The Hierarchy's work on Earth.'
- Sarah told the press that she was shocked at the level of planning that had gone into breaking up her mother's estate, and that Judith's gift to Benhayon of eight hundred thousand dollars in her final weeks 'was part of a strategy to make the estate look smaller and make the case for challenging the will weaker.'[117] Despite the jury's finding that Benhayon was a predatory charlatan who unduly influenced Judith, it was too late to remedy the injustice to Sarah and Seth. The family provision ruling could not be undone.

- ABC News' Josh Robertson reported that a child safety worker at the Lismore office of NSW's Department of Family and Community Services (FACS) had included a recommendation to attend Universal Medicine activities, including the Girl to Woman Festival, in the care plan of a vulnerable juvenile girl. The worker, a long-term UM member, remains employed at Lismore FACS.
- Deborah Benhayon stepped down from the Lismore Chamber of Commerce and Industry in November 2018. All the Chamber's business awards to Universal Medicine were rescinded.
- After the trial, Doctor Maxine Szramka resigned as spokeswoman for the Australian Doctors Federation and removed her testimonial material from UM websites. At the time of writing, Drs Malatt and Minford's material promoting Benhayon and UM remains online. Dr Samuel Kim remains an active promoter, citing his medical credentials in advertising himself as an Esoteric Practitioner.
- Sarah Broome became a registered psychologist and works for cult affiliated firm Fabic Behavioural Specialists that provides services to recipients of the National Disability Insurance Scheme. It operates in part from Benhayon's Unimed Brisbane premises.
- Serge Benhayon, Rachel Hall, Simon Asquith, and UM FACTS team members, Jonathan Baldwin, Isabella Benhayon, Désirée Delaloye, Alison Greig and Ray Karam published retractions of their defamations of Esther Rockett with apologies in 2019. Those remained online for twelve months.
- The published ruling in Benhayon versus Rockett has been used since the trial to make formal requests to educational institutions, community organisations and private employers that Unimed promoters among their staff or membership make undertakings not to introduce anything or anyone UM related to students, members, clients or staff without full disclosure.
- Late 2018, Professor Dwyer made a new complaint about UM to the NSW HCCC. The HCCC refused to publicly release its findings. A

complaint was also made to child safety authorities. The status of the Benhayons' Working with Children certifications are unknown.
- In 2019, Universal Medicine published a fine-print disclaimer on the home pages of its commercial websites stating that none of its beliefs or practices are evidence based.
- Evolve College's Chakra-puncture course was cancelled.
- Nick Farrow left Network Seven before the trial, but producer Stephen Rice, with reporter Matt Doran, completed a full *Sunday Night on Seven* episode on Universal Medicine which aired in February 2019. It included the footage taken at Lennox Head in 2017 and featured interviews with Esther, Pina, Matt Sutherland, and Sarah McIntyre, among others.
- In August 2019, state MP for Lismore, Janelle Saffin introduced a private members bill into New South Wales Parliament calling for a judicial inquiry into Universal Medicine's adverse influence in the Lismore region, particularly its promoters' infiltration of community groups and publicly funded workplaces. To date no inquiry has been launched.
- In 2019, Josh Robertson for ABC News reported on Sergeant Eric Walsh's involvement in UM's efforts to have Esther Rockett prosecuted. South Australian Police commenced an investigation, but did not release its findings.
- The media, including ABC News Australia, *The Australian Women's Weekly*, the BBC, *The Times of London*, and Vice World News continue to cover UM stories.
- Some footage of David Millikan's 2012 confrontation with the UM congregation was seen in an episode on Universal Medicine on Vice TV's *True Believers* series in 2022. It also showed Caroline Raphael, Ray Karam and Serryn O'Regan complaining to police after Millikan had left the premises.
- The University of Queensland refused to retract Christoph Schnelle's research papers. The editor of the *Journal of Medical Internet Research*

modified the authors' conflict of interest statements, and added corrigenda critical of the women's health paper's conclusions. Schnelle discontinued his doctoral studies, and in 2021, the authors retracted the papers on Esoteric Connective Tissue Therapy. Proposed hospital trials in Vietnam did not proceed.

o Ariana Ray was removed from the UK's register of social workers in April 2021 following an official finding that her continued promotion of Benhayon after the defamation trial constituted professional misconduct.[118] Janet Williams, mother of the fifteen year old girl who'd blogged in Benhayon's defence, continues to offer psychotherapy services to children and youth in Somerset.

o Lance's former wife, Anna, moved to Brisbane in 2021 to practise Esoteric healing, leaving their adolescent daughter in his full time care.

o Matthew Richardson was elevated to Senior Counsel in 2021. Lucy McCallum was appointed Chief Justice of the Australian Capital Territory. Louise Goodchild became a Federal Circuit Court magistrate.

o Henry di Suvero died in July 2020. A longtime, committed champion of civil liberties, he had a distinguished legal career in the United States and Australia. In 1974, he founded the not-for-profit Peoples College of Law in Los Angeles, a licensed, 'non-competitive, cooperative, student and community-run, progressive law school' dedicated to 'securing progressive social change and justice in society.' It continues to operate.[119]

List of characters

*An asterix indicates a pseudonym. Some names have been changed for privacy or legal reasons.
Those identified as UM acolytes were followers at the time of the events in this book.

Robert Anderson KC: Brisbane defamation barrister
Anna: UM acolyte, former wife of Lance
Simon Asquith: UM acolyte, UM media and publicity
Meri Ayala: Sydney paralegal
Alice A. Bailey: Edwardian era Theosophy author, Serge Benhayon's previous incarnation
Jonathan Baldwin: UM acolyte, UM FACTS Team, UM media and publicity, brother of Rebecca and Sarah
Rebecca Baldwin: UM acolyte, UM FACTS Team, UM media and publicity
Sarah Baldwin: UM acolyte, former partner of Matt Sutherland, wife of Ray Karam
Dr Jane Barker: General practitioner, UM acolyte and promoter
Mei Barnes: Brisbane barrister
Otto Bathurst: British film director, UM acolyte and promoter
Cameron Bell: Mullumbimby solicitor, Universal Law
Curtis Benhayon: Esoteric practitioner, youngest child of Serge Benhayon
Deborah Benhayon: First wife of Serge Benhayon, Universal Medicine Chief Financial Officer
Emmalee Benhayon: First wife of Michael Benhayon
Isabella Benhayon: Wife of Curtis Benhayon
Kelly Benhayon: Second wife of Michael Benhayon
Michael Benhayon: Esoteric practitioner, Glorious Music (GM Records) proprietor, third child of Serge Benhayon
Miranda Benhayon: Second wife of Serge Benhayon

Natalie Benhayon: Esoteric practitioner, director of UM companies, second child of Serge Benhayon

Serge Benhayon: Proprietor and leader of Universal Medicine

Simone Benhayon: Swim-coach, director of UM UK companies, eldest child (stepdaughter) of Serge Benhayon

Helena Blavatsky: Victorian era Theosophist

Hamish Broome: Journalist, UM acolyte, UM media and publicity

Sarah Broome: Psychologist, UM FACTS Team, UM event organiser and publicity

Mark Burton: Barrister, former army nurse and chaplain

Michelle Crowe: Esoteric practitioner, UM acolyte and promoter, sister of Odette

Désirée Delaloye: Serge Benhayon's personal assistant, UM FACTS Team, UM publicity

Dinah*: Mother of Joelle

Eric Dobbs*: Former husband of UM acolyte

Elizabeth Dolan: Registered nurse, Esoteric Breast Massage practitioner, UM acolyte and promoter

Matt Doran: Investigative journalist, Seven Network

Professor John Dwyer: Emeritus Professor of Medicine, UNSW

Ellen*: UM acolyte, former girlfriend of Heath

Tim Elliott: Investigative journalist

Jenny Ellis: Brisbane Esoteric Breast Massage practitioner, UM acolyte and promoter

Nick Farrow: Television producer

Paula Fletcher: Mullumbimby solicitor, Universal Law, wife of Cameron Bell, UM acolyte and promoter

Professor William Foley: Linguistics professor, UM acolyte

Fran*: UM acolyte, mother of Lara and former partner of Graham

Jean Gamble: Sydney psychotherapist, UM acolyte and promoter

Neil Gamble: Former casino boss, UM acolyte and promoter

Louise Goodchild: Sydney barrister for defence

Graham*: Former partner of UM acolyte, Fran; father of Lara
Kate Greenaway: Physiotherapist, UM acolyte and promoter
Alison Greig: Former law academic, UM FACTS Team, UM publicity, director of College of Universal Medicine charity
Haley*: child of UM acolytes, juvenile houseguest of Serge Benhayon
Hayes*: Byron Bay psychotherapist
Dr Rachel Hall: Brisbane dentist, UM acolyte and promoter
Louise Hay: New Age author
Heath: Former boyfriend of UM acolyte, Emma
Jane Hansen: Investigative journalist
Cynthia Hickman: Melbourne registered psychologist, UM acolyte and promoter
Ingrid: Housemate of Judith McIntyre, UM acolyte and promoter
Chris James: Musician, UM acolyte and promoter
Joelle*: Former tennis pupil of Serge Benhayon
Alan Johnston: Property developer, UM acolyte and promoter
Josephine Johnston: Wife of Alan Johnston, UM acolyte
Ray Karam: Ballina fruit shop owner, former police officer UM FACTS Team and UM promoter
Jane Keep: NHS HR consultant, Esoteric Breast Massage practitioner, UM acolyte and promoter
Dr Samuel Tae-Kyu Kim (Sam Kim): Lung specialist, UM acolyte and promoter
Klaus*: Investigator, Australian Not-for-profit and Charities Commission
Lance: Byron Bay business owner, former husband of UM acolyte, Anna
Lara*: child of UM acolyte
Leonie*: Lara's grandmother, Graham's mother
Nicola Lessing: Unimed Living company secretary, UM acolyte, UM publicity, wife of Christoph Schnelle
Clayton Lloyd: Second husband of Deborah Benhayon, UM acolyte, UM publicity

Justice Julia Lonergan: New South Wales Supreme Court judge, trial judge, Benhayon v Rockett
Associate Professor Rachel Lynwood: Sociology academic, UM acolyte and promoter
Madeline Shaw: Louise Goodchild's legal clerk
Dr Anne Malatt: Opthalmologist, UM acolyte and promoter
Marianna Masiorski: Registered psychologist, UM acolyte and promoter
Maura*: Esoteric practitioner, champion belcher
Justice Lucy McCallum: New South Wales Supreme Court judge
Judith McIntyre: UM acolyte, cancer patient
Sarah McIntyre: Daughter of Judith McIntyre
Seth McIntyre: Son of Judith McIntyre
Anne McRitchie: Director of College of UM charity, UM acolyte and promoter
Reverend Dr David Millikan: Uniting Church Minister, cult expert
Dr Eunice Minford: Belfast surgeon, UM acolyte and promoter
Tom Molomby SC: Senior Sydney barrister for defence
Brendan Mooney: Registered psychologist, UM acolyte and promoter
Mary-Louise Myers: Esoteric Breast Massage practitioner, UM acolyte and promoter
David Nicholson: Frome business owner, former husband of Simone Benhayon, UM acolyte
Michael Nicholson: Chartered accountant, owner of Upper Vobster Farm, UM acolyte and promoter
Tricia Nicholson: Wife of Michael Nicholson, owner of Upper Vobster Farm, UM acolyte
Stewart O'Connell: Sydney solicitor
Odette*: Sister of UM acolyte Michelle Crowe
Olga*: Former UM acolyte
Nick Olson: Sydney barrister
Serryn O'Regan: Solicitor, director of UM companies
Kieran Pehm: New South Wales Health Care Complaints Commissioner

Pina*: Former client of Serge Benhayon
Caroline Raphael: Registered psychologist, UM promoter
Ariana Ray: UK social worker, UM acolyte
Matthew Richardson: Sydney barrister for defence
Neil Ringe: Former acupuncturist, UM acolyte
Rosie*: Former patient of Dr Sam Kim
Riz*: Esther's longtime friend
Josh Robertson: Investigative journalist
Christoph Schnell: Financial planner, Biostatistics student, UM acolyte, husband of Nicola Lessing
Kieran Smark SC: Senior Sydney barrister for Serge Benhayon
Smith*: Sydney solicitor
Dr Amelia Stephens: Brisbane General Practitioner, UM acolyte and promoter
Amanda Stoker: Brisbane barrister
Matt Sutherland: Comedian, former partner of UM acolyte Sarah Baldwin
Henry di Suvero: Retired barrister
Dr Maxine Szramka: Rheumatologist, UM acolyte and promoter
Trish: Miranda Benhayon's mother
Sergeant Eric Walsh: South Australian police officer, UM acolyte
Janet Williams: Owner of The Lighthouse (UM hub in Somerset, England), UM acolyte and promoter, psychotherapist
Simon Williams: Chartered Accountant, owner of The Lighthouse, UM acolyte
Charles Wilson: Brisbane barrister, UM acolyte, director of College of Universal Medicine charity
David Wright: Mayor of Ballina

Acknowledgements

None of this, from exposure campaign to publication of this account, could have happened without the support of extraordinary people. I owe great thanks to the Rockett family, and in alphabetical order, Rob Anderson KC, Meri Ayala, Bruce Burke, Bruce Clarke, Kasha and Robin Clifford, JD, Diane D, Peter Daley, Jenny Dowell, Professor John Dwyer, Nick Farrow, Frederick Jordan Chambers, Friends of Science in Medicine, Heath Gibney, Louise Goodchild, Jane Hansen, Joelle and Dinah, Ros Hodgkins and Cult Information & Family Support, Dr Sue Ieraci, Mark J, Ros Keenan, Craig L, LawRight Brisbane, Robert Macindoe, Riley Martin, Carli McConkey, Sarah McIntyre, Ken McLeod, Reverend Dr David Millikan, Tom Molomby SC, Josie M, O'Brien Criminal and Civil Solicitors, Peter O'Brien, Stewart O'Connell, the late Mary Oldenburg, Olga, Stephen Rice, Matthew Richardson SC, Helen Roberts, Josh Robertson, Rosie and Joe, Janelle Saffin, Mattie S, the late Madeline Shaw, the Stevenson family, Amanda Stoker, Matt Sutherland, the late Henry di Suvero, Peter Tierney, Keith Williams.

Thank you to the supporters not named here who also helped with information, expertise, funds, and kindness.

Endnotes

Benhayon's self-published books are identified by the following abbreviations:

- o AOLTH: Benhayon, Serge. *An Open Letter to Humanity*. Unimed Publishing, Goonellabah, 2013.
- o ATOC: Benhayon, Serge. *A Treatise On Consciousness*. Unimed Publishing, Goonellabah, 2007.
- o ETR: Benhayon, Serge. *Esoteric Teachings & Revelations: A New Study for Mankind*. Unimed Publishing, Goonellabah, 2011.

- o LSH: Benhayon, Serge. *The Living Sutras of the Hierarchy*. Unimed Publishing, Goonellabah, 2009.
- o TWII: Benhayon, Serge. *The Way It Is: A Treatise on Esoteric Truth*. Unimed Publishing, Goonellabah, 2006.

---

[1] Reported by Hue Fortson Jr. American Experience. *Jonestown: The Life and Death of Peoples Temple*. US: PBS. 2007. https://www.pbs.org/wgbh/americanexperience/films/jonestown/
[2] https://chrisjames.net/store/silk-in-the-clouds/
[3] TWII, 2006, pp. 47-48.
[4] Ellingsen, Peter. 'The Guru, His Wife and the Followers', *The Age*, 26 June 2005. https://www.theage.com.au/national/the-guru-his-wife-and-the-followers-20050626-ge0erd.html
Funder, Rosie. 'Hillock of Peace', *Griffith Review*, October 2018. https://www.griffithreview.com/articles/hillock-of-peace/
[5] Benhayon, Serge. *Sermon 34*. Video. The Way of the Livingness, 30 April 2016.
[6] Leser, David. 'The Da Vinci Mode', *The Sydney Morning Herald*, 25 August 2012. www.smh.com.au/lifestyle/the-da-vinci-mode-20120820-24h50.html
[7] TWII, 2006, p.109.
[8] 'Cults, Sects and New Religious Movements: Universal Medicine', Cult Education Institute website, 15 January 2012. https://forum.culteducation.com/read.php?12,107998
[9] https://web.archive.org/web/20160619095343/http://www.courthousenews.com/2016/05/13/woman-drops-lawsuit-against-scientology.htm
[10] https://medicineandsergebenhayon.com/2012/09/03/illness-and-disease-are-healing/
[11] ETR, 2011, pp.273, 473.
[12] https://web.archive.org/web/20110201124734/http://www.esoteric-breast-massage.com/
[13] Benhayon, Serge. *The Study of Esoteric Medicine 1*. Audio. 20 February 2010.
[14] Serge Benhayon interviewed by Gayle Cue, *Interview 8*. Audio. 1 January 2012. https://study.universalmedicine.com.au/interviews
[15] TWII, 2006, pp.72, 77.
[16] ETR, 2011, p.615.
[17] ETR, 2011, pp.115, 428.
[18] ETR, 2011, pp.312, 406, 446.
[19] ETR, 2011, pp.283, 284.
[20] TWII, 2006, p.26; ETR, 2011, p.80, 296, 693.

21 ETR, 2011, p.599.
22 Jonestown survivor Laura Johnston Kohl - *AllOutAttack* Podcast w/ Harry Robinson - #2
https://youtu.be/LvJtjSD0J2g
23 LSH, 2009, p.240.
24 Benhayon, Serge. EDG Message 23, newsletter, undated.
25 Hume, Lynne. 'A Reappraisal of the Term "Cult" and Consideration of "Danger Markers" in Charismatic Religious Group', *Colloquium* 28, no. 1 (May 1996): 35—52.
26 Lifton, Robert Jay. *Destroying the World to Save It: Aum Shinrikyo, Apocalyptic Violence, and the New Global Terrorism*. 1st edition. New York: Picador, 2000, pp. 137, 138, 140-143.
27 https://thesoulfuldoctor.co.uk/blog/assisted-suicide-it-really-end/ 14 January 2012.
28 Hay, Louise. *Heal Your Body: The Mental Causes for Physical Illness and the Metaphysical Way to Overcome Them*. Hay House, 1984, p.4.
29 Ibid., p.21.
30 Woods, Judith. 'How positive thinking helped me beat cancer', *telegraph.co.uk*, 23 April 2007.
31 ETR, 2011, pp. 302, 587, 592, 606, 618.
32 Oppenheimer, Mark. 'The Queen of the New Age'; *New York Times Magazine*, 4 May 2008. http://www.nytimes.com/2008/05/04/magazine/04Hay-t.html
33 Hay, 1984, p.10.
34 Benhayon, Serge. *The Study of Esoteric Medicine*, 13, Part 1. Audio. 19 August 2011.
35 Benhayon, Serge. *Sermon 32*. Video. The Way of the Livingness, 26 March 2016; and ETR, 2011, p.296.
36 See Langone, M. D. *Recovery from Cults: Help for Victims of Psychological and Spiritual Abuse*. New York: W. W. Norton, 1995.
37 https://www.universalmedicine.com.au/questions/what-esoteric-breast-massage
38 Jung, Carl Gustav. 'The Philosophical Tree'. In *Alchemical Studies*, Vol. 13. The Collected Works of C. G. Jung. Princeton University Press, 1945, p.335.
39 Image: *Fury* by Yumiko Kayukawa.
40 Jung, Carl Gustav. *Psychology and Religion: West and East*. Vol. 11. 20 vols. The Collected Works of C. G. Jung. Princeton University Press, 1938, p.131. Jung, Carl Gustav. *Spirit in Man, Art, and Literature*. Vol. 15. 20 vols. The Collected Works of C. G. Jung. Princeton University Press, 1938, para 69.

Jung, Carl Gustav. *Aion: Researches into the Phenomenology of the Self.* Vol. 9, Part II. 20 vols. The Collected Works of C. G. Jung. Princeton University Press, 1951, p.14.

41 Benhayon, Serge. *The Study of Esoteric Medicine 1.* Audio. 20 February 2010.

42 ETR, 2011, p.526.

43 https://web.archive.org/web/20140211153649/http://womeninlivingness.com/2013/08/21/men-periods-and-the-our-cycles-period-app/

44 https://factsaboutuniversalmedicine.wordpress.com/2013/05/07/monopolizing-sexual-abuse-outrage-and-the-esoteric-kamikaze/

45 Benhayon, Serge. *The Study of Esoteric Medicine 11.* Part 2. Audio. 13 May 2011.

46 Storr, Anthony, *Feet of Clay: A study of gurus*, Harper Collins, 1997, p.232.

47 https://web.archive.org/web/20090602211743/http://lighthouse-uk.com/clinic/esoteric-body-work

48 ETR, 2011, pp.519, 544.

49 https://web.archive.org/web/20070829072525/http://universalmedicine.com.au/whatif

50 https://www.gov.uk/government/publications/the-way-of-the-livingness-the-religion-of-the-soul-trust/the-way-of-the-livingness-the-religion-of-the-soul-trust-charity-commission-decision

51 Dolan, Elizabeth. 'Esoteric Developers Group 18th Feb 2012' and 'EDG 17/12/2011' student notes.

52 The Sound Foundation is now 'Sound Foundation Community Care', not to be confused with several other UK charities named The Sound Foundation.

53 https://www.thirdsector.co.uk/charity-commission-hands-action-plan-health-charity/governance/article/1222011

54 Benhayon, 2007, ATOC, p.264.

55 Sydney had higher than average rainfall for six months out of twelve in both 1989 and 1990. However, days of high rainfall tended to be clustered. The rain was not constant.

56 https://truthaboutuniversalmedicine.com/2014/06/06/meeting-serge-benhayon-a-meeting-on-the-edge-of-eternity/

57 https://truthaboutsergebenhayon.com/2012/07/27/experience-as-a-cancer-patient/

58 Appendix 3 to Alison Greig's submission to NSW Parliamentary Inquiry in to False and Misleading Health Information and Practices, p.46 of 49.

59 https://truthaboutuniversalmedicine.com/2014/06/06/meeting-serge-benhayon-a-meeting-on-the-edge-of-eternity/

60 https://truthaboutsergebenhayon.com/2012/07/27/experience-as-a-cancer-patient/
61 https://truthaboutsergebenhayon.com/2012/07/27/experience-as-a-cancer-patient/
62 https://truthaboutuniversalmedicine.com/2014/06/06/meeting-serge-benhayon-a-meeting-on-the-edge-of-eternity/
63 Benhayon, Serge. *The Study of Esoteric Medicine 11*, Part 2, 13 May 2011.
64 https://medicineandsergebenhayon.com/2016/02/20/the-big-c-why-me/
65 https://medicineandsergebenhayon.com/2015/12/31/congratulations-you-have-cancer/
66 https://medicineandsergebenhayon.com/2013/07/10/getting-away-with-it/
67 https://medicineandsergebenhayon.com/2015/02/14/cancer-is-it-bad-luck-or-a-blessing-in-disguise/
68 ETR, 2011, p.619.
69 https://www.dailytelegraph.com.au/news/nsw/doctor-sent-woman-for-two-years-of-new-age-healing-in-a-galaxy-far-far-away-for-a-cough-costing-her-35000/news-story/1be290c03d2f44cdf8d87e42c0d8a62b
70 TWII, 2006, p.17. AOLTH, 2013, p.642.
71 'Final Report, Inquiry Into The Promotion of False and Misleading Health-Related Information and Practices' (New South Wales Parliament, November 2014), pp. 11, 15.
72 'Transcript Report of Proceedings, Day 2, Hearing, Inquiry Into The Promotion of False and Misleading Health-Related Information and Practices,' New South Wales Parliament, 3 September 2014, p.2.
73 Dolan, Elizabeth Esoteric Development Group notes, 20 August, 2011.
74 *Benhayon v Rockett* [2016] NSWSC 1210, 30 August 2016.
75 archival.sl.nsw.gov.au/Details/archive/110072497
76 Benhayon, Serge. *Esoteric Medicine 11*, Part 2, The Study of Esoteric Medicine, 13 May 2011.
77 *An Interview with Judith McIntyre*, Evolving Media, 2014. https://evolvingmedia.com.au/our-work/video-production/an-interview-with-judith-mcintyre/
78 https://www.universalmedicine.com.au/questions/what-esoteric-breast-massage
79 http://womeninlivingness.com/2013/08/25/my-first-esoteric-breast-massage-unveiling-the-hidden-harm-of-pornography/
80 Singer, Margaret Thaler, and Robert Jay Lifton. *Cults in Our Midst: The Continuing Fight Against Their Hidden Menace*. San Francisco, CA: Jossey-Bass, 2003, p.317.
81 ETR, 2011, p.695.

[82] https://www.pozible.com/project/196122
[83] *McIntyre v O'Regan* [2015] NSWSC 1985.
[84] https://www.ingridunfolding.com/single-post/2017/07/25/preparing-to-pass-over-and-having-fun-with-it
[85] https://www.smh.com.au/national/nsw/universal-medicines-serge-benhayon-to-inherit-bulk-of-devotees-milliondollar-estate-20151228-glvl7u.html
[86] TWII, 2006, p.110.
[87] *Kim, Samuel Tae-Kyu* [2017] NSWMPSC 4 (8 May 2017).
[88] Benhayon, Serge. *The Study of Esoteric Medicine 12*, Part 2. Audio. 29 July 2011.
[89] King Pyrrhus was an Ancient Greek opponent of the Roman Empire. While his army won several battles against the Roman forces, the victories resulted in catastrophic troop losses for victors. The Romans, however, had vast reserves. After winning the Battle of Heraclea, Pyrrhus is reported to have said words to the effect of 'another win like that and I'll be completely annihilated.'
[90] http://publichealth.jmir.org/2018/1/e6/
https://trialsjournal.biomedcentral.com/articles/10.1186/s13063-017-2055-8
[91] Forum. Video. The Way of the Livingness, 11 July 2015.
[92] Forum. Video. The Way of the Livingness, 9 April 2016.
[93] Benhayon, Serge. *Sermon 43*. Video. The Way of the Livingness, 1 January 2017.
[94] https://theconversation.com/why-consumers-need-better-protection-from-dodgy-health-care-the-case-of-universal-medicine-95144#comment_1608518
[95] Benhayon, Serge. *Sermon 37*. Video. The Way of the Livingness, 30 July 2016.
[96] https://web.archive.org/web/20130131131950/http://www.medicalobserver.com.au/news/government-blocks-ywca-documents
[97] Forum. Video. The Way of the Livingness. 1 January 2017.
[98] Benhayon, Serge. Esoteric Developers Group Presentation. Audio. 15 October 2011.
[99] *Benhayon v Rockett* [2018] NSWSC 1312, (No. 4).
[100] Benhayon, Serge. Esoteric Developers Group presentation. Audio. 27 September 2008.
[101] Benhayon, Serge. Relationships workshop presentation. Audio. 16 October 2011.
[102] Benhayon, Serge. *Sermon 32*. Video. The Way of the Livingness, 26 March 2016.

103 Benhayon, Serge. Sacred Esoteric Healing, Level 2 workshop. Audio. 7 May 2011.
104 Benhayon, Serge. *The Study of Esoteric Medicine 11*, Part 1. Audio. 13 May 2011.
105 Benhayon, Serge. Esoteric Developers Group presentation. Audio. 24 July 2010.
106 Eunice Minford, 'Entities, Spirits and Ghosts: Serge Benhayon offers a core religious understanding', *universalmedicinefacts.com*, 2 Sep 2016.
107 *Benhayon v Rockett* (No 6) [2018] NSWSC 1403.
108 ETR, 2011, p.715.
109 Benhayon, Serge. Sacred Esoteric Healing workshop. Audio. 7-8 May 2011.
110 ETR, 2011, p.479.
111 Benhayon, Serge. Esoteric Developers Group presentation. Audio. 15 October 2011.
112 Benhayon, Serge. Esoteric Developers Group presentation. Audio. 18 February 2012.
113 Benhayon, Serge. Sacred Esoteric Healing Level 2 workshop. Audio. 21 October 2011.
114 *Benhayon v Rockett* (No 8) [2019] NSWSC 169.
115 *Re S (Parental Alienation: Cult)* [2020] EWCA Civ 568, para 101, (UK Court of Appeal 2020).
Details of Family Court proceedings are confidential and only published when tried before the High Court. The parties are identified by pseudonyms to protect their privacy.
116 *Benhayon v Rockett* (No 9) [2019] NSWSC 172.
117 https://youtu.be/cUl-Ze67VQU
118 https://www.socialworkengland.org.uk/concerns/hearings-and-decisions/hearings-decisions/?SearchTerm=Ariana+Ray
119 https://www.peoplescollegeoflaw.edu

www.ingramcontent.com/pod-product-compliance
Lightning Source LLC
Chambersburg PA
CBHW031229290426
44109CB00012B/221